the

TAKE-OUT
MENU
COOKBOOK

How to Cook In the Foods You Love to Order Out

CARLA SNYDER
AND MEREDITH DEEDS

RUNNING PRESS
PHILADELPHIA · LONDON

9 8 7 6 5 4 3 2 1

Digit on the right indicates the number of this printing

Library of Congress Control Number: 2007920545

ISBN-13: 978-0-7624-3155-7

ISBN-10: 0-7624-3155-5

Cover and interior design by Amanda Richmond

Edited by Diana C. von Glahn

Typography: Cheltenham and Futura

Front cover (left column, top to bottom): Thai noodles: ©Ingram Publishing/Fotosearch; Mexican tacos: ©Image Source/Jupiter Images; Italian pizza: ©Burke/Triolo Productions/FoodPix/Jupiter Images; Chinese shrimp on rice: ©Paul Poplis/FoodPix/Jupiter Images; Middle-Eastern kebabs: ©Corbis/Fotosearch; (right column, top to bottom): Greek salad: ©FoodCollection/Fotosearch; French croissant: ©Eisenhut & Mayer/FoodPix/Jupiter Images; Japanese sushi: ©FoodCollection/Fotosearch; Jewish bagel: ©Brian Leatart/FoodPix/Jupiter Images; Spanish paella: ©iStockphoto.com/Rosen Dukov.

Back cover: ©Burke/Triolo/Brand X Pictures/Jupiter Images

This book may be ordered by mail from the publisher.

Please include $2.50 for postage and handling.

But try your bookstore first!

Running Press Book Publishers

2300 Chestnut Street

Philadelphia, PA 19103-4371

Visit us on the web!

www.runningpresscooks.com

To our husbands, Rick Snyder and David Deeds—
our partners, allies, helping hands, dishwashers, advocates, companions,
taste testers, sidekicks, sympathizers, endorsers, mainstays. . . .
We couldn't have done it without you.

❧ CONTENTS ❧

℘INTRODUCTION℘

YOU'VE GOT A SERIOUS CRAVING FOR KUNG Pao Chicken. Unfortunately, the nearest Chinese restaurant is more than thirty-five minutes away, and well, it's overpriced and just plain stinks. Come to think of it, you haven't found great, let alone decent, Chinese food since you moved from New Jersey to Ohio ten years ago. Indian would be good, but that would require airline tickets. Mexican would be divine, but the closest option is Chili's in the mall, twenty-five minutes away, and having been there before, you know that's not much of an option. And even if you could find good ethnic food nearby, you know a restaurant is not nearly as concerned as you are about your waistline or your wallet (especially after they've charged your credit card).

What to do? Why not cook it yourself? After all, you enjoy cooking and you know it'll be fresher, cheaper, and certainly healthier coming out of your own kitchen. Problem is, you're terrified at the thought of making your own Thai curry, or enchiladas verdes, or—heaven forbid!—sushi. The last ethnic cookbook you bought was so big, and had so many unfamiliar recipes that you felt lost before you even began. But what you don't realize is that you don't have to spend all your free time studying doorstop-sized tomes on individual ethnic cuisines, and you don't have to tackle fancy dishes that you've never even heard of, and definitely can't pronounce. All you need to do is turn the pages of this book, find the recipe you want, and step confidently into the kitchen.

As longtime cooking instructors, the bulk of our cooking classes have included ethnic cuisines and techniques because that's what our students want to learn—which is not too surprising, considering how deeply influenced American appetites have become by the multitude of enticing ethnic restaurants that have landed on our shores. What we've learned through our years of teaching these classes is that whatever the experience level of our students, their main interest usually resides in learning the quintessential recipes of a particular cuisine. Not that there aren't passionate foodies out there who want to know how to make *mee krob*, the elaborate crispy sweet rice noodle dish originating from the royal palaces of Thailand. But if we're teaching a class, and Thai food is on the menu but pad thai or a red curry isn't, we'd be hung from the pot racks if we couldn't at least tell our class where to find a good recipe for those dishes and where to get the necessary ingredients.

While the Internet is an option for finding one particular dish, it would take a considerable amount of surfing to garner enough information on techniques and ingredients to feel confident about making any ethnic dish. And even then, the information you find might be less than credible. You could try a good cookbook that focuses on your ethnic food of choice, but that comes with its own pitfalls, too. Not every cook is interested in being an armchair traveler. Although some of us read cookbooks like novels, the average home cook wants information to be concise and easily accessible.

That's what makes *The Take-Out Menu Cookbook* a practical tool for real cooks in real kitchens.

Although we're the first to agree that there is a

place for the large in-depth studies of the culinary practices of a particular country or region, we hope to cast a broader net with this cookbook. We are essentially cherry-picking from each cuisine to deliver the information and recipes that are of the most interest to the most readers. In choosing these recipes, we polled our students and colleagues on their favorites. But we didn't stop there—we spent a great deal of time online, comparing menus from ethnic restaurants all over the country to find which dishes popped up time and time again. Each chapter includes a wide variety of dishes to create a complete menu, but because each culture differs in the way it approaches a meal, not every chapter is weighted in the same way. For example, the Japanese chapter has less in the way of dessert than the chapter on French cuisine.

As our students have taught us, trying to make familiar dishes from an unfamiliar cuisine can be daunting. This book lowers the frustration and fear that often accompanies this task and helps you succeed in the kitchen by offering a simple approach that demystifies the culinary techniques of the world's leading cuisines. *The Take-Out Menu Cookbook* brings our classroom virtually into your kitchen and tells you, in an easy-to-understand format, how to execute a dish properly and get great results.

No restaurant specializing in an ethnic cuisine can replicate a dish exactly as it is made in the country of origin. Compromises, large and small, must be made in order to execute a dish using ingredients that can be readily obtained in this country. Also, techniques that have been used throughout the years may no longer make sense in today's modern kitchens. We make every effort to create authentic classic dishes, but also keep in mind the fact that you need to be able to buy the ingredients and execute the techniques in your own kitchen. Our recipes give you options and variations, making cooking these recipes less of a hair-pulling experience and much more fun.

Each chapter begins with a short cultural overview to help you understand each country's food, as well as some fun facts that liven up the dinner conversation—did you know that Americans eat 100 acres of pizza every day? We also offer a menu suggestion to get you started and tips for make-ahead planning and shopping. Each recipe also indicates start-to-finish and hands-on timelines to assist those of us who are time challenged.

Although neither one of us have spent a great deal of time in all twelve countries whose cuisines are covered in this book, as teachers, we have spent a great deal of time in the kitchen classroom teaching these dishes. We want to enjoy the world's flavors, too, and have spent years working to bring them into our own kitchens. Our experience has taught us that research and testing are the keys to developing credible recipes that will enable all of us to make the same dishes with confidence and success.

Of all the ethnic cookbooks in our personal collections, few qualify as favorites—those dog-eared, food-stained books we turn to year after year. Whether we're planning a dinner party or just pulling together Tuesday night dinner, favorite cookbooks are in a class by themselves . . . they are our trusted friends in the kitchen. We hope this book will become one of yours.

❧ACKNOWLEDGMENTS❧

ONCE WE FINISHED WRITING THIS BOOK, we realized how much fun we had researching, testing, and—most of all—eating the most delicious food in the world. There were many revelations that came about as we worked. One of the biggest was how delicious the food we normally ate in restaurants could be when we made it yourself in our own homes. We're not sure whether this came about as a result of nature (better ingredients) or nurture (making it ourselves in our own homes), but there was no mistaking that we had never eaten such a varied and bounteous diet in our lives. The recipes from this book added color and texture to diets and habits that had become a little staid and routine amid the busy background of families and work. *The Take-Out Menu Cookbook* took us places down a culinary highway we might never have ventured, and for that we are eternally grateful.

This book was a pleasure to write (and taste along the way) and many people helped to make it so. First we'd like to thank Diana von Glahn, our editor, and Jon Anderson, Craig Herman, and Amanda Richmond at Running Press for working with us to create the best cookbook possible, and letting us run with it, even when it grew to be much larger than originally intended.

Many thanks to our indefatigable agent, Lisa Ekus, who is always there when we need her, and all the wonderful people at The Lisa Ekus Group, especially Jane Falla for not only seeing to our literary concerns, but making it fun along the way.

Thanks to our recipe testers extraordinaire: Anne Norvell, Julie Neri, Alicia Ravens, and students Nancy Studebaker, Linda Irving, Michael Gentile, Jodi Wilson, Beth Balzarini, C. M. Shearer, Lloyd Shankland, Susan Cizmadji, Dan Collins, Tom Baird, Marilou Suszko, Dave McIlvaine, Iris Harvie, Sheryl Zangardi, Betsy Spak, Pam Huggett, and Scot Bowman. Thank you for always being willing to test just one more recipe. You provide an invaluable service to us and we can't thank you enough.

Thanks to our families for trying new things even when they thought they wouldn't like it. Jessica, Justin, and Corey Snyder: your willingness to eat Lamb Korma, Crêpes Suzette, Egg Rolls, and Black Forest Cake for dinner one fateful night in November designates you as record holders for the most multicultural cast-iron stomachs. Quinn, Connor, and Kyle Deeds: thank you for trusting your Mom when she told you you'd actually like Falafel, Bisteeya, Paprikash, and a whole lot of other dishes you've never heard of, for having the courage to put that first bite in your mouth, and better yet, for learning to love foods from around the world at such a young age. You're the best!

CHINESE

❧ CHINESE ❧

CHINESE FOOD HAS ENTERED THE AMERICAN psyche in the form of white cardboard boxes that always smell so good as they're pulled from their brown paper bag, but often don't contain the freshness and flavor we anticipated when we called in the order. Don't despair; the recipes in this chapter deliver in every way.

Confucius, born in 551 BC, taught that a man cannot be too serious about his eating. This concept lives on in modern China, where the Chinese continue to prepare fresh, seasonal food to nourish the body, the soul, and the mind. From this focus on food and the senses evolved a cuisine generally considered as one of the two greatest cuisines. (French being the other. Though the Italians would strongly disagree. Oh, and the Thai might have something to say about it too. And yes, so would the Germans. OK, our point is, the Chinese have really given food a lot of thought.)

Western societies are most familiar with the cuisine of Canton in the south, as most Chinese immigrants in the nineteenth century arrived from that region. They came to America and Australia to work in mines and railroads and brought with them a cuisine based upon a large variety of foods grown and raised in a subtropical climate. Freshness and fast cooking are hallmarks of Cantonese cuisine, which features favorites such as dim sum, colorful stir-fries, egg rolls, and roast pork. Rice is the staple food from this region, where a large bowl of rice is usually placed in the center of the table, and with vegetables rather than meat predominating in the meal.

The other most recognized regional Chinese cuisines come from the Szechuan and Hunan provinces. In these inland regions, wheat is the staple food and is found in noodles, steamed breads, and dumplings. This fare includes many sweet-and-sour dishes such as sweet-and-sour fish or pork, along with the strong flavors of garlic and chiles.

Many grocery stores now carry an assortment of Chinese vegetables and flavorings such as napa or Chinese cabbage, bok choy, wonton skins, hoisin sauce, rice vinegar and rice wine, fresh ginger, and Asian sesame oil. Though convenient, the brands found in most grocery stores are expensive and not of as high a quality as those found in an Asian market, where the products will be more authentic. In some communities, these Asian markets can be difficult to find, but they are worth the time it takes to search them out.

There are few desserts on the Chinese menu, and this chapter reflects that. The ubiquitous fortune cookie offered at the end of a meal is largely the device of Americanized Chinese establishments and, though fun, certainly doesn't satisfy a sweet tooth. To appease western tastes, we have included recipes for almond cookies and green tea ice cream, though fresh fruit would also be a nice finish to a Chinese meal.

We love the fresh taste of good, homemade Chinese food. It cannot be compared to most take-out Chinese. The variety of textures and colors feeds your eyes even before you crunch down on a crispy egg roll or spoon the velvety tofu into your mouth from the hot-and-sour soup.

Here's one of our favorite Chinese menus that could get you started in your own kitchen.

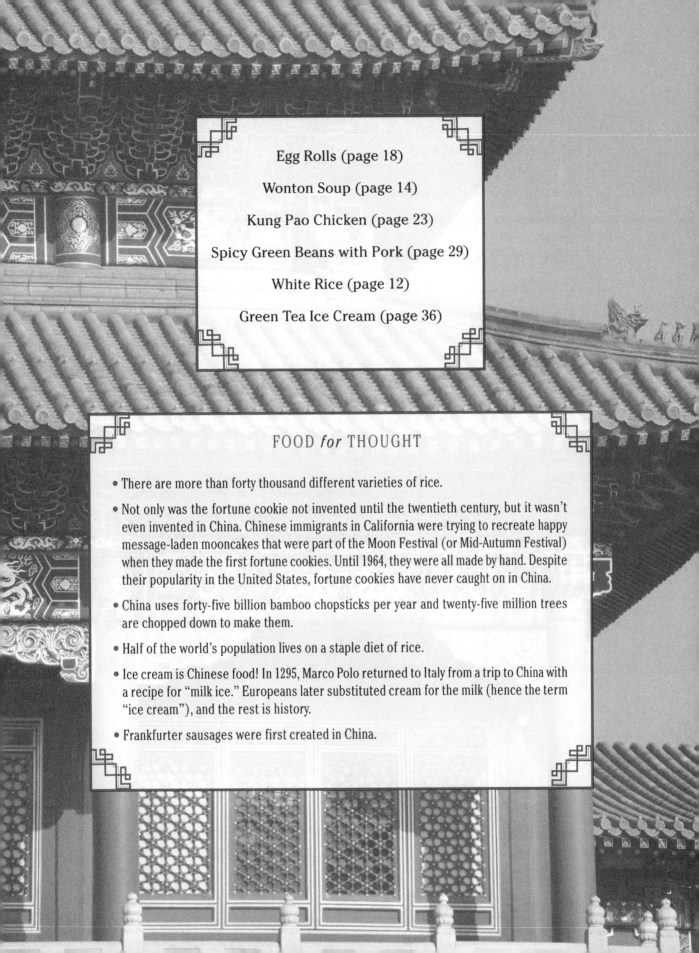

FOOD *for* THOUGHT

- There are more than forty thousand different varieties of rice.

- Not only was the fortune cookie not invented until the twentieth century, but it wasn't even invented in China. Chinese immigrants in California were trying to recreate happy message-laden mooncakes that were part of the Moon Festival (or Mid-Autumn Festival) when they made the first fortune cookies. Until 1964, they were all made by hand. Despite their popularity in the United States, fortune cookies have never caught on in China.

- China uses forty-five billion bamboo chopsticks per year and twenty-five million trees are chopped down to make them.

- Half of the world's population lives on a staple diet of rice.

- Ice cream is Chinese food! In 1295, Marco Polo returned to Italy from a trip to China with a recipe for "milk ice." Europeans later substituted cream for the milk (hence the term "ice cream"), and the rest is history.

- Frankfurter sausages were first created in China.

White Rice

Start to finish: 27 minutes • Hands-on time: 7 minutes

Rice has been cultivated in China since around 5000 BC and has spread to such a degree that half the world depends on it for survival. Rice is so important a staple that instead of saying "Hello," the Chinese greet each other by asking, "Have you had your rice yet?"

Leftover rice is a plus, so be sure to make enough so that you can make Fried Rice (opposite) the next day.

YIELD: 4 SERVINGS

1 cup long-grain rice

1¾ cups cold water

Pour the rice into a mesh strainer and run cold water through the rice while stirring it around with your hand. (This washes the excess starch from the rice.) When the water runs clear, combine the rice and water in a medium saucepan and bring to a boil over medium-high heat. Boil for 2 minutes, then cover and reduce the heat to low. Cook the rice for 18 minutes, remove it from the heat, and let it rest with the cover on for 5 minutes. Serve immediately.

TIP: To reheat rice, place it in a metal colander or mesh strainer set over 1 inch of boiling water in a large pot. Cover the pot and steam the rice for about 5 minutes. Do not refrigerate cooked rice unless you plan on using it for fried rice, rice pudding, etc. Refrigerated rice becomes hard and never regains its fluffy texture after being chilled. Cooked rice can be kept at room temperature for up to 2 hours.

Fried Rice

Start to finish: 30 minutes • Hands-on time: 30 minutes

Fried rice is what you make when you have leftover rice from the meal before. Though it is not traditional, we sometimes like to turn it into a one-pot meal by cleaning out the refrigerator and adding leftover diced cooked pork, chicken, or beef, or vegetables such as cabbage, broccoli, carrots, or red peppers. It's fast, easy, and delicious.

YIELD: 4 SERVINGS

3 tablespoons peanut oil

8 shrimp, peeled, deveined, and cut into ½-inch pieces

3 ounces ham, cut into ½-inch pieces (¼ cup)

½ cup frozen peas, thawed

1 tablespoon soy sauce, plus more for seasoning

2 large eggs, beaten

4 green onions, thinly sliced

Pinch of salt

Freshly ground black pepper

3 cups cold leftover rice

1 tablespoon rice wine or dry sherry

Heat 2 tablespoons of the oil in a wok or frying pan set over medium heat. Add the shrimp, ham, and peas and cook for 1 minute. Add the soy sauce and transfer to a plate to keep warm.

Heat the remaining tablespoon of oil in the pan. Add the eggs, green onions, and salt and pepper. Scramble the eggs in the pan. Once this mixture comes together into clumps, add the rice, shrimp mixture, and rice wine. Adjust the seasoning with soy sauce or salt and pepper. Serve hot.

VARIATION: Feel free to sauté cabbage, broccoli, bok choy, or diced carrots along with the shrimp, ham, and peas.

TIP: This recipe won't work as well with freshly cooked rice. It will be mushy and stick to the pan, a real mess. Use only cold leftover rice.

Wonton Soup

Start to finish: 1 hour • Hands-on time: 35 minutes

At a time when mu shu pork and kung pao dishes were too foreign for our unsophisticated palates, we children would eat wonton soup when dining in Chinese restaurants with our parents. The rich stock and "funny" Chinese noodles were non-threatening and fun to eat. But what makes this dish good for children can sometimes make it bland and uninteresting for adults. Our version of this traditional soup is perfumed with ginger and swimming with flavorful five-spice-flavored pork wontons. Although most chicken stock–based soups taste like a chicken was just waved over the pot, we get big chicken flavor in this recipe by enriching canned chicken stock with extra chicken and vegetables for that rich flavor that we remember so fondly.

YIELD: 6 SERVINGS

STOCK

2 pounds chicken
   necks and backs

10 cups chicken stock

5 whole peppercorns

4 quarter-sized slices fresh
   ginger, unpeeled

1 onion, quartered

1 carrot, quartered

1 stalk celery, quartered

1 bay leaf

WONTONS

½ pound boneless pork shoulder,
   finely ground

2 tablespoons plus ¼ cup finely
   chopped green onion

2 tablespoons dry white wine,
   like sauvignon blanc

1 tablespoon soy sauce

½ teaspoon five-spice powder

To make the stock: In a large stockpot, combine the chicken, stock, peppercorns, ginger, onion, carrot, celery, and bay leaf. Bring to a simmer over medium-high heat. Reduce the heat to low and continue to simmer the stock uncovered for 30 minutes, skimming the froth from the top every now and then and discarding it.

Strain the stock into another large pot, discarding the bones and vegetables. Skim and discard the fat from the top of the stock with a large spoon. Depending on how aggressively your stock has cooked, it may have reduced somewhat. Taste the stock. If it is a little salty, add water in ¼-cup increments until a balance has been achieved.

To make the wontons: In a large bowl, combine the pork, 2 tablespoons of green onion, the wine, soy sauce, five-spice powder, and pepper. Mix thoroughly. To taste for seasoning, heat a small skillet and fry a tablespoon-sized patty until it's no longer pink inside. Taste and adjust seasoning as desired.

On a work surface, lay out about 6 wonton wrappers, keeping the remaining wrappers covered with plastic so that they don't dry out. Moisten the edges with your fingertip dipped in water. Drop 1 tablespoon of the pork filling into the center of each wrapper and flatten it slightly, leaving a generous border. Press another wrapper on top (like ravioli). Press from the center out to the edges to remove any air from the wonton. Run your finger around the edges to seal.

¼ teaspoon freshly ground black
    pepper, plus more as needed
Salt, as needed
24 wonton wrappers

Arrange the wontons on a parchment-lined sheet pan and refrigerate while you continue with the remaining wrappers and meat mixture. (You may have some leftover filling. You can make more wontons and freeze them for up to 1 month or cook extra for larger appetites.)

Bring a large pot of water to a boil over medium-high heat. Add the wontons 6 at a time and cook for 4 minutes, stirring to keep them from sticking to the bottom of the pan. Remove the wontons from the pot and transfer them to a covered dish to keep warm. Repeat until all the wontons are cooked.

Ladle the stock into bowls and add 2 wontons to each serving. Garnish with the chopped green onions. Serve hot.

MAKE AHEAD: The stock can be made up to 2 days in advance. The wontons can be made and frozen for up to 1 month or wrapped and refrigerated for up to 24 hours. Thaw the wontons for 1 hour, then proceed with the recipe as directed.

Egg Drop Soup

Start to finish: 1 hour • Hands-on time: 15 minutes

If you have a cold, feel a little under the weather, or need comforting in any way, this is the soup for you. The success of this reviving soup depends largely upon the quality of your chicken stock. In order for this dish to sing we recommend that you enrich store-bought stock by simmering it with chicken backs and necks. This step gives your stock the deep, rich flavor that a soup of this simplicity demands.

YIELD: 4 TO 6 SERVINGS

1½ pounds chicken necks
   and backs, rinsed

6 cups chicken stock

3 whole peppercorns

2 quarter-sized slices fresh
   ginger, peeled

1 onion, quartered

1 carrot, quartered

1 stalk celery, quartered

1 bay leaf

2 tablespoons cornstarch mixed
   with 3 tablespoons cold water

2 large eggs, lightly beaten

Salt and freshly ground
   black pepper

2 green onions, thinly sliced,
   for garnish

In a large stockpot, combine the chicken, stock, peppercorns, ginger, onion, carrot, celery, and bay leaf. Bring to a simmer over medium-high heat. Reduce the heat to low and continue to simmer the stock uncovered for 30 minutes. Skim the froth from the top every now and then and discard.

Strain the stock into another large pot, discarding the bones and vegetables. Skim and discard the fat from the top of the stock with a large spoon. Depending on how aggressively your stock has cooked, it may have reduced somewhat. Taste the stock. If it is a little salty, add water in ¼-cup increments until a balance has been achieved.

Bring the chicken stock to a boil. Stir in the cornstarch mixture, stirring until the soup thickens slightly. Slowly drizzle in the eggs and give the soup one more light stir. Remove the pot from the heat and adjust the seasoning with salt and pepper to taste.

Garnish the soup with the green onions and serve hot.

> **MAKE AHEAD:** This soup can be made up to the cornstarch addition, cooled, covered, and refrigerated for 2 days. Return the soup to a simmer and add the eggs right before serving.

Hot-and-Sour Soup

Start to finish: 20 minutes • Hands-on time: 20 minutes

Hot-and-sour soup is one of those dishes (like a consommé) that is perfect on a cold day. It is quick to prepare, low in fat, and warms you up from the inside out. We like to keep a container of this soup in the freezer for those times when someone we know might need a bit of added warmth.

YIELD: 4 SERVINGS

6 dried Chinese mushrooms
  (shiitake are fine)
4 cups chicken stock
⅓ cup chopped bamboo shoots
4 ounces pork tenderloin or chicken
  breast, cut into thin strips
1 cup diced firm tofu
¼ cup cider vinegar
3 tablespoons soy sauce
1 teaspoon toasted Asian
  sesame oil
1 teaspoon chili garlic sauce
Salt and freshly ground
  black pepper
2 tablespoons cornstarch mixed
  with 3 tablespoons water
1 large egg, beaten
2 green onions, thinly sliced,
  for garnish

Soak the mushrooms in ⅓ cup boiling water for 15 minutes. With a slotted spoon, lift the mushrooms from the liquid and set aside. Strain the liquid through a coffee filter–lined strainer to remove the grit and set it aside. Discard the tough stems from the mushrooms. Squeeze the mushrooms dry. Cut into thin slices.

Pour the mushroom liquid and chicken stock into a large stockpot set over medium-high heat. Add the mushrooms, bamboo shoots, and meat. Bring the mixture to a simmer and add the tofu, vinegar, soy sauce, sesame oil, and chili sauce. Taste the soup and adjust the seasonings to taste.

Stir the cornstarch mixture and add it to the simmering soup. Cook for 2 minutes to thicken the soup. Drizzle in the egg while the soup is at a simmer, stirring gently. Do not boil.

Serve hot, garnished with green onions.

> **MAKE AHEAD:** The soup can be made up to the cornstarch addition up to 1 day ahead, covered, and refrigerated. To finish the soup, reheat over medium-high heat and once it reaches a simmer, resume the recipe.

Egg Rolls

Start to finish: 1 hour • Hands-on time: 1 hour

The egg rolls often served in Chinese restaurants can be poor imitations of what an egg roll should be. They suffer from what the restaurant industry refers to as "sandbagging." It means that your egg rolls have probably been made hours in advance, stacked and ready for a reheat after you order it. This process tends to result in soggy or tough exteriors, not to mention higher grease retention. Our version is crispy on the outside with lots of pork, shrimp, and well-seasoned vegetables, and is likely to be the best egg roll you've ever eaten. Our families sure think so!

YIELD: 12 EGG ROLLS

2 tablespoons oyster sauce

1 tablespoon soy sauce

1 tablespoon Asian sesame oil

1 teaspoon sugar

½ teaspoon salt

¼ cup vegetable oil

1 (1-inch) knob fresh ginger, peeled and minced

3 garlic cloves, minced (1 tablespoon)

1 bunch green onions, white and light green parts only, thinly sliced

1 rib celery, minced (½ cup)

1 carrot, minced (½ cup)

10 shiitake mushrooms, stems discarded and caps thinly sliced

½ head of napa or Chinese cabbage, thinly sliced (2 cups)

1 pound raw shrimp, peeled, deveined, and diced

½ pound ground pork

Combine the oyster sauce, soy sauce, sesame oil, sugar, and salt in a small bowl and set aside.

Heat the vegetable oil in a large skillet set over medium heat. Add the ginger, garlic, green onions, celery, carrot, and mushrooms and sauté for about 3 or 4 minutes, or until they soften. Add the cabbage and sauté for another minute or two. Add the shrimp and pork and cook, tossing and stirring vigorously, for about 2 minutes, or until they are cooked through.

Add the reserved sauce and toss to incorporate. Remove from the heat and set aside until cool to the touch.

Cover the egg roll wrappers with a piece of plastic wrap. Place 1 wrapper on a work surface with one point facing you. Spread ¼ cup of the filling horizontally across the lower third of the wrapper. Fold the bottom point over the filling, tightening the wrap over the filling, and fold in the side corners. Brush the top corner with the egg wash and roll up the wrapper tightly, sealing the roll closed. Transfer the rolls as they are made to a parchment-lined sheet pan and cover loosely with plastic wrap. Fill the rest of the wrappers in the same manner.

Preheat the oven to 200°F.

In a wide, heavy pot, heat 2 inches of oil to 360°F. over medium heat. Carefully add 4 egg rolls to the oil and fry, turning them with a slotted spoon after about 2 minutes as they brown on the bottom. Fry on the second side for another 2 minutes, or until they brown. Transfer the egg rolls to a sheet pan lined with a double thickness of paper towels. Fry the remaining egg rolls in batches of 4. When they are all browned, the egg rolls can be kept warm in the oven for up to 30 minutes.

1 (16-ounce) package egg roll
   wrappers
1 egg, beaten
2 to 3 cups peanut or vegetable
   oil, for frying
Chinese mustard, plum sauce, or
   sweet chile sauce, for serving

Serve hot with Chinese mustard, plum sauce, or sweet chile sauce.

VARIATION: To make vegetarian egg rolls, substitute 6 ounces of cubed tofu for the pork and shrimp.

MAKE AHEAD: The egg rolls can be assembled, but not cooked, covered, and refrigerated for up to 8 hours or frozen for up to 1 month. Thaw at room temperature for 3 hours before frying.

Pot Stickers FRIED PORK DUMPLINGS

Start to finish: 2 hours • Hands-on time: 2 hours

Pot stickers come from northern China. Their appeal lies in the tender, juicy filling and crispy skins. Don't get too caught up in trying to make these dumplings look perfect. They will be delicious no matter how unevenly shaped they are. There are many variations on this theme and to confuse us westerners even further, these delicious morsels can be boiled, steamed, or pan-fried. Some people like to boil or steam them first, then pan-fry, but we like the simpler version of frying them up in a little oil and then steaming them in the same pan with a little chicken stock.

It goes without saying that this is a dish well suited to group activity. Like grandma used to say, "Many hands make light work." We like to make these dumplings as part of a multicourse meal that could consist of a soup course, a stir-fry of vegetables, rice, and pot stickers. That way, there is truly something for everyone.

YIELD: 3 TO 4 DOZEN POT STICKERS

DUMPLINGS

- ½ head of Chinese cabbage (napa or celery cabbage), finely chopped (2 cups)
- 1 pound ground pork
- ½ green onion, minced (2 tablespoons)
- 2 tablespoons soy sauce
- 2 tablespoons minced cilantro
- 1 (1-inch) knob fresh ginger, peeled and minced
- 1 tablespoon minced fresh chives, plus more for garnish
- 1 tablespoon rice wine or dry sherry
- 1 tablespoon toasted Asian sesame oil
- 1 teaspoon light brown sugar
- 1 teaspoon salt

In a large bowl, combine the cabbage, pork, green onion, soy sauce, cilantro, ginger, chives, rice wine, sesame oil, brown sugar, salt, pepper, and garlic. Work the ingredients with your hands until completely mixed. Heat a frying pan over medium heat and fry a tablespoon of the mixture to check the seasoning. Adjust the seasoning as necessary.

Cover the dumpling wrappers with a damp towel. Place one wrapper on a work surface. With a finger dipped in water, dampen the edges of the wrapper to help it adhere. Place about 1 tablespoon of the filling into the center of each wrapper and fold it into a half-moon-shaped pouch. Make 3 or 4 pleats at each edge to gather the dough around the filling, and then pinch around the top of the dumpling to seal it tightly. Arrange the dumplings on a parchment-lined sheet pan. Assemble the remaining dumplings in the same manner.

Heat a large frying pan with a tight-fitting lid over medium-high heat and add the oil. When the oil is hot, add the dumplings to the pan and fry them on one side until browned, about 3 minutes. Shake the pan to move them around during cooking and keep them from sticking. Add the chicken stock to the pan and cover the pan tightly so that the pot stickers steam and cook through. Cook for about 5 minutes, or until the liquid has evaporated from the pan.

¼ teaspoon freshly ground
   black pepper
1 garlic clove, minced
1 (12-ounce) package dumpling
   wrappers or wonton skins,
   cut into rounds
¼ cup peanut or vegetable oil
1 cup chicken stock

DIPPING SAUCE

¼ cup soy sauce
2 tablespoons rice vinegar
1 teaspoon minced fresh ginger
¼ teaspoon chile oil
1 garlic clove, minced

To make the dipping sauce: Combine the sauce ingredients in a small bowl. Let the sauce sit for at least 5 minutes to let the flavors blend.

Transfer the dumplings to a heated platter, garnish with chives, and serve with the dipping sauce.

VARIATION: To make vegetarian pot stickers, substitute ½ pound of tofu for the pork and add ½ cup sliced snow peas, ¼ cup diced water chestnuts, and ¼ cup diced red bell pepper. Cook as directed in the recipe using water instead of chicken stock.

MAKE AHEAD: The dumplings can be frozen, uncooked, for up to 1 month and cooked directly from the freezer. Any unused sauce should be refrigerated and discarded after 2 days.

Barbecued Spareribs

Start to finish: 5 hours • Hands-on time: 30 minutes

As children, we loved the buffets often served on the weekends at our favorite Chinese restaurants. Not only was the se-lection vast, but one could munch on as many crispy pork spareribs as desired. At the time we loved their bright red color, but these days we choose to leave out the red dye #5. Our marinade for spareribs is sweet and salty. It's a mixture of soy sauce, honey, rice vinegar, and hoisin. Hoisin is China's take on barbecue sauce, which probably explains why Americans enjoy this dish so much.

YIELD: 6 SERVINGS

¼ cup soy sauce

¼ cup hoisin

3 tablespoons honey

2 tablespoons rice vinegar

3 garlic cloves, minced
(1 tablespoon)

1 (1-inch) knob fresh ginger,
peeled and minced

4 pounds pork spareribs,
trimmed of excess fat

Plum sauce, for serving

Combine the soy sauce, hoisin, honey, rice vinegar, garlic, and ginger in a large plastic zip top bag. Place the spareribs in the bag and shake to coat. Let the ribs marinate in the refrigerator overnight, or for 3 hours at room temperature.

Preheat the oven to 375°F.

Place a rack in a roasting pan and fill the pan with 1 inch water. Set the ribs on the rack and roast for 45 minutes, turning and basting frequently with the marinade. Raise the oven temperature to 450°F. and continue to roast for another 15 minutes.

Remove the ribs from the oven and cool until they can be handled. Cut into individual ribs and brush on more marinade. Return to the oven for an-other 15 minutes until they are crispy and brown.

Serve hot or room temperature with plum sauce.

> **MAKE AHEAD:** These ribs can be made up to 8 hours ahead and refrigerated. Reheat at 300°F. for 10 minutes.

Kung Pao Chicken

Start to finish: 45 minutes • Hands-on time: 45 minutes

One of the hottest of Chinese dishes, kung pao originates from Szechuan province, where the people's love for spicy cuisine is legend. If you're not such a fan of the hot stuff, just leave out a few of the chiles to make it milder. Or if you like your kung pao "China syndrome" hot, add a few more. Most of us agree that a large quantity of peanuts makes this dish irresistible.

YIELD: 4 SERVINGS

1 egg white, beaten

4 tablespoons soy sauce

1 tablespoon cornstarch

1 teaspoon plus 2 tablespoons
rice wine

4 chicken breasts, skinned, boned,
and cut into bite-sized pieces

3 tablespoons rice vinegar

2 tablespoons sugar

2 tablespoons hoisin

2 teaspoons Asian sesame oil

⅓ cup peanut or vegetable oil

1 cup peanuts, preferably boiled
and unsalted

5 dried hot chiles, or to taste

2 garlic cloves, minced

4 green onions, sliced

3 quarter-sized pieces of fresh
ginger, peeled and minced

White Rice (page 12), for serving

Combine the egg white, 1 tablespoon soy sauce, cornstarch, and 1 teaspoon rice wine in a large bowl. Add the chicken and stir to coat. Refrigerate for about 30 minutes.

In a separate bowl, combine the remaining 3 tablespoons soy sauce, and 2 tablespoons rice wine with the rice vinegar, sugar, hoisin, and sesame oil and set aside.

Heat the oil in a wok over high heat until it is hot and barely smoking. Add the peanuts and toss them for about 2 minutes, or until they begin to brown. Remove the peanuts from the oil and transfer them to a heatproof plate. Set aside.

Add the chicken to the oil and toss, cooking it until it is slightly browned on the outside, but not cooked all the way through, about 2 minutes. Remove the chicken from the wok and add it to the peanuts. (There will be some brown bits on the bottom of the wok. They will help thicken the sauce when it is added to the pan later. Be careful and don't let them burn, or your sauce will taste sharp.)

Add the chiles to the wok and cook them until they turn almost black, about 1 minute. Add the garlic, green onions, and ginger along with the peanuts, chicken, and sauce. Toss to incorporate the sauce and heat through. Serve with rice.

VARIATION: Sometimes we like to add vegetables to this dish to make it a one-dish meal. Try adding sliced water chestnuts and green or red bell peppers, broccoli, or bok choy along with the other vegetables in the dish. By swapping out the peanuts for cashews, the dish becomes cashew chicken. You can also vary the dish by using thinly sliced pork or beef, or whole shrimp.

Orange Beef

Start to finish: 45 minutes • Hands-on time: 45 minutes

Most Chinese restaurants use dried orange peel for this dish, which doesn't compare to what you get when making it with fresh oranges. Fresh orange peel will give you the best orange beef you've ever tasted. This dish relies heavily on the flavor of the orange zest and juice, so find the best oranges you can and you will be rewarded with a dish made of crispy, chewy meat fragrant with the scent of citrus.

YIELD: 4 SERVINGS

1 pound beef round or sirloin, thinly sliced and cut into 3-inch strips

3 tablespoons soy sauce

1 tablespoon plus 1 teaspoon cornstarch

½ teaspoon freshly ground black pepper

Zest from 2 organic oranges

2 garlic cloves, minced

1 (1-inch) knob fresh ginger, peeled and minced

½ cup freshly squeezed orange juice

2 tablespoons sugar

2 tablespoons dry sherry or white wine

1 tablespoon hoisin

2 teaspoons Asian sesame oil

3 cups vegetable oil

Green onion, thinly sliced, for garnish

In a medium bowl, toss the meat with 2 tablespoons of soy sauce, 1 tablespoon of cornstarch, and the pepper. Marinate the meat at room temperature while you assemble the rest of the ingredients.

Combine the orange zest, garlic, and ginger in a small bowl and reserve.

In a medium bowl, combine the remaining tablespoon of soy sauce, and the remaining teaspoon of cornstarch with the orange juice, sugar, sherry, hoisin, and sesame oil. Set aside.

Heat the oil in a heavy wok or pot to 360°F. Add one-third of the beef to the oil, one piece at a time (it's important not to add all the beef at once as the temperature of the oil will plummet and the beef will absorb more oil than necessary). Scrape the bottom of the pot as some of the meat may stick. Cook for 2 minutes or until crispy and brown. Transfer the meat with a slotted spoon to paper towels to drain and repeat with the rest of the meat. Discard all but 2 tablespoons of the oil.

Add the orange zest, garlic and ginger mixture to the wok and cook for about 1 minute, or until fragrant. Stir the orange juice mixture and add it to the wok, along with the fried beef. Stir until the sauce thickens, about 2 minutes.

Serve garnished with green onions.

VARIATION: For a faster dish with less fat, stir-fry the beef instead of deep-frying it. It won't be crispy, but the flavor is delicious. You can also substitute chicken, pork, or shrimp for the beef.

General Tso's Chicken

Start to finish: 1 hour • Hands-on time: 1 hour

General Tso's Chicken is one of those Chinese dishes that would be hard to find in China. It seems that this dish of battered, deep-fried chicken pieces bathed in a sweet, garlicky spicy sauce was born back in the seventies in a Chinese restaurant in New York. But even though it would be difficult to locate a recipe for it in a traditional Chinese cookbook, it stands as one of the most-ordered favorites on the Chinese-American menu. Just who is this General Tso guy anyway? Turns out he was a successful Chinese statesman back in the mid-1800's. We're not sure why this dish was named after him, since we can be pretty sure he never tasted it, but we're sure glad that someone came up with the recipe.

YIELD: 6 SERVINGS

1 large egg, beaten

4 tablespoons cornstarch

1 tablespoon plus ¼ cup soy sauce

3 tablespoons mirin

1½ pounds boneless chicken,
   cut into 1-inch cubes

¼ cup rice vinegar

¼ cup sugar

2 tablespoons hoisin

1 tablespoon chili paste with garlic

10 black peppercorns, crushed

2 teaspoons Asian sesame oil

2 to 3 cups vegetable oil, for frying

5 hot chiles, cut in half

1 (1-inch) knob fresh ginger,
   peeled and minced

3 garlic cloves, minced

2 cups broccoli florets

1 red bell pepper, seeded and
   thinly sliced

3 green onions, thinly sliced,
   for garnish

White Rice (page 12), for serving

In a medium bowl, combine the egg, 3 tablespoons of cornstarch, 1 tablespoon of soy sauce, and 1 tablespoon of mirin. Add the chicken and let it marinate at room temperature while you assemble the rest of the ingredients.

In a separate bowl, combine the remaining tablespoon of cornstarch, the remaining ¼ cup soy sauce, the remaining 2 tablespoons mirin, and the rice vinegar, sugar, hoisin, chili paste, peppercorns, sesame oil, and ½ cup of water. Set aside.

In a heavy pot over medium heat, heat 3 inches of oil to 360°F. Add about 10 pieces of chicken to the hot oil and fry until brown and crispy, about 2 minutes. Remove from the oil with a slotted spoon and drain on paper towels. Repeat with the remaining chicken. Set aside.

Remove all but 3 tablespoons of oil from the pot and add the chiles, ginger, and garlic, and cook for 30 seconds. Add the broccoli and bell pepper and stir-fry, tossing the vegetables for 2 minutes or until they are brightly colored and partially cooked.

Add the cooked chicken to the pot along with the reserved sauce and cook, stirring, until the sauce thickens and the vegetables are tender, about 2 minutes.

To serve, sprinkle green onions over the top and serve hot with rice.

Sweet-and-Sour Pork

Start to finish: 1 hour • Hands-on time: 1 hour

Though immensely popular, sweet-and-sour pork is not an authentic Chinese dish and was probably invented here in the United States to suit American tastes. It is most often served with a mix of carrot, green and red bell pepper, pineapple, and onion, and glazed with a sweet-and-sour sauce that includes a heavy of dose of good old ketchup. We've tried to make it successfully without the ketchup in order to stay truer to its Asian roots, but it just isn't the same as that old standby we used to eat as kids back in the heyday of the mom-and-pop Chinese restaurant.

YIELD: 4 SERVINGS

1 pound pork tenderloin, cut into bite-sized cubes

1 tablespoon rice wine or dry sherry

2 teaspoons soy sauce

¼ teaspoon Szechuan pepper or freshly ground black pepper

2 to 3 cups peanut or vegetable oil, for frying

1 cup ketchup

¼ cup sugar

¼ cup cider vinegar

½ cup chicken stock

1 tablespoon soy sauce

2 teaspoons dark sesame oil

½ teaspoon chili garlic sauce

⅓ cup unbleached all-purpose flour

2 tablespoons cornstarch

1 egg white

1 tablespoon vegetable oil

Pinch of salt

1 garlic clove, minced

1 green bell pepper, cut into 1-inch squares (1 cup)

In a medium bowl, toss the pork with the wine, soy sauce, and pepper. Marinate for at least 15 minutes.

Fill a wok or large frying pan with 3 inches of oil and heat to 360°F.

In a bowl, combine the ketchup, sugar, cider vinegar, stock, soy sauce, sesame oil, and chili sauce. Set aside.

In a separate bowl, combine the flour, cornstarch, egg white, vegetable oil, salt, and ¼ cup water to form a batter. Dip the pork in the batter, then carefully add about 10 pieces of pork to the wok and fry for 3 minutes. Remove the cooked pork with a slotted spoon and drain on paper towels. Continue to dip and cook the remaining pork in the same manner. (If you would like the pork to be extra crispy, fry it again in small batches for 1 minute. Be careful not to let the oil's temperature drop below 350°F or the pork will absorb oil.)

Pour off all but about 3 tablespoons of the oil in the wok or heat another pan with 3 tablespoons of oil. Add the garlic to the pan and cook for about 30 seconds, being careful not to burn it, then add the bell peppers, onion, and pineapple. Stir-fry the vegetables until they begin to soften, about 3 minutes.

Stir the reserved sauce and add it to the vegetables along with the fried pork. Toss until the sauce lightly coats the vegetables and meat.

Serve hot with rice and garnished with green onions.

1 red bell pepper, cut into
   1-inch squares (1 cup)
1 small onion, cut into
   ½-inch slices (1 cup)
5 slices pineapple, cut into
   1-inch squares
White Rice (page 12), for serving
2 green onions, thinly sliced,
   for garnish

VARIATION: You may substitute chicken, beef, or shrimp for the pork in this recipe.

FOOD *for* THOUGHT

ACCORDING TO press reports, China released a new set of stamps to celebrate the Year of the Pig, which began on February 18, 2007. They are scratch and sniff, lick and taste stamps that smell like sweet-and-sour pork when you scratch the front, and taste like the dish when you lick the back.

Cold Szechuan Noodles

Start to finish: 30 minutes • Hands-on time: 30 minutes

This fresh pasta salad is alive with the flavors of peanuts, sesame, and garlic. It is one of our favorite hot-weather salads to serve with simple grilled meats such as chicken and pork. But there are so many flavors in the peanut sauce that it can really dominate the plate, so keep the other flavors of the meal low-key. This recipe makes a lot, but don't worry about leftovers. Because it is eaten cold, the noodles keep in the refrigerator for days. They make a great high-protein snack or lunch and when made with the whole-wheat noodles, they are an even better choice.

YIELD: 6 TO 8 SERVINGS

⅓ cup chicken stock

½ cup smooth peanut butter

¼ cup soy sauce, plus more
   if necessary

¼ cup rice vinegar

2 tablespoons Chinese black
   vinegar or Worcestershire sauce

3 tablespoons toasted Asian
   sesame oil

2 tablespoons chili garlic sauce,
   plus more if necessary

1½ tablespoons sugar

4 garlic cloves, minced

1 pound Chinese # 3 wheat noodles,
   linguine, or whole-wheat linguine

1 red pepper, seeded and cut into
   matchsticks

1 carrot, peeled and cut into
   matchsticks

1 bunch green onions, thinly sliced

½ cup peanuts, chopped

2 cups bean sprouts

Bring a large pot of water (1 gallon) to a boil over high heat.

Meanwhile, combine the stock, peanut butter, soy sauce, rice vinegar, black vinegar, sesame oil, chili garlic sauce, sugar, and garlic in the bowl of a food processor. Pulse to combine well and transfer to a large bowl.

Cook the noodles for about 6 minutes, or until they are almost done but still have a little bite in the center. Drain the noodles and add them immediately to the sauce mixture. Toss the noodles, then add the red pepper, carrot, green onions, peanuts, and sprouts. Taste to adjust the seasoning with more soy sauce or chili sauce. If the mixture is dry, add a few tablespoons of hot water to make the mixing of ingredients easier. Let the noodles sit to come to room temperature. As they sit, they will absorb the extra sauce in the bottom of the bowl.

Serve at room temperature or chilled.

> **MAKE AHEAD:** These noodles will keep, covered and refrigerated, for 2 to 3 days. If you want to make the dish ahead of time, don't add the bean sprouts. They become slimy and lose their crunch.

Spicy Green Beans with Pork

Start to finish: 45 minutes • Hands-on time: 45 minutes

Garlic, ginger, and chiles are the main flavors in this Chinese classic. We could make a meal out of the crispy green beans, flavorful pork, and spicy sauce. Although this dish technically fills a portion of your daily allowance of vegetables, it doesn't taste like it. Serve this dish to the vegetable haters in your life. They might actually thank you for it.

YIELD: 4 SERVINGS

1 pound pork tenderloin, frozen for 30 minutes, then thinly shaved (see note)

3 tablespoons soy sauce

2 tablespoons rice wine

1 teaspoon Szechuan peppercorns, crushed, or ¼ teaspoon freshly ground black pepper

¼ cup chicken stock

1 tablespoon spicy bean sauce

1 tablespoon hoisin

1½ teaspoons chili garlic sauce

1½ teaspoons sugar

1 teaspoon Asian sesame oil

2 teaspoons cornstarch

¼ cup peanut or vegetable oil

1 pound green beans, trimmed and snapped in half

3 garlic cloves, minced (1 tablespoon)

1 (1-inch) knob of fresh ginger, peeled and minced

4 green onions, thinly sliced

¼ cup toasted white sesame seeds

In a small bowl, toss the pork with 2 tablespoons of soy sauce, 1 tablespoon of rice wine, and the peppercorns. Marinate at room temperature while assembling the rest of the ingredients.

In a separate bowl, combine the remaining tablespoon of soy sauce, the remaining tablespoon of rice wine, the stock, spicy bean sauce, hoisin, chili garlic sauce, sugar, sesame oil, and cornstarch. Set aside.

Heat a wok or large frying pan over medium-high heat and add the oil. When the oil is hot, add the beans and stir-fry them for 10 minutes, or until they begin to brown or blister. Remove the beans from the pan using a slotted spoon and pour off all but 2 tablespoons of the oil. Return the pan to the heat and add the pork, garlic, and ginger. Stir-fry for about 3 minutes, or until there is no longer any pink color to the pork. Add the green onions and cook for 1 minute. Add the reserved sauce and green beans and mix well. The sauce will begin to thicken and glaze the pork and beans.

To serve, sprinkle with sesame seeds.

VARIATION: Feel free to substitute chicken, beef, shrimp, or tofu for the pork.

NOTE: Meat is much easier to shave if it is partially frozen. When you need to slice meat very thin, freeze it for about 30 minutes, then use your sharpest knife to cut it.

Eggplant in Spicy Sauce

Start to finish: 40 minutes • Hands-on time: 35 minutes

We can't get enough of this spicy, hot eggplant dish studded with tender pork. Try to find the small Asian eggplants at your local market. They contain fewer of the seeds that tend to make eggplant bitter.

YIELD: 4 TO 6 SERVINGS

2 cups peanut or vegetable oil

1 pound eggplant, cut into sticks
   the size of French fries

1 tablespoon soy sauce

1 tablespoon light brown sugar

1 tablespoon spicy bean sauce

1 tablespoon rice vinegar

1 tablespoon rice wine

1 teaspoon Asian sesame oil

1 teaspoon cornstarch

3 garlic cloves, minced
   (1 tablespoon)

1 tablespoon chopped
   fresh ginger

4 whole dried chiles, soaked in
   water for 10 minutes, dried,
   and chopped

1 cup thinly sliced pork tenderloin

3 green onions, thinly sliced

In a wok set over medium-high heat, heat the oil to 360°F. Add half the eggplant to the oil and fry for about 5 minutes or until the eggplant is limp. Remove the eggplant with a slotted spoon or spider and drain on a paper-towel-lined sheet pan. Cook the remaining eggplant in the same manner.

In a small bowl, combine the soy sauce, brown sugar, bean sauce, rice vinegar, rice wine, sesame oil, and cornstarch. Set aside.

Pour off all but 2 tablespoons of the oil in the wok. Add the garlic, ginger, and chiles and cook for 1 minute. Add the pork and stir-fry for 2 minutes. Return the eggplant to the wok. Stir the sauce and add it to the pork. Boil until the sauce thickens, about 2 minutes.

To serve, garnish with green onions.

Chicken Chow Mein with Crispy Noodles

Start to finish: 45 minutes • Hands-on time: 40 minutes

Most historians agree that noodles have been consumed in China for over two thousand years. This dish probably came over in the mid-1800s with workers headed for the railroads and has about a thousand variations. One thing most foodies agree on is that the crispy noodles in the can are a big no-no. We are fans of frying these soft noodles until they are crispy on the outside, but soft on the inside.

YIELD: 4 SERVINGS

4 chicken breasts, thinly sliced

4 tablespoons rice wine

1 teaspoon plus ¼ cup soy sauce

½ cup chicken stock

3 tablespoons rice vinegar

1½ tablespoons Asian sesame oil

1 tablespoon oyster sauce

2 teaspoons sugar

1 teaspoon garlic red chili sauce

1½ tablespoons cornstarch

1 (10-ounce) package Chinese egg noodles or vermicelli

1 cup peanut or vegetable oil

2 garlic cloves, minced

1 (1-inch) knob of fresh ginger, peeled and minced

1 onion, thinly sliced (1 cup)

2 ribs bok choy, thinly sliced (1 cup)

1 cup broccoli florets

¼ head napa cabbage, shredded (1 cup)

1 cup snow peas

1 carrot, peeled and thinly sliced

Combine the chicken, 1 tablespoon of rice wine, and 1 teaspoon of soy sauce in a medium bowl. Marinate at room temperature while you assemble the rest of the ingredients.

In a separate bowl, combine the remaining ¼ cup of soy sauce, the remaining 3 tablespoons of rice wine, the stock, rice vinegar, sesame oil, oyster sauce, sugar, red chili sauce, and cornstarch. Set aside.

Bring 3 quarts of water to a boil in a large pot. Add the noodles and cook according to the directions on the package. Drain the noodles and rinse them under cold water to stop the cooking. Lay the noodles out on paper towels to dry.

Heat the oil in a wok or large frying pan to 360°F. and add the noodles. They will cling together forming a pancake of sorts. Fry this on one side for about 5 minutes, or until the bottom is crisp, then flip the noodle pancake with a spatula and fry the other side for 3 minutes. Drain the noodle pancake on paper towels, cover with aluminum foil, and keep in a warm place.

Drain all but 2 tablespoons of the oil from the wok and add the chicken. Stir-fry until it is almost cooked, about 2 minutes. Remove the chicken from the pan and add the garlic and ginger. Cook for 30 seconds, then add the onion, bok choy, broccoli, cabbage, snow peas, and carrot. Stir-fry the vegetables for 4 minutes or until the color brightens. Return the chicken to the pan, and stir in the sauce. Cover and cook for 3 minutes, or until the vegetables are tender and the sauce thickens.

Place the noodle cake on a large serving dish and top with the chicken and vegetables. Serve hot.

VARIATION: You may substitute beef, pork, tofu, or shrimp for the chicken in this recipe.

Peking Duck with Peking Pancakes

Start to finish: 2 hours • Hands-on time: 44 minutes

Peking duck is a real celebration dish, usually at the center of a Chinese banquet. While the dish can be a bit laborious to prepare, we've tried to simplify the process by using duck breasts instead of a whole duck. It makes less of a mess in your oven and cuts down significantly on the prep and cooking time. This is a delicious and fun dish to serve to a group, but don't forget the napkins!

YIELD: 6 SERVINGS, 24 PANCAKES

PEKING DUCK

4 duck breasts, skin on

2 tablespoons honey

2 tablespoons rice vinegar

1 tablespoon soy sauce

24 Peking Pancakes, for serving

Duck sauce, for serving

1 bunch green onions, green parts cut lengthwise, to form brushes

1 English cucumber, cut into 4-inch sticks

PEKING PANCAKES

2 cups unbleached all-purpose flour

¾ cup boiling water

1 tablespoon Asian sesame oil

To make the Peking Duck: Arrange the duck breasts on a rack over a baking pan, skin side up.

Mix the honey, rice vinegar, and soy sauce together in a small bowl and brush over the skin of the duck. Let the duck breasts sit at room temperature for 1 hour, then brush them again and let sit for 15 minutes.

Meanwhile, begin making the dough for the pancakes. Combine the flour and water in a large bowl and stir with a wooden spoon. When the dough comes together, turn it out onto a lightly floured surface and knead gently for 10 minutes, or until it is smooth and elastic. Divide the dough into 2 pieces, cover it with an inverted bowl or damp towel, and let it rest for 20 minutes.

Preheat the oven to 375°F.

Add ½ cup of water to the baking pan with the duck breasts. Bake for 30 minutes, or until the skin is crispy and the duck is cooked through. (If the skin isn't crispy enough, run the breasts under the broiler for about 3 minutes.) Remove the duck from the oven and let it rest until it is cool enough to handle, about 15 minutes.

While it cools, make the pancakes. On a lightly floured surface, roll out the dough until it is ⅛-inch thick. Cut out 24 rounds using a 2½-inch round cookie cutter.

Brush the tops of half of the dough rounds with sesame oil and top with the unbrushed rounds. Roll out the rounds until they are 6 inches in diameter, stack them on a plate, and cover them with a damp towel. Continue with the remaining dough. You can combine any scraps and roll them out one more time before discarding them.

To cook the pancakes, heat a skillet over medium heat and add a pancake to the hot pan. Cook for about 1 minute, then flip it and cook for 1 minute longer. The pancake will puff up and brown slightly. Gently separate the halves and stack the cooked pancakes on a dish. Cook the remaining pancakes in the same manner.

Peel the skin from the cooled duck and cut it into small slices. Carve the duck into thin slices and arrange it on a plate next to the skin.

Allow your guests to assemble their own pancakes. Spread about 1 teaspoon of duck sauce down the middle of each pancake. Top with green onion, cucumber, duck, and skin and roll the pancake up.

Mu Shu Pork

Start to finish: 1 hour 30 minutes • Hands-on time: 1 hour 30 minutes

Mu shu pork is a party on a plate. Don't let the long ingredient list scare you. Once assembled, this dish comes together quickly and disappears from plates even faster. The homemade pancakes are to die for, but if you are feeling pressed for time, don't hesitate to use frozen store-bought mu shu or Peking pancakes from your local Asian market.

YIELD: 6 SERVINGS

24 Peking Pancakes (page 32)

1 pound pork tenderloin, thinly sliced and cut into narrow strips

4 tablespoons dry sherry or dry white wine

4 tablespoons light soy sauce

8 tablespoons vegetable oil

4 garlic cloves, minced

¼ cup chicken stock

2 tablespoons Asian sesame oil

1 teaspoon light brown sugar

½ teaspoon chili paste with garlic

1 teaspoon salt, plus more as needed

Freshly ground black pepper

2 large eggs, beaten

1 head napa cabbage, thinly sliced (4 cups)

1 cup thinly sliced shiitake mushrooms, stems discarded

4 green onions, thinly sliced

1 (1-inch) knob fresh ginger, peeled and minced

1 tablespoon cornstarch mixed with 2 tablespoons water

½ cup hoisin, for serving

Prepare the pancakes according to the directions within the Peking Duck recipe on page 32. In a small bowl, combine the pork, 2 tablespoons of the sherry, 2 tablespoons of the soy sauce, 2 tablespoons of the vegetable oil, and half the garlic. Toss together, and refrigerate while assembling the remaining ingredients.

In a separate bowl, combine the remaining 2 tablespoons of soy sauce, and sherry, the stock, 1 tablespoon of the sesame oil, the sugar, chili paste, ½ teaspoon of salt, and black pepper. Set aside.

Heat 2 tablespoons of vegetable oil in a wok or sauté pan set over medium heat. Add the eggs and stir-fry until they become firm, about 1 minute. Transfer the eggs to a large bowl.

Add another 2 tablespoons of vegetable oil to the wok and heat. Add the cabbage, mushrooms, and green onion. Sauté the vegetables until they begin to soften, about 3 minutes. Add the remaining garlic, the ginger, and ½ teaspoon of salt, and continue to cook for another minute, or until the garlic and ginger are fragrant. Transfer the mixture to the bowl containing the eggs.

Heat the remaining 2 tablespoons of vegetable oil in the wok, then add the pork and its marinade and stir-fry until it is almost cooked, about 2 minutes. Return the cabbage and eggs to the wok along with the sauce. When the sauce boils, add the cornstarch mixture and cook for another minute, or until the sauce thickens. Transfer the mixture to a heated platter.

To serve, arrange a platter with mu shu pork, pancakes, and hoisin and let your guests make their own mu shu.

Almond Cookies

Start to finish: 3 hours • Hands-on time: 1 hour

Desserts and sweets don't figure prominently in Chinese cuisine, but here in the United States, we often have a yen for a sweet ending to a meal. These little almond cookies should fill that need, especially when accompanied by Green Tea Ice Cream (page 36).

YIELD: 48 COOKIES

2¾ cups unbleached
   all-purpose flour

¾ teaspoon baking powder

¾ teaspoon baking soda

½ teaspoon salt

1 cup vegetable shortening

½ cup sugar

½ cup light brown sugar, packed

2 large eggs

1 tablespoon almond extract

1 cup blanched almonds

1 egg, lightly beaten

In a medium bowl, sift together the flour, baking powder, baking soda, and salt. Set aside.

Using an electric mixer, beat together the shortening and sugars until light and fluffy, about 3 minutes. Add the eggs one at a time and, when incorporated, add the almond extract.

Slowly add the flour mixture to the bowl and mix until a firm dough develops. Divide the dough in half and roll each piece into a cylinder about 15 inches long. Wrap the dough in plastic wrap and refrigerate for at least 2 hours.

Preheat the oven to 325°F. Line a sheet pan with parchment paper

Remove the dough from the refrigerator and cut into ¼-inch slices. Lay the slices out on the prepared pan and press an almond into the center of each cookie. Brush the cookies with egg.

Bake for 10 minutes, or until the cookies are golden brown. Transfer to a rack to cool. Store in an airtight container.

> MAKE AHEAD: The cookies can be made 1 day in advance and kept tightly wrapped.

Green Tea Ice Cream

Start to finish: 24 hours • Hands-on time: 30 minutes

You caught us! This recipe has nothing to do with authentic Chinese cuisine, but it is sooo good. The green tea powder gives this ice cream a lovely tint. How could sugar, cream, and eggs be a bad thing?

YIELD: ABOUT 1 QUART,
   FOR 6 SERVINGS

2 cups half-and-half
1 vanilla bean, split lengthwise
¾ cup sugar
6 egg yolks
Pinch of salt
1½ tablespoons matcha
   green tea powder (see note)
1 cup heavy cream
1 cup milk

In a large saucepan set over medium heat, heat the half-and-half and vanilla bean until the milk steams. Remove the pan from the heat, cover it, and let the vanilla bean steep for 15 minutes. Remove the bean and scrape the vanilla seeds from the pod, adding them to the hot half-and-half.

In a large bowl, beat the sugar and egg yolks with a whisk until well-blended. Add the hot half-and-half in a stream, whisking constantly. Return the egg mixture back to the pan and whisk in the salt and green tea powder. Heat over medium heat, stirring constantly with a wooden spoon or heatproof spatula. When the mixture begins to thicken, after about 3 minutes, remove it from the heat and transfer it to a heatproof bowl. Add the cream and milk, and stir to cool the custard. Cover and refrigerate overnight.

Process the cold custard in an ice cream maker following the manufacturer's directions. When frozen (it will be the consistency of soft-serve ice cream), transfer the ice cream to a container and freeze for 2 hours to firm up before serving.

NOTE: Matcha tea powder can be found in Asian grocers or online.

❦EASTERN EUROPEAN❦
& JEWISH

EASTERN EUROPEAN AND JEWISH DISHES are the epitome of comfort food that makes you feel good from the inside out. Whether you grew up in New York City, enjoying a warm, flaky knish at your favorite deli, or in Madison, Wisconsin, coming in from the snow to the wonderful aroma of your mother's chicken noodle soup, these dishes will bring you home.

Maybe it's because Eastern Europe has cold winters, but we get warm just thinking about chicken paprikash, beef stroganoff, and stuffed cabbage rolls. Or, maybe those warm feelings have to do with the fact that these are the same foods that many of us in America shared at the dinner table as children. Even if your mom's family was from Scandinavia, she could probably make a pretty good chicken noodle soup or beef brisket.

In Eastern Europe, cooks prefer to season food so it tastes like what it is, rather than using herbs and spices that change the character of a dish. This practice probably explains why so many of their specialties, from healing soups to kugel to pierogi, have become comfort food. As Eastern Europeans sought work and a better life in America, they brought their culture and their culinary traditions with them. Dishes like goulash have become staples on the American dinner table, whether or not the family has any Eastern European heritage. This is because the food is good, hearty, and not too intimidating. These

affordable dishes all use everyday ingredients that are easy to find in your local grocery stores, and no one will leave the table hungry.

Unlike most cuisines, Jewish and Eastern European dishes share traditions from a host of nations. Many of the dishes cooked by the Jewish communities in Eastern Europe are the same as those of Christian or Catholic neighbors who live beside them. Jewish cooking shows the influence of Middle Eastern, German, Spanish, Mediterranean, and Eastern European styles of cooking, all subject to the dietary constraints of Jewish laws.

The Jewish deli had its start in large cities, but moved rapidly across America. That's where most of us first sampled "Jewish penicillin," or matzo ball soup, the Jewish mother's answer to all that ails you. (Recent studies show that she may be right!)

Who doesn't know what a bagel is today? We're not talking about those hockey pucks, or overly fluffy, flavorless disks that you find in the freezer section of the grocery store. If you've never had a freshly baked bagel, you haven't lived. To most New Yorkers, a chewy, dense bagel topped with a schmear of cream cheese is a thing of beauty. These are familiar dishes, nothing to be afraid of, so dig right in. You'll be making knishes before you know it!

Here's a menu to get you started in your own kitchen.

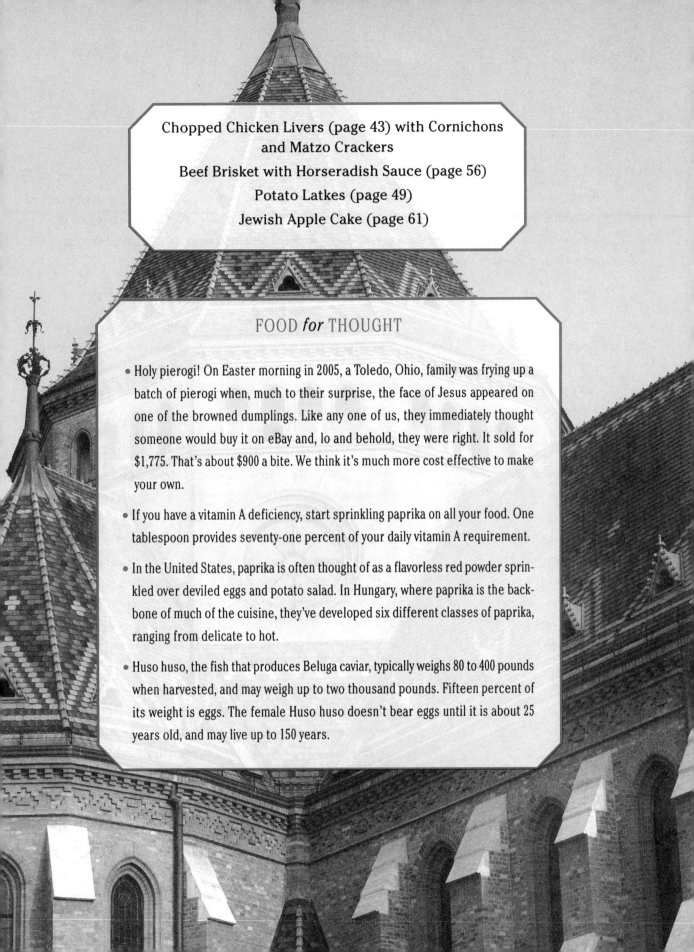

Chopped Chicken Livers (page 43) with Cornichons
and Matzo Crackers

Beef Brisket with Horseradish Sauce (page 56)

Potato Latkes (page 49)

Jewish Apple Cake (page 61)

FOOD *for* THOUGHT

- Holy pierogi! On Easter morning in 2005, a Toledo, Ohio, family was frying up a batch of pierogi when, much to their surprise, the face of Jesus appeared on one of the browned dumplings. Like any one of us, they immediately thought someone would buy it on eBay and, lo and behold, they were right. It sold for $1,775. That's about $900 a bite. We think it's much more cost effective to make your own.

- If you have a vitamin A deficiency, start sprinkling paprika on all your food. One tablespoon provides seventy-one percent of your daily vitamin A requirement.

- In the United States, paprika is often thought of as a flavorless red powder sprinkled over deviled eggs and potato salad. In Hungary, where paprika is the backbone of much of the cuisine, they've developed six different classes of paprika, ranging from delicate to hot.

- Huso huso, the fish that produces Beluga caviar, typically weighs 80 to 400 pounds when harvested, and may weigh up to two thousand pounds. Fifteen percent of its weight is eggs. The female Huso huso doesn't bear eggs until it is about 25 years old, and may live up to 150 years.

Bagels

Start to finish: 3 hours • Hands-on time: 1 hour

We really like the smaller, chewy New York–style bagels, but at most national bagel restaurant chains, you find the "bigger is better" philosophy of bagel-making, which often results in huge, fluffy, bland rings of dough. Not only are those bagels enormous in size, but they are also heavy in calories. These, in contrast, are typical of the flavorful, dense bagels you get in a really good New York bagel shop or delicatessen.

YIELD: 12 BAGELS

2 cups warm water, about 110°F.

2 (2¼ teaspoon) packages active
   dry yeast

3 tablespoons sugar

5 to 6 cups unbleached
   all-purpose flour

1 tablespoon salt

Vegetable oil

OPTIONAL TOPPINGS

Sautéed chopped onions

Poppy seeds

Sesame seeds

Caraway seeds

Kosher salt

In a large bowl, or the bowl of a stand mixer, stir together the water, yeast, and 2 tablespoons of the sugar and let stand until foamy, about 5 minutes. Using a wooden spoon or the paddle attachment on the mixer, gradually add 4½ cups of the flour and the salt, and combine until the mixture comes together.

Continue to work more flour in, ¼ cup at a time, using either the dough hook attachment of your mixer or kneading with your hands, until you have dough that is no longer sticky and is smooth and elastic. (Bagel dough is a bit heavier and stiffer than most other bread dough.) Bring the dough together into a ball.

Oil a large bowl and place the dough in the bowl, turning to coat with the oil. Cover with a clean kitchen towel and let the dough rise in a warm area until it doubles in size, about 1 hour and 15 minutes.

Uncover the dough and punch it down several times to work out the air bubbles. Form it into a ball and divide the dough into 12 equal pieces. Cover the balls with a damp cloth and allow them to rest for 5 to 10 minutes for easier shaping.

Lightly coat your hands with vegetable oil. Find the middle of one dough ball and push a finger through to make a hole. Gently widen the hole by twirling the bagel on your finger. Be careful not to rip the wall of the bagel in the process. The walls should be approximately 1 inch thick, and the hole 2 inches wide. Repeat with the remaining dough balls. Place them on a large, lightly greased baking sheet, cover with a clean cloth, and let rest 20 to 30 minutes, until risen but not doubled, in a draft-free spot.

MAKE AHEAD: The unbaked, formed bagels can be frozen with their toppings, on a parchment-lined baking sheet until solid. Then transfer to a zip top freezer bag for up to 1 month. Remove the bagels from the freezer for 1 hour before baking as directed.

Preheat the oven to 400°F.

In a large, heavy pot, bring 12 cups of water and the remaining tablespoon of sugar to a boil. In batches, add the bagels to the water and boil, turning once, for 30 seconds to 1 minute. Remove the bagels from the water, shake off any excess, and place back on the greased baking sheet.

Sprinkle any desired toppings on top of the bagels (or if you like a lot of poppy or sesame seeds, you can dip the bagel directly into the topping for extra coverage). Bake for 20 to 25 minutes, or until golden brown.

Remove from the oven and let cool on a wire rack.

FOOD *for* THOUGHT

IN 1610, the community of Krakow, Poland, stated that *beygls* (or bagels, as we know them today) would be given as gifts to women in childbirth. There's no way to know if the bagels arrived pre- or postpartum.

DON'T EAT a poppy seed bagel before a drug test. Tests suggest that ingesting just two poppy seed bagels may produce a positive result for opiates.

Challah Bread

Start to finish: 2 hours 45 minutes • Hands-on time: 30 minutes

A rich bread made with lots of eggs, challah is not only wonderful with a meal, but also is the perfect base for bread pudding and French toast. Challah is usually formed in a braid. Although you can make the braid any size you like, making one large loaf seems more practical because it allows you to make sandwich-size slices.

YIELD: 1 LARGE LOAF

1 cup warm water, about 110°F.

2 tablespoons sugar

1 (2¼ teaspoon) package active dry yeast

5 cups unbleached bread flour

1 tablespoon salt

¼ cup oil, plus more as needed

2 large eggs

3 egg yolks

MAKE AHEAD: Challah is best eaten the day you bake it, unless you are going to use it for bread pudding or French toast. You can make the dough the night before you plan to bake it. Place the dough in a bowl and cover tightly with plastic wrap. The next day, remove the bowl from the refrigerator and let the dough come to room temperature. Shape the loaf, let it rise, and bake as directed.

In a small bowl, mix together the warm water, sugar, and yeast. Allow to sit until foamy, about 5 minutes.

In a large bowl or the bowl of a stand mixer, combine the flour and salt. Add the yeast mixture, oil, eggs, and 2 of the egg yolks and stir to combine. If you are using a mixer, attach the dough hook and knead for about 4 minutes, until the dough is stretchy and smooth. If you are mixing by hand, knead the dough on a lightly floured surface for about 10 minutes.

Oil a mixing bowl and place the dough in the bowl, coating it with the oil. Cover it with a moist towel or plastic wrap and leave it to rise until it doubles in size, about 45 minutes to 1 hour.

Punch the dough down to work out the air bubbles, then use a dough cutter or knife to cut it into three equal sections. Work each section into a ball, cover the dough with a moist towel or plastic wrap, and let rest for 15 minutes.

With your hands, roll each ball into a long cylinder by rolling in and pulling out until the dough is the desired length. The cylinders should be slightly longer than the length of the baking sheet.

To begin braiding, place all three pieces of dough alongside each other, pinching them together at one end. Start braiding the dough loosely, right over left. Once you have finished braiding, fold the ends together and tuck them under the loaf so both ends of the loaf match.

Carefully place the braided dough on a parchment-lined baking sheet, cover it with a dish towel, and let it rise for 45 minutes.

Preheat the oven to 400°F.

Prepare an egg wash by mixing the remaining egg yolk and 1 tablespoon of water. Brush the mixture over the unbaked, risen challah. Bake for 30 minutes, or until the challah is golden brown on top and the internal temperature is 200°F. when tested with an instant thermometer.

Chopped Chicken Livers

Start to finish: 2 hours 20 minutes • Hands-on time: 20 minutes

The Jewish version of pâté, this rich spread gets a flavor boost from the sweet caramelized onions and the rendered chicken fat. Not a dish for the faint of heart, literally. It's wonderful on little pumpernickel squares with cornichons, but in a Jewish deli you can also find it spread between two slices of rye for lunch.

YIELD: 4 TO 6 SERVINGS

6 tablespoons Schmaltz (page 44)
1 pound chicken livers, trimmed of any visible fat and membrane
1 medium onion, coarsely chopped (1 cup)
2 large eggs, hard-cooked and chopped
¾ teaspoon salt
¼ teaspoon freshly ground black pepper
Toasted rye or pumpernickel bread, crackers, matzo, and cornichons, for serving

Prepare the schmaltz as directed in the recipe. Rinse the livers and pat them dry with paper towels.

In a large sauté pan set over medium heat, heat 2 tablespoons of the schmaltz and sauté the livers until browned, turning once, about 2 to 2½ minutes per side. They should be just barely pink inside. Don't overcook them, or they will be dry. Transfer the livers to a cutting board to cool.

Using the same pan, heat another 2 tablespoons of the schmaltz and add the onion. Cook, stirring occasionally, until golden brown, about 10 minutes.

Transfer the cooked onions and livers to the bowl of a food processor. Add the eggs, salt, pepper, and the remaining 2 tablespoons of schmaltz. Pulse 6 to 8 times, until coarsely chopped. Do not purée. Taste for seasoning and chill for at least 2 hours before serving.

Serve with toast, crackers, or matzo and cornichons.

MAKE AHEAD: Can be made 1 day ahead and kept covered in the refrigerator.

Schmaltz RENDERED CHICKEN FAT

Start to finish: 35 minutes • Hands-on time: 5 minutes

Schmaltz is highly flavorful rendered chicken fat, often used in Jewish cooking. It's easy to make and worth the effort as it tastes quite a bit different than butter or other similar fats.

YIELD: ABOUT ½ CUP

½ pound chicken fat and/or skin, cut into small pieces

1 sprig fresh thyme

1 medium onion, sliced

2 tablespoons cold water

Combine all the ingredients in a medium saucepan. Partially cover the pan and bring the mixture to a simmer over medium heat. The fat will begin to crackle as it cooks. When you no longer hear the fat crackle, remove the lid, reduce the heat to low, and continue to cook until the skin becomes crispy, about 15 to 25 minutes. (Lower the heat, if necessary, to keep the skin from browning too quickly.) Set aside to cool slightly.

Strain into a small bowl. If desired, reserve the crispy skin. Refrigerate, covered, for up to 1 week.

TIP: Trim the chicken fat and skin from whole birds before roasting and store it in the freezer until there is enough to render, or ask your butcher for some.

If you are making chicken schmaltz at the same time as the chopped chicken liver, feel free to add the brown onions and cracklings to the liver in place of the sautéed onions.

Borscht ROASTED BEET SOUP

Start to finish: 1 hour 30 minutes • Hands-on time: 30 minutes

Although everyone has heard about borscht, very few people who are not of Eastern European heritage have actually tasted this satisfying, jewel-toned soup. Roasted beets lend their magenta hue and sweet, earthy flavor, along with smoky bacon, cabbage, and rich chicken stock. The sweet-tart addition of vinegar, honey, and green apple at the end of this soup high-lights all the other flavors, making it a soup everyone should try.

YIELD: 6 TO 8 SERVINGS

1 pound medium-sized beets, with tops cut off

Salt and freshly ground black pepper

3 tablespoons extra-virgin olive oil

3 slices bacon, finely chopped

1 medium onion, finely diced

2 carrots, peeled and cut into ¼-inch dice

2 parsnips, peeled and cut into ¼-inch dice

3 sprigs fresh thyme

7 cups chicken stock

½ head savoy cabbage, shredded (3 cups)

3 tablespoons red wine vinegar

1½ tablespoons honey

1 Granny Smith apple, peeled and grated

1 tablespoon chopped fresh dill, plus more for garnish

½ cup sour cream

Preheat the oven to 400°F.

Scrub the beets and put them on a large sheet of aluminum foil; season with salt and pepper, and drizzle with 2 tablespoons of olive oil. Enclose the beets in the foil, place them on in a baking pan (to prevent dripping), and bake until the beets are tender, about 1 hour. Set aside. When the beets are cool enough to handle but still warm, peel off their skins and cut them into ¼-inch dice.

In a large, heavy-bottomed pot set over medium heat, add the bacon and cook until it begins to brown, about 3 minutes. Add the remaining table-spoon of olive oil, the onion, carrots, and parsnips, and cook until the veg-etables are softened and just starting to color, about 10 minutes. Add the thyme, stock, cabbage, and beets and simmer until the vegetables are ten-der, about 20 minutes. Remove the thyme sprigs. Add the vinegar, honey, and apple. Season with salt and pepper.

To serve, mix the dill and sour cream. Serve the borscht, hot or cold, in bowls, garnished with a dollop of dilled sour cream, and sprinkled with a little fresh dill.

> MAKE AHEAD: The soup can be made up to 2 days ahead and kept covered in the refrigerator. Reheat over medium heat if serv-ing warm. Garnish with the dilled sour cream right before serving.

Matzo Ball Soup

Start to finish: 2 hours 20 minutes • Hands-on time: 30 minutes

The sign of a great matzo ball soup lies in the lightness of the matzo ball and the richness of the stock. A matzo ball is the Jewish version of a dumpling, and in this recipe we've used a good bit of baking powder to make sure the matzo ball resembles a dumpling more than a hockey puck. We ensure a golden, rich stock by essentially making a double stock, first cooking chicken bones and vegetables together and then adding a whole chicken to boost the flavor.

YIELD: 8 TO 10 SERVINGS

STOCK

2 pounds chicken parts (wings, necks, and back bones)

2 stalks celery, including leafy tops, cut into large chunks

1 large onion, halved, with skin

3 large whole carrots, trimmed, peeled, and cut into large chunks

1 medium parsnip, peeled, and cut into large chunks

1 whole chicken

10 sprigs flat-leaf parsley

2 teaspoons salt

¼ teaspoon freshly ground black pepper

MATZO BALLS

1 tablespoon plus ¼ teaspoon salt

5 large eggs

⅓ cup vegetable oil

¼ teaspoon freshly ground black pepper

1 tablespoon baking powder

1⅓ cups matzo meal

To make the stock: Pour 4 quarts cold water into a large stockpot and add the chicken parts, celery, onion, carrots, and parsnip. Bring to a boil over medium-high heat, then reduce heat to low and simmer, uncovered, for 1 hour.

Add the whole chicken, parsley, salt, and pepper. Cover and simmer gently for 45 minutes. Transfer the chicken to a large platter. When it cools, remove the skin and bones, and cut the meat into bite-sized pieces. Add it to the soup just before serving, or save it for another use.

To make the matzo balls: Beat the eggs in a large bowl, then add the ¼ teaspoon of salt, the oil, pepper, baking powder, and matzo meal. Mix until completely blended. Cover and chill for 15 minutes to allow the dough to become firm.

Bring a large pot of water to boil, then add the remaining tablespoon of salt.

With wet hands, shape the dough into balls about 1 inch in diameter. Gently place the balls in the boiling water and reduce the heat to low. Simmer for 25 minutes, turning once so both sides cook evenly.

Strain the soup, reserving the carrots and discarding the other solids. Let the soup sit for 5 minutes, then skim off the fat that has risen to the surface. Taste and reseason with salt and pepper, if necessary. Thinly slice the carrots on the diagonal and return to the soup. Add the chicken meat, if desired. Remove the matzo balls from the hot water with a slotted spoon, place 1 or 2 in each soup bowl, and ladle the hot soup on top. Serve immediately.

> **MAKE AHEAD:** The soup can be made up to 2 days ahead and kept covered in the refrigerator. Although you can make the matzo balls ahead of time and store them in the soup, they are better made just before serving.

Goulash

Start to finish: 1 hour 30 minutes • Hands-on time: 30 minutes

Although we typically think of this dish as Hungarian, it's made all over Eastern Europe, with each country and region having its own take on the dish. Sometimes it's a soup and sometimes it's a thick stew served with spätzle or mashed potatoes. Our version is somewhere in between. It can be served as a thick, hearty soup, but it's equally wonderful spooned on top of buttery spätzle (page 112).

YIELD: 4 TO 6 SERVINGS

2 pounds boneless chuck, trimmed and cut into ½-inch cubes

Salt and freshly ground black pepper

3 slices bacon, chopped

1 tablespoon vegetable oil

2 medium onions, finely chopped

2 garlic cloves, minced

2 tablespoons Hungarian sweet paprika

2 tablespoons unbleached all-purpose flour

2 tablespoons red wine vinegar

2 tablespoons tomato paste

2 cups beef stock

½ teaspoon salt

1 red bell pepper, finely diced

¼ cup chopped flat-leaf parsley

Sour cream, for serving

Season the beef with salt and pepper. In a large, heavy pot set over medium heat, cook the bacon, stirring, until crisp. Transfer to a large bowl with a slotted spoon.

Raise the heat on the pot to medium-high, add the beef, and brown it in small batches in the bacon fat. When the meat browns, after 3 to 4 minutes, use a slotted spoon to transfer it to the bowl with the bacon.

Reduce the heat to medium and add the oil, onions, and garlic, and cook, stirring, until the vegetables are golden, about 6 minutes. Stir in the paprika and flour and cook, stirring, for 2 minutes. Whisk in the vinegar and tomato paste and cook, whisking, for 1 minute. Stir in the stock, salt, bell peppers, bacon, beef, and 1 cup of water, and bring to a boil, stirring. Reduce the heat to low and let the soup simmer, covered, for 1 hour, or until the meat is tender.

Taste and reseason with salt and pepper if necessary.

To serve, stir in the parsley, ladle the soup into bowls, and top with a dollop of sour cream. Serve immediately.

TIP: Good paprika is the key to this dish. We tend to think of paprika as something you sprinkle on top of a dish for color, but quality paprika, usually from Hungary, has a wonderful flavor all its own and adds a deep earthiness to the goulash. Look for sweet Hungarian paprika in the spice aisle of your grocery store. You can also use hot Hungarian paprika or a mixture of both if you want to make the soup spicy.

MAKE AHEAD: The soup may be made 3 days ahead and kept covered in the refrigerator. Reheat the soup, thinning with water if necessary.

Chicken Noodle Soup

Start to finish: 2 hours 20 minutes • Hands-on time: 30 minutes

There is almost no ill that this chicken noodle soup won't cure. From colds to broken hearts, Jewish mothers have always known what doctors are just now proving, that chicken noodle soup has restorative powers. The added bonus is that it tastes good, too.

YIELD: 8 TO 10 SERVINGS

2 pounds chicken parts (wings, necks, and backbones)

2 stalks celery, including leafy tops, cut into large chunks

1 large onion, halved, with skin intact

1 large whole carrot, trimmed, peeled, and cut into large chunks

1 medium whole parsnip, peeled and cut into large chunks

1 whole chicken

4 thyme sprigs

1 bay leaf

10 sprigs flat-leaf parsley

2 teaspoons salt

¼ teaspoon freshly ground black pepper

2 celery ribs, halved lengthwise and cut into ¼-inch-thick slices

12 ounces wide egg noodles

Pour 4 quarts cold water into a large stockpot and add the chicken parts, celery stalks, onion, carrot, and parsnip. Bring to a simmer and cook, uncovered, for 1 hour.

Add the whole chicken, thyme, bay leaf, parsley, salt, and pepper to the pot, cover, reduce the heat, and simmer gently for 45 minutes.

Transfer the chicken to a large platter. When it cools, remove the skin and bones and shred the meat into bite-sized pieces.

Strain the stock, reserving the carrot chunks, and discard all other solids. Cut the carrots into ¼-inch slices. Let the stock sit for 5 minutes and then skim off any excess fat that has risen to the surface. Bring to a simmer and add the carrots and celery ribs. Cook for 10 minutes. Add the noodles and simmer for another 5 minutes, or until they are just tender. Stir in the shredded chicken. Taste and reseason with salt and pepper, if necessary. Serve hot.

TIP: This soup is delicious made with store-bought noodles, but for a special treat, make homemade noodles using the Basic Egg Pasta recipe on page 182. You can use a pasta roller or simply roll the dough out with a rolling pin and cut into the desired size. We like ours on the thicker side, a luxury you get only when you make it from scratch!

> MAKE AHEAD: The stock and shredded chicken can be prepared 1 day ahead. Cover the chicken meat and stock separately and refrigerate. Bring the stock to a boil before continuing with the recipe.

Potato Latkes

Start to finish: 45 minutes • Hands-on time: 45 minutes

The hardest thing about making latkes is waiting for these crisp, slightly salty potato cakes to cool down just enough for you to eat them. Although they are traditionally eaten during Hanukkah, we love them year-round, served with applesauce and sour cream or alongside any kind of roasted meat. They also make a great accompaniment to beef brisket with horseradish sauce.

YIELD: 35 TO 40 LATKES

3 pounds russet potatoes, peeled
1 small onion, grated
   (½ cup)
2 large eggs, lightly beaten
2 teaspoons salt
½ teaspoon freshly ground
   black pepper
Vegetable oil, for frying

In a food processor or using a box grater, grate the potatoes. Line a strainer with cheesecloth and transfer the potatoes to the strainer. Set it over a large bowl and twist the cheesecloth tightly into a pouch. Continue twisting to squeeze as much moisture out of the potatoes as possible. Pour the liquid out of the bowl and add the potatoes, onion, eggs, flour, salt, and pepper. Toss to combine.

Preheat the oven to 200°F. Line a baking sheet with paper towels.

In a large skillet, heat ¼ inch of oil over medium-high heat. Drop heaping tablespoonfuls of the potato mixture into the skillet, flatten them slightly with a fork, and cook until golden brown, about 3 to 4 minutes a side. Place the cooked latkes on the baking sheet and keep them warm in the oven until ready to serve, up to 30 minutes. See headnote for serving suggestions.

Pierogi

Start to finish: about 2 hours • Hands-on time: about 1 hour 45 minutes

When Meredith started teaching cooking classes, the first thing she was asked to teach was a class on pierogi. Never having eaten a pierogi, much less made one, she had to jump into the subject with both feet. The dough in this recipe is adapted from a recipe by Janice Daltorio, a fellow cooking teacher. It is made with sour cream, which keeps it tender and adds a wonderful flavor. Filling options for pierogi are endless, but two of our favorites are sweet cabbage (as opposed to sauerkraut, also a nice option) that is flecked with fresh dill, and the winner of the pierogi popularity contest, potato-cheddar filling. Serving pierogi is a matter of taste. Some people like to keep it simple and toss their cooked pierogi in unadorned melted butter. Most prefer to serve them with onions that have been caramelized in butter. You can carefully toss your pierogi in with the onions just to warm them, or you can add them to the sauté pan and continue cooking them until they are nice and crispy. To gild the lily, serve them with sour cream on the side.

YIELD: ABOUT 50 PIEROGI

SWEET CABBAGE FILLING

1 tablespoon olive oil

2 tablespoons unsalted butter

1 large onion, finely chopped

½ head cabbage, finely shredded
   (3½ cups)

½ teaspoon salt

¼ teaspoon freshly ground
   black pepper

1 tablespoon cider vinegar

3 tablespoons finely chopped
   fresh dill

To make the cabbage filling: Heat the oil and butter in a large sauté pan set over medium heat. Add the onion and cook, stirring, for 5 minutes. Add the cabbage and sauté until tender, about 20 minutes, stirring often. Add the salt, pepper, vinegar, and dill and stir to combine. Remove from the heat. Taste and reseason if necessary. Allow the mixture to cool before filling the pierogi.

To make the potato-cheese filling: In a large pot, add the whole, unpeeled potatoes and cover with cold water. Place the pot over medium-high heat and bring to a boil. Add 2 teaspoons of salt and cook until the potatoes are tender, about 20 minutes. Drain. While the potatoes are still warm but cool enough to handle, peel them and run them through a potato ricer or food mill, or mash with potato masher.

Sauté the onion in the butter until golden brown.

Add the browned onions, the remaining teaspoon of salt, the pepper, buttermilk, and cheese to the potatoes and stir to combine. Taste and reseason with salt and pepper if necessary. Allow the potato mixture to cool before filling the pierogi.

POTATO-CHEDDAR FILLING

1½ pounds russet potatoes

3 teaspoons salt

1 large onion, chopped

2 tablespoons unsalted butter

½ teaspoon freshly ground
   black pepper

⅓ cup buttermilk

4 ounces cheddar cheese, grated

DOUGH

4 large eggs

1 teaspoon plus 1 tablespoon salt

1 cup sour cream

3 cups unbleached
   all-purpose flour

Filling

Cornmeal

> **MAKE AHEAD:** Pierogi can be frozen uncooked in a single layer on a cornmeal-dusted baking sheet. Once frozen solid, transfer the pierogi to a freezer bag. Cook directly from the freezer in gently boiling, salted water for 10 minutes, or until the dough is just tender (take one out and test it).

To make the dough: In a large bowl or the bowl of a stand mixer, beat together the eggs, 1 teaspoon of salt, and the sour cream. Gradually mix in the flour. The dough will be soft and slightly sticky. Knead the dough with your hands on a floured surface or with the dough hook attachment on the mixer until the dough is smooth and no longer sticky, but still soft. Allow it to rest loosely covered for 10 minutes.

Divide the dough into 2 pieces. Work with one piece at a time, keeping the other half covered to prevent drying out. Roll the dough out on a well-floured surface to ⅛-inch thickness. Cut into 2-inch rounds and fill the center of each with ½ tablespoon of filling. Fold the dough over to make a half round, making sure you pinch all around the edges to seal the pierogi. Place the filled pierogi on a large baking sheet that has been dusted with cornmeal. Make sure they don't touch one another or they will stick together.

In a large pot, bring 4 quarts of water to a boil. Add the remaining tablespoon of salt. Add a dozen pierogi and bring the water back to a gentle boil. Don't cook at a rolling boil, or you will surely burst your pierogi (not a pretty sight!). Cook for about 8 minutes, or until the dough is just tender (take one out and test it). Carefully transfer the cooked pierogi to a warm serving platter with a slotted spoon and cool slightly before serving.

TIP: Each pierogi has only ½ tablespoon of filling that's surrounded by dough. In order to taste the filling, it needs to be well-seasoned. Although we're not suggesting you oversalt the filling, it is important to season it enough so the flavor of the filling stands out.

Potato Knishes

Start to finish: 2 hours 15 minutes • Hands-on time: 1 hour

Almost every cuisine has a version of knishes. In India they're called samosas, in Spain and Mexico, you can find empanadas. The filling may change, but the heart of the dish remains the same. There are lots of different options when it comes to filling your knish. Sometimes you'll find them with meat, or kasha, or sauerkraut, or cheese. We like the popular potato-filled knish. You can't help but feel decadent when you're eating this carb-on-carb delight. The warm, flavorful potato-and-caramelized-onion filling, encased in a buttery, flaky pastry dough, is too good to pass up.

YIELD: ABOUT 22 KNISHES

DOUGH

2 cups unbleached all-purpose
flour, plus more for rolling

¼ pound (1 stick) unsalted
butter, chilled

3 tablespoons shortening, chilled

½ teaspoon salt

2 large eggs

FILLING

1¼ pounds russet (baking) potatoes

2 teaspoons salt

2 tablespoons vegetable oil

1 large onion, diced

1 large egg

¼ cup chopped flat-leaf parsley

1 teaspoon salt

Freshly ground black pepper

To make the dough: Combine the flour, butter, shortening, and salt in the bowl of a food processor and pulse about 7 or 8 times, until the butter and shortening form pea-sized pieces. Mix one egg with ⅓ cup cold water and add to the processor in a steady stream through the feed tube while pulsing 4 to 6 times to incorporate it into the flour mixture. Remove the dough from the food processor and shape it into 3 balls. Cover with plastic wrap and chill for 1 hour.

To make the filling: Peel the potatoes and cut them in half. Put them in a large pot filled with cold water. Add the salt and bring to a gentle boil. Cook until the potatoes are tender, about 15 minutes.

Meanwhile, heat the oil in a medium skillet set over medium heat. Add the onions and sauté until they are golden brown, about 8 to 10 minutes.

Drain the potatoes, then push them through a potato ricer into a large bowl. Add the egg, parsley, salt, pepper, and onions and mix well. Set aside to cool.

Preheat the oven to 375°F.

To assemble: Remove the dough from the refrigerator. Working with one dough ball at a time, roll into a 14 x 4-inch rectangle on a lightly floured work surface. Spread a third of the cooled filling down the length of the dough, leaving a 1-inch border. Bring both sides up around the filling and pinch to close the sides and ends of dough, creating a log. Roll the log over so that the sealed edge is on the bottom.

Using the side of your hand like a knife, divide the log into 2-inch sections. Cut them with a knife and use a fork to seal the edges. Repeat with the remaining dough and filling. Place the knishes, flat-side-down, on parchment-lined baking sheets.

Mix the remaining egg and 1 tablespoon of water together with a fork. Brush the tops of the knishes with the egg wash. Bake for 25 to 35 minutes, or until the knishes are golden brown.

Stuffed Cabbage Rolls

Start to finish: 2 hours 15 minutes • Hands-on time: 40 minutes

Carla grew up in a West Virginia steel mill town that had a large Eastern European community. She remembers large electric roasters filled to the brim with cabbage rolls at the Serbian picnic grounds. No matter how many cabbage rolls were made, it was never enough. The sweet-and-sour tomato sauce in this recipe gives a tangy edge to these meat-and-rice stuffed rolls that we find irresistible.

YIELD: 6 TO 8 SERVINGS

TOMATO SAUCE

2 tablespoons olive oil

1 small onion, finely chopped
   (½ cup)

2 garlic cloves, chopped

1 (28-ounce) can crushed tomatoes

2 tablespoons cider vinegar

2 tablespoons light brown sugar

1 teaspoon salt

½ teaspoon freshly ground black
   pepper

FILLING

1 tablespoon olive oil

1 medium onion, chopped

1 garlic clove, minced

½ pound ground beef

½ pound ground pork

1 large egg

2 tablespoons chopped
   flat-leaf parsley

⅔ cup cooked white rice

To make the sauce: Heat the oil in a large saucepan over medium heat. Add the onion and garlic and sauté until translucent, about 3 minutes. Reduce the heat to low and add the tomatoes and 1 cup of water. Cook, stirring occasionally, for 5 minutes. Add the vinegar and brown sugar. Simmer until the sauce thickens, about 20 minutes. Season with salt and pepper and remove from the heat.

To make the filling: Heat the oil in a medium skillet over medium heat. Add the onion and garlic and sauté until translucent, about 3 minutes. Stir in ½ cup of the tomato sauce and remove from the heat. Combine the beef and pork in a large mixing bowl. Add the egg, parsley, rice, onion mixture, salt, and pepper. Use your hands to mix the filling together.

Bring a large pot of salted water to a boil. Add the cabbage leaves and cook until tender, about 3 to 4 minutes. Drain the leaves in a colander and refresh under cold running water. Blot each leaf dry with paper towels. Cut out the thick part of the center vein from the leaves.

Preheat the oven to 350°F. Spread ½ cup sauce on the bottom of a 13 x 9-inch baking pan and set aside.

Put about ⅓ cup of filling in the center of a cabbage leaf and fold the sides in and roll up, starting at the stem end, to enclose the filling. Place the rolls side-by-side, seam-side-down, in the prepared baking pan. Pour the remaining sauce over the rolls and cover the pan with foil.

Bake for 45 minutes. Remove the foil, baste the rolls with sauce, and continue cooking for 30 minutes. Serve hot.

¾ teaspoon salt

¼ teaspoon freshly ground
   black pepper

8 large savoy or green
   cabbage leaves

TIP: We find savoy cabbage easier to work with, but if you want to make them just like grandma did, go ahead and use regular green cabbage.

> MAKE AHEAD: The cabbage rolls can be assembled and kept covered in the refrigerator up to 1 hour. Bake as directed, adding 5 to 10 minutes to the baking time.

Chicken Paprikash

Start to finish: 1 hour • Hands-on time: 20 minutes

Which came first . . . the paprikash or the spätzle? Who cares. What's important is that they're together now. This dish is an all-time favorite with both of our families. What's not to love? The creamy, rich, paprika–sour cream sauce is served over tender, braised chicken and homemade spätzle. This is comfort food at its best.

YIELD: 4 TO 6 SERVINGS

4- to 5-pound chicken,
   cut into 8 pieces
Salt and freshly ground
   black pepper
2 tablespoons vegetable oil
1 medium onion, chopped
2 tablespoons sweet Hungarian
   paprika
2 cups chicken stock
½ cup sour cream
2 tablespoons unbleached
   all-purpose flour
Spätzle (page 112), for serving

Rinse and dry the chicken pieces. Season with salt and pepper.

Heat the oil in a large skillet over medium-high heat. Working in two batches, add the chicken to the skillet and brown, about 3 minutes per side. Remove the chicken from the skillet and set aside.

Reduce the heat to medium. Add the onion and sauté until it is softened, about 6 minutes. Add the paprika and cook, stirring constantly to prevent burning, for 1 minute. Stir in the stock and return the chicken to the skillet. Reduce the heat to low and simmer, partially covered, for 40 minutes, or until the chicken is completely cooked.

In a small bowl, whisk together the sour cream and flour until smooth. Add the sour cream mixture to the skillet and bring back to a low simmer. Cook for 5 minutes or until the sauce is slightly thickened. Season with salt and pepper. Serve with the spätzle.

> MAKE AHEAD: The recipe can be made up to the point of adding the sour cream 1 day ahead, then cooled and kept covered in the refrigerator. Bring back to a simmer until heated through and then proceed with the recipe.

Beef Brisket with Horseradish Sauce

Start to finish: 4 hours • Hands-on time: 40 minutes

If your idea of pot roast is a plate of tough beef served with mushy vegetables, give this recipe a try. What makes it special is the process of reducing the red wine, which concentrates its flavor, and combining it with a liberal dose of honey. This gives the sauce and meat an intense, robust flavor you won't find in the pot roast special at most roadside diners.

YIELD: 8 TO 10 SERVINGS

4- to 5-pound beef brisket
Salt and freshly ground
  black pepper
1 cup unbleached all-purpose flour
2 tablespoons olive oil
2 large onions, thinly sliced
4 garlic cloves, sliced
1 (6-ounce) can tomato paste
2 cups dry red wine
2 bay leaves
1 teaspoon dried thyme
3 cups beef stock, homemade
  or low-sodium
¼ cup honey

HORSERADISH SAUCE

⅓ cup prepared horseradish
1 tablespoon white wine vinegar
1 cup mayonnaise
2 tablespoons chopped
  fresh chives
Kosher salt and freshly ground
  black pepper

Preheat the oven to 325°F.

Season the brisket with salt and pepper. Place the flour in a large, shallow dish. Dredge the brisket in the flour and shake off the excess.

Heat the oil in a large Dutch oven over medium-high heat. Add the brisket and cook until well-browned, about 6 to 8 minutes per side. Transfer the brisket to a plate.

Add the onions to the pot and cook until softened, about 6 minutes. Add the garlic and tomato paste and continue to cook for another 3 minutes. Add the wine, bay leaves, and thyme. Increase the heat to high and bring to a boil. Cook rapidly, stirring often, until almost all the liquid has evaporated. Pour in the stock and honey and bring back to a boil. Reduce the heat to medium and add the brisket. Move the pot to a rack in the lower third of the oven and braise the beef, covered, until a fork comes out easily when the meat is pierced, about 3 hours.

Meanwhile, make the horseradish sauce. Mix the horseradish, vinegar, mayonnaise, and chives in a small bowl. Stir well to blend and season with salt and pepper. Refrigerate until ready to use.

Transfer the brisket to a cutting board and cut it into thin slices. Place the meat on a serving platter, pour the pan juices over the meat and serve with horseradish sauce.

> MAKE AHEAD: Both the brisket and the horseradish sauce can be made the day before. Reheat the meat in the sauce on the stovetop over medium heat until warm.

Beef Stroganoff

Start to finish: 30 minutes • Hands-on time: 30 minutes

Although the name conjures images of czars and onion-domed palaces, the currently accepted history of this dish places its origin in the 1890s, when a chef working for Count Pavel Alexandrovich Stroganov (a famous Russian general) invented it for a cooking competition. It's a deceptively simple dish that is essentially strips of beef tenderloin in a rich and earthy mushroom-and-sour-cream sauce.

YIELD: 4 TO 6 SERVINGS

2½-pound piece beef tenderloin, well trimmed, cut into 3 x 1 x ½-inch strips

Salt and freshly ground black pepper

2 tablespoons vegetable oil

6 tablespoons butter

¼ cup finely chopped shallots

1 pound small button mushrooms, thickly sliced

2 cups beef stock, homemade or low-sodium

2 tablespoons Cognac

12 ounces wide egg noodles

¼ cup heavy cream

½ cup sour cream

1 tablespoon unbleached all-purpose flour

1 tablespoon Dijon mustard

1 tablespoon chopped fresh dill

Pat the meat dry with paper towels, then sprinkle with salt and pepper.

Heat the oil in a heavy, large skillet over high heat until very hot. Working in batches, add several slices of the meat in a single layer (do not crowd the pan) and brown about 1 minute per side. The meat should be rare at this point. Transfer to a warm plate. Cook the remaining meat in the same manner.

Lower the heat to medium-high and melt 2 tablespoons of butter in the same skillet. Add the shallots and sauté until tender, about 2 minutes. Add the mushrooms and sauté until brown, about 10 minutes. Add the stock, then the Cognac. Simmer until the liquid thickens and just coats the mushrooms, about 15 minutes. Remove from the heat.

Bring a large pot of salted water to a boil, then cook the noodles until tender, about 6 to 8 minutes. Drain and transfer to a bowl. Add the remaining 4 tablespoons butter and toss to coat. Season with salt and pepper.

Meanwhile, in a medium bowl, whisk together the cream and sour cream. Sprinkle the flour on top and whisk to combine. Stir the sour cream mixture and the mustard into the mushroom-stock mixture in the pot. Add the meat and any accumulated juices from the plate. Simmer over medium-low heat until the meat is heated through but still medium-rare, about 2 minutes. Stir in the dill and season to taste with salt and pepper.

To serve, divide the noodles among the plates. Top with the beef and sauce.

TIP: Although using beef tenderloin makes a wonderfully tender dish, it is a luxury. You may substitute a good quality sirloin. To ensure its tenderness, cut the sirloin into thin slices against the grain and make sure you don't overcook the beef.

Potica NUT ROLLS

Start to finish: 4 hours 20 minutes • Hands-on time: 1 hour 10 minutes

One of Carla's favorite family recipes, these nut rolls are especially nice to have in your freezer over the holidays. The dough is easy to work with and the nut filling is rich and sweet. We like lots of filling in our nut rolls, and the recipe reflects that fact. Make sure you slather it onto the dough generously, and reap the rewards.

YIELD: 5 LARGE ROLLS

DOUGH

2 (2¼ teaspoon) packages
    active dry yeast

2 cups scalded milk, cooled
    to lukewarm

½ pound (2 sticks) unsalted butter,
    softened

1 cup sugar

1 teaspoon salt

2 large eggs, beaten

7 cups unbleached all-purpose
    flour, plus more as needed

FILLING

2 pounds walnuts, finely ground

2 cups sugar

½ pound (2 sticks) unsalted
    butter, melted

2 large eggs, beaten

¼ teaspoon salt

1⅓ cups milk

1 egg, beaten, for egg wash

To make the dough: Dissolve the yeast in 1 cup of the milk.

Combine the butter, sugar, and salt in the bowl of a stand mixer. Mix on speed 4 with the flat beater until light and fluffy, about 2 minutes. Turn the mixer to stir (speed 2), add the yeast-milk mixture and 3 cups of the flour, and beat until well mixed, about 1 minute.

Exchange the flat beater for the dough hook and add the remaining flour in ¼-cup additions, interspersed with the remaining cup of lukewarm milk. Knead the dough with the dough hook on speed 2 until smooth and elastic, about 10 minutes. Remove the bowl from the mixer, cover it with plastic, and let the dough rise in a draft-free spot until it doubles in size, about 2 hours.

To make the filling: Add the walnuts, sugar, butter, eggs, salt, and milk to a large pot. Cook slowly over medium heat, stirring constantly until thick, about 4 to 6 minutes. Be careful that the bottom doesn't scorch. Cool.

Punch down the risen dough and divide it into 5 equal parts. Roll out each piece on a lightly floured surface into a 12 x 12-inch rectangle. The dough will be thin. Spread about a fifth of the filling over the dough, leaving a 1-inch margin along the edges. This will help the nut roll to seal. Start from the far edge and roll the dough up tightly toward you. Pinch the ends together and lay the nut roll seam-side-down on a parchment-lined baking sheet. Repeat with the remaining dough and filling, leaving 4 to 5 inches of space between the rolls. Cover and let the rolls rise for 30 minutes.

Preheat the oven to 350°F.

Brush the rolls with the egg wash. Bake them for 45 to 50 minutes. Cool before slicing.

TIP: These rolls are great to give as gifts during the holidays. They freeze, baked and tightly wrapped, for up to 2 months.

Sweet Noodle Kugel

Start to finish: 1 hour 30 minutes • Hands-on time: 30 minutes

If you enjoy bread pudding, this noodle pudding will be right up your alley. It is the perfect comfort food. Although kugel is sometimes a savory side dish, we are featuring it as a dessert. The sour cream and cottage cheese blend together with sugar, vanilla, and cinnamon to make a sweet, creamy base for the bow-tie noodles.

YIELD: 8 SERVINGS

16 ounces bow-tie noodles (farfalle)

16 ounces cottage cheese

2 cups sour cream

6 tablespoons unsalted butter, melted

1 cup sugar

5 large eggs, beaten

¼ teaspoon salt

1 teaspoon vanilla extract

1 teaspoon cinnamon

2 cups cornflakes

Preheat the oven to 350°F.

Bring a large pot of salted water to a boil. Cook the noodles until al dente, about 8 minutes, and drain.

In the bowl of a food processor, combine the cottage cheese, sour cream, 4 tablespoons of the butter, ¾ cup of the sugar, the eggs, salt, vanilla, and ½ teaspoon of the cinnamon. Pulse until smooth. Pour into a large bowl. Add the cooked noodles and toss well. Transfer the mixture to a buttered 13 x 9 x 2-inch baking dish.

Add the cornflakes to the bowl of a food processor and pulse to make crumbs.

In a large bowl, mix the remaining ¼ cup sugar and remaining ½ teaspoon cinnamon. Add the cornflake crumbs and the remaining 2 tablespoons butter and toss to combine. Top the noodle mixture with the cornflake mixture.

Bake for 1 hour, or until the kugel is cooked through and the top is puffy and golden. Remove from the oven and let rest for 15 minutes before cutting into squares. Serve warm or at room temperature.

VARIATION: Try soaking raisins, currants, chopped dried apricots, or any other dried fruit that you enjoy in brandy or rum and toss them with the noodles and sour cream mixture before baking. You can also add chopped walnuts or pecans.

Cheese Blintzes

Start to finish: 2 hours 15 minutes • Hands-on time: 45 minutes

Cheese blintzes are crêpes filled with a sweetened blend of cheeses and topped with a fruit sauce. They're a mainstay of the Sunday brunch buffet table. Unfortunately, a blintz's life in a chafing dish can be long, which can make it greasy and tough. Making them at home gives you the chance to taste a freshly made, tender crêpe wrapped around a not-too-sweet filling and dappled with a vibrant blueberry sauce . . . a totally different take on an often mistreated classic.

YIELD: 12 BLINTZES, 6 TO 8 SERVINGS

1¼ cups milk

3 large eggs

1¼ cups unbleached
   all-purpose flour

2 tablespoons granulated sugar

¾ teaspoon salt, plus a pinch

5 tablespoons unsalted butter,
   melted and cooled

2 tablespoons oil

16 ounces farmer's cheese

4 ounces cottage cheese

¼ cup confectioners' sugar

Zest of 1 lemon

1 egg yolk

2 (11.5-ounce) jars good-quality
   blueberry preserves or jam

2 tablespoons fresh lemon juice

4 tablespoons butter

Sour cream, for serving

> **MAKE-AHEAD:** Can be made up to 1 day ahead and kept covered in the refrigerator until ready to fry.

To make the crêpes: Combine the milk, eggs, flour, sugar, ¾ teaspoon salt, and 3 tablespoons of butter in a blender. Blend at high speed for 10 seconds. Scrape down the inside of the jar with a spatula and blend again for 30 seconds. The batter should be the consistency of heavy cream. Transfer the batter to a bowl and let it sit covered at room temperature for 1 hour before using.

Have a large plate or platter ready. Place a large skillet over moderately high heat, brush lightly with melted butter, and heat until the butter begins to smoke. Pour ¼ to ⅓ cup of batter into the pan, tilting to spread into a thin, even layer. Cook about 1 to 2 minutes, until the edges curl slightly away from skillet and the underside is lightly browned. Use a flexible spatula to flip the crêpe out of the skillet onto a plate, cooked-side-up. Repeat with the remaining batter and melted butter.

To make the filling: In a food processor, combine the farmer's cheese, cream cheese, confectioners' sugar, lemon zest, and egg yolk and blend until smooth. Chill for about 30 minutes.

Place 1 crêpe, cooked-side-up, on a plate. Place 2 tablespoons of filling in the center and fold up the bottom to cover the filling. Fold down the top, fold in the sides, then roll it up. Place it seam-side-down on a large plate. Repeat with the remaining crêpes and filling.

To make the sauce: In medium saucepan, heat the preserves over low heat until melted, about 3 minutes. Remove from the heat and stir in the lemon juice. Heat 1 tablespoon of the butter in an iron skillet over moderately high heat. Add 3 blintzes and fry until golden brown on both sides, about 1 to 2 minutes per side. Repeat with remaining blintzes and butter. Serve hot with blueberry sauce and sour cream.

Jewish Apple Cake

Start to finish: 1 hour 10 minutes • Hands-on time: 20 minutes

This simple vanilla pound cake filled with cinnamon, apples, and walnuts goes well with a cup of coffee in the morning and a glass of dessert wine after dinner. Meredith's neighbor brought one over when Meredith's son was born. That cake lives in her memory as the only thing that made those first few sleepless nights bearable.

YIELD: 12 SERVINGS

- 3 Granny Smith apples, peeled, cored, and cut into ½-inch chunks
- 1 tablespoon lemon juice
- ¼ cup plus 2 cups sugar
- 1 teaspoon cinnamon
- ½ cup coarsely chopped walnuts
- 1 cup of vegetable oil
- 1 teaspoon vanilla extract
- 4 large eggs
- 3 cups unbleached all-purpose flour
- 2 teaspoons baking powder
- 1 teaspoon salt
- ½ cup orange juice

Preheat the oven to 350°F. Generously butter a 10-inch tube pan and dust with flour.

In a large bowl, mix together the apples, lemon juice, ¼ cup of the sugar, the cinnamon, and walnuts. Set aside.

Using a mixer, beat together the oil, vanilla, and remaining 2 cups of sugar. Beat in the eggs one at a time.

In a separate bowl, whisk together the flour, baking powder, and salt.

Drain any excess liquid that has accumulated in the bottom of the apple bowl and combine with the orange juice.

Gradually beat portions of the flour mixture into the egg batter alternately with portions of the orange juice mixture, beginning and ending with the dry ingredients. Mix well after each addition.

Pour three-fourths of the batter into the prepared pan. Top with the apple-walnut mixture and spoon the remaining batter on top of the apples.

Bake until golden and a wooden skewer inserted in the middle of the cake comes out with a few crumbs adhering, about 50 minutes. Cool the cake in the pan on a rack for 20 minutes. Run a thin knife around the inner and outer edges of the cake, then place the rack over the pan and invert the cake onto the rack to cool.

> MAKE AHEAD: This cake can be made 1 day ahead and kept covered at room temperature.

❧ FRENCH ❧

WHY DOES FRENCH COOKING SEEM SO SCARY? Maybe, in the back of our minds, we all have a little French chef yelling, "Your soufflé is falling, your crêpes suzette will never flambé, St. Jacques would be ashamed of your coquilles!" Never fear, this chapter will clear your culinary head and get rid of your kitchen demons. So roll up your sleeves, don your toque, and dive in to some of the best food this side of the Eiffel Tower.

In *la belle* France, cooking is viewed as an art form . . . where a meal in a four-star restaurant is regarded as theater you can eat. But make no mistake, this reverence for fine dining begins at home in the traditional family gatherings around the table, where meals are lovingly prepared and then leisurely consumed amid multiple courses, wine, cheese, and spirited conversation.

In order to simplify (due to time and space constraints), we have classified French cuisine into two basic categories: haute cuisine (sophisticated, refined food) and provincial cuisine (simple, country cooking). Up until the last twenty years, most French restaurants in the United States served the classic haute cuisine, but now we see more and more restaurants or bistros featuring the regional foods of the French countryside, such as cassoulet, croque monsieur, quiche, or roast chicken. These diverse regions afford the French many culinary options with varied dishes rich in culture and tradition.

The French are choosy about their food and nowhere is this fact more evident than in their consumption of bread, wine, and cheese. Bread, bought daily from the neighborhood bakery, accompanies every meal. They like their long, skinny baguettes, with a dense interior and a crispy crust.

Wine is synonymous with France, home of the most celebrated vineyards in the world. The fruit of the grape is not saved for special occasions, but consumed as a standard part of everyday meals, and great care is taken to match the wines with the style of food served. Cheese can accompany a meal or can even be a course by itself, served after the meal, but before the dessert. The cheese course usually includes three or four cheeses, bread, and fruit.

Many have the mistaken impression that French food is all cream and butter. They couldn't be more wrong—there are also copious amounts of wine! Really though, most French dishes are straightforward and simple, made from the freshest seasonal ingredients. Many of the recipes in this chapter can be made from ingredients that are probably already in your pantry or refrigerator.

Because French culinary technique is taught as the basis for the curriculum in most cooking schools across the country, there is a coherence to the work environment. Everyone who knows the French culinary technique knows how to perform certain tasks in the same way. It is the universal language of the kitchen. At the beginning of our culinary careers, it was by using these techniques that we learned how to cook. We like to say that once you learn a technique, you can adapt it to make a hundred different recipes. In this chapter, we offer you a basic introduction to the complex cuisine that was the beginning of our love affair with cooking. We hope to ignite the same passion in you.

Try the following menu for French cuisine.

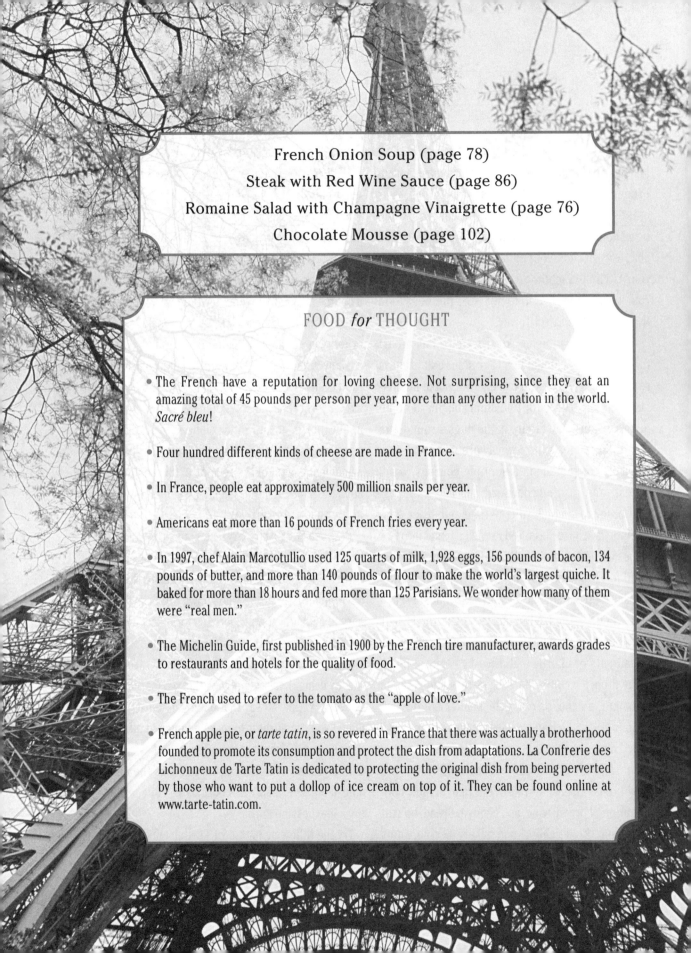

FOOD *for* THOUGHT

- The French have a reputation for loving cheese. Not surprising, since they eat an amazing total of 45 pounds per person per year, more than any other nation in the world. *Sacré bleu*!

- Four hundred different kinds of cheese are made in France.

- In France, people eat approximately 500 million snails per year.

- Americans eat more than 16 pounds of French fries every year.

- In 1997, chef Alain Marcotullio used 125 quarts of milk, 1,928 eggs, 156 pounds of bacon, 134 pounds of butter, and more than 140 pounds of flour to make the world's largest quiche. It baked for more than 18 hours and fed more than 125 Parisians. We wonder how many of them were "real men."

- The Michelin Guide, first published in 1900 by the French tire manufacturer, awards grades to restaurants and hotels for the quality of food.

- The French used to refer to the tomato as the "apple of love."

- French apple pie, or *tarte tatin*, is so revered in France that there was actually a brotherhood founded to promote its consumption and protect the dish from adaptations. La Confrerie des Lichonneux de Tarte Tatin is dedicated to protecting the original dish from being perverted by those who want to put a dollop of ice cream on top of it. They can be found online at www.tarte-tatin.com.

Flaky Pastry PÂTE BRISÉE

Start to finish: 2 hour 20 minutes • Hands-on time: 20 minutes

It is so easy to make your own pastry, and yet, so many people are afraid to try. As encouragement, we offer two ways. The results will surprise you, and there is no limit to the dishes you can crank out of your kitchen that feature pastry as an ingredient.

YIELD: 1 (10-INCH) PIECRUST

1½ cups unbleached all-purpose
    flour, chilled in freezer for 1 hour
¼ teaspoon salt
¼ pound plus 1 tablespoon
    unsalted butter, cut into ½-inch
    pieces and chilled in freezer
    for 1 hour
⅓ cup ice water

MAKE AHEAD: The pastry can be kept in the refrigerator, tightly wrapped in plastic, for up to 2 days. It may also be rolled out, wrapped, and frozen for up to 2 months.

To make in a stand mixer: Combine the flour, salt, and butter in the bowl of a stand mixer. Using the paddle attachment, mix for 30 seconds on low speed. Turn the mixer to medium speed and mix until the butter is cut into the flour and only small lumps of butter remain, about 1 minute. Quickly add the ice water and stop the machine when the dough begins to come together. Remove the dough from the bowl and compress it into a disk with your hands. Wrap it in plastic and refrigerate for 1 hour.

To make in a food processor: Place the flour, salt, and butter in the bowl of a food processor and pulse about 10 times, until the butter is reduced to pea-sized pieces. Add the ice water in a steady stream through the feed tube while pulsing 4 to 6 times, just enough to incorporate the water into the flour and butter. Transfer the dough onto a cool work surface. The mixture will not have come together yet and will look shaggy and dry. Using the heel of your hand, smear the pastry mixture against the counter, bit by bit, until it comes together and forms a rough dough. Shape it into a disk and wrap it in plastic. Refrigerate the pastry for 1 hour.

TIP: We make 4 or 5 dough discs at a time, roll them out, and freeze them layered between parchment and wrapped in plastic. When a recipe calls for pastry, we just take a layer out of the freezer, defrost it for about 30 minutes, and use it as directed in the recipe.

Croissants

Start to finish: 10 to 24 hours • Hands-on time: 1 hour 30 minutes

To most French people, the best croissants are made by the local baker. Unfortunately, the lack of French bakeries in most American neighborhoods means that most of us have never tasted a freshly baked, all-butter croissant. The sad fact is that most rolls passed off as croissants at the local grocery arrive at the store frozen and are not made with butter, but with hydrogenated fats, which is bad news for our health and even worse news for our taste buds.

The taste of a freshly baked croissant, though not life-changing, will convince you never to eat a subpar croissant again. We like to start this recipe a day ahead so it can easily take a starring role in celebratory dinners. This ethereal pastry will take some time to produce, but most of it is hands-off rising and cooling times spent in the refrigerator.

Thanks to Julia Child and Simone Beck's Mastering the Art of French Cooking *for the inspiration of this recipe.*

YIELD: 20 CROISSANTS

1 (2¼ teaspoon) package active dry yeast

2 tablespoons sugar

1½ cups warm milk (110°F.)

3½ cups unbleached all-purpose flour, plus more as needed

2½ teaspoons salt

½ pound plus 4 tablespoons (2½ sticks) unsalted butter, chilled

1 large egg, beaten with 2 tablespoons water

In a small bowl, combine, but do not stir, the yeast, sugar, and warm milk. Let it sit undisturbed for 5 minutes, at which time the top of the milk will be foamy and the yeast activated. Stir to dissolve the sugar.

In a large mixing bowl or a stand mixer bowl, combine the flour and salt. Make a well in the center of the flour and add the yeast mixture. If you are using a stand mixer, attach the paddle and mix on speed 2 until the dough comes together, about 1 or 2 minutes. Change to the dough hook and knead for about 2 minutes. If you are making the dough by hand, mix the dough with a wooden spoon until combined, then turn it out onto a work surface and knead until the dough is smooth and elastic, about 4 minutes.

Place the dough in a large (12-cup) bowl and cover with plastic wrap. Let rise in a warm place (75°F.) until it triples in size, about 2½ hours.

Punch the dough down to deflate it and let it rise again until it doubles in size, about 1½ hours.

Deflate the dough by loosening up the sides with a rubber scraper. Cover with plastic wrap and refrigerate for 30 minutes.

Remove the dough from the refrigerator and turn it out onto a floured surface. Roll the dough out into a rectangle measuring 20 x 14 inches.

Flour a work surface near the dough and lay out the butter, with two sticks side by side and the half stick across the top end to form what looks like a letter T. Flour the butter. (The flour keeps the butter from melting and becoming messy, so use however much sticks on the butter.) Pound it with a rolling pin, trying to keep it together in one piece until it measures roughly 14 x 12 inches. (It's okay if the butter breaks into pieces, just push it back together.)

Lay the butter on the top two-thirds of the dough, leaving a 1-inch border around the edges. The bottom third of the dough won't have any butter on it. Starting at the bottom third that isn't covered with butter, fold the dough into three layers, like a business letter. Fold the dough up and over to cover part of the butter-covered dough. Pat down to secure it and fold the other end of the butter-covered dough up and over the previous fold. You now have three layers of dough covering two layers of butter. This is turn #1.

To make the next turn, position the dough so that an open end faces you, then roll out the dough with a rolling pin into a rectangle about 18 x 10 inches. Brush any flour from the top of the dough with a dry pastry brush. Fold it into thirds as before. Wrap the dough in plastic wrap and place it in a bag. At this point, you can store the dough in the refrigerator overnight to bake the next day or, to continue with the recipe, chill the dough for 1 hour.

When you're ready to proceed, remove the dough from the refrigerator, unwrap it, and let it sit for 10 minutes to warm up. Roll out the dough again into an 18 x 10-inch rectangle. Fold it into thirds, roll it out again, and fold it into thirds one more time, for a total of four turns. Rewrap the dough and chill for 1 hour.

About 2 hours before you are ready to bake the croissants, remove the dough from the refrigerator, unwrap it, and let it sit for 10 minutes to warm up.

On a lightly floured surface, roll out the dough into a 30 x 5-inch rectangle. Cut the dough in half crosswise, making two 15 x 5-inch rectangles, and refrigerate one half while you use the other to shape your first batch.

Roll the dough into a 25 x 5-inch rectangle and cut it into 5 (5-inch) squares. Refrigerate 4 squares while you work with one.

Cut the square on the diagonal to make 2 triangles and use your rolling pin to roll out each triangle so that, from the wide end to the tip, it is about 7 inches long.

Using your fingers, roll each dough triangle from the wide end to the tip into a tube, then bend the two ends down to form a crescent shape. Arrange the croissants on a parchment paper–lined sheet pan about 3 inches apart. Repeat with the remaining squares. *While you work, it is important to keep the dough cold. If it starts to look oily or becomes difficult to work with, return it to the refrigerator to firm up.*

Cover the croissants with a clean kitchen towel and let them rise for 1 hour.

Preheat the oven to 450°F.

Brush the risen rolls with the egg wash and bake them for 12 to 15 minutes. Serve hot or at room temperature.

MAKE AHEAD: Since they are so full of butterfat, croissants freeze surprisingly well. Freeze baked croissants on a baking sheet, then transfer them to a freezer bag and keep frozen for up to 2 weeks. To reheat them, place them, still frozen, on a baking sheet and warm them up in a 400°F. oven for 5 minutes. Croissants can also be frozen unbaked. Thaw on a parchment-lined baking sheet in the refrigerator overnight.

French Bread BAGUETTE

Start to finish: 24 hours • Hands-on time: 30 minutes

We shouldn't be surprised when a country that reveres bread as France does gives its bakers superstar status. At a time when the American way of doing business—more machinery, fewer people, faster production—might have forever changed the quality of bread eaten by the French, bakers such as Lionel Poilâne proved that quality bread cannot be rushed, poked, or prodded into submission. Fast bread = poor quality and taste.

Classic French bread needs only four ingredients: flour, salt, leaven or yeast, and water. The quality of the resulting bread is determined by the length of the rise and the temperature of the dough during fermentation. There are many books on the subject and we encourage you to read more about it once you become "seduced by dough." We can guarantee that every time you make this bread it will be a little different, but it will always be delicious and better than any that you might buy at your neighborhood bakery or grocery store.

YIELD: 4 LOAVES

1 (2¼ teaspoon) package
    active dry yeast
⅓ cup warm water
    (not over 110°F.)
4½ cups all-purpose unbleached
    flour, plus more as needed
1 tablespoon salt

Stir the yeast into the warm water along with a pinch of flour. Allow to sit until the yeast becomes creamy and foamy on the surface, about 7 minutes.

In the bowl of a stand mixer, with the flat beater attachment, combine the flour and salt.

Mix the yeast water with 1½ cups cool water.

Add the water-yeast mixture to the flour-salt mixture with the mixer on Speed 2. Stop the mixer from time to time and push the loose flour on the sides of the bowl into the wet dough mass in the center. Stir until the dough comes together, about 1 minute.

Exchange the flat beater attachment for the dough hook attachment, turn the mixer to Speed 2, and work the dough for 8 minutes. The dough will begin to look satiny and will become very elastic.

Remove the dough hook and scrape the loose dough from it. Remove the bowl from the mixer, cover it with plastic, and allow the dough to rise in a draft-free spot for 2 hours.

Remove the plastic and punch down the dough to deflate it. Return the plastic wrapping and place the bowl in the refrigerator for an overnight rise.

Remove the dough from the refrigerator 5 hours before you plan to bake the bread, and allow it to warm up, still in the bowl, on the kitchen counter for about 2 hours.

Gently remove the dough from the bowl and turn it out onto a floured surface. Pat the dough into a rough rectangle shape and cut it into 4 pieces. Using your hands, roll each piece into a loaf or baguette about 12-inches long.

Lay parchment paper onto 2 inverted sheet pans lying side-by-side. Arrange 2 lengths of dough on each sheet pan, leaving 5 inches of space between the loaves. Pull the paper between the dough to form a hill between the loaves. This will keep the loaves from sticking to each other as they rise. Spray the dough with nonstick spray and cover loosely with a linen or cotton towel (one with no fuzz). Allow the dough to rise to almost double in size, about 1½ hours.

Place unglazed clay oven tiles on the oven racks, leaving a little space around each tile for the air to circulate. Alternately, place a pizza stone on the middle rack of the oven. Preheat the oven to 450°F.

When the dough has risen, mist the loaves with water and bring them to the oven. Carefully slide the parchment and loaves onto the clay tiles or pizza stone in the oven. Maintain space between the loaves so they don't stick together as they puff in the oven.

Mist the loaves again in 2 minutes and again 2 minutes after that. Bake the bread for about 22 to 25 minutes, or until an instant-read thermometer inserted into the bottom of a loaf reads 200°F. Remove the bread from the oven and allow it to cool at least 1 hour before cutting. (If you only have enough tiles for one rack in your oven you may bake the first 2 loaves, and when they are removed, the second batch can be placed in the oven to bake. The extra 20 or so minutes of rise won't hurt them.)

Quick Puff Pastry PÂTE FEUILLETÉE

Start to finish: 2 hours 30 minutes • Hands-on time: 30 minutes

This simple and delicious recipe is a great substitute for store-bought puff pastry, which can taste flat and definitely not buttery. And while it does take some time to roll out, fold, and chill, it's faster to make than classic puff pastry. Feel free to use it as an even flakier substitute for piecrust.

YIELD: 1 (25 X 10-INCH) RECTANGLE

1½ cups unbleached
    all-purpose flour
½ cup cake flour
½ teaspoon salt
½ pound (2 sticks) unsalted butter,
    each stick quartered length-
    wise, then cut into 10 slices
½ cup ice water

MAKE AHEAD: The pastry can be kept in the refrigerator, tightly wrapped, for up to 2 days. It can also be rolled out, wrapped, and frozen for up to 2 months. We like to roll it out and freeze it on a sheet pan between sheets of parchment paper. Then when we want to use it, all we have to do is separate the pastry from the parchment, and let it thaw on the counter for 20 minutes.

In a medium-sized bowl, combine the flours, salt, and butter, cover with plastic wrap, and freeze for 30 minutes.

Pour the cold flour mixture into the bowl of a food processor and pulse about 10 times. While you're pulsing, add the ice water through the feed tube in a steady stream and pulse until the dough comes together in 2 or 3 clumps. Do not overmix. There should be lots of chunks of butter visible in the dough.

Turn the dough out onto a lightly floured work surface and press it with a floured rolling pin until you can shape it into an 8 x 4-inch rectangle. (The dough might still be crumbly at this point, but don't worry, it will come together as you fold and will hydrate evenly as it sits in the refrigerator.)

Using a metal spatula for support, fold the short ends of the dough like a letter—bring the top third down and the bottom third up over the top third to make a three layer rectangle. This is called a turn.

Slide the dough around so that the open, shorter end is facing you. Lightly flour the dough and use your a rolling pin to press the dough into an 8 x 4-inch rectangle. (You'll have to press the dough so that it begins to stick together. The pastry can be a little crumbly at first.) Give the dough another turn, folding as before. Turn the pastry again so that the open end is facing you and roll the pastry out to a 12 x 4-inch rectangle. At this point, the dough should be holding together better.

Beginning at the short end of the rectangle and using a spatula to get started, roll the pastry to a tight cylinder. Flatten it a little, wrap it in plastic, and refrigerate it for at least 1 hour before using as directed in any subsequent recipe.

Hollandaise and Béarnaise Sauces

Start to finish: 20 minutes • Hands-on time: 5 minutes

Hollandaise is one of those sauces that always elicits groans of pleasure. It is a sinful indulgence sure to elevate fish, vegetables, and even steaks to kingly status. Don't be put off by the length of the method. There are lots of details, but it won't take you much longer to make than it takes to read the whole recipe. Once you get the hang of it, making hollandaise is one of the easiest and quickest sauces to grace a table. Béarnaise sauce is hollandaise's dressed up cousin. It is simply hollandaise with a reduction of fresh herbs, wine, and vinegar. It is great on a steak or poached eggs or vegetables like asparagus, broccoli, or cauliflower.

YIELD: ABOUT 1½ CUPS

HOLLANDAISE SAUCE

3 pasteurized egg yolks (see note)

Salt and freshly ground black
  pepper

½ pound (2 sticks) unsalted butter,
  clarified and cooled (see page
  153 for directions)

2 teaspoons fresh lemon juice

BÉARNAISE REDUCTION

1 shallot, minced

¼ cup dry white wine

¼ cup good quality
  white wine vinegar

5 black peppercorns, crushed

3 large sprigs tarragon

2 teaspoons finely minced tarragon

To make hollandaise sauce: Combine the egg yolks, 3 tablespoons water, and a pinch of salt in a heavy-bottomed saucepan over medium heat. Whisk rapidly and watch closely—too little heat and your hollandaise will be runny; too much heat and it will scramble. The sauce will become airy, and will double in volume. Once the whisk leaves a clean path on the bottom of the pan, remove the pan from the heat and immediately whisk in the butter. Pour the butter slowly and whisk quickly. The sauce will emulsify and thicken. Season with lemon juice, salt, and pepper.

To make béarnaise sauce: Make the reduction first. Combine the shallot, wine, vinegar, peppercorns, and tarragon in a shallow frying pan over high heat. Cook until only a tablespoon of liquid remains. Set aside.

Make the hollandaise sauce as directed above. Strain the béarnaise reduction into the hollandaise, then add the tarragon.

NOTE: Eating raw or undercooked eggs is a risk for foodborne illness. Pasteurization reduces the risk of egg-borne illness caused by salmonella. Not all eggs are pasteurized. Buy only pasteurized egg products that bear the USDA inspection mark.

> MAKE AHEAD: These sauces can be kept warm over a pan of warm, not hot, water for 1 hour. They can also be stored in a thermos for up to 1 hour.

Veal and Ham Pâté TERRINE DE CAMPAGNE

Start to finish: 24 hours • Hands-on time: 1 hour

This pâté is very closely related to meatloaf . . . but oh what a meatloaf! We hope you try this recipe, because unless you live in New York City or some other metropolis, you have a slim chance of finding this delicacy for purchase. It does take some time to finish, but the most involved part takes only 1 hour. Your friends and family will keel over when they taste this simple, country dish.

YIELD: 1 (9 X 5-INCH) LOAF
OR 3 (4½ x 2¾ x 1¼-INCH)
MINI LOAVES

3 tablespoons unsalted butter

1 medium onion, finely minced

Dash of salt

3 garlic cloves, minced

½ cup port or Madeira wine

2 carrots, trimmed into ¼-inch
  wide, 5-inch long strips

8 slices bacon

¾ pound lean ground pork

¾ pound ground veal

¾ pound ground pork fat

2 large eggs

1 tablespoon minced fresh chives

2 teaspoons salt

1 teaspoon dried marjoram

¼ teaspoon freshly ground
  black pepper

¼ teaspoon five-spice powder

2 tablespoons Cognac

¼ pound ham, sliced into 9 thin
  strips ¼ inch wide, 5 inches long

½ cup natural pistachios, shelled

Preheat the oven to 350°F.

Heat a medium skillet over medium heat. Add the butter, and when it melts, add the onions and salt. Sauté the onions until they are tender, about 10 minutes. Add the garlic and cook for another 2 minutes. Add the wine and cook until the liquid is reduced by half. Remove the pan from the heat and let it cool.

Add 2 cups of water to a medium saucepan and bring to a boil. Add the carrots and boil for about 5 minutes, or until crisp-tender. Using a slotted spoon, transfer the carrots to paper towels and pat them dry; set aside. Add the bacon to the same saucepan of water and cook for about 5 minutes to remove some of the smoky flavor. Remove the bacon and pat it dry with paper towels; set aside.

In a large bowl, combine the onion mixture, pork, veal, pork fat, eggs, chives, salt, marjoram, pepper, five-spice powder, and Cognac and mix with your hands or a wooden spoon until well mixed. Cook a small amount of this mixture to taste for seasoning, and adjust if necessary.

Line the bottom and sides of the loaf pan(s) with bacon. Divide the pâté mixture into thirds and place one-third along the bottom of the pan(s). Top with half the ham and half the carrot. Arrange pistachios between the rows. Repeat the layers, using the remaining ingredients and ending with a layer of pâté mixture. Cover with the remaining bacon.

Cover the pâté with aluminum foil and set it in the center of a 13 x 9-inch pan. Add boiling water to the pan so that the water comes halfway up the sides of the loaf pan. Place the pan in the oven and bake for 1 hour and 30 minutes or until a thermometer reads 160°F. (The mini-loaf pans

Rustic bread, mustard, and
cornichons, for serving

will be done in about 45 minutes to 1 hour.) The pâté will have shrunken from the sides of the pan and will be full of liquid fat.

Carefully remove the pan(s) from the water bath. Place a piece of wood or cardboard cut to fit inside the loaf pan(s) on top of the pâté and place a 4-pound weight on top. (Cans of food work well for this. This compacts the pâté, giving it a better texture.) Let the pâté sit out until it cools to room temperature, then refrigerate the weighted pâté overnight.

Unmold the pâté and serve it sliced on a platter accompanied by rustic bread, mustard, and cornichons.

TIP: If you keep the pâté in its pan, covered with its fat, it will keep for up to 1 week. Once it is removed from the pan and the fat is disturbed, the pâté will keep for 3 or 4 days. The pâté may be frozen but the texture will suffer and become a bit grainy.

Salade Niçoise

Start to finish: 1 hour • Hands-on time: 1 hour

Like many iconic dishes, salade niçoise has thousands of adaptations. Originating in Nice, this salad's usual suspects are anchovies, eggs, tomatoes, potatoes, green beans, and tuna. The salade niçoise most often served in Paris and New York always includes tuna, though at some of the more upscale establishments, the tuna can be fresh and cooked rare. The French often make meals out of salads incorporating leftovers. Ever frugal, they waste nothing and are ingenious about turning yesterday's leftovers into today's plat du jour. With its vivid colors and bright taste, this salad makes a terrific lunch or even a light dinner. Feel free to add more or less anchovies, as your taste dictates.

YIELD: 6 SERVINGS

VINAIGRETTE

3 tablespoons white wine vinegar

¼ teaspoon salt

1 teaspoon Dijon mustard

½ cup extra-virgin olive oil

1 tablespoon mixed fresh herbs, such as chives, thyme, basil, and/or parsley

Freshly ground black pepper

SALAD

2 large waxy or red-skinned potatoes

Pinch of salt, plus more to taste

½ pound green beans, trimmed

1 pint grape or cherry tomatoes, halved

5 ounces mixed salad greens

2 large eggs, hard-boiled, peeled, and quartered

4 ounces jarred roasted red peppers, cut into strips

To make the vinaigrette: Add the vinegar and salt to a medium bowl and let sit for a few minutes to dissolve the salt. Add the mustard and whisk in the olive oil, pouring in a steady stream, until the dressing is emulsified. Stir in the herbs and season with pepper to taste. Set aside.

In a pot large enough to hold them, cover the potatoes with water by 2 inches. Cook over medium heat until the water boils, then turn the heat down to low and simmer until the potatoes are tender or easily pierced with the point of a knife, about 30 to 40 minutes. Remove the potatoes from the water and let cool.

Peel and cut the potatoes into medium-sized chunks. Toss with about 3 tablespoons of the vinaigrette, and salt and pepper to taste.

Bring a medium pot of water to a boil, then add a pinch of salt and the green beans. Simmer for 2 minutes, drain, and immerse them in ice water to stop the cooking. Lay them out on a clean dish towel and roll them up to dry for at least 5 minutes. Place the beans in a medium bowl and toss with 2 tablespoons of the vinaigrette. Season with salt and pepper to taste.

Toss the tomatoes in about 2 tablespoons of the vinaigrette and season with salt and pepper. Toss the salad greens with about 3 tablespoons of the dressing and season with salt and pepper.

Arrange the greens in the center of six plates. Lay the potatoes, tomatoes, and eggs around the perimeter of the plate. Arrange the green beans in the center and the red peppers around the edges. Divide the tuna among the plates and sprinkle the olives over all. Arrange the anchovies in a

2 (6-ounce) cans tuna packed in
  olive oil, preferably imported,
  drained
⅓ cup niçoise or kalamata olives
15 anchovy fillets, rinsed and
  patted dry if salt-packed

crisscross pattern on top of the tuna. Drizzle the plates with the remaining dressing and serve immediately.

NOTE: The success of this salad lies in the freshness of the ingredients and adequate seasoning with salt and pepper. It may seem like a lot of salt and pepper while you are preparing the ingredients, but if you season each component individually, you will be assured of a well-seasoned dish that your guests won't have to doctor up with the salt-cellar at the table.

MAKE AHEAD: This salad can be assembled up to 2 hours ahead, kept covered, and refrigerated. The dressing and vegetables can all be prepared at least 4 hours ahead of time, kept covered, and refrigerated and assembled just before service.

Romaine Salad with Champagne Vinaigrette

Start to finish: 15 minutes • Hands-on time: 15 minutes

We like to serve fresh, vibrant salads the French way: after the main course. There, it doesn't spoil our appetites for the main event and our palates are refreshed by the salad after the meal.

YIELD: 4 SERVINGS

1 small shallot, minced

2 tablespoons Champagne vinegar

½ teaspoon fresh thyme, tarragon, or flat-leaf parsley

½ teaspoon Dijon or whole grain mustard

¼ teaspoon salt

⅓ cup extra-virgin olive oil

1 head romaine lettuce, torn into bite-size pieces

Combine the shallot, vinegar, herbs, mustard, and salt in a large bowl and let sit for 5 minutes for the flavors to blend and the salt to dissolve.

Whisk in the olive oil, pouring it in a slow, steady stream, until the vinaigrette is emulsified.

Moments before serving, add the lettuce to the bowl of vinaigrette and toss with your hands to coat the leaves. Serve immediately.

VARIATION: We like to serve this salad topped with sliced grapefruit sections, orange sections, olives, crumbled goat cheese, or toasted walnuts.

Vichyssoise POTATO AND LEEK SOUP

Start to finish: 45 minutes • Hands-on time: 15 minutes

One of the best characteristics of this velvety, creamy soup is that it can be served either hot or cold. We prefer it hot in the winter and cold in the summer, making it a year-round favorite.

YIELD: 4 SERVINGS

2 tablespoons olive oil

3 leeks, white and light
  green parts only, trimmed
  and thinly sliced

1 pound Yukon Gold potatoes,
  peeled and thinly sliced

4 cups chicken stock, plus more for
  thinning the soup if necessary

1 teaspoon minced fresh thyme
  or ½ teaspoon dried thyme

½ cup heavy cream

1 teaspoon white wine vinegar

Pinch of cayenne pepper

Pinch of ground nutmeg

Salt and freshly ground
  black pepper

1 tablespoon finely minced
  fresh chives

Heat the olive oil in a large pot over medium heat and add the leeks. Cook until the leeks soften, about 4 minutes. Add the potatoes, chicken stock, and thyme. Bring to a boil, then turn the heat to low. Simmer for about 25 minutes, or until the potatoes are tender.

Using an immersion blender, regular blender, or food processor, blend the soup so that it is creamy and thick. (If you are using a blender or food processor, make sure not to overfill the jar or work bowl, and always put a kitchen towel over the top so if pressure from the steam builds and soup escapes, you are not burned.) Add the cream, vinegar, cayenne pepper, and nutmeg and taste for seasoning, adding salt and pepper if desired.

Serve the soup hot or chilled with a sprinkling of fresh chives. (If you are serving the soup chilled, you may want to thin it with a bit of extra stock or milk.)

NOTE: We like the creamy texture of Yukon Golds, but any potato will make a nice soup.

MAKE AHEAD: This soup can be made two days ahead and kept covered in the refrigerator. It may need to be thinned with a bit of extra chicken stock or milk after reheating. Garnish right before serving.

French Onion Soup SOUPE À L'OIGNON

Start to finish: 2 hours • Hands-on time: 30 minutes

Onion soup is probably on most people's top ten favorite foods list. If you live in a wintry climate, nothing can surpass the power of this rich stock, heavily laced with caramelized onions and topped with crusty bread and melted cheese. If you have it, whip out your homemade stock for this classic, but canned stock still makes a pretty good soup.

YIELD: 6 SERVINGS

4 tablespoons unsalted butter

2 tablespoons vegetable oil

4 large white onions, thinly sliced

4 leeks, trimmed and thinly sliced

Pinch of salt

2 garlic cloves, minced

½ cup Madeira wine

6 cups beef stock

1 bay leaf

6 slices crusty white bread

Salt and freshly ground
   black pepper

½ pound Gruyère cheese, grated

Heat a large soup pot over medium heat and add the butter and vegetable oil. When the fat is hot, add the onions, leeks, and salt. Cook the onions and leeks, stirring occasionally, until they begin to brown. Turn down the heat and continue to cook, scraping the bottom of the pot to release the browned bits. Continue cooking in this manner until the onions are soft and brown, about 30 minutes. Add the garlic and cook for another 2 minutes, or until the garlic is fragrant.

Return the heat to medium and add the wine to the pot. Scrape up all the brown bits and cook until the wine has reduced to a few tablespoons. Add the stock and bay leaf, stir, and cook for about 30 minutes.

While the soup is cooking, turn the broiler on and toast the bread on both sides.

Taste the soup and season with salt and pepper to taste. Arrange heat-proof bowls on a baking sheet and ladle the soup into them, so the bowls are about three-quarters full. Sprinkle half the cheese over the soup, top with the toasted bread, and then sprinkle the rest of the cheese on top. Put the soup bowls under the broiler and broil until the cheese has melted and becomes lightly browned. Serve immediately.

> MAKE AHEAD: The soup can be made 1 day in advance, minus the bread and cheese topping, and kept covered and refrigerated. Reheat over medium heat.

Croque Monsieur and Croque Madame

Start to finish: 30 minutes • Hands-on time: 30 minutes

Croque Monsieur is a heavenly little grilled ham-and-cheese sandwich served in bistros all over France. The name comes from the French verb "croquer", which means to crack or crunch, and literally translated means "crunchy mister." Who knows why the French name their dishes so whimsically! Just know that this little snack will make you feel as marvelous as that grilled cheese your mom used to make for you after a long day of cold or rainy weather. (Maybe you had the tomato soup from that familiar can to go along with it?)

A true croque monsieur consists of ham, Gruyère cheese, and béchamel sauce between two pieces of butter-slathered bread, which is then grilled on a hot pan to a toasty brown color. The croque madame is the same sandwich with a fried egg served either on top or inside the sandwich.

YIELD: 2 SERVINGS

6 tablespoons unsalted butter, softened

1 tablespoon unbleached all-purpose flour

Pinch of salt

1 cup whole milk, warmed in the microwave

Freshly ground black pepper

4 slices homemade-style bread, sliced ½-inch thick

Dijon mustard

¼ pound deli ham, thinly sliced

4 slices Gruyère cheese

In a medium saucepan, melt 2 tablespoons of butter over medium-high heat. Add the flour and salt and cook until the flour foams. Whisk in the milk and continue to cook the béchamel sauce until it boils and thickens, about 2 minutes. Remove the sauce from the heat and add more salt and pepper to taste.

Spread the remaining 4 tablespoons butter over one side of each bread slice. Place two slices of bread butter-side down and spread the other side with mustard and a tablespoon or so of the béchamel sauce. Divide the ham and cheese among the two slices. Drizzle the cheese with more of the sauce and top with the remaining bread slices, butter side out.

Heat a skillet over medium-high heat and add the sandwiches to the pan. Brown them on one side, about 4 minutes, then flip and brown the second sides. Transfer the sandwiches to plates and top with more of the sauce. Serve hot.

VARIATION: To make a croque madame, fry an egg and serve it atop the sandwich, drizzled with béchamel sauce.

Quiche Lorraine

Start to finish: 3 hours 40 minutes (includes the time needed to make the pastry) • Hands-on time: 35 minutes

Quiche was born a hundred years ago in rural France as a rustic lunch for farmers. It came to be the toast of the town back in the seventies, giving birth to such clichés as "Real men don't eat quiche." Even though the seventies are long gone, quiche remains a lunchtime favorite, and shows up frequently as a mini appetizer at cocktail parties. The traditional quiche from Lorraine consists of a plain custard filling with no cheese or bacon. Cooks in the Alsace region first added bacon, cheese, and onions, which resulted in the dish most recognized today as quiche Lorraine. Thanks to the Alsatians, nutty Gruyère cheese, smoky bacon, and savory sautéed leeks improve on the original version.

YIELD: 1 (8-INCH) TART,
FOR 6 SERVINGS

1 recipe Flaky Pastry (page 65)

8 slices bacon, chopped

1 leek, white part only,
thinly sliced

¾ cup heavy cream

½ cup whole milk

2 large eggs plus 2 yolks

¼ teaspoon salt

¼ teaspoon freshly ground
black pepper

⅛ teaspoon cayenne pepper

⅛ teaspoon freshly ground nutmeg

4 ounces Gruyère cheese, grated

MAKE AHEAD: The quiche can be made 2 hours ahead and kept at room temperature.

Prepare the pastry as directed in the recipe.

Preheat the oven to 375°F.

Roll out the pastry and fit it into an 8-inch fluted tart pan with a removable rim or a pie plate. Using a fork, poke holes into the bottom of the crust. Line the pastry with parchment paper and fill it about 1-inch deep with pie weights, dried beans, or rice. (The weights keep the bottom of the tart from rising as hot air pushes it up from the bottom.) Bake for 20 minutes.

Remove the shell from the oven and transfer the weights to a heatproof dish. Return the shell to the oven and bake for another 15 minutes, or until the pastry is set and a light golden brown. Remove from the oven and cool.

In a medium skillet, cook the bacon over medium heat until it is crisp and brown. Transfer it to a plate lined with paper towels and pour off all but about 2 tablespoons of the bacon fat. Add the leek to the pan and sauté until it is softened and begins to brown, about 5 minutes.

In a medium bowl, combine the cream, milk, eggs and egg yolks, salt, pepper, cayenne pepper, and nutmeg and whisk until combined.

Place the pastry shell on a baking sheet. Spread a layer of leek over the bottom of the shell and top with bacon. Sprinkle the cheese over the top of the bacon, then carefully pour in the milk-egg mixture to fill the tart. Bake for 25 minutes or until the custard is set. Remove the quiche from the oven and let cool for 15 minutes. Cut and serve warm or at room temperature.

Cheese Soufflé SOUFFLÉ AU FROMAGE

Start to finish: 1 hour 10 minutes • Hands-on time: 35 minutes

Few dishes are as impressive as a soufflé. We're not sure why so many cooks are timid about making them, as they are really easy to assemble and require only a few ingredients. For this cheese soufflé, most any cheese will do, but we like the combination of nutty Gruyère and salty Parmigiano-Reggiano.

YIELD: 6 SERVINGS

6 tablespoons unsalted butter, softened

¾ cup grated Parmigiano-Reggiano cheese

4 tablespoons unbleached all-purpose flour

1½ cups whole milk, heated

¼ teaspoon salt

Freshly ground black pepper

Pinch of ground nutmeg

Pinch of cayenne pepper

6 large eggs, plus 2 large egg whites, separated, at room temperature

Pinch of salt

1 cup grated Gruyère cheese

MAKE AHEAD: The soufflé base can be prepared up to 3 hours ahead, kept covered, and refrigerated. Bring it back to room temperature before continuing with the recipe.

Place an oven rack in the lower third of the oven. Preheat the oven to 400°F.

Butter an 8-cup soufflé dish with 1 tablespoon of butter, then coat it with ¼ cup of the Parmigiano-Reggiano cheese. Set aside.

Melt the remaining 5 tablespoons of butter in a medium saucepan over medium heat. Add the flour and cook, stirring, until the butter foams. Cook for 1 minute, then add the hot milk and whisk until blended. Add the salt, pepper, nutmeg, and cayenne pepper and whisk at a simmer for 1 minute. Remove from the heat and cool for 3 minutes. Beat in the egg yolks one at a time, then fold in the remaining ½ cup of Parmigiano-Reggiano cheese. Set aside. This is your soufflé base.

Whisk the egg whites and pinch of salt until the whites are stiff. Add one-third of the egg whites to the soufflé base. Using a large spatula, gently turn and fold the soufflé base up and over the top of the egg whites. Fold in all but 2 tablespoons of the Gruyère, then fold in half of the remaining whites, leaving some streaks of white. Add the remaining egg whites and gently fold them in completely. (Avoid over-mixing the whites or they will deflate. Fold until each addition of egg whites is almost incorporated, then add the next addition until all the whites are incorporated.)

Gently transfer the soufflé batter to the prepared dish and flatten the top with the spatula. Sprinkle the remaining cheese over the top. Run a finger or a spoon around the edge of the soufflé, leaving a trough about ½-inch deep.

Transfer the soufflé to the oven and immediately turn the heat down to 375°F. Bake for 30 to 35 minutes without opening the oven door.

Check the soufflé after 30 minutes and gently jiggle it. If it moves slightly in the center, it is done. If it is loose on the edges, bake it for another 5 minutes. It should be browned and crusty on top. Serve immediately.

Gratin Dauphinois CREAMY POTATO GRATIN

Start to finish: 1 hour 30 minutes • Hands-on time: 30 minutes

A creamy potato casserole can elevate a simple meal to master status. Perfect with grilled or roasted meats, gratin dauphinois is one of those dishes whose appearance and taste belie its simplicity. It looks much more difficult to assemble than it is, and the gratin tastes like the angels whipped it up in the clouds . . . a little piece of heaven on your plate.

YIELD: 6 SERVINGS

1 garlic clove, peeled and
    cut in half
1 tablespoon unsalted butter,
    softened
2 cups heavy cream
⅛ teaspoon cayenne pepper
2 pounds red-skinned or
    Yukon Gold potatoes,
    peeled and thinly sliced
1 teaspoon salt
Freshly ground black pepper
Freshly grated nutmeg
½ pound Gruyère cheese, grated

Preheat the oven to 350°F.

Rub the cut side of the garlic clove all over the bottom and sides of a large gratin dish, preferably enameled cast iron such as Le Creuset. Spread the butter over the bottom and sides of the pan.

Combine the cream, cayenne pepper, and garlic in a heavy saucepan over medium heat until it steams, about 4 minutes. Remove from the heat.

Arrange one-third of the potato slices so that they overlap in the bottom of the pan. Sprinkle with salt, pepper to taste, and a light sprinkle of nutmeg. Spread a thin layer of cheese over all and ladle about ⅓ cup of the hot cream over all. Repeat with the remaining potatoes and ingredients until you have made three layers. If you are using a cast-iron pan, place it on the stove over medium heat until the cream simmers. (If you are using a ceramic or glass pan, skip this step, but add 10 minutes to the baking time.)

Bake for 50 minutes, or until the gratin is browned and the potatoes are tender when pierced with a knife. Remove from the oven and let sit for 10 minutes so the potatoes can absorb some of the cream. Serve hot.

> **MAKE AHEAD:** The potato casserole can be assembled up to 1 day ahead, covered, and refrigerated. When you're ready to bake it, just add a few minutes to the baking time.

Pommes Frites FRENCH FRIES

Start to finish: 1 hour 30 minutes • Hands-on time: 30 minutes

Sacré bleu! How can it be that French fries are not French, but were first made in Belgium? Wherever they come from, they've been widely popularized all over the world by fast-food chains and have recently become a gourmet sensation. Restaurants are popping up that serve only pommes frites *along with numerous mayonnaise-based condiments flavored with chipotle, wasabi, roasted garlic, and even mango. Whether you prefer French fries with ketchup or hollandaise sauce, from shoestring to curly, thick-cut to waffle-cut, they must be crispy on the outside and tender and fluffy on the inside. To that end, we fry them not once, but twice. The extra step results in tender, crispy fries so easy to make, you'll wonder how you've lived so long without them.*

YIELD: 2 TO 4 SERVINGS

2 Yukon Gold or russet potatoes per person, about 5 ounces per potato (you will have some waste)

4 to 5 cups peanut or vegetable oil

Sea salt

> **MAKE AHEAD:** After the first fry, you can let the fries sit at room temperature for up to 4 hours. Reheat the oil and finish frying moments before service.

Peel the potatoes and cut them in half, then into ¼-inch slices. Stack them and cut them into ¼-inch square sticks. (It is very important that the potatoes be uniform in size or you will end up with a mixture of crispy and soggy fries.) Immerse the potatoes in cold water, rinse, and immerse them two more times to remove the starch from the outside. After three rinses, allow the potatoes to soak in cold water for 30 minutes.

While the potatoes are soaking, heat 4 inches of oil in a heavy pot over medium-high heat to 340°F.

Drain the potatoes and pat them dry to reduce splattering. Carefully add a handful of potatoes to the hot oil (add fewer rather than more) and fry them for 3 minutes, or until they are tender, but not brown. Remove the potatoes with a slotted metal spatula and transfer them to a sheet pan lined with paper towels. Repeat the process with the rest of the potatoes.

When all of the potatoes have had their first fry, increase the temperature of the oil to 360°F. Fry the potatoes again, in batches, for 5 minutes, or until they are crispy and brown. Drain on fresh paper towels and sprinkle with sea salt to taste. Serve hot.

NOTE: The type of potato that you use is important. We have good results with Yukon Golds and russets, but waxy or red-skinned potatoes don't have that light texture that you're looking for in a French fry.

Boeuf à la Bourguignonne

BEEF STEW WITH PEARL ONIONS, BACON, AND MUSHROOMS

Start to finish: 3 hours 10 minutes • Hands-on time: 1 hour

Once familiar with French food, you become aware of how simple it really is and boeuf à la bourguignonne *is a prime example of a simple, but sensational dish. The technique for cooking this stew is called braising. Most of us grew up eating braises, as a matter of fact—remember pot roast? To braise means to cook a less tender cut of meat for a few hours in enough liquid to cover it at a gentle simmer over slow, even heat. The type of pots generally used for braises are heavy enameled cast iron like Le Creuset, but any heavy pot or Dutch oven will do. The cooking liquid will impart a good bit of flavor to the sauce. The traditional liquid for this dish is red wine, but other regions of France may use white wine, tomatoes, cider, or even water, along with vegetables more plentifully grown in that region. We love to make this dish for company because the leftovers are even better. All you have to do is reheat.*

YIELD: 6 SERVINGS

3½ pounds beef chuck roast, cut
   into 1½-inch chunks

2¼ cups dry red wine (see note)

2 medium onions, chopped

2 carrots, peeled and cut
   into 1-inch sections

1 stalk celery, cut into
   1-inch sections

3 garlic cloves, smashed

Bouquet garni (1 bay leaf and
   3 sprigs flat-leaf parsley, tied
   together with a piece of string)

Salt and freshly ground
   black pepper

8 slices thick-sliced bacon, diced

1 cup beef stock

5 tablespoons unsalted butter

2 cups (10 ounces) pearl or
   boiling onions, blanched and

In a large bowl, combine the beef, 2 cups of wine, the chopped onions, carrots, celery, garlic, and bouquet garni. Marinate at room temperature for at least 2 hours, or up to 12 hours in the refrigerator.

Strain the meat and vegetables from the wine, reserving the wine. Separate the meat from the vegetables. Pat the meat dry and season it with salt and pepper.

Heat a large, heavy pot over medium heat and add the bacon. Cook until it is crispy and brown, then transfer the bacon to paper towels.

Slowly add the marinated beef to the hot bacon fat. Don't crowd the pan or the meat won't brown. Depending on the size of the pan, you may want to brown the meat in two or three batches. Let the meat brown on one side before turning it.

Once all the meat is browned, return it to the pan, add the marinated vegetables, reserved wine marinade, and beef stock. Bring the mixture to a simmer, cover, and turn the heat to low. Check the pot after about 5 minutes to make sure that it isn't simmering too high. You want a little bubble every few seconds, but not a boil. Cook for about 2 hours, or until the meat is very tender when pierced with the point of a knife.

Meanwhile, heat a sauté pan over medium heat. Add 3 tablespoons of the butter, the pearl onions, and a pinch of salt and pepper. Brown the onions, giving them a toss every now and then to keep them from burning.

peeled, or frozen pearl onions

½ pound cremini or button
   mushrooms, quartered

1 tablespoon unbleached
   all-purpose flour

¼ cup chopped flat-leaf parsley

MAKE AHEAD: The dish is ex-
cellent made 1 day in advance,
covered, and refrigerated. Reheat over low heat.

After 5 minutes, add the mushrooms and continue to cook until they are soft, about 5 minutes. Add the remaining ¼ cup wine and cook until no liquid remains in the pan, about 1 minute. Set aside.

When the stew is done, strain the meat and vegetables, being sure to reserve the liquid. Cool the meat and vegetables, cover with plastic wrap, and set aside. Pick out the bouquet garni and discard. Return the liquid to the pan and heat over medium heat until it boils, then cook down until about 1½ cups of liquid remain, about 10 minutes. Season with salt and pepper.

Mix the flour and the remaining 2 tablespoons butter together with a fork, then whisk into the simmering sauce. The sauce will thicken and become velvety. Return the meat and vegetables to the pot and add the onion-mushroom mixture along with the bacon. Heat the stew to a simmer to reheat all the ingredients.

Sprinkle the parsley over the stew and serve hot directly from the pot.

NOTE: In this recipe, use a wine that you might be drinking with this dish. Typically the French would use a Burgundy wine (pinot noir) in this recipe, but feel free to use a merlot, zinfandel, Syrah, or Shiraz. They all work just fine.

TIP: Because we like the meat cut into smaller pieces than the butcher at the grocery store usually cuts it, it makes sense to buy a chuck roast and cut it up yourself. That way, you can cut away some of the tougher sinew that they leave on.

Steak with Red Wine Sauce ENTRECÔTE À LA BORDELAISE

Start to finish: 20 minutes • Hands-on time: 20 minutes

The French have come up with so many variations of this dish that it almost boggles the mind. Its genius is that one need only pan-fry a steak and then, with only a few ingredients—depending on your cravings, what's in the pantry, or the season—make a pan sauce that elevates your steak to master status. Believe us, the grill has its place, and steaks cooked on it are delicious, but you forfeit the sauce on the grill. For this reason, pan-fried steaks with a reduction sauce are worth the time it takes to learn the technique, which is really très simple.

YIELD: 4 SERVINGS

4 (8-ounce) Delmonico or rib-eye
  steaks, about 1 inch thick, or
  2 (1-pound) porterhouse steaks,
  about 1 inch thick, or
  4 (8-ounce) strip or rib steaks,
  about 1 inch thick
Salt and freshly ground
  black pepper
3 tablespoons unsalted butter
2 tablespoons olive oil
1 large shallot, minced
1 cup dry red wine, such as
  merlot, pinot noir, or zinfandel
1 cup prepared reduced beef or
  veal stock (see tip)

Remove the steaks from the refrigerator about 1 hour before you intend to cook them.

Pat the steaks dry and salt and pepper them liberally on both sides.

Heat a large sauté pan over medium-high heat and add 1 tablespoon of the butter, along with the olive oil. When the fat is hot, carefully arrange the steaks in the pan. Cook the steaks for 3 to 4 minutes, or until they have browned and no longer stick to the pan. Turn the steaks and cook for another 3 to 4 minutes on the second side for medium-rare, or 5 to 6 minutes for medium-well. (Regulate the heat so that the juices in the pan don't burn.) Transfer the steaks to a plate and cover loosely with aluminum foil.

Remove the fat from the pan, add the shallot, and cook for 30 seconds. Add the wine and cook, stirring up the browned bits by scraping the bottom of the pan with a spatula. Cook for about 5 minutes, or until the wine is reduced by half, then add the stock and continue to reduce until reduced again by at least half. (Your goal is to have about 1 cup of liquid in the pan.) Remove the sauce from the heat and add the remaining 2 tablespoons butter. Season with salt and pepper. (You may not need to add salt if the stock was salted.) Keep the sauce warm.

Cut the steaks crosswise into strips and arrange them on plates. Pour the sauce over the steaks and serve hot.

NOTE: When you want to grill a steak and serve it with a sauce, try it with Béarnaise Sauce (page 71). Buttery béarnaise goes beautifully with a juicy, char-grilled steak as well as with eggs Benedict or roasted asparagus.

VARIATION: *Entrecôte au Poivre Vert* (Steak with Green Peppercorn Sauce)—Crush 2 tablespoons whole black peppercorns with the bottom of a heavy pan and press them into both sides of the meat along with the salt. Follow the recipe, substituting ⅓ cup Cognac for the wine. Finish the sauce with the 2 tablespoons of butter plus ¼ cup heavy cream and 2 tablespoons brined green peppercorns, chopped.

TIP: Thanks to store-bought reduced stocks, such as those made by More Than Gourmet, many of these normally difficult dishes have become quite simple. Without the reduced stocks, this dish (like many other French dishes) would be a two-day marathon of roasting bones, simmering them with vegetables and herbs in water for 8 to 10 hours, straining, degreasing, and then reducing the liquid into manageable storage quantities. There is no way that salted, canned stocks can be reduced to these levels and you will only end up with what amounts to a bouillon cube. Reduced stocks can be found at many higher-end grocery stores and specialty stores or online. They are a great resource for those of us who may not have the time or inclination to go the whole route for these types of dishes, but who are curious to try them. A 1.5-ounce jar of demi-glace mixed with 1 cup water makes a very nice demi-glace or reduced stock.

Duck Breasts à l'Orange MAGRETS DE CANARD À L'ORANGE

Start to finish: 1 hour • Hands-on time: 1 hour

After ordering duck à l'orange in a restaurant setting, you will most often be presented with an entire half of a duck on your plate. For the home cook, thawing out a frozen duck and cutting it in half is a challenging experience. To make life easy, we use duck breasts instead, which we sauté until the skin is crispy, leaving the meat still a bit rosy in the center. The sauce consists of caramelized sugar, orange juice and zest, and sherry vinegar, all of which give it that sweet-and-sour taste, along with a mellow, rich stock base that gives the sauce a nice, thick consistency.

Since it is now possible to buy duck breasts in many grocers' meat cases, this is a dish that more and more cooks can make at home. This is a celebratory dish that makes your guests says, "Wow," but at the same time is not too difficult to pull off. We like to serve this dish with a creamy potato casserole and a salad for special meals with friends and family.

YIELD: 6 SERVINGS

2 Seville or Valencia oranges

3 tablespoons sugar

1 teaspoon corn syrup

⅓ cup sherry vinegar

1 cup reduced duck, chicken, or veal stock (see tip on page 87)

Salt and freshly ground black pepper

2 tablespoons unsalted butter

6 duck breasts

Orange slices, for garnish

Using a potato peeler, sharp knife, or zester, peel only the colored zest from the oranges (the white pith is bitter). Cut the zest into thin strips. In a small saucepan, bring 2 cups of water to a simmer over medium heat and add the zest. Boil for 30 seconds, strain, and rinse the zest with cold water. Set aside.

Juice the oranges into a medium pan. Boil the juice over medium heat until it has reduced to about ¼ cup. Set aside.

In a separate medium saucepan, combine the sugar, 1 tablespoon of water, and the corn syrup, and place over medium heat. Don't stir, but swirl the pan as the sugar melts. When the syrup has caramelized and turns amber, after about 4 minutes, quickly pour the vinegar into the pan. The mixture will bubble and harden. Continue to cook over medium heat until the caramel has melted into the vinegar and it has reduced to a syrup consistency, about 4 minutes. Set aside. (French food 101: This mixture of caramelized sugar and vinegar is called a *gastrique*.)

Add the stock to the reduced orange juice and boil, reducing until about ¾ cup remains. Taste the reduction. (At this point, you'll begin adding the *gastrique* a little at a time, tasting between each addition so you can get the balance of sweet and sour right.) Add 2 tablespoons of the *gastrique*. Taste again and season with salt and pepper. Add more *gastrique* (we generally use it all) until the sauce tastes a little sharp from the vinegar and orange.

Duck is probably one of the most misunderstood foods in the United States. It has the reputation of being "greasy and tough" only because of mishandling. There is a huge difference between French ducks and those found in America's freezers. The American Pekin, or Long Island duckling, has a thicker coating of fat covering its body, which makes it unsuitable for roasting. The best use for these ducks is to separate breasts from legs and cook them individually. The best way to cook the breasts is to sauté them, and the best way to cook the legs is to either make a confit (simmer in their own fat) or braise them (cook over low heat in a small amount of liquid).

Add the butter and orange zest and set aside over low heat.

Score the duck skin by making a series of slashes diagonally across the breast, cutting through the skin, but not into the meat. Make another series of slashes from the opposite direction so that the skin now has a crosshatch of about 14 slashes. (The cuts help the skin to render the fat more efficiently.) Season the breasts with salt and pepper.

Heat a large sauté pan over medium-high heat. When the pan is blazing hot, arrange the duck breasts in the pan skin side down. They will spit and sizzle a little until the pan cools down a bit. Fat will render from the skin immediately, so there's no need to add fat to the pan. Cook the breasts for 7 minutes or until the skin is crispy and brown. Turn and cook the other side for 3 or 4 minutes longer. Transfer the breasts to a plate, cover with foil, and let rest for 5 minutes to complete the cooking and let the juices resettle throughout the meat.

To serve, slice the meat on the diagonal and pour the sauce over the top. Garnish with orange slices.

Coq au Vin CHICKEN WITH WILD MUSHROOMS, BACON, AND PEARL ONIONS

Start to finish: 1 hour 30 minutes • Hands-on time: 20 minutes

Originally, coq au vin would have been made with a tough, wiry rooster. Since we no longer find roosters in modern-day grocery stores, chicken thighs are a tasty substitute. The bones give up delicious texture and thickness to the sauce, while the slow cooking in wine renders the sometimes tough meat tender, juicy, and full of flavor. We like to add a bit of color to the stew by roasting some vegetables to add at the end of cooking. They add texture, sweetness, and vibrancy to this iconic French country favorite.

YIELD: 6 SERVINGS

5 tablespoons olive oil

4 slices bacon, cut into pieces

3 pounds (12 large) bone-in chicken thighs, skinned

Salt and freshly ground black pepper

1 teaspoon dried thyme

1 cup diced onion

½ cup diced carrot

¼ cup diced celery

2 cups pearl onions, skinned

3 garlic cloves, minced

½ pound cremini mushrooms, halved

1½ cups dry red wine (see note)

2 cups chicken stock

1 bay leaf

2 carrots, peeled, halved lengthwise, and cut into quarters

3 parsnips, peeled, halved lengthwise, and cut into quarters

2 turnips, peeled and cut into

Heat a large, heavy pot over medium heat, add 2 tablespoons of the olive oil, and cook the bacon in it until it renders its fat.

Meanwhile, season the chicken liberally with salt, pepper, and thyme and add it to the bacon. Sauté until the chicken it begins to color lightly, about 4 minutes. Add the diced onion, carrot, and celery and cook until very lightly browned, about 4 minutes. Add the pearl onions, garlic, and mushrooms and cook for another 3 minutes. Using a slotted spoon, transfer the chicken and vegetables to a plate and keep warm.

Pour the wine into the hot pot and cook until the wine reduces by half, about 10 minutes. Add the chicken stock, bay leaf, and chicken and vegetables. Cover and cook at a bare simmer on low heat for at least 1 hour.

While the chicken is cooking, preheat the oven to 400°F.

In a bowl, toss the carrots, parsnips, and turnips with the remaining 3 tablespoons olive oil, salt, and pepper, then spread them out on a parchment-lined sheet pan. Bake for 20 to 25 minutes or until tender and lightly browned. Remove from oven and set aside.

Remove the cooked chicken from the pot and, when it is cool enough to handle, separate the meat from the bones.

Bring the sauce to a boil and cook until the flavors have intensified and are full and rich, about 4 minutes. Taste the sauce and adjust the seasoning with salt and pepper. Lower the heat to medium and bring to a simmer.

With your fingers or a fork, combine the butter and flour, creating a paste. Whisk the butter mixture in chunks into the sauce. The butter and

quarters, then halved

3 tablespoons unsalted butter

2 tablespoons unbleached
all-purpose flour

¼ cup minced flat-leaf parsley,
for garnish

Rice, noodles, risotto, polenta,
or couscous, for serving

flour will enrich and thicken the sauce. Return the chicken and roasted vegetables to the pot to reheat.

Garnish with parsley right before serving. Serve hot with rice, noodles, risotto, polenta, or couscous.

NOTE: We suggest a Shiraz, Syrah, or zinfandel wine for this dish because those wines typically feature rich, fruity, and spicy flavors. When reducing a more tannic wine like cabernet sauvignon, the resulting sauce can have a sharp or astringent quality. There's no need to break the bank on a boutique wine here since there are countless bottles available in the $10 to $15 range, plus you should have enough left over in the bottle to whet your whistle while pulling the meal together.

Roast Chicken POULET RÔTI

Start to finish: 1 hour 30 minutes • Hands-on time: 15 minutes

Roast chicken is one of the easiest meals to prepare. The oven obviously does most of the work for you, creating a luscious brown bird, with tender, juicy meat within. Most of the time, we roast free-range fryers of about 3 or 4 pounds, but when we want lots of leftovers we've been known to roast a 5-pound roasting chicken. It does take a little longer, but it is often possible to reconstruct a second meal from the leftover meat if you hide it from late-night snackers in the refrigerator. The best way we've found to roast a chicken is to remove the backbone and splay the chicken open, breast-side up, over a rack. This technique allows the heat to reach the leg meat more easily, cooking it faster so that the breast meat, which usually cooks in less time than the dark meat, doesn't overcook and become dry. It also makes it easier to infuse the meat with flavor by inserting herbs, spices, or stuffings between the meat and the skin, which we believe is the best way to flavor a bird. Lastly, we are fond of laying vegetables underneath the chicken so they cook with it and pick up that chickeny flavor that we love. The vegetables—usually onion, carrot, and celery—can be mashed up in the juices to thicken the jus, or gravy, or they can be served on the side as an accompaniment to the meat.

YIELD: 4 TO 6 SERVINGS

- 3 to 4 pound fryer chicken, giblets removed
- 3 garlic cloves, minced
- 3 tablespoons minced fresh tarragon
- 4 tablespoons unsalted butter, softened
- ½ teaspoon salt
- ¼ teaspoon freshly ground black pepper
- 2 medium carrots, peeled, halved, and quartered lengthwise
- 2 medium onions, peeled and cut into 8 pieces
- 1 stalk celery, peeled, halved, and quartered lengthwise

Preheat the oven to 400°F.

Lay the chicken on a work surface, breast side down. Using a pair of poultry or kitchen shears, begin to cut from just to the right of the tail along the spine of the chicken. There is a "sweet spot" that the shears can easily cut through along the spine. If you hit hard bone, move the shears a centimeter to the right or left and you will find the spot that the shears can penetrate. Cut down the right side and then do the same with the left side of the spine. Turn the chicken over, breast side up, laying it as flat and open as possible.

In a small bowl, combine the garlic, tarragon, 3 tablespoons of the butter, the salt, and pepper until it forms a paste. Using your index finger, separate and loosen the skin from the breast meat without tearing it or removing it. Slide some of the butter mixture between the skin and meat.

Repeat this process with the legs and thighs, beginning at the outer edge of the thigh where the backbone was removed. Slide your finger between the skin and meat as far up the leg as is possible without tearing the skin. Slip the remaining butter mixture over the legs and thighs.

Add about ½ cup of water to a roasting pan and put a roasting or cooling

Salt and freshly ground black
   pepper
2 teaspoons unbleached
   all-purpose flour
Flat-leaf parsley, for garnish

rack over the top so it fits inside of the pan. Salt and pepper the carrots, onions, and celery, and place them on the rack. Top the vegetables with the chicken and roast for 1 hour, or until the drumstick wiggles freely or the meat between the thigh and breast registers 165°F. on an instant-read thermometer. Remove the chicken from the oven, tent with foil, and let it rest for 10 minutes.

In a small bowl, combine the remaining tablespoon of butter and the flour to make a paste.

While the bird is resting, pour or skim off most of the fat in the roasting pan and transfer the juices to a saucepan. Bring them to a simmer and add the butter paste in small chunks, whisking to incorporate. Continue to add the paste until the gravy is velvety and slightly thickened. (Depending on how much juice the bird rendered, you might not use it all.) Taste for seasoning and adjust with salt and pepper.

To carve the chicken, begin by cutting off the wings at the joint where they meet the breast. The legs should just about pull off the carcass. If they don't, sever them at the hip joint, then cut the leg from the thigh. Carve the breast meat by cutting along the side of the breastbone as close to the bone as possible. Continue to cut the meat away from the bone and detach the breast meat. Cut the breast meat into 4 slices.

Arrange the chicken and vegetables on a platter and garnish with parsley. Drizzle some gravy over all and serve the remaining gravy in a heated gravyboat.

NOTE: There is some hysteria over the dangers of food-borne illness that has made many home cooks reluctant to handle poultry. Salmonella is a bacteria that lives on the surface and inside the cavities of infected chickens. Roasting a chicken to an internal temperature of 165°F. kills salmonella bacteria (salmonella dies at 140°F.). The main culprit of salmonella poisoning lies in cross contamination. To avoid this danger, we clean all poultry-contaminated items (especially our hands) with very hot, soapy water and give the cutting boards a rinse with a touch of bleach. An even better solution is to keep a separate cutting board that you use only for poultry and meats. This should keep cross contamination at a minimum.

Cassoulet

Start to finish: 4 hours • Hands-on time: 30 minutes

Cassoulet is a country dish that was most likely created by necessity. It is composed largely of white beans and whatever meat might be lying around. Imagine a French housewife, about two hundred years ago, assembling the ingredients for this dish and then taking it down to the baker—who often had the only oven in the village—to let it sit in his oven for a few hours. She would send one of the children to fetch the hot earthenware pot, which would then be wrapped tightly in a cloth so the child wouldn't burn his hands. What a warm and satisfying meal to feed a hungry family. This is earthy country food at its best. Our thanks go out to Jim Peterson for the bones of this classic recipe.

YIELD: 4 SERVINGS

2 cups dried cannellini beans, flageolets, or great Northern beans

1 (8-ounce) pork rind, cut into about 10 strips, 8 tied together with string

4 flat-leaf parsley stems

4 garlic cloves

2 bay leaves

8 black peppercorns, crushed

3 onions, peeled and stuck with 3 whole cloves

2 carrots, peeled and quartered

2 stalks celery, quartered

2 teaspoons salt

1½ pounds pork shoulder, cut into bite-sized pieces

1 teaspoon dried thyme

½ pound andouille or other spicy sausage

2 cups fresh breadcrumbs

Rinse the beans and put them in a large saucepan. Cover with water by about 2 inches and bring to a boil over medium heat. Remove the pan from the heat and let the beans sit for 1 hour.

Drain the beans, leaving them in the pot, and refill the pot with fresh water. Add 2 strips of the pork rind, 1 parsley stem, 1 garlic clove, 1 bay leaf, 2 peppercorns, 1 onion, 4 pieces of carrot, and 4 pieces of celery. Bring to a simmer, then add 1 teaspoon of salt. Cover and cook for 1 hour over low heat at a bare simmer.

Meanwhile, in a large Dutch oven, place the remaining pork rind, parsley, garlic, bay leaf, peppercorns, onions, carrots, celery, and salt, plus the pork shoulder and thyme. Cover with water by about 1 inch and bring to a boil over medium heat. Skim the scum from the top of the water, cover, and cook on low heat at a bare simmer for 1 hour.

Reserving the liquid, strain the beans, vegetables, and rind and add them to the pot with the pork shoulder. Add enough of the bean liquid to the pot to cover and cook covered for another hour. Taste the beans and add more salt and pepper as needed.

Preheat the oven to 325°F.

Remove and discard the pork rind, parsley stems, bay leaf, onion, carrot and celery from the pot. Cut the sausage into 3-inch pieces and add them to the pot, pushing them down into the beans. Top with half the breadcrumbs and bake uncovered for 30 minutes or until the breadcrumbs brown. Remove the pot from the oven, turn the crust over and let it fall into the cassoulet. Top with the remaining breadcrumbs and bake for another 30 minutes. Serve hot.

Sole Meunière SOLE IN BUTTER AND LEMON SAUCE

Start to finish: 20 minutes • Hands-on time: 20 minutes

One of France's most widely known dishes, sole meunière was the dish that started Julia Child on the path to gastronomy. A dish so simple requires perfectly fresh fish, which can be a bit dicey for many. Purists would dictate that it must be made with a whole Dover sole, flown in tout de suite *from the icy waters of the English Channel. We see no need to break the bank when you can make a delicious and fabulous sole meunière using easily procured fillets of sole, flounder, or even tilapia.*

YIELD: 4 SERVINGS

Salt and freshly ground
   black pepper
4 (6- to 8-ounce) fillets of sole,
   flounder, or tilapia, skinned
⅓ cup unbleached all-purpose flour
¼ pound (1 stick) unsalted butter
Half a lemon
2 tablespoons minced flat-leaf
   parsley, for garnish

Salt and pepper the fish on both sides. Spread the flour out on a large plate and dredge the fish in it, shaking off the excess.

Heat 4 tablespoons of butter in a large sauté pan over medium-high heat. When it foams, arrange the fish in the hot pan. Cook the fish for about 3 minutes, or until the cooked side becomes a light golden color, then turn it and cook it on the second side for 2 minutes. Transfer the fish to a platter and cover to keep warm.

In a small skillet, heat the remaining 4 tablespoons butter over medium-high heat until it becomes foamy, about 3 minutes. Squeeze the lemon over the fish and immediately pour the hot butter over all.

Garnish with parsley and serve immediately.

Crème Anglaise CUSTARD SAUCE

Start to finish: 30 minutes • Hands-on time: 15 minutes

This vanilla custard sauce is simplicity itself. It can serve as a sauce for fresh fruit or you can choose to gild the lily by serving it with chocolate soufflé or tarte tatin. One thing is certain: once you are aware of the wonders of crème anglaise, you will find many uses for it, not the least of which is eating it out of the bowl with a spoon.

Of the hundreds of crème anglaise recipes floating around, our favorite by far is adapted from a recipe by our friend and the author of Cookwise, *Shirley Corriher, who can always be counted on to come up with something sinfully rich with eggs and cream.*

YIELD: ABOUT 2 CUPS

1 cup milk

½ cup heavy cream

1 vanilla bean,
   split down the middle

⅓ cup sugar

Pinch of salt

5 large egg yolks

In a large saucepan, heat the milk, cream, vanilla bean, sugar, and salt over medium heat until it steams. Turn off the heat, cover with a lid, and let the milk sit for 15 minutes to infuse the flavor of the vanilla bean.

Remove the bean from the liquid and, using the back of a knife, scrape the pod's seeds into the pan. Return the pod to the pan and stir to combine.

In a large heatproof bowl, whisk the yolks, then add the hot milk mixture in a steady stream, whisking constantly. Return the mixture to the pan and heat over medium heat. Stir constantly with a wooden spoon until the mixture begins to thicken slightly and look velvety, about 4 minutes. Cook for 1 minute longer, remove from the heat, and transfer to a large bowl set inside another large bowl filled with ice. Stir the custard until it is cool. Remove the pod and discard it. Cover and refrigerate until serving.

MAKE AHEAD: The custard keeps for up to 3 days, covered and refrigerated.

Grand Marnier Soufflé SOUFFLÉ AU GRAND MARNIER

Start to finish: 1 hour • Hands-on time: 20 minutes

Who can resist the sight of a beautifully risen dessert soufflé arriving at the table? Light and fluffy with a hint of orange, Soufflé au Grand Marnier is certainly one of the most glorious conclusions to a meal and a perfect pairing with Champagne. Like most French desserts, soufflés are an impressive pièce de résistance whose appearance is quickly diminished once it is dug into with a serving spoon. So, ante up the drama when transporting your spectacular dessert to the table. Dim the lights and turn up the music; perhaps an étude by Chopin. Your guests (or family) will love it.

YIELD: 6 SERVINGS

4 tablespoons unsalted butter, softened

¾ cup plus 2 tablespoons granulated sugar

¾ cup whole milk

Grated zest of 2 oranges

3 tablespoons unbleached all-purpose flour

Pinch of salt

6 large eggs plus 1 large egg white, separated

3 tablespoons Grand Marnier liqueur

2 tablespoons confectioners' sugar

Preheat the oven to 425°F. Move an oven rack to the lower third of the oven.

Coat the inside of an 8-cup soufflé dish with 2 tablespoons of butter. Add 2 tablespoons of granulated sugar and roll it around the inside of the dish to coat. Discard the remaining sugar and set the dish aside.

In a small saucepan, heat the milk, ½ cup of granulated sugar, and the orange zest until the mixture steams. Remove from the heat and set aside.

While the milk is warming up, heat a 2-quart saucepan over medium heat and add the remaining 2 tablespoons butter. Let the butter melt, then add the flour and salt and cook, stirring, until the mixture is foamy, about 2 minutes. With the saucepan still over the heat, whisk the flour mixture and add the hot milk all at once. Whisk until the mixture becomes thick and velvety, about 2 minutes. Remove from the heat and transfer to a large bowl. Let the mixture cool for 5 minutes. This is the base for your soufflé.

Whisk the egg yolks, one at a time, into the soufflé base. Add the Grand Marnier and set aside.

Using a mixer set on medium speed, beat the 7 egg whites until they are foamy. Turn the speed to high. When the whites form soft peaks, add the remaining ¼ cup granulated sugar slowly. Continue to beat on high speed for 1 minute. The whites should become glossy and firm.

To assemble the soufflé, add one-fourth of the egg whites to the soufflé base. Using a large, flat spatula, gently turn and fold the soufflé base up and over the top of the egg whites to lighten the mixture. Add half the remaining egg whites and fold, leaving some streaks of white. Then add the remaining egg whites and gently fold them in completely. Be careful not to

(continued on next page)

overmix or the whites will deflate, leaving you with an under-risen soufflé. The secret to success here is in folding until each addition of egg whites is almost incorporated, then adding the next batch and so on until all the whites are incorporated.

Gently transfer the soufflé batter into the prepared dish and flatten the top with the spatula. Run a finger or a spoon around the edge of the soufflé, leaving a trough about ½ inch deep. This will allow the soufflé to rise even higher.

Put the soufflé in the oven and immediately turn the heat down to 375°F. Bake for 20 minutes, the pull out the oven rack, and carefully dust the soufflé with the confectioners' sugar. Gently push the rack back into the oven and close the door. (Don't over worry about a stray noise or bump affecting your soufflé. They are much hardier than you think.) Check the soufflé after 15 minutes and gently jiggle it. If it moves slightly in the center the soufflé is done. If it is loose on the edges, bake for another 5 minutes. It should be browned and crusty on top

Remove the soufflé from the oven and serve immediately.

TIPS FOR EGG WHITES:

- Sometimes egg whites don't beat properly because a trace of yolk has bled into them when you separated the eggs. To avoid this, break your eggs and separate the whites from the yolks into a clean dish. Once you've made sure there are no traces of yolk or shell, add the white to a communal bowl.

- Be sure to beat your egg whites in a clean glass or stainless steel bowl. Because fat can adhere to plastic bowls, it can prevent your egg whites from gaining volume.

- Room-temperature egg whites beat more efficiently than cold ones.

Chocolate Soufflé

Start to finish: 1 hour • Hands-on time: 30 minutes

If we had to make one showstopping dessert that matches its flamboyant theatrics with great taste, we would have to choose a chocolate soufflé. This dish has lots of chocolaty flavor along with a light and fluffy texture, not to mention a dramatic rise and fall to thrill your tablemates. For an extra indulgence, serve this dish with Crème Anglaise (page 96) and a few raspberries tossed on the plate for good measure. The delicious vanilla sauce and sharp berries offset the rich chocolate to good effect.

YIELD: 4 SERVINGS

4 tablespoons unsalted butter, softened

5 tablespoons plus ⅓ cup sugar

1¼ cups whole milk

¼ cup unbleached all-purpose flour

½ pound bittersweet chocolate, chopped

¼ cup strong brewed coffee

1 tablespoon vanilla extract

6 large eggs, separated

Pinch of salt

Preheat the oven to 425°F.

Use 1 tablespoon of the butter to coat an 8-cup soufflé dish. Add 3 tablespoons of the sugar to the dish and roll it around to coat the sides and bottom evenly. Discard the excess and set the dish aside.

Warm the milk in a medium saucepan or in the microwave.

In another saucepan, add the flour and the ⅓ cup sugar. Whisk in the hot milk until the mixture is completely blended. Set the saucepan over medium-high heat and cook until the milk mixture comes to a boil. Boil for 30 seconds; the mixture will be thick.

Remove the saucepan from the heat and add the chocolate, coffee, and vanilla. Stir until the heat from the milk mixture melts the chocolate completely. This is your soufflé base.

Let the base cool for 5 minutes, then add the egg yolks, one at a time. Mix in 2 tablespoons of the butter and dot the top with the remaining tablespoon of butter to keep a skin from forming on top.

In a glass or stainless steel mixer bowl, beat the egg whites with the salt until soft peaks form. Sprinkle the remaining 2 tablespoons sugar over the whites and beat until stiff peaks form.

Add one-fourth of the egg whites to the soufflé base. Using a large, flat spatula, gently turn and fold the soufflé base up and over the top of the egg whites to lighten the mixture. Add half the remaining egg whites and fold, leaving some streaks of white. Then add the remaining egg whites and gently fold them in completely. Be careful not to overmix or the whites will deflate, leaving you with an under-risen soufflé. The secret to success here is in folding until each addition of egg whites is almost incorporated, then adding the next batch and so on until all the whites are incorporated.

(continued on next page)

Gently transfer the soufflé batter into the prepared dish and flatten the top with the spatula. Run a finger or a spoon around the edge of the soufflé, leaving a trough about ½ inch deep. This will allow the soufflé to rise even higher.

Put the soufflé in the oven and immediately turn the heat down to 375°F. Bake for 40 to 45 minutes. At this point, the top of the soufflé should look nicely browned. To check for doneness, poke a thin knife or long straw into the soufflé center; it should come out clean. Remove the soufflé from the oven and serve immediately.

Tarte Tatin UPSIDE-DOWN APPLE TART

Start to finish: 3 hours 30 minutes (including time needed to make the pastry) • Hands-on time: 40 minutes

Invented by the Tatin sisters more than one hundred years ago in their hotel-restaurant in the Lamotte-Beuvron region of France near the Loire River, this rich upside-down apple tart is a lesson in simplicity. As with many simple dishes, the quality of ingredients is très important. We find Granny Smiths to be the best apples for tarte tatin since they keep their shape, and their tartness is a nice counterpoint to the sweet buttery caramel. Once baked, the tart is flipped so that the crispy crust is on the bottom, revealing the beautiful glazed fruit. Constructed of nothing more than apples, butter, and sugar in a pastry-topped skillet, this culinary tour de force is sure to become one of your family's favorite desserts.

YIELD: 8 TO 10 SERVINGS

Flaky Pastry (page 65)

16 Granny Smith apples
    (12 if they are large), peeled

¼ pound (1 stick) plus 2 table-
    spoons unsalted butter, softened

1½ cups sugar

Pinch of salt

Crème fraîche or Crème Anglaise
    (page 96), for serving

Prepare the pastry as directed in the recipe.

Cut a thin slice from the bottom of each apple so they stand up straight. Halve the apples lengthwise, then core them.

In a 3 quart (10-or 11-inch) skillet with straight sides, melt the butter over medium-high heat. Sprinkle the sugar and salt over the butter and cook, stirring occasionally until the sugar begins to brown, about 4 minutes. Lower the heat and cook for 3 minutes, stirring every now and then to ensure even caramelization. When the mixture becomes a deep golden caramel, remove it from the heat.

Carefully stand the apples around the outside of the pan (cut insides facing inward), then fill in the center with the remaining apples, bottoms down, so the apples are as snug as possible. It may be necessary to cut some of the apple halves in half again so they fit.

Return the pan to medium-low heat and cook for about 3 minutes. The apples will begin to give off some of their liquid, thinning the hard caramel. Using a turkey baster, baste the apples with the caramel. It will be thick at first, but will thin as the apples cook. Cook and baste for about 10 minutes and add any leftover apples, cut into quarters, to fill in spaces that open up as the apples soften. (If you don't have a turkey baster, just skip the basting.) Remove the pan from the heat.

Preheat the oven to 400°F.

Lightly flour a work surface. Place the pastry dough on top of the flour and dust the top of the dough with an additional light dusting of flour. Roll the dough gently but firmly, picking it up after each roll and rotating it a quarter turn. This rotation keeps the dough from sticking and also helps the dough keep a round shape.

Roll the dough to about 14 inches in diameter and trim the round so that it is 2 inches larger than the skillet. Fold the dough in half, then into a quarter, and transfer it to the skillet, placing the folded point in the center of the apples. Quickly open the dough and fold the sides down between the apples and the pan. Cut three vent holes in the top. Carefully place the skillet on a sheet pan with sides (to catch any drips).

Bake for 25 to 30 minutes, or until the pastry is brown and crisp. Remove from the oven and let cool for at least 20 minutes before carefully inverting the skillet onto a large serving platter. Cut the tart at the table and serve warm with crème fraîche or crème anglaise.

NOTE: Though a simple dessert, this French apple pie is not uncomplicated. Browning the sugar and butter to the perfect color caramel is key. If you are using a dark skillet, spoon some of the caramel as it is cooking to get an idea of how dark it is. If it is too dark, your tart will be bitter. If it is too light, it will lack depth and richness.

TIP: The correct size skillet is also important. We find that a 10- or 11-inch skillet with straight sides works best. If you use a skillet with sloping sides (like a frying pan) the tart may not hold together when unmolded and may look a bit messy on the sides, although it will still taste great. Traditionally, tarte tatin was made in cast-iron pans. If you find an old seasoned cast-iron pan with straight sides, by all means use it. It will cook your tarte tatin to perfection. Le Creuset also makes special tarte tatin pans that can be found in some cookware stores.

MAKE AHEAD: The tart may be baked 8 hours in advance and kept in the skillet at room temperature. It should be warmed in a 350°F. oven for about 20 minutes before serving.

Chocolate Mousse MOUSSE AU CHOCOLAT

Start to finish: 2 hours 30 minutes • Hands-on time: 30 minutes

There are countless chocolate mousse recipes circulating in the universe, but we think this is one of the best. For choco-holics, digging in to a really fine chocolate mousse is one of those transcendent moments of which songs are sung ("Heaven! I'm in heaven!"), poetry written (Ode to Chocolate), and stories told ("I can't believe I ate the whole thing!"). Leave it to the French to concoct a dessert so rich and heavy with butter and chocolate, yet light at the same time.

YIELD: 6 TO 8 SERVINGS

4 large pasteurized eggs,
    separated, at room temperature
    (see note)

⅓ cup plus 2 tablespoons
    extra-fine granulated sugar

2 tablespoons strong brewed coffee

Pinch of salt

2 tablespoons Grand Marnier,
    Cointreau, Frangelico, or
    Kahlúa liqueur

6 ounces bittersweet chocolate,
    chopped into small pieces

4 tablespoons unsalted butter,
    diced

1 teaspoon vanilla extract

Whipped cream, for garnish

Bring a medium saucepan filled with about 2 inches of water to a simmer.

Meanwhile, in a large stainless steel bowl, beat the egg yolks and ⅓ cup of the sugar until the mixture is pale yellow and thick. Whisk in the coffee, salt, and your choice of liqueur.

Set the bowl over the simmering water and continue to whisk until the sugar melts, about 5 minutes. Remove the bowl from the heat and add the chocolate, butter, and vanilla. Continue to whisk (off the heat) until the chocolate and butter have melted. You may need to return the bowl to the saucepan to finish melting the chocolate. Let the mixture cool to room temperature.

Using an electric mixer, beat the egg whites until soft peaks form. Add the remaining 2 tablespoons sugar and beat until firm peaks form, about 1 minute. Fold one quarter of the egg whites into the cooled chocolate leaving it streaky with white. Add half of the remaining egg whites and fold gently, leaving it streaky again. (Don't overmix the mousse, or you will deflate the air in the egg whites.) Add the remaining egg whites and fold until they are completely incorporated.

Pour the mousse into a serving dish or dessert cups. Refrigerate for at least 2 hours or overnight. Garnish with whipped cream.

NOTE: Eating raw or undercooked eggs is a risk for foodborne ill-ness. Pasteurization reduces the risk of egg-borne illness caused by salmonella. Not all eggs are pasteurized. Buy only pasteurized egg products that bear the USDA inspection mark.

TIP: Use the best bittersweet chocolate for this recipe. Look for Callebaut, Des Alpes, Valhrona, Scharffen Berger, or other high-quality chocolate. It really does make a difference. Chocolate is very finicky when it comes to heat. Be careful not to overheat it or it will become grainy and lose its velvety texture. Once chocolate is overheated, there is nothing you can do to fix it but start over, so watch carefully and don't melt the chocolate completely over the heat. Melt it partially over the heat, then stir it off the heat. If you must return the bowl to the hot water, do it off the heat and stir constantly.

Crème Brûlée

Start to finish: 6 hours 25 minutes • Hands-on time: 25 minutes

What is the best part of crème brûlée? The creamy, sinfully rich custard or the crackly caramelized sugar topping? Whatever your choice, crème brûlée is one of the most hedonistic desserts ever. The brûlée is achieved by caramelizing the sugar with a propane torch. It might look a little scary, but your guests and family are sure to enjoy the result.

YIELD: 6 SERVINGS

1½ cups heavy cream, chilled

1 cup half-and-half

½ cup granulated sugar

Pinch of salt

1 vanilla bean, halved lengthwise,
   or 2 teaspoons vanilla extract

8 large egg yolks

6 tablespoons Turbinado
   or Demerara sugar

MAKE AHEAD: The custards can be made up to 2 days ahead. Flame the tops no more than 2 hours ahead or the caramel won't have that celebrated crack.

Adjust your oven rack to the lowest position and preheat the oven to 325°F.

In a medium saucepan over medium heat, combine the cream, half-and-half, granulated sugar, salt, and vanilla bean and heat until the mixture steams. Remove the vanilla bean and, with the back of a paring knife, scrape the beans from the pod. Return the pod and beans to the hot milk and bring to a simmer. Remove the pan from the heat, cover, and let sit for 15 minutes.

Bring 5 cups of water to a boil. Place a kitchen towel in a 13 x 9-inch pan and arrange 6 (4-ounce) ramekins in the bottom of the pan. (The towel will keep the ramekins from sliding around in the pan.) Place the pan on a sheet pan for easier transport.

In a large bowl, whisk the egg yolks. Add 1 cup of the cream mixture, whisking vigorously. Add the remaining cream mixture while whisking. Strain the resulting custard through a mesh strainer. (If you're using vanilla extract, add it now.) Ladle the custard evenly into the ramekins.

Pull the oven rack halfway out of the oven and set the pan of ramekins on it. Carefully pour the hot water into the pan until it comes halfway up the sides of the ramekins. Bake the custard until it is set, about 30 minutes. The custard will still look jiggly, but not liquid and loose.

Carefully remove the ramekins from the water and let them cool on a wire rack (canning tongs work well for this step). Transfer them to a sheet pan, cover with plastic, and refrigerate until cold, at least 4 hours and up to 2 days.

About an hour before serving, sprinkle each ramekin with 1 tablespoon of Turbinado sugar and flame with a propane torch until the sugar caramelizes. Refrigerate the custards for 45 minutes. Serve cold.

Crêpes Suzette

Start to finish: 2 hours 45 minutes • Hands-on time: 45 minutes

As children, we were fascinated by desserts that flamed: cherries jubilee, baked Alaska, and crêpes Suzette. We eventually grew out of our pyromania (well, almost), but we never grew tired of little crêpes flamed in Grand Marnier, sugar, and orange. This iconic French dessert not only provides a sweet ending to a meal, but was presented with more than a little bit of theater, including pyrotechnics! A trolley would roll to the table with all the accoutrements necessary to bathe the crêpes in a delicious orange butter sauce. Carla remembers dining as a child with her grandparents at an old Pittsburgh bastion of fine dining, where "the waiter would then pour over the sugar and brandy or Grand Marnier and, with a flourish, light the chafing dish with a whoosh . . . every eye in the restaurant would be on our table. We would feel so special, our faces bathed in that golden glow. After the flames subsided, we would eat those perfect crêpes Suzette, the sauce dribbling down our chins."

YIELD: 4 TO 6 SERVINGS

CRÊPES

2 large eggs

½ cup milk

½ cup unbleached all-purpose flour

4 tablespoons unsalted butter, melted

½ teaspoon sugar

⅛ teaspoon salt

1 tablespoon vegetable oil

ORANGE BUTTER

4 sugar cubes

2 organic navel oranges

3 tablespoons sugar

4 tablespoons unsalted butter, at room temperature

3 tablespoons Grand Marnier liqueur

To make the crêpes: Combine the crêpe ingredients, minus the oil, in a blender and blend until mixed well. Transfer the batter to a bowl, cover, and let rest on the counter for at least 2 hours or refrigerate for up to 24 hours. (If refrigerated, let it rest at room temperature for 1 hour before continuing with the recipe.)

Just before you're ready to make the crêpes, preheat the oven to 325°F. Butter the bottom of a shallow ceramic or porcelain heatproof dish.

To make the orange butter: Rub the sugar cubes over the skin of the oranges. The grainy cubes will absorb the fragrant oil in the skin and turn orange. Be careful not to rub in one place too long or you will pick up the flavor of the white pith, which is bitter. Using a microplane or grater, grate the remaining orange zest into a sauté pan. Add the sugar cubes, sugar, butter, and Grand Marnier. Juice the oranges into the pan and crush the sugar cubes with the back of a fork. Set aside.

Heat a crêpe pan or 7-inch nonstick skillet over medium heat. Fold a paper towel to a few layers of thickness and dip the end into the vegetable oil, then rub the oily towel over the bottom of the hot pan. Test the pan's heat by flicking a few drops of water onto it. If the water sizzles away immediately, the pan is ready.

Pour about 1½ ounces (about 3 tablespoons or a scant ¼ cup) of batter into the pan. Tilt and rotate the pan to spread the batter just so it coats the

(continued on next page)

MAKE AHEAD: Crêpes Suz-
ette can be assembled up to 24
hours ahead, kept covered, and
refrigerated. Bake as directed,
adding a few minutes to the
cooking time.

entire surface of the bottom of the pan. If you've added too much batter, pour out the excess. If you've added too little batter, just add a bit more the next time. Return the pan to the stove for about 1 minute. The crêpe's surface will be matte and no longer shiny. Using a fork or your fingers, pick up an edge of the crêpe and lift it off the pan, then flip the crêpe over. It will cook for about half a minute on the second side. (For some reason first crêpes tend to be ugly. By the time you roll it up, it shouldn't matter. It'll still taste great.) Transfer the finished crêpe to a plate and continue until you have used up all the batter.

Heat the orange butter over medium heat.

Dredge both sides of each crêpe in the sauce. Carefully fold the crêpes into quarters and arrange them in the buttered dish so they overlap slightly. When all the crêpes are folded, pour the remaining orange sauce overtop. Cover the dish with foil and bake for 10 minutes or until heated through. Serve hot.

NOTE: If you want to flame the crêpes, arrange them in a flameproof chafing dish or skillet. Measure out 2 tablespoons of Cognac—never pour directly from the bottle, or the flame can shoot up the liquor and into the bottle, creating a Molotov cocktail—and add them to the dish. Carefully light the dish with a long match. The flames will be high, so make sure that you are far from the vent hood, curtains, or hanging lights. Let the flames burn down, after about 10 seconds, then serve hot.

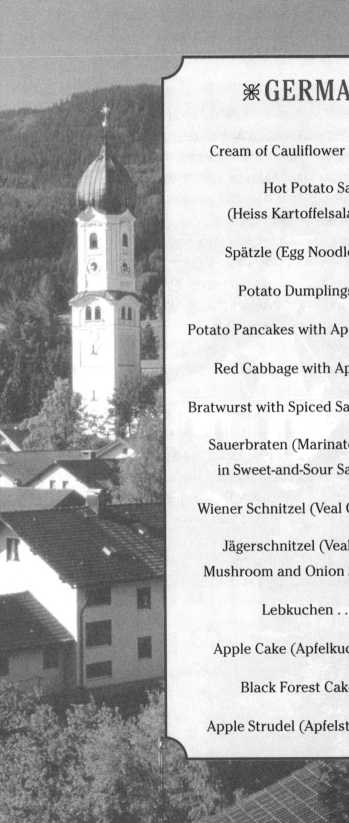

�֍ GERMAN �֍

❊ GERMAN ❊

NOBODY UNDERSTANDS THAT "EVERYTHING tastes better with an excessively large beer stein in your hand" like the Germans. Okay, we made the concept up, and you don't really need a beer stein to enjoy the cuisine of Germany. In fact, it tastes great with a glass of Riesling, too. Either way, these recipes will bring the oom-pa-pa right into your kitchen.

Don't let the stereotype fool you. German cuisine consists of much more than sauerkraut, sausages, and beer. Hearty food for big appetites is the basic rule of thumb, and meat and potato dishes are always a favorite. From schnitzel and sauerbraten to stews and spätzle, the food of Germany is as varied as the history and culture of its people.

In the United States, German restaurants can take on a Disneyesque quality, with the gables, half-timbering, and gingerbread trim, and the polka music playing loudly in the background. Once you get past all that kitsch and the loud clanking of beer mugs, there is genuinely good food to be found. To us, German dishes hearken back to the good, honest, straightforward food of the American Midwest. If you've ever had chicken-fried steak, Wiener schnitzel will be familiar. The same goes for sauerbraten, just a gingersnap away from marinated pot roast.

Although most people think about downing an icy beer with their bratwurst, the Germans are also well known for their winemaking. Germany is famous for its white wines, particularly riesling, grown up and down the Rhine. When looking for a nice German wine to accompany your potato pancakes, keep in mind that the term *trocken* on a wine label signals that it is dry, while *halbtrocken* refers to semi-dry wine.

The Germans love their sweets and we love them for it. The *kaffeeklatsch* is a daily custom and a good excuse to get together with friends for a cup of coffee, a sweet treat, and a dose of the daily gossip. The best thing about German food is that it is simple, hearty fare that warms you up from the inside out.

Here is one of our favorite German menus that can get you started in your own kitchen.

FOOD *for* THOUGHT

- From the earliest times right up into the 1800s, beer was considered to be important for the constitution. Many believed beer was a drink from the gods that had the ability to encourage strength, health, and relaxation.

- German chocolate and German chocolate cake are misnomers, originally called German's chocolate and German's chocolate cake, as the man who developed this chocolate was named Mr. German—the cakes have nothing to do with Germany.

- Duke Wilhelm IV of Bavaria decreed, in 1516, that beer could only be brewed from barley malt, hops, and water. This Rheinheitsgebot (purity law) was the world's first consumer protection law.

- While Frankfurter sausages might have come to Germany via the Chinese, they came to America via the Germans. The American hot dog traces its roots to Austrian/German immigrants who settled in our country in the nineteenth century.

Cream of Cauliflower Soup

Start to finish: 1 hour • Hands-on time: 30 minutes

This cold-weather favorite is sure to satisfy hearty appetites. We love the comforting, creamy texture of this cauliflower soup enriched with egg yolks and brightened with lemon juice. Nothing would be finer after a day spent hiking through the Black Forest, maybe hunting down wild mushrooms. We like to serve this soup as a first course with Wiener schnitzel (page 118), followed by Apfelkuchen (page 121).

YIELD: 6 SERVINGS

1½ pounds (about 1 small head) cauliflower

3 tablespoons unsalted butter

3 slices bacon, diced

1 medium onion, diced (1 cup)

⅓ cup unbleached all-purpose flour

4 cups chicken or vegetable stock

1½ cups milk

1½ teaspoons salt, plus more as necessary

¼ teaspoon white pepper, plus more as necessary

¼ teaspoon ground nutmeg, plus more as necessary

2 large egg yolks

½ teaspoon fresh lemon juice

Dash of cayenne pepper

¼ cup minced flat-leaf parsley or chives, for garnish

Cut away the thick stem base of the cauliflower and trim the florets from the head. Wash the cauliflower under cold water and chop it into 1-inch pieces.

In a 3-quart pot set over medium-high heat, melt the butter, then add the bacon and onion and cook until the onion is translucent, about 3 minutes. Add the flour and cook for 2 minutes. Whisk in the stock and 1 cup of water and bring to a boil. Add the cauliflower and turn the heat to medium-low. Simmer until the cauliflower is tender, about 20 minutes. Remove from the heat and allow the soup to cool for about 10 minutes.

Purée half of the soup in a food processor or blender. Return the purée to the pot and add the milk, salt, white pepper, and nutmeg. Return to a simmer over medium heat, then remove from the heat.

Beat the egg yolks in a heatproof bowl. Ladle a cup of the hot soup into the yolks while whisking. Repeat with another cup of hot soup, then quickly stir the egg mixture back into the soup and stir for about 1 minute. Do not boil the soup or the eggs will curdle. Add the lemon juice, taste, and adjust the seasonings if necessary. Add the cayenne pepper and garnish with minced parsley or chives. Serve hot.

> MAKE AHEAD: The soup can be made 1 day in advance to the point of adding the eggs. Reheat the soup over medium heat and continue with the recipe as directed.

Hot Potato Salad HEISS KARTOFFELSALAT

Start to finish: 50 minutes • Hands-on time: 10 minutes

Though not of German descent, Carla's mother would make a version of this rich potato salad for special occasions. The not-so-secret ingredient in this recipe is the bacon fat, which carries the sweet, sour, and onion flavors to great effect. The following recipe is the simplest, though the addition of diced celery or celery seed results in a tasty version as well. We like to serve this salad with everything from hamburgers and bratwurst cooked on the grill to simple roasted meats and poultry.

YIELD: 6 SERVINGS

2½ pounds red skin potatoes
   (about 8 to 10)

6 slices bacon, diced

1 medium onion, diced
   (1 cup)

¼ cup cider vinegar

¼ cup chicken stock or water

3 tablespoons sugar

½ teaspoon salt

½ teaspoon freshly ground
   black pepper

2 tablespoons chopped
   flat-leaf parsley

In a large pot set over medium heat, cover the potatoes with cool water. Bring to a boil, then lower the heat to a simmer and continue to cook the potatoes for 40 minutes, or until they are tender when pierced with a knife. Drain the potatoes, and when they are cool enough to handle but still warm, peel and slice them into a large bowl.

In a large skillet set over medium heat, cook the bacon until it is crispy and brown. Add the onion and cook for 3 minutes. Add the vinegar, stock, and sugar and continue to cook for 1 minute.

Pour the dressing over the warm potatoes, add the salt and pepper, and toss to coat until the potatoes have absorbed the liquid. Sprinkle with the parsley and serve warm.

> **MAKE AHEAD:** Though we enjoy this salad most when warm, it can be made up to 1 day ahead, kept covered, and refrigerated. Bring to room temperature before serving.

Spätzle EGG NOODLES

Start to finish: 45 minutes • Hands-on time: 30 minutes

Move over gnocchi, noodles, and mashed potatoes. We want spätzle for dinner! A surprisingly savory dish consisting of tiny noodles made with flour, eggs, milk, salt, and nutmeg, spätzle literally translated from German means "little sparrow." We don't know what these dumplings have to do with birds, but they sure do pair up well with braises and stews. As with most ethnic dumplings, these rate very high on the comfort food rankings. We especially like them fried in butter so they are a little crispy on the outside and soft and chewy on the inside.

YIELD: 6 SERVINGS

4 large eggs

1 cup whole milk

1½ teaspoons salt

¼ teaspoon freshly ground
   black pepper

⅛ teaspoon freshly ground nutmeg

3 cups unbleached
   all-purpose flour

4 tablespoons unsalted butter

Combine the eggs, milk, ½ teaspoon of the salt, the pepper, and nutmeg in a large bowl. Add the flour and mix by hand until a smooth dough forms. Let the dough rest, covered with a dish towel, for 15 minutes.

Meanwhile, bring a large pot with about 4 quarts of water to a boil over high heat and add the remaining teaspoon of salt.

Use a spätzle machine, a ricer, a colander with large holes, or a flat grater with large holes to make the spätzle. Place about ½ cup of the dough onto the device, lay it over the boiling water, and press the dough through the holes directly into the boiling water. Stir the spätzle gently to prevent it from sticking together, and boil rapidly for 2 or 3 minutes, or until the noodles float. Remove the noodles from the water with a slotted spoon and transfer them to a bowl of ice water. Repeat with the remaining dough, then drain the noodles from the ice water.

Melt the butter in a large sauté pan and add the cooled and drained noodles. Cook over medium-high heat until the spätzle begin to brown and crisp slightly, about 5 minutes. Don't stir too often, or they won't get a chance to crisp up. Serve hot as a side dish or add to soups and stews.

> MAKE AHEAD: The noodles can be drained, covered, and refrigerated for 1 day before they are fried. Continue with the recipe as directed.

Potato Dumplings

Start to finish: 1 hour 15 minutes • Hands-on time: 30 minutes

Since we never met a potato we didn't like, these plump little balls of über-comfort can be found on our tables through-out the winter months. Part of their charm is their simplicity, which makes them pair famously with dishes such as Sau-erbraten (page 117) and many soups and sauces. The trick to keeping them light instead of leaden is in refraining from overworking the dough. Once you have it combined, give it a rest before forming the balls, and you will be rewarded with puffy pillows of potato goodness.

YIELD: 8 TO 10 SERVINGS, ABOUT 20 DUMPLINGS

4 tablespoons unsalted butter

3 slices thick-sliced, homemade-type bread, crusts removed, cut into ¾-inch pieces

1½ pounds (about 3 to 4) russet potatoes, boiled in their jackets, cooled, peeled, and mashed

2 large eggs, lightly beaten

1 cup unbleached all-purpose flour, plus more if needed

2 tablespoons salt

Pinch of nutmeg

Pinch of pepper

MAKE AHEAD: The dumplings can be assembled up to 4 hours ahead, kept covered, and refrig-erated.

Melt the butter in a skillet set over medium heat. Add the bread and toss to coat. Brown the croutons until they are crispy and colored, about 10 min-utes. Remove from the heat and set aside.

In a large bowl, combine the potatoes, eggs, flour, 1 tablespoon of the salt, the nutmeg, and pepper. You should have a dough that can easily be shaped into balls. If the dough is thin, add more flour, 1 tablespoon at a time, until the desired consistency is achieved. Chill the dough for at least 30 minutes.

In a large pot set over medium-high heat, bring 1 gallon of water to a boil and add the remaining tablespoon of salt.

Divide the dough into golf-ball-sized rounds. Take a crouton and use your finger to push it into the center of a ball, completely covering the bread with dough. Continue with the remaining dough and croutons.

Add the dumplings to the boiling water. Give the pot a stir once or twice to make sure that the dumplings don't stick to the bottom of the pan or to each other. Cook the dumplings at a simmer until they float to the surface, about 10 minutes. Cook 5 minutes longer and remove the dumplings from the water with a slotted spoon. Serve hot with sauced meats and poultry.

TIP: It is necessary to really chill the mashed potatoes before making the dumplings, otherwise the potatoes will be too loose and the dough will lack texture.

Potato Pancakes with Applesauce

Start to finish: 45 minutes • Hands-on time: 45 minutes

Potato pancakes have to be one of the most frequently ordered items in a German restaurant. They are the perfect accompaniment to just about any dish, but when you pair them with applesauce, a line has been crossed—potato pancakes with applesauce is a match made in heaven. We can't get enough of these crispy cakes with sweet-tart homemade applesauce like you've never tasted before.

YIELD: 6 TO 8 SERVINGS

APPLESAUCE

6 Crispin, Mutsu or Braeburn
    apples, peeled, cored, and diced
Pinch of salt
Pinch of nutmeg
¼ cup apricot preserves
Sugar, as needed

POTATO PANCAKES

3 large russet or baking potatoes
1 large egg, beaten
2 tablespoons unbleached
    all-purpose flour
1½ teaspoons salt
Freshly ground black pepper
1 medium onion
About 1 cup bacon fat or
    vegetable oil, or frying

> **MAKE AHEAD:** The pancakes can be made up to 4 hours ahead and kept covered and refrigerated. Reheat in a 350°F. oven for 10 minutes.

To make the applesauce: Combine the apples and salt in a large pot set over medium heat, and cook until the apples begin to give off some of their liquid, about 5 minutes. Turn the heat down and cook the apples until they are soft and most of the liquid has cooked off, about 25 to 30 minutes.

Add the nutmeg and apricot preserves and stir to mix well. Taste the applesauce and add sugar as your taste dictates. Set aside.

To make the pancakes: Peel the potatoes and finely grate them into a colander. Push down on the grated potatoes with your hands to press some of the liquid from them, then transfer the potatoes to a large bowl. Immediately add the egg, flour, salt, and pepper and mix well. Grate the onion and add it to the potatoes. Mix well.

Preheat the oven to 200°F.

Heat 2 to 3 tablespoons of the fat in a large skillet set over medium heat. Using an ice cream scoop, scoop 3 or 4 mounds of potato into the hot pan. Press down on the potatoes with a fork to flatten them and tidy up the sides. Fry the potato cakes on one side for about 3 minutes or until browned. Flip the pancakes and brown the other side for about 3 minutes. Transfer the browned pancakes to a paper-towel-lined sheet pan and keep warm in the oven while you cook the remaining pancakes. Serve hot with applesauce.

TIP: It is worth the time to fry some bacon so you have bacon fat in which to cook the pancakes. We sometimes crumble up the bacon and add it to the pancake mix, which makes for a nice variation.

Red Cabbage with Apples

Start to finish: 2 hours 20 minutes • Hands-on time: 20 minutes

This has to be everyone's favorite way to eat cabbage. It is braised with apples, bacon, and onions so it is tender and moist, with an appealing sweet-and-sour tang. This cabbage goes especially well with schnitzel, ham, and simply grilled wurst.

YIELD: 6 SERVINGS

1 (2 to 3 pound) head of
  red cabbage

4 tablespoons unsalted butter

4 slices bacon, chopped

1 small onion, sliced

3 tablespoons light brown sugar

¼ cup red wine vinegar

2 teaspoons salt, plus more as
  needed

2 Crispin, Mutsu, or Granny
  Smith apples, peeled, cored,
  and sliced

Freshly ground black pepper

¼ cup red currant jelly

Tear off any unsightly outer leaves from the cabbage, quarter it and cut the core from each quarter. Thinly slice the quarters and set aside.

Heat a large Dutch oven over medium heat and add the butter and bacon. Cook the bacon until it is limp and has rendered some of its fat, then add the onion to the pan and cook for 3 minutes, or until the onion is soft. Add the brown sugar and cabbage, tossing the cabbage to coat it with the fat. Add the vinegar and cook the cabbage, stirring constantly until it turns bright magenta, about 3 minutes. Add 1 cup of water, the salt, and apples, and stir to mix. Cover the pot and simmer on low for about 2 hours, or until the cabbage is tender. If there is still liquid in the bottom of the pot, remove the lid and cook over medium heat until it cooks off.

Season the cabbage with salt and pepper. Stir in the red currant jelly, and serve hot.

TIP: The red currant jelly gives the cabbage a slightly sweeter note, but it still has that edgy tang.

> MAKE AHEAD: The cabbage can be made 1 day in advance and kept covered and refrigerated.

Bratwurst with Spiced Sauerkraut

Start to finish: 2 hours 30 minutes • Hands-on time: 30 minutes

The only exposure many Americans have had to bratwurst is at the ballpark, where it is smothered in bright yellow mustard. Although bratwursts can be deeply satisfying in the bottom of the seventh inning, we've hit a home run with this recipe. Bratwurst with sauerkraut is one of those simple dishes that can define an entire cuisine. Brats are common in most regions of Germany, but they can vary a great deal. Most consist of blends of beef, pork, or veal and are spiced with a variety of seasonings such as ginger, nutmeg, coriander, and caraway.

YIELD: 4 SERVINGS

1 pound bag sauerkraut

¼ cup bacon fat, lard,
   or unsalted butter

1 medium onion, minced

2 teaspoons sugar

2 Crispin, Mutsu, or Ginger
   Gold apples, peeled, cored,
   and sliced

2 cups beer, dry white wine, or
   chicken stock

5 juniper berries

6 peppercorns

2 bay leaves

2 allspice berries

⅓ pound boneless smoked
   pork butt

Potato Pancakes (page 114),
   for serving

2 pounds bratwurst,
   cooked variety, for serving

Drain the sauerkraut and rinse it under cold running water. Squeeze it dry.

In a large Dutch oven or pot set over medium heat, melt the fat, then add the onion and cook for 3 minutes, or until the onion is soft. Add the sugar and cook for about 5 minutes, or until the onions have browned. Add the apples, beer, and sauerkraut, and stir to mix well.

Crush the juniper berries and peppercorns with the bottom of a heavy pan and lay them out on a small square of cheesecloth with the bay leaves and allspice. Tie up the bag and tuck it into the sauerkraut mixture. Lay the pork butt on top, cover, and cook over low heat at a bare simmer for about 1 hour 30 minutes, or until most of the liquid has been absorbed.

Meanwhile, make the potato pancakes as directed in the recipe. Tuck the bratwurst into the sauerkraut, cover, and cook for another 30 minutes.

Remove the bratwurst and pork butt from the pan, and slice both into bite-sized pieces. Return them to the pan and mix into the sauerkraut. Serve hot as a one-pot meal along with Potato Pancakes.

TIP: The French make a dish very similar to this called *choucroute garni*. When we make *choucroute*, we like to use wine instead of beer and substitute garlic sausages instead of bratwurst.

> MAKE AHEAD: This dish can be made 1 day ahead and kept covered and refrigerated. Reheat over medium heat until hot.

Sauerbraten MARINATED POT ROAST IN SWEET-AND-SOUR SAUCE

Start to finish: 3 days • Hands-on time: 30 minutes

German for sour (sauer) meat (braten), this dish from the Rhineland is simple, filling, and delicious with potato dumplings or spätzle. The beef is marinated for days in a wine and vinegar mixture accented with juniper berries, bay leaves, and garlic. We love that the marinade becomes the sauce with the unlikely addition of crushed gingersnaps. It is surprisingly good.

YIELD: 6 SERVINGS

MARINADE AND ROAST

1½ cups dry red wine

½ cup red wine vinegar

1 large onion, quartered

4 whole cloves

2 bay leaves

4 black peppercorns, crushed

5 juniper berries, crushed

2 garlic cloves, crushed

3 to 4 pounds boneless beef roast,
  rump, top or bottom round, tied

2 teaspoons salt

½ teaspoon freshly ground
  black pepper

STEW

5 slices bacon, chopped

1 large onion, sliced

2 large carrots, peeled and sliced

1 bay leaf

GRAVY

2 tablespoons honey, or to taste

½ cup raisins

½ cup gingersnap crumbs

2 tablespoons unsalted butter

Salt and freshly ground pepper

To marinate the roast: Combine the wine, vinegar, onion, cloves, bay leaves, juniper berries, and garlic in a large pan and bring to a boil. Remove the pan from the heat, add 2 cups of water, and set aside to cool.

Rub the roast with salt and pepper, and put it in a nonreactive pot or heavy ziptop bag. Add the marinade and refrigerate for 2 or 3 days, turning it 2 times each day so the roast marinates evenly.

Remove the meat from the marinade and pat it dry with paper towels. Strain and reserve the marinade, discarding the solids.

To make the stew: Heat a heavy, 5-quart Dutch oven over medium heat and cook the bacon until it is crispy. Remove the bacon from the pan and add the roast, browning it in the fat, about 5 minutes. Turn the roast and brown the other side, about 5 minutes. Remove the roast from the pan and add the onion and carrots. Cook the vegetables until they color lightly, about 3 or 4 minutes. Return the roast to the pan, along with the bacon and enough marinade to come halfway up the sides of the meat. Add the bay leaf and bring to a boil. Cover the pan, reduce the heat to low, and let the stew simmer for 3 to 3½ hours, or place in a 325°F. oven for the same amount of time. Check to make sure that there is enough liquid in the pan and add more marinade as needed. The meat is done when it is tender and shows no resistance when pierced with the tip of a knife. Transfer the meat and vegetables to a heated platter.

To make the gravy: Bring the sauce to a boil and add the honey and raisins. Cook for about 5 minutes, or until the raisins soften. Add the gingersnap crumbs and butter and stir until lightly thickened. Taste and adjust the seasonings with salt and pepper.

To serve, carve the roast into slices and top with the gravy.

Wiener Schnitzel VEAL CUTLETS

Start to finish: 1 hour • Hands-on time: 30 minutes

Schnitzel is an Austrian dish, but don't tell that to the millions of Germans who rank it as one of their favorite dishes. Called veal milanese in Italy and escalope in France, schnitzel has two widely known variations. Wiener schnitzel consists of breaded and fried veal cutlets. Jägerschnitzel, on the next page, features veal cutlets appear with a pan sauce made of mushrooms and onions. The one constant rule for schnitzel is that the veal must be pounded thin with a mallet or veal pounder in order for it to be delicate and tender.

YIELD: 6 SERVINGS

1 cup unbleached
    all-purpose flour

2 large eggs, beaten

1½ cups fine dry breadcrumbs
    (see tip)

6 veal cutlets, no more than
    ¼-inch thick

Salt and freshly ground
    black pepper

4 tablespoons unsalted butter

Lemon wedges, for serving

¼ cup finely minced flat-leaf
    parsley, for garnish

Create an assembly line, starting with the flour on a plate, the eggs in a large bowl, the breadcrumbs on a plate, and a cooling rack last.

Lay the cutlets between two sheets of plastic wrap and pound them thin. Season with salt and pepper, then dredge the cutlets in the flour, shaking off the excess. Dip the flour-coated cutlets into the eggs, and then dredge them in the breadcrumbs. Lay the breaded cutlets out on the rack and let them dry for 30 minutes at room temperature.

In a large skillet set over medium-high heat, melt 2 tablespoons of the butter. Add 3 cutlets to the pan and cook for 3 to 4 minutes on the first side, or until they are crispy and browned. Turn and cook on the second side for another 3 minutes. Transfer the cutlets to a heated plate and cook the remaining cutlets in the remaining 2 tablespoons butter. Keep the finished cutlets hot in a 200°F. oven while the remaining cutlets cook.

Serve with a squeeze of lemon and a sprinkling of parsley.

TIP: Store-bought breadcrumbs from the cylindrical can (you know what they are) are not going to yield good results here. Just toast some day-old bread and whir it up in a food processor until it forms fine crumbs. Japanese panko breadcrumbs also work beautifully.

Jägerschnitzel VEAL CUTLETS IN MUSHROOM AND ONION SAUCE

Start to finish: 45 minutes • Hands-on time: 35 minutes

Schnitzel made in the hunter's style isn't breaded, but is instead quickly sautéed, then cooked in a light mushroom and onion sauce. In German restaurants in the United States, you will often see the Wiener schnitzel served with Jägerschnitzel sauce. Feel free to serve yours any way you please.

YIELD: 6 SERVINGS

6 veal cutlets, no more than
    ¼-inch thick
Salt and freshly ground
    black pepper
3 tablespoons unsalted butter
1 small onion, minced
1 small carrot, minced
1 cup sliced mushrooms
1 tablespoon unbleached
    all-purpose flour
1 cup white wine
1 tablespoon lemon juice
¼ cup flat-leaf parsley, for garnish

Lay the cutlets between two sheets of plastic wrap and pound them thin. Season them with salt and pepper.

In a large skillet set over medium-high heat, melt the butter until it sizzles. Add half the veal and fry it on one side until browned, about 3 minutes. Turn the cutlets and fry the second side for another 2 or 3 minutes. Remove the veal from the pan and continue in the same manner with the remaining veal.

Add the onion and carrot to the pan and cook for 1 minute. Add the mushrooms and cook for 2 minutes. Add the flour and cook for 1 minute, then add the wine and lemon juice, stirring until the sauce thickens lightly. Return the veal to the pan and cover. Simmer for 10 minutes, or until the veal is tender.

Season with salt and pepper and garnish with parsley. Serve hot.

Lebkuchen

Start to finish: 1 hour 10 minutes • Hands-on time: 45 minutes

This traditional German Christmas cookie can appear either soft in bar form, or rolled and baked until crisp. This precursor to gingerbread is thought to have been made first by monks who kept beehives in order to be supplied with wax for candles. Its popularity spread fast and these "honey cakes" fast became a favorite treat at Christmas time. These bar cookies are even better the day after you bake them.

YIELD: ABOUT 36 BARS

3 cups all-purpose flour

2 teaspoons cinnamon

2 teaspoons ground ginger

1 teaspoon baking powder

1½ teaspoons salt

½ teaspoon ground cloves

½ teaspoon ground nutmeg

½ teaspoon white pepper

2 teaspoons almond extract

1 cup light brown sugar

¼ pound unsalted butter, softened

3 large eggs

½ cup honey

1 teaspoon orange zest

¾ cup buttermilk

½ cup ground almonds

½ cup finely chopped candied lemon peel

GLAZE

1½ cups confectioners' sugar

1 pasteurized egg white (see note on page 102)

1 teaspoon almond extract

Preheat the oven to 350°F.

Sift together the flour, cinnamon, ginger, baking powder, salt, cloves, nutmeg, and white pepper. Set aside.

In a mixer bowl, combine the almond extract, brown sugar, and butter. Beat on medium speed until the mixture is light and airy. Add the eggs, one at a time, and beat until well mixed, then beat in the honey and orange zest. Add the buttermilk alternately with the flour mixture ⅓ cup at a time, ending with the flour. Stir in the almonds and lemon peel.

Butter an 18 x 12 x 1-inch sheet pan and cover it with parchment paper, pressing down on it so it sticks to the butter. Butter and flour the parchment paper, tapping out the excess flour.

Pour the batter into the pan and spread it so it covers the pan and is level. Bake for 25 minutes, or until the top is firm to the touch. Remove from the oven and let cool.

Meanwhile, make the almond glaze by combining the confectioners' sugar, egg white, and almond extract in a medium bowl. Using an electric mixer, mix until a smooth glaze forms.

When the lebkuchen is just slightly warm, drizzle the glaze over it and let dry for about 20 minutes before cutting. Cut the lebkuchen into squares and store in an airtight container.

MAKE AHEAD: The bars keep for up to 1 week, kept in a tightly sealed container.

Apple Cake APFELKUCHEN

Start to finish: 2 hours • Hands-on time: 40 minutes

Apfelkuchen is really more of an apple custard tart than a cake. The pastry is rich with egg yolks and the custard filling contains not only apples, but more eggs, sour cream, spices, and rum-steeped currants. Apfelkuchen is a terrific dessert to serve at a party becuase it could easily serve 16 diners a moderate slice. Apfelkuchen should be made and served on the same day.

YIELD: 10 SERVINGS

1¾ cups unbleached
    all-purpose flour

Grated zest of 1 lemon

4 tablespoons plus ⅓ cup sugar

¼ teaspoon salt, plus a pinch

3 large egg yolks

¼ pound (1 stick) unsalted
    butter, softened

½ cup currants

⅓ cup rum or Cognac

3 Braeburn apples (or other firm,
    sweet-tart apple), peeled,
    cored, and sliced ¼-inch thick

3 large eggs, beaten

¾ cup sour cream

Pinch of nutmeg

¼ teaspoon ground cinnamon

In a food processor, combine the flour, lemon zest, 2 tablespoons of the sugar, ¼ teaspoon salt, and 1 tablespoon water and pulse to incorporate the ingredients. Add the egg yolks and butter and process until well mixed and a clump of dough holds together when squeezed.

Pat the dough into the bottom and 2 inches up the sides of an 8-inch springform pan. Refrigerate until ready to fill.

Preheat the oven to 375°F.

Heat the currants and rum in a small pan over medium heat and let the currants sit until they have absorbed most of the rum.

Spread the apples over the bottom of the springform pan, overlapping them. Strain the currants, reserving the liquid, and scatter them over the top of the apples. Sprinkle with 1 tablespoon of sugar. Bake for 35 minutes, or until the apples are tender.

Beat the eggs and ⅓ cup of sugar until lemon-colored and thick. Whisk in the sour cream, reserved rum (from the currants), and a pinch of salt. Pour half the mixture over the apples and bake for 20 minutes, or until the custard is set. Pour the remaining custard mixture over the custard and bake for 15 minutes longer, until the custard is set.

Combine the remaining 1 tablespoon of sugar with the nutmeg and cinnamon and sprinkle over the top of the cake. Bake again for 10 minutes, or until the sugar has melted.

Remove the cake from the oven and cool on a wire rack before removing the springform sides of the pan. Slide the cake to a serving plate and serve slightly warm or at room temperature.

Black Forest Cake

Start to finish: 1 hour 10 minutes • Hands-on time: 35 minutes

There are many different versions of this cake. The most authentic, of course, hails from cherry country… the Black Forest region of southern Germany. Typically Black Forest cake consists of several layers of chocolate sponge brushed with Kirschwasser, a high grade form of cherry brandy, filled with sweetened whipped cream and sour cherries then topped with chocolate shavings. This impressive celebration cake is sure to make your short list.

YIELD: 12 SERVINGS

6 large eggs,
    at room temperature
5 large egg yolks,
    at room temperature
1⅓ cups plus ¼ cup
    granulated sugar
2 teaspoons vanilla extract
Pinch of salt
¾ cup unbleached all-purpose flour
½ cup cocoa powder
3 tablespoons plus ⅓ cup kirsch
1 (¼-ounce) package gelatine
    powder
3 cups heavy cream, chilled
¾ cup confectioners' sugar
1 (18-ounce) jar cherry preserves
6 ounces semisweet chocolate
10 maraschino cherries, drained
    and patted dry, for garnish

Preheat the oven to 350°F.

Grease three 8-inch round cake pans, line the bottoms with parchment paper, then butter the parchment.

Bring a medium saucepan half full of water to a simmer over medium heat.

In a large stainless steel or glass mixing bowl, whisk together the eggs, egg yolks, 1⅓ cups of the sugar, the vanilla, and salt. Set the bowl over the simmering water, making sure that the bottom of the bowl doesn't touch the water. Continue to whisk the egg mixture until it becomes warm to the touch. Using an electric mixer ot a stand mixer with the whisk attachment, whip on medium speed for about 10 minutes or until the mixture becomes thick and triples in volume.

In a separate bowl, sift the flour and cocoa powder together. Using a large spatula, fold the flour mixture into the eggs in three additions. Make sure there are no unmixed dry ingredients at the bottom of the bowl.

Divide the batter among the prepared pans and bake for 20 to 25 minutes or until the tops spring back when lightly touched. Cool on racks, invert, and carefully remove the parchment paper. Let cool completely before continuing with the recipe.

While the cakes are cooling, make the syrup. Heat the remaining ¼ cup sugar and ⅓ cup water in a small saucepan over medium heat until the sugar melts. Remove the pan from the heat, add 3 tablespoons of the kirsch, and set aside.

To make the topping, combine the remaining ⅓ cup kirsch and the gelatine in a small saucepan. Let it sit for 5 minutes, then heat it gently over low heat until the gelatine dissolves. Remove from heat.

MAKE AHEAD: The cake can be assembled up to 24 hours in advance.

Using an electric mixer or a stand mixer with the whip attachment, beat the cream, confectioners' sugar, and gelatine mixture until firm peaks form.

Transfer one of the cake rounds to a serving plate bottom side up and brush about one-third of the kirsch-flavored syrup over the bottom of one the cake. Spread half of the cherry preserves on top of the cake and top with about 1 cup of the whipped cream. Arrange the second layer over the first, bottom side up and brush half the remaining syrup over the second layer, topping it with the remaining cherry preserves and another 1 cup of cream. Layer on the third cake, bottom side up and brush on the remaining sugar syrup. Reserve about 1 cup of the remaining whipped cream for garnish. Frost the cake with the rest. Refrigerate the cake while you make the chocolate curls.

To make the chocolate curls, melt the chocolate in a double boiler over hot water. Be careful not to overheat. Spread the chocolate out evenly on the bottom of an inverted sheet pan with sides. Chill the pan in the refrigerator for 10 minutes. Remove the pan from the refrigerator and quickly push the edge of a stiff spatula against the firmed up chocolate, scraping it up from the sheet pan. It should roll into curls. (If the chocolate flakes, it is too cold. Let it sit at room temperature for 5 minutes, then try to scrape the chocolate into curls again.) Scrape the chocolate until you have enough to cover the top of the cake. Try not to touch the chocolate with your hands, as it will melt.

Transfer the remaining whipped cream to a pastry bag with a star tip. Pipe rosettes around the outer edge of the top of the cake. Place a maraschino cherry in the center of each rosette. Top the center of the cake with the chocolate curls. Refrigerate until you are ready to serve.

Apple Strudel APFELSTRUDEL

Start to finish: 1 hour 25 minutes • Hands-on time: 50 minutes

Strudel has been known as the cement that keeps families together, brokers peace, and generally makes a hard life worth living. There are many variations on the theme, the constant being phyllo or strudel dough, apples, nuts, and raisins.

Thank heavens we don't have to make the strudel dough, which is truly an art form. The frozen, boxed phyllo pastry from the grocery store is a fine substitute for homemade. The apples used will dictate the texture and sweetness you crave. We like to use Crispin, Mutsu, or Granny Smith apples because they keep their shape and have a nice acidic edge that, when sweetened with sugar and raisins, have a little more zing than most. Try a mixture of all three for a sensational balance of sweet, tart, perfumy goodness.

YIELD: 2 (12-INCH) STRUDELS,
8 SERVINGS

¼ cup rum

½ cup raisins

3 slices homemade-style bread,
    crusts removed

4 tablespoons plus ¼ pound
    (1½ sticks) unsalted butter

⅔ cup sugar

1 teaspoon cinnamon

Dash of nutmeg

Grated zest of 1 lemon

1½ pounds (about 3 large)
    Crispin, Mutsu, or Granny Smith
    apples, or a mix of all three

½ cup chopped walnuts, toasted

½ pound (17 x 2-inch) phyllo
    pastry sheets, thawed if frozen

Preheat the oven to 350°F.

Combine the rum and raisins in a medium saucepan set over medium heat, and bring to a simmer. Remove the pan from the heat and set aside while you prepare the remaining ingredients.

In a food processor, pulse the bread to form fine crumbs.

Melt the 4 tablespoons of butter in a medium sauté pan set over medium heat. Add the breadcrumbs. Sauté until the crumbs are browned and crispy, about 3 minutes. Set aside to cool.

In a small bowl, combine the sugar, cinnamon, nutmeg, and lemon zest.

Peel and core the apples and thinly slice them (about 20 slices per apple). Toss the apples with the sugar mixture and add the walnuts.

Melt the remaining ¼ pound of butter in a small saucepan set over medium heat.

Unwrap the phyllo dough, unroll it, and cover it with a sheet of plastic wrap. Cover the wrap with a dampened towel to prevent the phyllo from drying out. Lay out 1 sheet of phyllo on a parchment-lined sheet pan. Brush the phyllo with melted butter, then lay another sheet on top of it. Butter the sheet, then continue layering and buttering each layer until you have a stack of 10 sheets.

Drain the raisins and toss them with the apples.

Sprinkle half the breadcrumbs over the stack of phyllo pastry sheets. Place half of the apple mixture along one long side of the phyllo, leaving a few inches clear on each short end. Lift the parchment and roll the phyllo over the apples in a jelly-roll fashion, tilting it so the phyllo doesn't tear. Fold the ends over the apple strudel to encase it and brush the ends with butter so the phyllo adheres. Continue to roll the phyllo into a log shape.

Make another strudel in the same manner with the remaining phyllo and apple filling.

Brush the strudels with butter. Bake for 35 to 40 minutes, or until the strudel is golden brown and crispy. Serve warm or at room temperature.

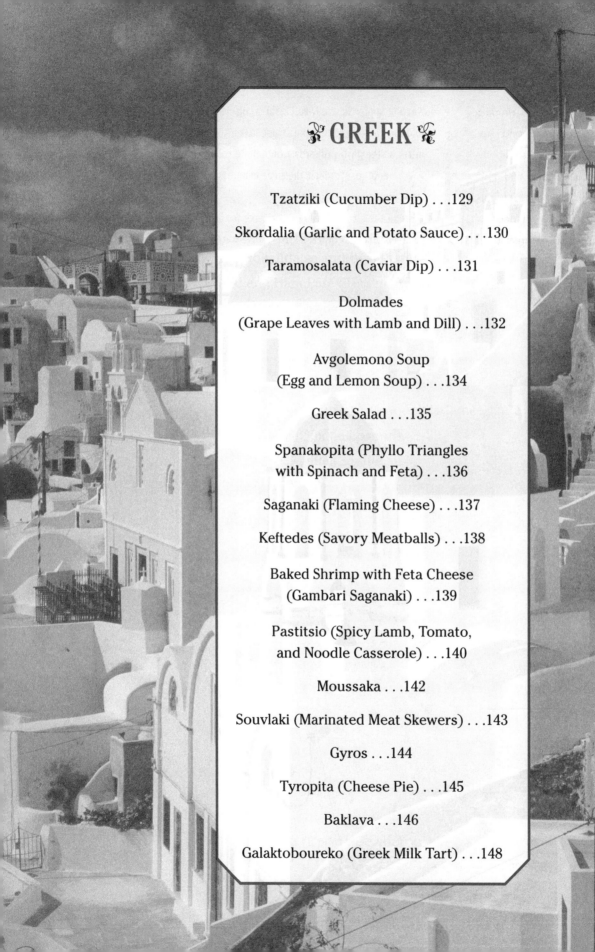

❦ GREEK ❧

THE GREEKS KNOW HOW TO HAVE A GOOD time. They eat, they drink, they sing, they dance, and instead of washing their dishes . . . they just break them on the floor. Actually, the breaking of dishes is not meant to get you out of a chore. It signifies passion and joy, and nowhere are those feelings more apparent than in Greek cooking. The flavors are intense and satisfying, and if you cook the dishes in this chapter, you can count on the fact that everyone will have cleaned their plates before smashing them on your dining room floor.

Situated at the doorstep of Europe, Asia, and Africa, Greece and its cuisine has evolved over the centuries to reflect the tastes of its neighbors. For this reason, many Greek dishes are known by numerous spellings, such as dolmades, dolma, or dolmathes; tyropita or tiropita; keftedes or keftethes; and so on. While this can sometimes be confusing, don't worry—if the spelling of a dish is close to what you recognize, it's probably what you think it is. Even if it's not, all Greek food is delicious so you're bound to love it anyway.

Generally considered the cradle of Western civilization, Greece consists of a mountainous mainland and about three thousand islands. Since no part of Greece is more than eighty-five miles from the sea, much of its climate is ideal for growing olive and lemon trees, raising sheep and goats, and, where the land is flat enough, growing wheat, tomatoes, potatoes, and eggplant. The country's cuisine reflects this abundance. Because Greece is surrounded by so much water, seafood also forms a large part of coastal Grecian meals.

It is impossible to talk about Greek cuisine without mentioning its famous *mezethes* (meze), or appetizers, consisting of platters of lusty food that can serve as a meal in itself. Typically served with wine or *ouzo* (a clear 80-proof anise-flavored beverage—remember all the broken dishes?), meze can consist of stuffed grape leaves, feta cheese, olives, pita bread, *tzatziki* (yogurt dip with cucumber), and buttery phyllo-wrapped *spanakopita* (cheese and spinach filling). The meze table is the hallmark of the Greek philosophy of sharing meals, a deeply rooted social event, strictly adhered to in a relaxed atmosphere.

The Greeks love to eat, and simplicity and freshness are the hallmarks of Greek cuisine. Who can resist *souvlaki* (tender lamb marinated in lemon juice and olive oil), or *pastitsio* (a lasagna-like dish covered with tomato-meat sauce topped with béchamel)? Certainly not us, as our waistlines will attest. As for the country's desserts, you can't talk about Greek desserts without talking about honey. Almost all their sweets include it. Topping the list is the famous baklava, a dish that is a testament to how the blending of cuisines occurs in a region. Baklava would be equally at home in the Middle Eastern chapter as it is here.

In the end, we don't know what we love best—the flamboyant food, or the energetic and enthusiastic way in which the Greeks consume it. Once you've cooked your way through a few of these dishes, we feel confident that you, too, will fall in love with the simple, bright flavors of the Greek Isles.

Here's a menu to get you started making Greek food in your own kitchen.

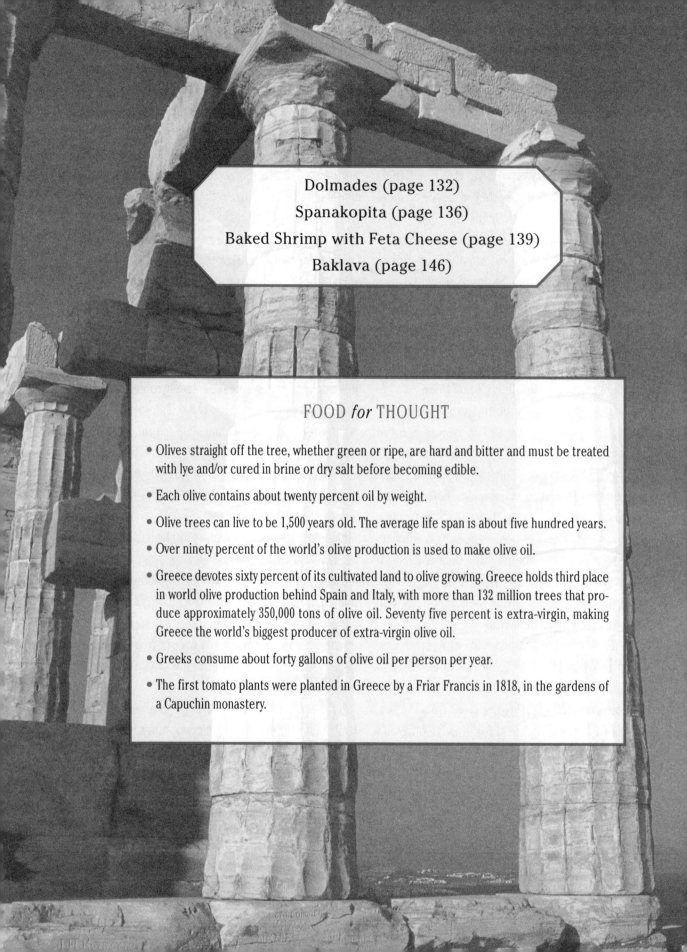

FOOD *for* THOUGHT

- Olives straight off the tree, whether green or ripe, are hard and bitter and must be treated with lye and/or cured in brine or dry salt before becoming edible.

- Each olive contains about twenty percent oil by weight.

- Olive trees can live to be 1,500 years old. The average life span is about five hundred years.

- Over ninety percent of the world's olive production is used to make olive oil.

- Greece devotes sixty percent of its cultivated land to olive growing. Greece holds third place in world olive production behind Spain and Italy, with more than 132 million trees that produce approximately 350,000 tons of olive oil. Seventy five percent is extra-virgin, making Greece the world's biggest producer of extra-virgin olive oil.

- Greeks consume about forty gallons of olive oil per person per year.

- The first tomato plants were planted in Greece by a Friar Francis in 1818, in the gardens of a Capuchin monastery.

Tzatziki CUCUMBER DIP

Start to finish: 3 hours • Hands-on time: 15 minutes

Tzatziki is the well-loved Greek cucumber dip that goes with everything, but is especially great with char-grilled meat such as souvlaki and gyros. We make the sauce thick and rich by draining the yogurt of its excess liquid. This keeps the tzatziki from becoming watery.

YIELD: 2 CUPS

2 cups plain yogurt
  or Greek yogurt

1 large cucumber, peeled
  and seeded

1 large garlic clove, minced

1 tablespoon olive oil

1 tablespoon lemon juice
  or white vinegar

Salt and freshly ground
  black pepper

Line a colander with a few coffee filters and place it over a bowl, leaving a clearance of 3 inches (so that the draining yogurt doesn't sit in its whey). Add the yogurt to the colander and place the whole thing in the refrigerator to sit for at least 3 hours or overnight. This process will thicken the yogurt and give it a richer texture. (If using Greek yogurt, this step can be omitted.)

Grate the cucumber and place it in a strainer. Squeeze the cucumber, to release some of the liquid and dry it out a bit. Set aside.

When the yogurt has thickened, place it in a bowl, add the cucumber and the remaining ingredients, and adjust the seasoning with salt and pepper.

> MAKE AHEAD: Tzatziki can be made up to 24 hours in advance and kept refrigerated.

Skordalia GARLIC AND POTATO SAUCE

Start to finish: 1 hour • Hands-on time: 10 minutes

Skordalia is a garlicky, potato-based dip that goes well with vegetables or topping grilled chicken, beef, or lamb. We are addicted to its smooth and rich olive oil flavor and ease of preparation.

YIELD: 2 CUPS

2 medium russet potatoes

½ head of garlic, peeled

3 slices of bread, crusts removed, moistened with 2 tablespoons water

½ cup olive oil

¼ cup vinegar

Salt and freshly ground black pepper

Put the potatoes in a large saucepan set over medium-high heat and cover them with cold water. Bring the water to a simmer, turn the heat down to low, and keep the potatoes at a simmer until they are cooked, about 45 minutes. Check for doneness by piercing the potato with the tip of a sharp knife. It should be tender to the center of the potato.

Remove the potatoes from the water and let cool. Peel and cut the potatoes in half and force them through a potato ricer or a food mill. Set aside.

In the bowl of a food processor, process the garlic until finely chopped. Add the bread, olive oil, and vinegar, and continue to process until smooth. Add the potatoes and process until smooth. Season with salt and pepper to taste. Serve at room temperature as a dip for vegetables.

MAKE AHEAD: Skordalia can be made up to 24 hours before serving, covered and refrigerated. Bring to room temperature before serving.

Taramosalata CAVIAR DIP

Start to finish: 20 minutes • Hands-on time: 20 minutes

One of the most popular of Greek hors d'oeuvres, taramosalata is made of olive oil, bread, lemon, garlic, and the salted roe, or fish eggs, of mullet, tuna, or cod. It is eaten as a dip for vegetables or flatbread. There are hundreds of variations, some using potato instead of stale bread and onion instead of garlic. We suggest that you make this rendition before you try other combinations. You will be sure to find a version that suits you to a T.

YIELD: ABOUT 2 CUPS

4 slices homemade-style white
    bread, crusts removed

3 ounces tarama or caviar
    (see note)

¼ cup fresh lemon juice

2 garlic cloves, minced

¾ cup extra-virgin olive oil

Soak the bread in ½ cup water for a minute or two, and squeeze it dry.

Combine the bread, tarama, lemon juice, and garlic in a medium bowl and smash with the back of a fork. Whisk in the olive oil in a steady stream and continue to mix until emulsified.

NOTE: Tarama can be found at some ethnic grocery stores or online.

MAKE AHEAD: This dip keeps for 4 days in the refrigerator.

Dolmades GRAPE LEAVES WITH LAMB AND DILL

Start to finish: 2 hours 30 minutes • Hands-on time: 1 hour

In the best Greek food, one can taste the fresh flavors of the sun-kissed isles, and there is no food that exemplifies those attributes more than this iconic appetizer. Whenever we find ourselves making these rolls, we imagine the women in small Greek villages coming together to assemble the food for a celebration, but also to share the stories, worries, victories, and comedies of their lives. We find ourselves doing much the same thing when we gather with friends: opening a bottle or two of wine and pitching in to make a delicious meal. Try making a batch or two up with a few friends. You'll be surprised at how quickly a platter of stuffed grape leaves appears!

YIELD: ABOUT 80, 10 TO 16 SERVINGS

2 (1-pound) jars brine-packed
  grape leaves, drained
1½ teaspoons salt
1 cup long-grain rice
4 tablespoons olive oil
1 medium onion, minced
3 garlic cloves, minced
1 pound lamb, finely ground
¼ cup pine nuts, toasted
¼ cup chopped fresh dill
¼ cup chopped fresh mint
¼ cup chopped flat-leaf parsley
½ cup currants
Zest of 2 large lemons
⅓ cup fresh lemon juice
2 teaspoons whole coriander
  seeds, freshly ground
⅛ teaspoon cayenne pepper
¼ teaspoon freshly ground
  black pepper

Soak the grape leaves in a large bowl filled with cold water for about 30 minutes.

Remove the leaves from the water and separate them carefully, laying them out on cloth towels to dry. Separate the largest and nicest leaves to use for rolling. Reserve the remaining leaves to line the bottom of a 4-quart saucepan and to place between the layers of the stuffed leaves.

Bring 1 cup of water and ½ teaspoon of the salt to a boil over medium-high heat. Add the rice, then cover and reduce the heat to low. Cook the rice until the water is absorbed, about 10 to 12 minutes. Transfer the partially cooked rice to a large bowl.

In a medium skillet, heat 2 tablespoons of the olive oil. Add the onion and garlic and cook for 3 minutes, or until the onion is translucent. Add the onion mixture to the rice along with the remaining teaspoon of salt, the lamb, pine nuts, dill, mint, parsley, currants, lemon zest, 3 tablespoons of the lemon juice, coriander seeds, cayenne pepper, and pepper. Toss to combine.

To roll the grape leaves, arrange one of the larger grape leaves shiny side down on a work surface, stem end toward you. Trim the stem if there is one. Spoon 1 tablespoon or so of the meat filling onto the leaf near the stem end and tightly roll the leaf, folding in the sides about halfway up and squeezing to pack the filling. Make more rolls in the same manner. The size of the rolls and stuffing amounts will vary according to the size of the

2 cups chicken stock

Pita bread, for serving

Greek yogurt, for serving

> **MAKE AHEAD:** The dolmade filling can be made and refrigerated 24 hours in advance. The rolled, cooked grape leaves keep for up to 3 days, covered and chilled. Remove the dolmades from the refrigerator 30 minutes before serving.

leaves. Try not to overstuff them, but add enough filling to make two bites. Be sure to roll them snugly, since loosely rolled grape leaves have a tendency to fall apart.

Line the bottom of a 4-quart saucepan with some of the smaller grape leaves and stack the stuffed rolls in layers, drizzled with the remaining 2 tablespoons of olive oil, and separated by more leaves. Add the chicken stock and remaining lemon juice to the pot so that the stock comes up almost to the top layer of grape leaves. Add water if needed. Cover the rolls with an inverted heatproof plate to weigh them down, and bring the stock to a simmer. Cover the pot with a lid and turn the heat to the lowest setting so that the rolls cook at a bare simmer for about 1 hour.

Remove the pan from the heat and let the rolls sit undisturbed for at least 30 minutes. Using tongs, transfer the hot rolls to a large platter to cool to room temperature.

Serve the dolmades with soft pita bread and rich Greek yogurt as accompaniments. We like to top a pita with a dolmades and yogurt, roll it up, and eat it like a Greek burrito. It's delicious!

TIP: Greek yogurt is thicker and richer than most American brands. If you can't find it, try lining a fine strainer with cheesecloth and set it in a bowl to catch the liquids. Then pour in the yogurt, cover, and refrigerate for at least 3 hours or overnight. The yogurt in the strainer will be thicker and richer the next day as a result of the liquid whey that drained off overnight.

Avgolemono Soup EGG AND LEMON SOUP

Start to finish: 30 minutes • Hands-on time: 10 minutes

Nothing could be more simple than this classic soup, rich with the addition of eggs and bright with lemon. As with any simple soup, the better your stock, the better the soup. If you have the time, make your own stock from scratch, but if you don't, enrich store-bought stock by cooking some chicken backs and necks in it for about 30 minutes (as in Wonton Soup, page 14).

YIELD: 6 SERVINGS

8 cups chicken stock

½ cup long-grain rice

3 large eggs

¼ cup fresh lemon juice

Salt and freshly ground
    black pepper

Bring the stock to a simmer and add the rice. Cover and lower the heat to cook at a bare simmer for 20 minutes. Remove from the heat and let sit for 10 minutes, uncovered.

Whisk the eggs in a large, heatproof bowl. Add 2 cups of the hot stock to the eggs in a thin stream, whisking constantly. Transfer the egg mixture quickly to the hot pot of soup, whisking constantly so that the eggs don't curdle. Add the lemon juice, and salt and pepper to taste. Serve hot.

Greek Salad

Start to finish: 30 minutes • Hands-on time: 30 minutes

Heaven knows, you don't have to be in a Greek restaurant to order a Greek salad. With all the variations, it can be a bit confusing as to just what a Greek salad is. From our experience, the main criterion is freshness of ingredients. The best tomatoes, cucumbers, peppers, kalamata olives, and feta cheese are the constants. Whether the salad contains lettuce is up to you, but we find romaine to be the best lettuce to hold its own with the other chunky ingredients and tangy dressing.

YIELD: 4 SERVINGS

¼ cup red wine vinegar

2 garlic cloves, minced

1 shallot, minced

½ teaspoon salt

Freshly ground black pepper

1 tablespoon Dijon mustard

2 teaspoons minced fresh oregano

2 teaspoons minced fresh basil

¾ cup extra-virgin olive oil

1 large cucumber, peeled, seeded,
    and cut into ½-inch slices

3 medium tomatoes, each cut into
    about 8 pieces

1 green bell pepper, seeded
    and cut into about 12 pieces

½ red onion, thinly sliced
    into rings

1 cup feta cheese

½ cup kalamata olives

2 tablespoons chopped fresh mint

Romaine lettuce, torn into bite-
    sized pieces

In a large bowl, combine the vinegar, garlic, shallot, salt, and pepper. Let the mixture sit for about 5 minutes to combine the flavors.

Whisk in the mustard, oregano, and basil. Pour the olive oil into the mixture in a thin stream, constantly whisking to form an emulsion. Set the dressing aside.

In a large bowl, combine the cucumber, tomato, bell pepper, onion, feta, olives, and mint. Toss with about ⅓ cup of the dressing, reserving the rest for later use. Let the salad sit for about 30 minutes at room temperature so the vegetables soak up the dressing.

Serve the salad on top of torn romaine leaves.

> **MAKE AHEAD:** The dressing keeps covered and refrigerated for 2 days.

Spanakopita PHYLLO TRIANGLES WITH SPINACH AND FETA

Start to finish: 1 hour 30 minutes • Hands-on time: 1 hour 30 minutes

Feta and spinach are a favorite Mediterranean combination often found sandwiched between buttery layers of phyllo. This filling shows up in appetizers and large pies alike, as in this, the most-recognized Greek dish in America. Phyllo appetizers are always a welcome addition to a party table and since they are good hot or at room temperature, they are also easy on you. While this recipe makes a lot, trust us, it will disappear fast.

YIELD: ABOUT 72 PIECES

3 tablespoons olive oil

4 green onions, trimmed
   and thinly sliced

2 (10-ounce) packages frozen
   chopped spinach, thawed
   and squeezed dry

3 garlic cloves, minced

¼ cup chopped flat-leaf parsley

¼ cup chopped fresh mint leaves

1½ cups crumbled feta cheese

Salt, as needed

¼ teaspoon freshly ground
   black pepper

⅛ teaspoon freshly ground nutmeg

½ cup pine nuts, toasted

24 (17 x 12-inch) sheets of phyllo
   pastry, thawed if frozen

¼ pound (1 stick) unsalted butter,
   melted

Heat the oil in a large sauté pan set over medium heat. Add the green onions and spinach and sauté until the spinach breaks up and the onions are soft, about 5 minutes. Add the garlic, parsley, and mint and cook for another minute or so, until fragrant. Remove the pan from the heat and stir in the feta cheese. Taste to see if it needs salt. (Feta can be very salty.) Add the pepper, nutmeg, and pine nuts. Stir to combine and set aside to cool.

Preheat the oven to 400°F. Line a baking sheet with parchment paper.

Unroll the phyllo onto a work surface and cover it with plastic wrap. Cover the plastic wrap with a damp towel to weigh it down and keep the pastry from drying out.

Working quickly, carefully remove one sheet of phyllo dough and lay it out on the work surface with the long side facing you. Brush the sheet with butter, lay a second sheet of phyllo on top, and brush with butter. Using a pizza cutter or a sharp knife, cut the phyllo into 8 strips. Place about 1 teaspoon of filling on the short end of each strip. Fold the phyllo over the filling to form a triangle, or as you would fold a flag, and continue to fold, leaving a seam on the bottom. Brush each triangle with butter and place on the prepared baking sheet, about ½-inch apart. Repeat with the remaining phyllo and filling.

Bake for 12 to 15 minutes, or until golden. Serve hot or at room temperature.

MAKE AHEAD: The unbaked stuffed triangles can be arranged on a parchment-lined baking sheet, frozen, and wrapped in plastic for 1 month. They may be baked frozen without thawing; just add 3 to 5 more minutes to the baking time.

Saganaki FLAMING CHEESE

Start to finish: 10 minutes • Hands-on time: 10 minutes

It's almost impossible to eat dinner in a Greek restaurant and not see flaming cheese floating through the dining room, precariously perched on a waiter's shoulder. Everyone at the table shouts, "Opa!" while the waiter extinguishes the flames with lemon juice. While these theatrics are fun, the cheese is fabulous. If you can't find kefalotyri cheese, just use feta: it will still be delicious.

YIELD: 6 SERVINGS

¼ cup olive oil

1 pound kefalotyri or feta cheese

1 large egg, beaten

½ cup unbleached
   all-purpose flour

2 tablespoons brandy

1 lemon

Pita bread, for serving

Heat the oil in a large skillet set over medium-high heat.

Cut the cheese into strips about ⅛ inch wide. Dip the cheese slices into the egg and dredge them in the flour, shaking off the excess. Add the cheese to the oil and brown on one side, about 1 minute. Turn and brown the other side of the cheese, about 1 minute.

Pour the brandy over the cheese and carefully ignite. Douse the flames with a squeeze or two of lemon juice.

Serve in the pan so the cheese stays hot. Accompany with pita bread.

Keftedes SAVORY MEATBALLS

Start to finish: 1 hour • Hands-on time: 40 minutes

Keftedes are meatballs made with either lamb or beef, and studded with onion, parsley, mint, tomato, and sometimes a touch of ouzo. Whether you make them small or large, round or flattened into disks, as an appetizer or as a stuffing for a pita sandwich, these versatile nuggets are sure to transport you to cloudless and sunny Greek skies. There are as many methods of cooking keftedes as there are variations in ingredients. The following recipe is our favorite version, which can be adapted to serve as an appetizer or, with the addition of rice, can be a main-course entrée.

YIELD: 6 SERVINGS

4 slices homemade-style bread, crusts removed

2 pounds ground lamb, beef, or a mixture of the two

1 large egg

6 garlic cloves, minced

¼ cup minced fresh mint

2 tablespoons unsalted butter, melted

1 teaspoon dried oregano

1 teaspoon salt, plus more as needed

¼ teaspoon cayenne pepper

⅛ teaspoon nutmeg

Freshly ground black pepper

¼ cup olive oil

1 large onion, sliced

1 (28-ounce) can diced tomatoes with juice

1 cup dry white wine

White Rice (page 12), for serving

Preheat the oven to 375°F.

Put the bread in the bowl of a food processor and pulse until fine crumbs are formed. Pour into a large bowl and add the meat, egg, 4 cloves of garlic, mint, butter, oregano, salt, cayenne pepper, nutmeg, and black pepper to taste. Mix well. Form a teaspoon-sized patty of meat and fry it in a hot pan. Taste and correct seasoning with salt and pepper if necessary.

Form the meat mixture by heaping tablespoons into round balls. Lay them out on a baking sheet, leaving space between them so they cook evenly. Bake the meatballs for 10 to 12 minutes, or until they are firm.

While the meatballs are baking, heat the oil in a large skillet or Dutch oven over medium-high heat. Add the onion and a pinch of salt. Sauté for 3 minutes, or until the onion is transparent. Add the remaining 2 garlic cloves and cook another 2 minutes. Add the tomatoes and wine, and bring to a simmer.

Add the meatballs to the tomato mixture, tucking them into the sauce so they are somewhat submerged. Simmer the meatballs for 20 minutes. Season to taste.

Serve hot with toothpicks as an appetizer, or over rice as a main-course entrée.

> **MAKE AHEAD:** The meatballs can be cooked 1 day in advance and kept covered in the refrigerator. Reheat over medium heat.

Baked Shrimp with Feta Cheese GAMBARI SAGANAKI

Start to finish: 30 minutes • Hands-on time: 30 minutes

Nothing could be easier than this dish of briny shrimp perfumed with oregano and mint. We can't decide whether we like it most as an appetizer or a main-dish entrée. Any way you serve it, it's delicious.

YIELD: 8 APPETIZER SERVINGS OR 4 AS A MAIN DISH

⅓ cup olive oil

1 large onion, minced

Pinch of salt

2 garlic cloves, minced

½ teaspoon oregano

¼ teaspoon red pepper flakes

1 (14½-ounce) can diced tomatoes with juice

½ cup dry white wine

2 pounds medium-sized (28 to 30) uncooked shrimp, peeled and deveined

6 ounces feta cheese, cut into ½-inch cubes

2 tablespoons minced flat-leaf parsley, for garnish

2 tablespoons ouzo

White Rice (page 12), for serving

In a large sauté pan, heat the oil over medium-high heat until it shimmers. Add the onion and salt, and sauté until the onion is soft, about 3 minutes. Add the garlic and continue to cook for another 2 minutes. Add the oregano, red pepper flakes, and tomatoes and cook for 5 minutes, or until the sauce reduces somewhat and thickens.

Add the shrimp, tucking them into the mixture so they cook evenly. Stir a few times and cook at a bare simmer for 2 minutes, or until the shrimp turns pink and opaque. Stir in the feta cheese and cook 1 minute longer. Remove the pan from the heat, garnish with parsley, and drizzle with ouzo.

Serve as an appetizer, or with rice as a main dish.

Pastitsio SPICY LAMB, TOMATO, AND NOODLE CASSEROLE

Start to finish: 2 hours 30 minutes • Hands-on time: 1 hour

Pastitsio is a lasagna-like casserole often served at celebrations or large gatherings. Redolent with warm spices, lamb, tomato sauce, buttery noodles, and creamy béchamel sauce, pastitsio is so worth the effort. It is easily made a day or so ahead and refrigerated. We like to serve this decadent dish with a simple salad, bread, and a nice medium-bodied red wine.

YIELD: 8 SERVINGS

6 tablespoons unsalted butter

1 tablespoon plus ½ teaspoon salt

1 pound bucatini or penne pasta

1 cup grated kefalotyri or
   Parmigiano-Reggiano cheese

¼ teaspoon nutmeg

Freshly ground black pepper

2 large eggs, beaten

TOMATO SAUCE

¼ cup olive oil

1 large onion, chopped

4 garlic cloves, minced

1½ pounds ground lamb

½ teaspoon dried oregano

½ teaspoon dried marjoram

½ teaspoon dried basil

1½ teaspoons salt

¼ teaspoon cinnamon

Freshly ground black pepper

2 (14.5-ounce) cans diced
   tomatoes with juice

¼ cup tomato paste

1 cup dry white wine

½ teaspoon sugar

Bring 4 quarts of water to a boil in a large pot.

Melt the butter in a medium saucepan over medium heat. Cook until the butter begins to brown, about 3 minutes. Remove from the heat and set aside.

Add 1 tablespoon of the salt to the boiling water, then add the pasta and cook for about 8 minutes, or until al dente. (The pasta will finish cooking in the oven.) Drain the pasta and return it to the pot. Add the browned butter and ½ cup of the kefalotyri cheese, the remaining ½ teaspoon salt, the nutmeg, and pepper to taste and toss to coat. Mix in the eggs and set aside.

To make the tomato sauce: Heat the oil in a large skillet over medium heat. Add the onion and garlic and cook for about 2 minutes, or until the onions begin to soften. Add the lamb, breaking it up into small bits. Add the oregano, marjoram, basil, salt, cinnamon, and pepper to taste. Cook for about 3 minutes or until the vegetables are tender and the lamb is no longer pink. Add the tomatoes, tomato paste, wine, and sugar, lower the heat and cook at a simmer for 15 minutes, or until the liquid cooks down and the mixture is thick. Taste and adjust the seasoning if necessary.

To make the béchamel: Melt the butter in a medium saucepan over medium heat. Stir in the flour and cook for 2 minutes, or until the flour is foamy. Add the warm milk all at once and whisk until the sauce boils and thickens, about 2 minutes. Remove from the heat and add the salt, nutmeg, cayenne pepper, and black pepper to taste. Stir the sauce to cool it for a few minutes, then whisk in the egg. Add about ½ cup of the béchamel to the tomato sauce and stir to blend. Taste and adjust the seasoning if necessary.

Preheat the oven to 350°F.

To assemble the pastitsio: Arrange half the pasta into the bottom of a

BÉCHAMEL

4 tablespoons unsalted butter

¼ cup unbleached
   all-purpose flour

2 cups warm milk

½ teaspoon salt

¼ teaspoon nutmeg

Dash of cayenne pepper

Freshly ground black pepper

1 large egg, beaten

2-quart baking dish. Top with the tomato sauce, then top with the rest of the pasta. Pour the remaining béchamel over the top of the casserole, then sprinkle the remaining ½ cup of the cheese on top.

Bake for 50 minutes to 1 hour, or until bubbly and hot. Let rest for 5 to 10 minutes before serving hot.

> MAKE AHEAD: The pastitsio can be assembled 1 day in advance and kept covered and refrigerated.

Moussaka

Start to finish: 1 hour 45 minutes • Hands-on time: 45 minutes

Where we come from, moussaka is what you make in the late summer when gardens are bursting with eggplant, zucchini and tomatoes. If you, like us, serve this homey dish at neighborhood potlucks, we guarantee you won't be taking home any leftovers. Sometimes moussaka contains ground meat and béchamel, and stands in as a main course. This is a lighter vegetarian version so you can use up all of late summer's bounty.

YIELD: 8 SERVINGS AS A SIDE DISH

2 medium eggplants, peeled
    and sliced ½ inch thick
1 teaspoon salt, plus more
    as necessary
¼ cup olive oil
1 onion, chopped
2 zucchini, sliced
3 garlic cloves, minced
3 ripe tomatoes, peeled, seeded,
    and chopped
¼ teaspoon ground cinnamon
Freshly ground black pepper
¼ cup dry breadcrumbs
½ cup grated kefalotyri or
    Parmigiano-Reggiano cheese

> **MAKE AHEAD:** Moussaka can be assembled or made up to 24 hours in advance and refrigerated. Reheat or bring back to room temperature before serving.

Toss the eggplant with the salt, then place it in a colander set over a bowl, and let it stand for 30 minutes.

Rinse the eggplant and pat dry. Heat 2 tablespoons of the oil in a large skillet over medium heat. Fry half the eggplant until lightly browned on both sides, about 2 minutes each side. Transfer to a plate and cook the remaining eggplant.

Add the onion and a pinch of salt to the skillet and sauté until translucent, about 3 minutes. Add the zucchini and cook for 5 minutes, or until it softens. Add the garlic, tomatoes, and cinnamon and cook until the tomatoes give off their juices, about 5 minutes. Season with salt and pepper to taste.

Preheat the oven to 350°F.

Spread the remaining oil over the bottom of a 3-quart casserole and sprinkle the breadcrumbs over the oil. Place half the eggplant on top of the breadcrumbs and top with half the zucchini-tomato mixture, then half the cheese. Repeat the layers with the remaining eggplant, zucchini mixture, and cheese.

Bake for 45 minutes, or until the top is crispy and the vegetables are tender. Serve hot or at room temperature.

TIP: If you prefer the meat-eater's version of this dish, add 1 pound ground lamb or beef to the skillet with the onion and cook for 2 minutes, then continue with the recipe as directed.

Souvlaki MARINATED MEAT SKEWERS

Start to finish: 24 hours • Hands-on time: 1 hour

Souvlaki consists of marinated meat grilled on skewers. Lamb is the most popular version, though beef and chicken run a close second and third. The nicer the meat, the better the souvlaki, so pick well-marbled, high-quality sirloin for the most tender, juicy kebabs. For a hearty pita sandwich, grill the meat only and use it as a filling with tzatziki, sliced ripe tomatoes, and sweet onions.

YIELD: 4 TO 6 SERVINGS

2 pounds boneless leg of lamb,
  beef sirloin, or chicken breast,
  cut into 2-inch cubes

3 garlic cloves, chopped

2 lemons, zested and juiced

⅓ cup olive oil, plus more
  for brushing

1 teaspoon freshly ground black
  pepper, plus more to taste

1 teaspoon salt,
  plus more to taste

3 tablespoons chopped
  fresh rosemary

Wooden skewers, preferably flat,
  soaked in water for 1 hour

1 pint cherry tomatoes

1 red onion, cut into large chunks

2 green bell peppers,
  cut into large chunks

½ pound mushrooms,
  cut in half if large

Tzatziki (page 129), for serving

In a large bowl, combine the meat, garlic, lemon zest and juice, pepper, salt, rosemary, and the ⅓ cup of oil. Toss to combine, cover with plastic wrap, and refrigerate up to 24 hours for lamb or beef, 8 hours for chicken.

Prepare a charcoal grill, preheat a gas grill, or preheat the broiler.

Using separate skewers for each kind of food, place the meat, tomatoes, onion, bell pepper, and mushrooms loosely onto skewers (don't put too much on each skewer to insure proper cooking). Brush the skewered food with olive oil and season with salt and pepper to taste.

Since the vegetables will take longer to cook, begin cooking them first. Cook on one side for 4 minutes, then turn and cook for 3 minutes on the second side.

When the vegetables are almost done, start the meat skewers. Cook on one side for 3 minutes, then turn them and cook the second side for 2 minutes for medium-rare meat.

Transfer the cooked kebabs to a heated plate.

Remove the meat and vegetables from the skewers and toss together in a large heated bowl or plate. Serve hot with tzatziki.

VARIATION: To make a shrimp variation, peel and devein 28 to 30 medium-sized shrimp. Marinate for 2 hours, then continue with the directions.

Gyros

Start to finish: 30 minutes • Hands-on time: 30 minutes

Gyros (pronounced yeer-ohs) are made from minced lamb or beef that has been molded around a spit into twenty-pound cones and roasted vertically. The meat is sliced and wrapped in a pita and served with onions, tomatoes, and tzatziki. Sold as street food in Greece, gyros were introduced to America in Chicago back in the sixties. Now, chicken, pork, and even falafel gyros are options in some Greek-American restaurants. Because roasting twenty pounds of meat isn't practical for most home cooks, we've come up with a recipe that embraces the spirit of the dish without the unwieldiness. While having a different shape, these little flat burgers are to be eaten in the traditional way. The important thing to remember is that a gyro is basically healthy food that can be grabbed and eaten on the run.

YIELD: 4 SERVINGS

¼ cup olive oil

½ onion, minced (½ cup)

2 garlic cloves, minced

1½ pounds ground lamb

2 tablespoons lemon juice

2 teaspoons fresh oregano,
　or ½ teaspoon dried

1 teaspoon fresh rosemary,
　or ¼ teaspoon dried

1 teaspoon ground cumin

1 teaspoon salt

¼ teaspoon freshly ground
　black pepper

Pita bread, cut in half
　to form pockets

Lettuce, for serving

Tomato, sliced, for serving

Red onion, thinly sliced, for serving

Fresh mint leaves, for serving

Tzatziki (page 129), for serving

Heat 2 tablespoons of the oil in a large sauté pan over medium heat. Add the onion and cook until translucent, about 2 minutes. Add the garlic and cook for another 2 minutes. Transfer the onion mixture to a large bowl and let cool.

Add the lamb, lemon juice, oregano, rosemary, cumin, salt, and pepper to the onion and mix well. Form the meat into 8 thin patties.

Heat the remaining oil in a sauté pan over medium-high heat. Add the lamb patties and cook for 3 minutes on one side, then turn and cook 2 minutes on the second side. (Or grill the patties for even flavor.)

Fill each pita pocket with a meat patty, lettuce, tomato, onion, mint, and tzatziki. Serve hot.

TIP: Sometimes we like to add Greek Salad (page 135) to the gyros instead of the lettuce, tomato, and onion. It works really well.

Tyropita CHEESE PIE

Start to finish: 2 hours 15 minutes • Hands-on time: 45 minutes

Tyropita is a simple and delicious cheese pie held together between buttered layers of phyllo. This extremely versatile dish can also include vegetables, meats, or herbs and spices for hundreds of variations. This basic recipe will give you a good start to making your own tyropita to suit your individual tastes.

YIELD: 1 (13 X 9-INCH) PIE,
6 TO 8 SERVINGS

6 tablespoons unsalted butter

⅓ cup unbleached all-purpose flour

⅓ cup warm milk

½ teaspoon salt

Dash of nutmeg

Freshly ground black pepper

5 large eggs

½ pound feta cheese, crumbled

1 cup grated kefalotyri or
    Parmigiano-Reggiano cheese

1 cup fresh anthotiros
    or ricotta cheese

2 tablespoons minced
    flat-leaf parsley

¼ pound (1 stick) unsalted
    butter, melted

½ pound (17 x 12-inch) phyllo
    pastry sheets, thawed if frozen

MAKE AHEAD: The tyropita can be assembled and refrigerated, unbaked for up to 8 hours. It can also be assembled and frozen, unbaked, for 1 month. Thaw for 24 hours in the refrigerator before baking.

To make the filling: Melt the 6 tablespoons of butter in a medium saucepan over medium heat. Add the flour and stir until the mixture becomes foamy. Whisk in the milk and cook until the sauce thickens, about 2 minutes. Remove from the heat and stir, adding the salt, nutmeg, and pepper to taste. Cool the sauce for 5 minutes, then add the eggs, beating them in one at a time. Stir in the cheeses and parsley. Set aside.

Preheat the oven to 350°F. Brush a 13 x 9-inch baking pan with melted butter.

Unfold the phyllo dough onto your work surface and cover it with a sheet of plastic wrap topped by a damp towel to keep from drying out. Trim the phyllo sheets so they fit the pan without overlapping.

To assemble the tyropita: Place 6 phyllo sheets in the pan, brushing each sheet with butter. Spread half the cheese mixture evenly over the sheets and press lightly. Cover with 3 sheets of phyllo, brushing each sheet with butter, then top with the remaining cheese mixture. Top the last layer of cheese with 6 sheets of phyllo dough, brushing each sheet with butter.

Cover and refrigerate for 30 minutes so the butter sets, making the tyropita easier to cut. (Tyropita is more difficult to cut after it is cooked because the pastry becomes so flaky.)

Using a sharp knife, make 6 to 8 diagonal cuts lengthwise through the top few layers of pastry, then cut diagonally from the opposite direction to form diamonds.

Bake for about 45 minutes, until golden and flaky. Remove from the oven and, following the cuts already made, cut completely through the tyropita. Serve warm or at room temperature.

Baklava

Start to finish: 2 hours, plus several hours to cool • Hands-on time: 50 minutes

Memories of golden, honey-drenched baklava gobbled up on the island of Santorini kicked off a quest to recreate this sinfully sweet dessert. Versions of baklava exist throughout the Mediterranean region, incorporating all manner of nuts and syrups, but the most recognized in America has to belong to the Greeks, who use honey and a mixture of walnuts and almonds. The best baklava uses the freshest nuts and most aromatic of honeys, so don't skimp on quality. Remember, the fewer the ingredients, the more important the quality of those ingredients. Within no time you'll also be swooning over this timeless classic.

YIELD: ABOUT 30 PIECES

¼ pound plus 4 tablespoons (1½ sticks) unsalted butter, melted

1 pound shelled walnuts, toasted

¼ pound blanched almonds, toasted

⅓ cup sugar

½ teaspoon ground cinnamon

¼ teaspoon ground cloves

Pinch of salt

½ pound (17 x12-inch) phyllo pastry sheets, thawed if frozen

SYRUP

1 cup sugar

1 cup water

⅓ cup orange blossom honey

2 large strips orange zest

1 cinnamon stick

2 whole cloves

Preheat the oven to 375°F. Brush a 13 x 9-inch baking pan with butter and set aside.

Combine the nuts, sugar, cinnamon, cloves, and salt in the bowl of a food processor and process until finely ground. Set aside.

Unroll the phyllo dough and cover it with a sheet of plastic wrap topped by a damp towel. This will weigh it down and keep it from drying out. Keep the pastry covered when you are not working with it. Trim the phyllo sheets so they fit the pan without overlapping.

To assemble the baklava, place 8 phyllo sheets in the pan, brushing each sheet with butter. Spread half the nut mixture evenly over the sheets and press lightly. Cover with 4 sheets of phyllo dough, brushing each with butter, then top with the remaining nut mixture. Top the last layer of nuts with 8 sheets of phyllo dough, brushing each sheet with butter.

Cover and refrigerate for 30 minutes so the butter sets and makes the baklava easier to cut (it is more difficult to cut after it is cooked because the pastry becomes so flaky).

Using a sharp knife, make 6 to 8 diagonal cuts lengthwise through the top few layers of pastry, then cut diagonally from the opposite direction to form diamonds.

Bake for about 40 minutes, until golden and flaky.

Meanwhile, make the syrup. Combine the syrup ingredients in a saucepan over medium-high heat and bring to a boil. Reduce the heat and

TIP: Phyllo (filo) pastry is readily available in your grocer's freezer case. It consists of very thin sheets of pastry made of water and flour.

simmer for 10 minutes, until thickened. Remove the orange zest, cinnamon stick, and cloves. Set aside to cool.

Remove the baklava from the oven and, following the cuts already made, cut completely through the baklava. Pour the syrup evenly over the hot baklava. Allow to stand for at least 1 hour before serving. Cover and store at room temperature for up to 3 days.

FOOD *for* THOUGHT

BAKLAVA IS THE ancestor of strudel. It was brought to Hungary by Turkish invaders in the sixteenth century.

Galaktoboureko GREEK MILK TART

Start to finish: 1 hour 20 minutes • Hands-on time: 30 minutes

Most of us are familiar with baklava—that buttery, crispy, nutty, honey-drenched dessert—but galaktoboureko? It's a sweet semolina custard baked between sheets of buttery phyllo pastry, then drenched in a sweet lemon-flavored syrup. Whenever we make this, our families devour every last crumb and clamor for more. Move over baklava, we've found a new favorite!

YIELD: 1 (13 X 9-INCH) TART

2 cups milk

1 cup semolina flour

2½ cups sugar

5 large eggs

1 teaspoon vanilla extract

½ pound (17 x 12-inch) phyllo
   pastry sheets, thawed if frozen

¼ pound (1 stick) unsalted
   butter, melted

2 tablespoons fresh lemon juice

Preheat the oven to 350°F.

In a large saucepan set over medium heat, combine the milk, semolina, and 1 cup of the sugar. Simmer, whisking continuously, until the mixture thickens to the consistency of pudding, about 30 seconds. Remove from the heat and let cool for 5 minutes (it will thicken more upon sitting). Whisk in the eggs, one at a time, then the vanilla. Set the custard aside.

Brush the bottom of a 13 x 9-inch pan with butter.

Unroll the phyllo dough and cover it with a sheet of plastic wrap topped by a damp dish towel. This will keep the air from drying out the pastry. Keep the pastry covered when you are not working with it.

To assemble the galaktoboureko, place 6 phyllo sheets in the pan, slightly overlapping the ends and sides of the pan with the phyllo and brushing each layer with butter. Spread the custard mixture evenly over the stacked sheets. Top with 6 sheets of phyllo dough, brushing each sheet with butter. Flip any overlapping dough on top of the pastry to completely enclose the custard.

Cover and refrigerate for 30 minutes so the butter sets and makes it easier to cut (it is more difficult to cut after it is cooked because the pastry becomes so flaky).

Using a sharp knife, make 6 to 8 diagonal cuts lengthwise through the top few layers of pastry, then cut diagonally from the opposite direction to form diamonds.

Bake for about 45 minutes, until golden and flaky.

Meanwhile, make the syrup. Combine the remaining 1½ cups sugar and 1 cup water in a medium saucepan and bring to a boil. Boil for about 5 minutes, or until the mixture is syrupy. Remove from the heat and add the lemon juice.

Remove the pastry from the oven and, following the cuts already made, cut completely through the galaktoboureko. Pour the syrup over the pastry and let it soak for at least 1 hour before serving.

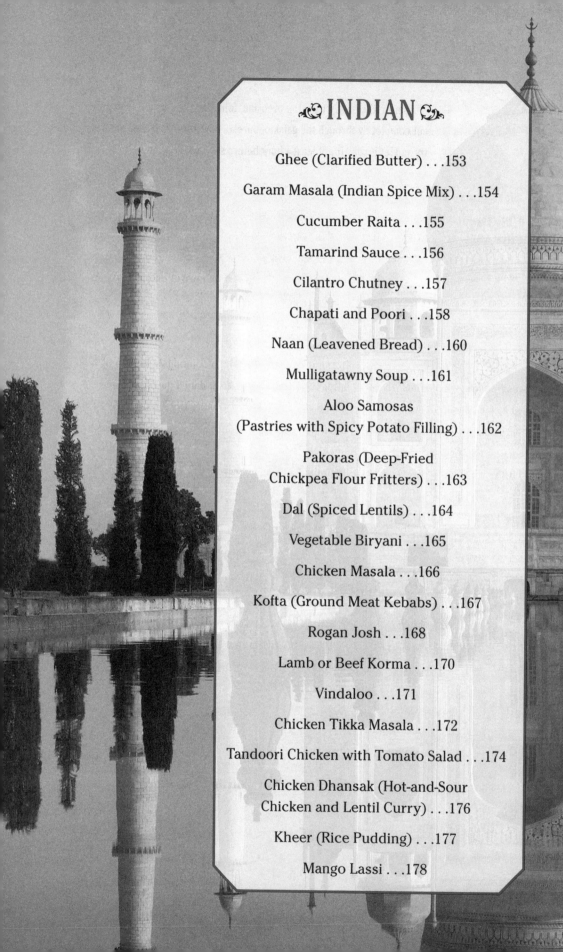

❧INDIAN☙

THE COMPLEX FLAVORS CREATED BY THE combination of exotic spices is what makes Indian food such an intoxicating dining experience. That's also what can make it seem too intimidating to recreate in your own kitchen. The good news is, once you bring India into your pantry and the spices into your culinary lexicon, Indian food is easy to incorporate into your everyday cooking.

Indian cuisine differs greatly according to region, religion, and caste (social order) and over the centuries, it has been altered by traders, including the British, Portuguese, Turks, Arabs, and Persians. Each foreign trader introduced ingredients or cooking styles that have become key components of Indian cookery.

The foods of Northern India (Punjab) are most often featured in restaurants in the United States. Northern Indian staples are rice, legumes such as lentils and chickpeas, and dairy products such as butter, cheese, and yogurt. Meats and flatbreads are cooked in large, round, coal or wood-fired ovens called *tandoors*.

The essence of fine Indian cuisine lies in the appropriate use of mixed aromatic spices. The most often-used spice blend is *garam masala*, made up of cinnamon, clove, cardamom, coriander, and various other spices. Other spices used in Northern Indian cuisine are fenugreek, black mustard seed, turmeric, cayenne pepper, black pepper, nutmeg, and saffron. As if these spices weren't enough to get your palate's attention, Indian dishes often add fresh ginger and garlic along with hot green chiles to the mix.

Indian cooking categorizes foods into tastes: sweet, sour, salty, spicy, and bitter. A well-balanced Indian meal contains all of these tastes. This is often done through the use of pickles, chutneys, side dishes, and condiments. This principle explains the use of countless spice combinations, adding depth and explosive flavor to Indian dishes.

As with other Asian cultures, in India all the dishes in a meal are served at once. An Indian meal usually includes a meat dish, vegetable dish, legume dish, and a variety of accompaniments. Fruit is usually served as a dessert. Most Indians eat with their hands, using flatbreads as tasty vehicles to get the food from the plate to their mouths.

In many parts of the United States, good Indian food is hard to find and is often unexplored by a large percentage of our students. It's always fun to watch how they appreciate the seductively spiced dishes we've prepared. The combination of spices and herbs is so unique that we think Indian cuisine is in a class by itself.

Here's a menu to get you started making Indian food in your own kitchen.

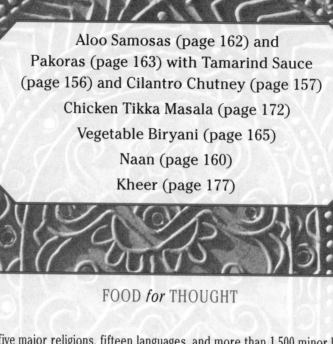

FOOD *for* THOUGHT

- India has five major religions, fifteen languages, and more than 1,500 minor languages and dialects—now that's big!

- There are 9,800 Indian restaurants in the UK, in which diners spend £3.2 billion every year.

- India is the largest democracy in the world, the sixth largest country in the world, and one of the oldest living civilizations (at least ten thousand years old).

- No country in the world has developed as elaborate and flavorful a range of vegetarian cuisine as India.

Ghee CLARIFIED BUTTER

Start to finish: 10 minutes • Hands-on time: 10 minutes

Ghee, known in the United States as clarified butter, is the magic fat that cooks Indian dishes and flavors them. By elim-inating the water and milk solids in butter (butter is about eighty percent fat and twenty percent water and milk solids), it can be heated to higher temperatures without burning. Ghee also has a longer shelf life than butter, so it's a good idea to always have some on hand.

YIELD: ABOUT 1 CUP

½ pound (2 sticks) unsalted butter

MAKE AHEAD: Ghee can be made and kept covered in the refrigerator for up to 2 weeks.

In a medium saucepan, melt the butter over medium heat. When it begins to spit and pop, watch it carefully so it doesn't burn. The idea is to cook out the water and brown the milk solids so that they sink to the bottom of the pan. It should take about 10 minutes. The top of the ghee will look foamy. Tilt the pan to check and, when the bottom of the pan is golden, remove the pan from the heat and pour off the liquid fat, or ghee, into a storage con-tainer. Use as directed in the recipes.

TIP: It is best to cook ghee in a stainless-steel or light-colored saucepan. Black-lined pans will make it difficult to assess when the milk solids begin to brown.

Garam Masala INDIAN SPICE MIX

Start to finish: 20 minutes • Hands-on time: 20 minutes

Garam masala is probably the most used Indian spice blend, so it makes sense to assemble the ingredients and make enough to last for a few weeks of cooking. Though you may find this spice combination on a grocery shelf, grinding fresh spice mixtures such as this are worth the extra effort. You will be rewarded with fragrant and pungent dishes more closely resembling those of authentic Indian cuisine, and usually with better flavor than those you would find in most restaurants.

YIELD: ABOUT 1 CUP

2 cinnamon sticks, broken into
  small pieces
2 tablespoons cardamom seeds
  (see note)
¼ cup whole cloves
¼ cup coriander seeds
¼ cup peppercorns
¼ cup cumin seeds

Heat a large skillet over medium heat. Add the spices and stir until fragrant, 3 or 4 minutes. Watch the spices carefully so they don't burn. They should begin to color and smoke. Remove from the heat and let the spices cool.

Grind the garam masala in a spice mill (see note). Store at room temperature in an airtight container. The fresh flavor of garam masala will keep for 3 or 4 months.

NOTE: One of the best tools to invest in is a coffee grinder that you dedicate to grinding spices (unless you enjoy the flavor of cumin-scented coffee and coffee-scented cumin!). Any inexpensive coffee mill will do. It makes for more finely ground spices with little effort. For grinding small quantities of spices, a mortar and pestle are invaluable pieces of equipment. If they are not available, spices can be crushed with a meat pounder or the bottom of a heavy pot.

NOTE: Cardamom pods look like fat little pumpkin seeds and are filled with the tiny black cardamom seeds. Desiccated cardamom only includes the seeds. If you can find it, it will save you the time spent crushing the pods to extract the seeds.

Cucumber Raita

Start to finish: 15 minutes • Hands-on time: 15 minutes

Raita is meant to cool the heat of hot curries. It generally consists of cucumber, yogurt, and mint, but many variations are possible, such as yogurt with grapes or other cooling fruits.

YIELD: ABOUT 2½ CUPS

1 cucumber, peeled, seeded,
   and grated
½ teaspoon coriander seeds
   (see note on previous page)
½ teaspoon cumin seeds
1½ cups whole-milk yogurt or
   Greek yogurt
1 tablespoon finely
   chopped fresh mint
Salt and freshly ground
   black pepper

Place the cucumber in a strainer and push down on it to remove any excess moisture, or place the cucumber in a towel and twist it to remove the water.

Heat the coriander and cumin seeds in a small frying pan until they are aromatic, about 3 minutes. Remove the spices from the heat and cool for 5 minutes. Grind the spices (see note on page 154).

Combine the cucumber with the spices, yogurt, and mint in a bowl. Stir to combine and season with salt and pepper to taste.

> MAKE AHEAD: Raita can be made up to 24 hours in advance, kept covered, and chilled.

Tamarind Sauce

Start to finish: 1 hour 30 minutes • Hands-on time: 30 minutes

This sweet and tart relish is usually served with samosas, but it goes well with pakoras as well. It keeps for days in the refrigerator, but will disappear fast since you will be dipping all manner of tidbits into its tangy depths.

YIELD: ABOUT 2 CUPS

½ cup tamarind paste,
   chopped into pieces

1½ cups boiling water

¼ cup light brown sugar

¼ cup molasses

⅓ cup golden raisins

2 teaspoons finely minced
   fresh ginger

2 teaspoons salt

1 teaspoon Garam Masala
   (page 154)

½ teaspoon cayenne pepper

Place the tamarind paste in a large bowl and cover with 1 cup of the boiling water. Let the paste soak until the water is cool enough so you can break apart the tamarind with your fingers. Add the remaining ½ cup boiling water and let stand again until just warm. Strain the mixture into a medium bowl, discarding the fibrous pulp.

To the tamarind liquid, add the brown sugar, molasses, raisins, ginger, salt, garam masala, and cayenne pepper. Taste and adjust the seasoning if necessary. Let the sauce sit for at least 1 hour at room temperature or overnight in the refrigerator.

Bring the sauce to room temperature before serving.

TIP: Tamarind paste comes in a plastic-wrapped block. It contains seeds and fibers that must be filtered out before it can be eaten.

MAKE AHEAD: This sauce can be made up to 1 week ahead, and kept in the refrigerator.

Cilantro Chutney

Start to finish: 20 minutes • Hands-on time: 20 minutes

If you love cilantro (most people either love it or hate it), you will want to have this bright and spicy accompaniment on hand to lend extra flavor to an assortment of dishes. Not only is it delicious dolloped on curries, it is also delicious with samosas and pakoras.

YIELD: ABOUT 1 CUP

2 cups cilantro leaves, lightly packed

1 (2-inch) knob fresh ginger, peeled

¼ cup sweetened shredded coconut

¼ cup fresh lemon juice (about 2 lemons)

1 teaspoon salt

¼ teaspoon freshly ground black pepper

1 serrano chile, seeded, optional

Combine all the ingredients in a food processor and pulse until finely chopped.

NOTE: We've specified sweetened coconut because the unsweetened can be difficult to find. Cilantro chutney usually has a little sugar in it, so the addition of the sweetened coconut works just fine.

TIP: This chutney can also be made by finely chopping all of the ingredients by hand or grinding them to a paste in a mortar.

Chapati and Poori

Start to finish: 1 hour • Hands-on time: 30 minutes

A chapati is the Indian equivalent of a tortilla. It's an unleavened whole wheat bread that is rolled out into a circle and cooked on a griddle. In India, chapati is served with light meals to fill you up, but we could make a meal out of nothing but these floury disks of homespun goodness. If you are feeling like a splurge, brush them with melted ghee and sprinkle with kosher salt as you stack them after cooking. Many people don't include salt in a traditional chapati recipe, but we think it improves the taste of the bread.

Poori is chapati's uptown cousin. It is essentially the same dough rolled in the same way, but fried instead of cooked on a griddle. The dough puffs as it is fried, so poori is lighter than chapati; because of the hot oil coating, it is savory and soft with a pretty shine. Poori and dal (page 164) make a great appetizer or can be part of a multicourse meal.

CHAPATI

YIELD: 12 SERVINGS

1 cup whole wheat flour

1 cup unbleached all-purpose
   flour, plus more for rolling

1 teaspoon salt

Ghee (page 153), for brushing

Kosher salt, for sprinkling

Combine the flours and salt in a large bowl and add ¾ cup water. Mix with your hands until a dough forms. Add more water if needed to make a moist, soft dough.

Turn the dough out onto a lightly floured work surface and knead for about 2 minutes, until it tightens up or doesn't stick to your hands or the work surface. Put the dough in a clean bowl, cover with plastic wrap, and let rest for at least 20 minutes.

Remove the dough from the bowl and, on a lightly floured work surface, roll it into a rope about 16 inches long. Cut the rope into 12 pieces and cover with a damp towel.

Take a piece of dough and lay it cut side down on your work surface. Press it down with the palm of your hand to flatten it, sprinkle with a touch of flour, and use a rolling pin to roll it into a thin, 6-inch round. Place the chapati on a plate and cover with plastic wrap. Continue to make the remaining chapati in the same manner, layering them between plastic so they don't stick together.

Heat a large skillet over medium-high heat. Place a chapati on the skillet and cook for about 30 seconds, or until bubbles form underneath the surface of the dough. Using tongs, turn the chapati and cook on the second side for 15 seconds. Transfer the chapati to a plate, brush it with ghee, sprinkle with salt, and cover it with a towel. Cook the remaining chapati in the same manner. Serve warm.

POORI

YIELD: 12 SERVINGS

Chapati dough (opposite)

Vegetable oil

Make the chapati dough as directed. Cut it into 12 pieces, but roll each piece to only 5 inches in diameter so that the dough rounds are a little thicker than the chapati rounds.

In a large skillet, heat 1 inch of vegetable oil to 360°F. Gently slide one of the poori rounds into the oil. It will sink and begin to puff in about 10 seconds. Using tongs, turn the poori over. It will puff immediately. Let it cook for 10 seconds, then remove the poori from the oil and lay it on a paper-towel-lined pan. Continue to fry the remaining poori in the same manner.

Serve immediately.

> MAKE AHEAD: The chapati and poori can be made earlier in the day and kept wrapped in aluminum foil. Reheat wrapped in foil in a 375°F. oven for 5 minutes.

Naan LEAVENED BREAD

Start to finish: 3 hours • Hands-on time: 20 minutes

Naan is an enriched, leavened flatbread that is traditionally cooked on the inside walls of a tandoor oven. It's a fascinating technique to watch. The dough is laid out on a pillow that has a pocket on the bottom, into which the baker slides his hand. He very quickly shoves the pillow into the blazing hot tandoor and sticks the dough onto the inside side wall of the oven. The dough sticks until it is done, at which time the baker peels it off with a long metal spike. Obviously, we can't cook naan in a tandoor, but a regular oven can give good results.

The interesting technique of using water instead of flour to keep the dough from sticking when being shaped is counterintuitive, but it works. Less flour on the outside of the dough makes for a more tender texture and interesting surface on the bread. Naan can be made simply as we have given the recipe here, or garnished with nigella seeds (black sesame seeds) and fresh cilantro.

YIELD: 4 FLATBREADS

1 (2¼ teaspoon) package
   active dry yeast
1 teaspoon sugar
1¼ cups warm milk
3¾ cups unbleached
   all-purpose flour
1 teaspoon salt
1 large egg, beaten
¼ cup Ghee, melted (page 153)
Kosher salt

Mix the yeast, sugar, and milk in a small bowl. Let sit for 5 minutes, or until foamy.

In a large bowl, combine the flour and salt. Add the egg and the yeast mixture and mix until a dough forms. If you are using a stand mixer, mix on speed 2 with the paddle attachment until the dough comes together, then change to the dough hook and mix on speed 2 for 2 or 3 minutes, or until the dough is smooth. If you are making the dough by hand, remove the dough from the bowl and knead it for about 5 minutes or until the dough is smooth.

Place the dough in a large bowl, cover it with plastic wrap, and let it sit in a warm (76°F. to 80°F.) place until it doubles in size, about 2 hours.

Preheat the oven to 400°F.

Punch the dough down and divide it into 4 pieces. Sprinkle a work surface with water and lay down one of the pieces of dough. Wet your hands and press out the dough to form a flat oval about 8 inches wide and 12 inches long. Transfer to parchment-lined sheet pans, brush with ghee, and repeat with the remaining dough. Bake for 10 to 12 minutes, or until browned and cooked through. Brush with ghee when removed from the oven and sprinkle with kosher salt. Serve hot.

Mulligatawny Soup

Start to finish: 1 hour • Hands-on time: 35 minutes

Mulligatawny soup became popular with the British about two hundred years ago during their stay in India. It is a version of a south Indian soup called a rasam*. Like so many Indian dishes popularized by the Brits, there are many versions of mulligatawny, but it generally consists of a stock (usually chicken), vegetables, and cream or coconut milk. This is the only dish where we advocate using a store-bought curry powder because that is the familiar seasoning most of us have tasted in restaurant mulligatawny soup.*

YIELD: 4 SERVINGS

¼ cup Ghee (page 153)

1 cinnamon stick

2 tablespoons curry powder

3 onions, 1 chopped, 2 sliced

Salt

2 carrots, peeled and chopped
   (1 cup)

1 rib celery, chopped (½ cup)

1 parsnip, chopped (½ cup)

3 garlic cloves, minced

8 cups chicken stock

1 teaspoon Garam Masala
   (page 154)

1 (14-ounce) can unsweetened
   coconut milk

Freshly ground black pepper

¼ cup minced fresh cilantro
   leaves

Heat 2 tablespoons of ghee in a large soup pot set over medium heat. When the ghee is sizzling, add the cinnamon stick and curry powder. Cook for 1 minute, then add the chopped onion and a pinch of salt. Cook for 1 minute, or until the onion begins to soften.

Add the carrot, celery, parsnip, and garlic to the pot and cook for 3 minutes, or until the vegetables soften. Add the chicken stock and bring the mixture to a simmer. Turn the heat to low and simmer the soup until the vegetables are tender, about 20 minutes.

Remove the cinnamon stick and blend the soup in a food processor or blender to a smooth consistency. (Don't fill the processor or blender more than one-third full, or the soup might run out the sides while processing.) Return the soup to the pot and keep at a low simmer.

Heat the remaining 2 tablespoons ghee over medium heat in a sauté pan. When it is hot, add the sliced onions and a pinch of salt. Cook until the onions begin to brown, about 5 minutes. Add the garam masala, turn the heat to low, and cook so the onions caramelize to a rich brown, about 20 minutes.

Add the coconut milk and raise the heat to high. Bring the mixture to a boil and cook until it becomes thick and reduces by half, about 7 minutes.

Add the coconut milk mixture to the puréed soup and season with salt and pepper. Garnish with cilantro and serve hot.

> **MAKE AHEAD:** The soup can be made 1 day ahead and kept covered and refrigerated. Reheat over medium heat until hot.

Aloo Samosas PASTRIES WITH SPICY POTATO FILLING

Start to finish: 2 hours 15 minutes • Hands-on time: 1 hour 45 minutes

A traditional snack that sometimes serves as a meal, a samosa is an irresistible, fried, flaky pastry that surrounds a spicy potato filling. Samosas can be quite time consuming to make, but are worth every minute. Homemade pastry makes a big difference in texture and flavor, but in a time crunch, store-bought spring roll pastry is an adequate substitute.

YIELD: 32 SAMOSAS, 6 TO 8 SERVINGS

PASTRY

1½ cups unbleached
    all-purpose flour

½ teaspoon salt

⅓ cup vegetable shortening

⅓ cup ice water

FILLING

3¼ cups vegetable oil

1 small onion, minced

1 tablespoon coriander seeds,
    crushed

1 serrano chile,
    seeded and minced

3 large potatoes,
    boiled and mashed

½ cup frozen peas

1½ teaspoons Garam Masala
    (page 154)

1 teaspoon salt

Freshly ground black pepper

2 tablespoons minced fresh cilantro

2 tablespoons fresh lemon juice

Cilantro Chutney (page 157), or
    Tamarind Sauce (page 156),
    for serving

To make the pastry dough: Combine the flour, salt, and shortening in a food processor and pulse until the mixture resembles cornmeal. Pour the water through the feed tube while continuing to pulse until the dough comes together in a ball. Transfer to a bowl and cover with a piece of plastic or a damp towel. Let the dough rest for 30 minutes.

To make the filling: In a large skillet, heat ¼ cup of the vegetable oil over medium heat, then add the onion and coriander seeds and cook for 2 or 3 minutes, or until fragrant and the onion is softened. Add the chile and cook for 2 minutes. Add the potatoes and cook, mixing well, for 2 minutes. Add the peas, garam masala, salt, pepper, cilantro, and lemon juice. Taste and adjust the seasonings if necessary. Set aside.

To assemble the samosas: Divide the dough in half and roll each piece into a 12-inch rope. Cut each rope into 8 pieces and roll into balls. Cover with a damp towel.

On a lightly floured surface, use a rolling pin to roll a dough ball into a 6-inch round. Cut the round in half. Moisten half of one cut edge with a little water. Make a cone by bringing the two pointed ends together, pressing the overlapped edges to seal. Fill the cone with 1 tablespoon of the filling. Moisten the inside rim of the cone and seal it, forming a triangle-shaped packet. Lay the samosa out on a parchment-lined sheet pan and repeat with the remaining pastry and filling.

In a wok or large pan, heat the remaining oil to 360°F. Fry about 5 samosas, turning them as they brown, for about 8 to 10 minutes, or until golden brown. Using a slotted spoon, transfer the samosas to paper towels. (They can be kept warm in a 200°F. oven while you cook the rest.) Fry the remaining samosas. Serve hot with Cilantro Chutney or Tamarind Sauce.

Pakoras DEEP-FRIED CHICKPEA FLOUR FRITTERS

Start to finish: 40 minutes • Hands-on time: 30 minutes

Chickpea flour is the base for these delectable vegetable fritters. We like to serve a platter of pakoras and aloo samosas as a start to an Indian meal, but we must admit that sometimes they serve as a meal themselves. The pakora is another snack that, like the samosa, can be found in many variations. It usually contains potatoes, but can contain all manner of vegetables, such as cauliflower, peas, broccoli, or squash.

YIELD: ABOUT 12, 4 SERVINGS

½ teaspoon cumin seed
½ teaspoon coriander seed
¼ teaspoon fenugreek
6 whole black peppercorns
½ teaspoon salt
½ teaspoon Garam Masala
    (page 154)
¼ teaspoon cayenne pepper
1 cup chickpea flour
¼ teaspoon baking soda
1 small onion, thinly sliced
1 medium potato,
    peeled and grated
¼ cup minced fresh cilantro
Vegetable oil, for frying
Cilantro Chutney (page 157) or
    Tamarind Sauce (page 156),
    for serving

In a medium skillet set over medium-high heat, toast the cumin, coriander, fenugreek, and peppercorns until they are aromatic, about 3 minutes. Cool and grind the spices to a fine powder (see note on page 154). Add the salt, garam masala, and cayenne pepper to the spice mixture.

Combine the spices, chickpea flour, and baking soda in a large bowl. Add ¾ cup water, the onion, potato, and cilantro and mix well. You should have a lumpy batter.

Heat 3 inches of vegetable oil in a heavy pan or skillet to 360°F. Drop the batter by ¼-cupfuls into the hot oil, about 3 at a time. Cook for 2 minutes. Turn the pakoras and cook on the second side for 2 minutes. Remove the pakoras from the oil with a slotted spoon and transfer them to a paper towel–lined sheet pan. Keep the fried pakoras warm in a 200°F. oven while you continue making the rest.

Serve the pakoras as an appetizer or a snack with Cilantro Chutney or Tamarind Sauce on the side.

VARIATION: 1 cup cooked, diced cauliflower, broccoli, squash, or carrot can be added to the basic recipe.

> MAKE AHEAD: Pakoras can be made up to 30 minutes ahead and kept warm in a 200°F. oven.

Dal SPICED LENTILS

Start to finish: 45 minutes • Hands-on time: 15 minutes

Simply cooked lentils, beans, and split peas (all legumes) are referred to as dal in Indian cuisine. Legumes are really the backbone of Indian meals and supply much-needed protein to what is often a vegetarian diet. Dal figures prominently in soups, stews, and rice dishes, and is ground to a flour to make batters and doughs.

The following dal recipe is one of the most flavorful we have found. If you make it thicker, it is great to use as a dip with chapati, while a thinner consistency makes it ideal to serve over rice as a delicious main-course meal. We like to have dal on hand in the refrigerator for a quick and easy lunch with fresh fruit.

YIELD: 6 SERVINGS

1 (1-inch) piece of cinnamon stick

2 whole cloves

½ teaspoon cardamom seeds

½ teaspoon cumin seeds

½ teaspoon coriander seeds

2 tablespoons vegetable oil

1 teaspoon salt, plus more as needed

½ teaspoon turmeric

1 cup lentils

3 cups chicken stock or water

Freshly ground black pepper

¼ cup Ghee (page 153)

1 small onion, chopped (½ cup)

1 (1-inch knob) fresh ginger, minced (1 tablespoon)

2 garlic cloves, minced

¼ teaspoon cayenne pepper

2 tablespoons fresh lemon juice

2 tablespoons fresh cilantro

Chapati (page 158), for serving

Jasmine Rice (page 307) or basmati rice, for serving

Heat a small skillet over medium-high heat and add the cinnamon, cloves, cardamom, cumin, and coriander. Toast until fragrant, about 3 minutes. Remove from the heat and let cool. Grind to a fine powder (see note on page 154).

Heat the vegetable oil in a large saucepan. Add the spice powder, salt, and turmeric and cook until toasty and fragrant, about 3 minutes. Add the lentils and chicken stock and bring to a boil. Reduce the heat and simmer for 20 minutes, or until the lentils are tender. Using a potato masher, smash the lentils to a rough purée. Adjust the seasoning with salt and pepper.

Heat the ghee in a medium skillet set over medium-high heat. Add the onion and cook for 5 minutes, or until the onion is soft and starts to brown. Add the ginger, garlic, and cayenne pepper, lower the heat, and continue to cook for another 3 minutes, or until the ginger and garlic are soft.

Pour the onion mixture over the top of the lentil mixture and sprinkle with lemon juice and cilantro.

Serve warm or at room temperature with chapati or rice.

> MAKE AHEAD: The dal can be made 1 day ahead, kept covered, and refrigerated.

Vegetable Biryani

Start to finish: 30 minutes • Hands-on time: 15 minutes

Biryani is a rice dish that can contain chicken, beef, shrimp, pork, or just vegetables. It is similar to a pilaf, but more likely to be a main dish than a side. Biryani is usually mildly spiced, but feel free to make it hotter with chiles or cayenne pepper, as your taste dictates. We like to serve this as a vegetarian rice dish alongside Chicken Masala (page 166) or Tandoori Chicken (page 174).

YIELD: 4 TO 6 SERVINGS

1½ cups basmati rice

1 teaspoon cumin seed

1 teaspoon coriander seed

⅛ teaspoon cardamom seeds

1 (2-inch) piece of cinnamon stick

2 whole cloves

¼ cup Ghee (page 153)

1 large onion, sliced

2 garlic cloves, minced

1 (1-inch) knob of fresh ginger, minced

2½ cups vegetable stock

¼ cup warm milk

10 saffron threads

1½ cups broccoli florets

1½ cups cauliflower florets

¼ cup cashews

¼ cup golden raisins

¼ cup candied ginger, chopped

Rinse the rice under cold running water until the water runs clear. Set aside.

Heat the cumin, coriander, cardamom, cinnamon, and cloves in a small skillet over medium heat until fragrant, about 3 minutes. Let cool for 5 minutes, then grind finely (see note on page 154).

Heat the ghee in a large skillet set over medium heat. Add the spice mixture and cook until fragrant, about 3 minutes. Add the onion, garlic, and fresh ginger. Cook for about 3 minutes, or until the onions start to wilt. Add the stock and rice.

Combine the milk and saffron and pour over the rice mixture. Cover, reduce the heat to low, and cook for about 10 minutes. Uncover and add the broccoli and cauliflower without stirring or disturbing the rice. Cover and cook for another 5 minutes.

Stir to combine the vegetables with the rice. Garnish the dish with cashews, raisins, and candied ginger. Serve hot.

VARIATION: You can make this dish into a meat biryani by adding 1 pound of beef chuck, lamb shoulder or leg, cubed chicken breast, or shelled shrimp. For the beef or lamb variation, cook the meat for 30 minutes in the stock before adding the rice in order for the meat to become tender. For the chicken variation, cook the chicken in chicken stock for 10 minutes before adding the rice. For the shrimp variation, add the shrimp along with the rice and cook according to the directions.

Chicken Masala

Start to finish: 1 hour • Hands-on time: 30 minutes

Masala is just another name for a mixture of many spices, and chicken masala is probably one of the most recognized Indian dishes in the United States. This version is a little spicy, but shouldn't hurt anyone who enjoys a little spice. The main difference between chicken masala and tikka masala is that the chicken here is cooked with the sauce and spices, while in tikka masala, the chicken is baked separately in the oven after being coated in ghee.

YIELD: 6 TO 8 SERVINGS

1 whole fryer chicken

1 cup plain whole-milk or
  Greek yogurt

1 teaspoon salt

Freshly ground black pepper

1 teaspoon cumin seeds

1 teaspoon coriander seeds

1 teaspoon turmeric

½ teaspoon fennel seeds

½ teaspoon cayenne pepper

¼ teaspoon cardamom seeds

¼ cup Ghee (page 153)

1 large onion, sliced (1½ cups)

2 garlic cloves, minced

2 teaspoons grated fresh ginger

1 (14.5-ounce) can diced
  tomatoes, with juice

2 tablespoons chopped cilantro,
  plus more for garnish

1 teaspoon Garam Masala
  (page 154), for garnish

White Rice (page 12) or basmati
  rice, for serving

Skin the chicken and cut it into 8 pieces (cut the breasts in half). In a large bowl, combine the chicken with ½ cup of the yogurt and the salt and pepper. Marinate at room temperature while you proceed with the recipe.

In a large skillet over medium heat, combine the cumin, coriander, turmeric, fennel seeds, cayenne pepper, and cardamom. Heat until fragrant, about 3 minutes. Remove from the heat and allow to cool. Grind the spices and set aside (see note on page 154).

Heat the ghee in a large skillet over medium heat and add the spice mixture. Cook for about 3 minutes, or until very fragrant. Add the onion, garlic, and ginger, and cook for 3 minutes, or until the onion is softened. Add the chicken and cook for 5 minutes, turning them after a few minutes, or until they begin to firm up. Add the tomatoes and juices, the remaining ½ cup yogurt, ⅓ cup water, and the cilantro, stirring to combine. Cover and simmer over low heat for 30 minutes.

Taste and adjust the seasoning with salt and pepper. To serve, garnish with a sprinkling of garam masala and cilantro, and accompany with rice.

VARIATION: You can make this dish into beef or lamb masala by substituting 1 pound of beef chuck or lamb shoulder for the chicken. Increase the cooking time by 30 minutes. A shrimp version can be made by substituting 1 pound of shrimp for the chicken. Cook for 5 minutes after adding the tomatoes to the pan.

> MAKE AHEAD: The masala can be made 1 day ahead, kept covered and refrigerated.

Kofta GROUND MEAT KEBABS

Start to finish: 1 hour • Hands-on time: 40 minutes

It seems that most cultures have their own version of meatballs. The Greeks have keftethes, *the French have* bitoques, *the Germans have Rheinpfalz meatballs, and the Indians have* kofta. *These little meatballs pack a spicy wallop that is cooled down by a side of cucumber raita. For further heat, we enjoy them with a side of cilantro chutney.*

YIELD: 4 SERVINGS

1 pound ground beef or lamb

1 medium onion, minced
(1 cup)

1 large egg

2 garlic cloves, minced

1 (1-inch) knob of fresh ginger,
peeled and finely minced

2 tablespoons minced
fresh cilantro

2 serrano chiles, seeded
and finely minced

2 teaspoons Garam Masala
(page 154)

1 teaspoon salt

1 medium potato, peeled and
finely grated

Freshly ground black pepper

¼ cup vegetable oil

Cilantro Chutney (page 157),
for serving

Cucumber Raita (page 155),
for serving

Combine the meat, onion, egg, garlic, ginger, cilantro, chiles, garam masala, salt, potato, and pepper in a large bowl and mix until well blended. Roll the mixture into golf-ball-sized rounds and let rest for 20 minutes at room temperature.

Heat the oil in a large skillet or wok set over medium-high heat. Add about 10 meatballs to the pan and brown them on all sides until they are cooked through, about 10 minutes. Continue to cook the remaining kofta in the same manner.

Serve hot with Cilantro Chutney and Cucumber Raita.

NOTE: If you make the meatballs smaller, they can serve as an appetizer, speared with toothpicks. Serve the raita as a dip.

MAKE AHEAD: The meatballs can be assembled up to 24 hours ahead and kept covered in the refrigerator.

Rogan Josh

Start to finish: 2 hours • Hands-on time: 40 minutes

Rogan josh, an aromatic lamb curry, is one of our favorite Indian dishes, but like a woman with many children, we find it hard to pick a favorite. This dish wins us over with its creamy texture and subtle spices. Rogan josh is not a spicy curry, which makes it a good choice for those unfamiliar with Indian food. We especially like it made with lamb, but chicken and beef are also high on our list.

YIELD: 6 SERVINGS

1 (2-inch) knob fresh ginger, peeled and finely chopped

6 garlic cloves, finely chopped

1 cup whole-milk plain or Greek yogurt

1¼ teaspoons cayenne pepper

2 teaspoons salt

2 pounds boneless lamb leg or shoulder, cut into 1-inch pieces

1 tablespoon cumin seed

2 teaspoons coriander seed

2 teaspoons paprika

½ teaspoon cardamom seeds

6 whole cloves

6 black peppercorns

1 bay leaf

1 stick cinnamon

¼ cup Ghee (page 153)

2 onions, peeled and sliced

1 serrano chile, finely minced

1 (14.5-ounce) can diced tomatoes, with juice

½ cup heavy cream

In a large bowl, combine the ginger, garlic, yogurt, ¼ teaspoon cayenne pepper, 1 teaspoon of salt, and the lamb. Marinate for 1 hour at room temperature, or 2 hours refrigerated.

While the lamb marinates, combine the remaining teaspoons of salt and cayenne pepper, and the cumin, coriander, paprika, cayenne pepper, cardamom, cloves, peppercorns, bay leaf, and cinnamon in a skillet over medium heat. Cook until the spices are fragrant, about 3 minutes. Cool and grind the spices (see note on page 154).

Heat the ghee in a large skillet over medium-high heat. Add the spice mixture and cook until fragrant, about 2 minutes. Add the onions and chile, and cook until they are soft, about 3 minutes. Add the lamb, stir, and cook for 3 minutes.

Add the tomatoes and cream to the skillet and bring to a simmer. Turn the heat to low, cover, and cook for 45 minutes, or until tender. Stir every now and then to make sure the sauce isn't burning on the bottom of the pan.

Remove the lid, increase the heat to medium-high, and cook until the sauce thickens, about 10 to 15 minutes. Taste and adjust the seasonings, if necessary.

To serve, sprinkle with garam masala and fresh cilantro and accompany with cilantro chutney and cucumber raita.

VARIATION: To make chicken or beef rogan josh, substitute 2 pounds diced chicken breast or 2 pounds diced beef chuck for the lamb. For the chicken variation, reduce the cooking time to 20 minutes; cook as directed for beef.

1 tablespoon Garam Masala
(page 154)
2 tablespoons chopped cilantro
leaves,
Cilantro Chutney (page 157),
for serving
Cucumber Raita (page 155),
for serving

MAKE AHEAD: Rogan josh can be made 1 day ahead and kept covered and refrigerated. Reheat over medium-low heat.

FOOD *for* THOUGHT

IN ENGLAND, curry has been suggested as the "National Dish" by none other than the British Tourist Authority.

MOST PEOPLE in India believe that eating with their hands makes the food taste better.

Lamb or Beef Korma

Start to finish: 1 hour 30 minutes • Hands-on time: 45 minutes

Korma is a mild, creamy, and fragrant dish that says "celebration." The almonds in the dish add to its rich character, while the mild and subtle spicing is unique among most Indian curries.

YIELD: 4 TO 6 SERVINGS

¼ cup almonds

2 tablespoons coriander seed

1 teaspoon cumin seed

10 black peppercorns

½ teaspoon cardamom seeds

4 whole cloves

2 pounds lean lamb or beef,
cut into 1-inch pieces

¼ cup Ghee (page 153)

3 onions, chopped

1 serrano chile, seeded
and chopped

3 garlic cloves, minced

1 (2-inch) knob fresh ginger,
minced

1 cinnamon stick

1 teaspoon Garam Masala
(page 154)

2 teaspoons salt

¼ teaspoon cayenne pepper

½ cup whole-milk yogurt
or Greek yogurt

¼ cup heavy cream

2 tablespoons chopped
fresh cilantro

Jasmine rice (page 307) or
basmati rice, for serving

Combine the almonds, coriander, cumin, peppercorns, cardamom, and cloves in a small skillet and heat over medium heat. Cook until the spices are aromatic, about 3 minutes. Remove the pan from the heat and let the spices cool. Grind the spices (see note on page 154) and add them to a large bowl along with the meat. Mix well and set aside.

Heat the ghee in a large skillet or Dutch oven set over medium heat. Add half the meat. Brown about 10 minutes, then transfer it to a plate. Brown the remaining meat in the same manner.

Return the meat to the pan and add the onions, chile, garlic, ginger, cinnamon stick, garam masala, salt, and cayenne pepper. Cook for about 5 minutes, or until the onion begins to soften. Add the yogurt and cook, stirring until the oil comes to the top of the mixture, about 3 minutes. Add 1 cup water and bring the mixture to a simmer. Cover the pan and cook over low heat for 1 hour.

Remove the lid and add the cream. Raise the heat to medium-high and cook until the sauce has thickened, about 5 minutes. Season to taste with salt and pepper.

To serve, garnish with fresh cilantro and serve with rice.

> **MAKE AHEAD:** The korma can be prepared 1 day ahead and kept covered in the refrigerator. Reheat over medium-low heat.

Vindaloo

Start to finish: 4 hours 30 minutes •Hands-on time: 30 minutes

Vindaloo's spicy roots go back to the Portuguese, who traded with India back in the early part of the sixteenth century. Classic vindaloo is made with pork, but most of the time on American menus we see it made with lamb or beef. This is one of the spicier Indian curries, but if you like your curry less spicy, seed the chiles before adding them.

YIELD: 4 TO 6 SERVINGS

1 teaspoon cayenne pepper

1 (2-inch) piece cinnamon stick

2 teaspoons coriander seed

2 teaspoons cumin seed

3 whole cloves

½ teaspoon cardamom seeds

1 teaspoon salt

1 teaspoon turmeric

½ teaspoon fenugreek

½ teaspoon black mustard seed

½ cup vegetable oil

2 pounds beef chuck, lamb shoulder, pork butt, or boned chicken thighs, cut into 1-inch cubes

2 garlic cloves, minced

1 (1-inch) knob of fresh ginger, minced

¼ cup cider vinegar

2 tablespoons tomato paste

2 tablespoons tamarind paste

1 cup boiling water

1 medium onion, diced

2 serrano chiles, minced

Jasmine rice (page 307) or basmati rice, for serving

Cucumber Raita (page 155), for serving

In a medium skillet set over medium heat, combine the cayenne pepper, cinnamon, coriander, cumin, cloves, cardamom, salt, turmeric, fenugreek, and mustard seed. Cook until fragrant, about 3 minutes. Remove the pan from the heat and let the spices cool. Grind the spices and set aside (see note on page 154).

Heat ¼ cup of the vegetable oil over medium heat and add the spice mixture. Cook until it is bubbly and fragrant. Remove from the heat and let cool.

Combine the cooled spice paste with the meat, garlic, ginger, cider vinegar, and tomato paste in a bowl or a zip top bag and let marinate, refrigerated, for 2 hours.

Place the tamarind in a heatproof bowl and add the boiling water. When the water has cooled, smash the tamarind so it blends with the water. Strain out the fibers and seeds through a wire mesh strainer and save the tamarind juice.

Heat the remaining ¼ cup vegetable oil in a large Dutch oven or heavy pan set over medium-high heat, then add the onion and chiles. Cook for about 3 minutes, or until the onion softens. Add the meat to the pan and cook for about 5 minutes, or until it begins to brown. Reduce the heat to medium, add the tamarind juice and heat until it comes to a simmer. Lower the heat, cover, and simmer for 2 hours (1 hour for chicken).

Taste for seasoning and adjust if necessary. Serve hot with rice and cucumber raita.

> MAKE AHEAD: The vindaloo can be made a day ahead, covered, and refrigerated. Reheat over medium heat.

Chicken Tikka Masala

Start to finish: 2 hours • Hands-on time: 1 hour

Probably the most-loved dish on Indian restaurant menus, chicken tikka masala isn't a true Indian dish. It is thought to have come about in response to the inability of the British to suffer through the spicy curries of India during their tenure there. It is usually a mild tomato-sauce curry perfumed with spices and a little cream for richness. The chicken is marinated in yogurt and spices and can be grilled or baked in the oven. We like to cut the chicken into small pieces so the marinade can penetrate more thoroughly, then bake it in the oven before adding it to the sauce. However you decide to make it, tikka masala is sure to make your short list of favorites.

YIELD: 4 SERVINGS

½ cup plain whole-milk yogurt

1 teaspoon Garam Masala (page 154)

½ teaspoon salt, plus more as needed

5 cloves garlic, minced

1 (3-inch) knob fresh ginger, minced

½ teaspoon cayenne pepper

1½ pounds boneless, skinless chicken breast (about 3), cut into 1-inch pieces

2 teaspoons coriander seed

1 teaspoon cumin seed

6 black peppercorns

½ teaspoon turmeric

¼ cup plus 2 tablespoons Ghee (page 153)

1 cinnamon stick, broken into 3 pieces

1 medium onion, thinly sliced

1 (14½-ounce) can diced tomatoes with juice

In a large bowl, combine the yogurt, garam masala, salt, half the garlic, half the ginger, ¼ teaspoon of the cayenne pepper, and the chicken. Marinate in the refrigerator for at least 1 hour, or up to 4 hours.

Heat a skillet over medium heat, add the coriander, and cumin seeds, and the peppercorns, and toast until fragrant, about 3 minutes. Remove the pan from the heat and let the spices cool. Grind the spices (see note on page 154). Combine with the turmeric and the remaining ¼ teaspoon cayenne pepper and set aside.

Preheat the oven to 400°F.

Heat ¼ cup of the ghee in a large sauté pan or Dutch oven. When the ghee is sizzling, add the cinnamon stick and spice mixture and cook for 1 minute. Add the onion and cook for 3 minutes, or until the onion becomes translucent. Add the remaining garlic and ginger and cook for 1 minute. Add the tomatoes with their juice. Simmer for 10 minutes.

While the sauce is simmering, place the chicken on a parchment-lined sheet pan, season with salt and pepper, and drizzle with the remaining 2 tablespoons ghee. Bake for 10 minutes.

Add the chicken and cream to the sauce and simmer for about 10 to 15 minutes, or until the oil rises to the surface of the sauce. Season with additional salt and pepper, if necessary.

Garnish with cilantro, and serve with rice or lentils.

Freshly ground black pepper

½ cup heavy cream

¼ cup minced fresh cilantro
leaves, for garnish

Jasmine Rice (page 308),
basmati rice or lentils,
for serving

MAKE AHEAD: Tikka masala can be made 1 day ahead, kept covered, and refrigerated. Reheat over medium-low heat.

FOOD *for* THOUGHT

INSTEAD OF MULTIPLE COURSES, Indian meals are based around rice or bread served with an assortment of savory dishes; this type of meal is called a thali, and in the South of India, it's often served on a large banana leaf.

Tandoori Chicken with Tomato Salad

Start to finish: 26 hours • Hands-on time: 40 minutes

A tandoor is a barrel-shaped clay oven that is wide at the bottom and narrow at the top. It is fired by hot coals and reaches super-hot temperatures that home ovens could never reach. The advantage of the super-high heat is that it cooks food quickly by searing it in seconds, resulting in crispy, flavorful crusts. You will love the flavor of this Indian classic when cooked on a grill. Even roasted in a conventional oven, tandoori chicken is one of our favorites with one caveat: traditional tandoori chicken is marinated in spices, yogurt, and an alarming red dye. If you want your tandoori chicken red, just add a half teaspoon of red food coloring to the marinade, but we prefer to leave it out.

YIELD: 6 SERVINGS

2 pounds bone-in chicken pieces,
  skin removed

¼ cup fresh lemon juice

2 teaspoons salt

2 teaspoons coriander seed

2 teaspoons cumin seed

½ teaspoon cardamom seed

½ teaspoon cayenne pepper

½ cup whole-milk yogurt
  or Greek yogurt

1 (1-inch) knob fresh ginger,
  peeled and chopped

3 garlic cloves, chopped

¼ cup Ghee (page 153)

Tomato Salad (recipe follows),
  for serving

Make four ½-inch slashes into each of the chicken pieces so the marinade can penetrate. Rub the chicken with the lemon juice and salt, pushing the lemon juice down into the slashes. Let the chicken marinate while you assemble the remaining ingredients.

In a skillet set over medium-high heat, toast the coriander, cumin, cardamom, and cayenne pepper until fragrant, about 3 minutes. Remove the pan from the heat and let the spices cool. Grind the spices (see note on page 154).

In a large bowl, combine the spice mixture, yogurt, ginger, and garlic. Add the chicken to the spice paste, cover with plastic, and refrigerate for 24 hours.

Preheat the oven to 450°F.

Remove the chicken from the marinade and wipe it dry. Arrange it on a wire rack placed over a shallow roasting pan or sheet pan. Brush the chicken with ghee and roast for 35 to 40 minutes, or until the meat registers 165°F. on an instant-read thermometer and the juices run clear when pierced with the tip of a knife. Remove the chicken from the oven and let sit for 5 minutes to allow the juices to settle.

Serve the chicken hot with Tomato Salad.

TOMATO SALAD

Start to finish: 20 minutes

Hands-on time: 20 minutes

YIELD: 2 CUPS

3 tablespoons fresh lime juice

½ teaspoon sugar

¼ teaspoon salt

1 serrano chile, minced

1 medium onion, finely chopped

2 tomatoes, finely chopped

½ cucumber, peeled, seeded,
and finely chopped

2 tablespoons minced
fresh cilantro

In a large bowl combine the lime juice, sugar, and salt. Let sit for 10 minutes to dissolve the sugar and salt.

Add the chile, onion, tomato, cucumber, and cilantro and toss to mix well. Refrigerate up to 4 hours until serving.

Chicken Dhansak HOT-AND-SOUR CHICKEN AND LENTIL CURRY

Start to finish: 1 hour • Hands-on time: 30 minutes

We can't get enough of this irresistibly spicy and sweet-and-sour dish of lentils and meat. Pair it with poori and you won't even have to use a fork.

YIELD: 4 SERVINGS

1 cup red or yellow lentils

1 small onion, diced

1 bay leaf

Salt

½ teaspoon cumin seed

½ teaspoon coriander seed

¼ teaspoon fenugreek seed

½ teaspoon cayenne pepper

½ teaspoon turmeric

¼ cup Ghee (page 153)

2 garlic cloves, minced

1 (2-inch) knob fresh ginger,
    peeled and minced

1 serrano chile, seeded and
    minced

1½ pounds boneless, skinless-
    chicken breasts, cut into
    1-inch pieces

1 teaspoon Garam Masala
    (page 154)

1 (14½-ounce) can diced
    tomatoes, including juice

¼ cup light brown sugar

2 tablespoons tamarind concentrate

Salt and freshly ground
    black pepper

¼ cup chopped fresh cilantro

In a medium saucepan over medium-high heat, combine the lentils, onion, bay leaf, a pinch of salt, and 2 cups water. Bring to a simmer, reduce the heat to low, and simmer until the lentils are tender, about 30 minutes. Remove from the heat and set aside.

In a skillet over medium heat, toast the cumin, coriander, and fenugreek until fragrant, about 3 minutes. Remove the pan from the heat and let the spices cool. Grind the spices (see note on page 154). Add the cayenne pepper and turmeric and mix.

Heat the ghee in a large pot or Dutch oven set over medium heat. Add the garlic, ginger, and chile. Sauté for 1 minute, then add the chicken, spice mixture, and garam masala. Cook until the chicken turns opaque, about 3 minutes. Add the tomatoes, brown sugar, and tamarind. Lower the heat, cover, and cook for 10 minutes.

Drain the cooked lentils and add them to the chicken. Cover and cook for 10 minutes. Taste and adjust the seasonings if necessary. Garnish with cilantro.

VARIATION: To make beef or lamb dhansak, substitute 1 pound of beef chuck or lamb shoulder cut into 1-inch pieces for the chicken. Add at the same time as you would add the chicken and cook with the tomatoes for 30 minutes, or until tender. For vegetarian dhansak, add diced tofu, cauliflower, zucchini, eggplant, or green beans in any combination and amount you choose, adding them at the same point as you would add the chicken.

NOTE: Tamarind concentrate can be found in Indian grocery stores or online.

Kheer RICE PUDDING

Start to finish: 1 hour 30 minutes • Hands-on time: 30 minutes

Kheer is an Indian-style rice pudding studded with raisins and spiced with cardamom and saffron. Most Indian rice puddings do not include eggs. Our take on this recipe is that the addition of eggs creates a richer, denser consistency. The Middle Eastern rice pudding, Roz bi Laban, on page 284 is also similar to an eggless Indian rice pudding. If you prefer your rice pudding without eggs, try that recipe and omit the rose water.

3 tablespoons Ghee (page 153)

1½ cups long-grain rice

¾ cup sugar

3 cups whole milk

1 cup heavy cream

1 teaspoon ground cardamom

5 to 6 strands saffron

3 large eggs

¼ cup golden raisins

In a large saucepan set over medium heat, melt the ghee. Add the rice, stirring constantly for about 2 minutes. Add the sugar, milk, cream, cardamom, and saffron and continue to stir until the mixture simmers. Reduce the heat to low and cook at a bare simmer for 1 hour, stirring occasionally to keep the bottom from burning.

In a large heatproof bowl, beat the eggs. Slowly add 3 ladlefuls of the hot rice mixture to the eggs, whisking after each addition to heat the eggs slowly. Pour the egg mixture into the remaining rice and mix well, stirring for another 2 minutes, or until the mixture thickens. Stir in the raisins.

Transfer the pudding to a large dish and let it cool slightly before serving warm. Refrigerate for 2 hours to serve the pudding cold.

MAKE AHEAD: This kheer keeps for 2 days, covered and refrigerated.

Mango Lassi

Start to finish: 20 minutes • Hands-on time: 20 minutes

Lassi is a cold, refreshing yogurt-based drink originating from Punjab. A lassi can be sweet, such as this mango lassi, or savory, with cumin and turmeric.

YIELD: 2 SERVINGS

1½ cups plain whole-milk
   or low-fat yogurt

¾ cup low-fat or whole milk

3 tablespoons sugar

1 mango, peeled, pitted,
   and diced

Pinch of salt

⅛ teaspoon ground cardamom

Combine all ingredients in a blender and purée the mixture. Serve cold.

❦ITALIAN❦

☙ITALIAN❧

TO AN ITALIAN, COOKING IS NOT JUST ABOUT putting food on the table; rather, it's an expression of a love of the good life. Perhaps that and all of its extraordinary flavors are why Italian cuisine is almost as popular in America and the rest of the world as it is in Italy. This particular culinary philosophy certainly puts us in touch with our "inner Italians." Lord knows, no two people love the good life more than we do!

This love of food, family, conversation, and camaraderie binds many of the Mediterranean cuisines, whether Moroccan, Greek, or Italian. But, according to the National Restaurant Association, Italian reigns supreme in the United States as the most popular of ethnic cuisines. Maybe it's the visions of al fresco meals in Italy, taken in the flower-filled outdoor trattorias and cafés, or perhaps it's just really easy to call out for pizza. We're not judging.

Italian food is generally served in courses. There's no need to hurry anything in Italy. After all, the only thing on the schedule after dinner is making love and thinking about breakfast. Oh, how we love Italians! The first course, antipasti, loosely translated means "before pasta." Consisting of sausages, olives, and colorful marinated vegetables, this course is supposed to entice the eye and prepare the stomach for the meal to come. Bruschetta or crostini is a familiar form of antipasti that consists of toasted bread topped with anything from white beans to sun-dried tomatoes or grilled eggplant. The main theme of these beginning courses is freshness, color, a savory bite, and, of course, an excuse to pop open the Chianti.

The next course is called *primi piatti*, or "first plates," and consists of small portions of pasta, risotto, soup, or polenta. Nourishing and filling, these plates are meant to satisfy you before the more expensive meat course that may or may not follow, depending on the occasion and depth of the cook's pocketbook.

Dessert in Italy usually consists of fresh fruit and cheese, sometimes drizzled with honey or zabaglione (a foamy custard made from wine, sugar, and egg yolks), accompanied by fortified wine or strong black coffee. For special occasions or feast days, there is the molded *cassata Siciliana* or the more familiar tiramisu, both consisting of sponge cake or ladyfingers soaked in liqueur and layered between sweetened mascarpone cheese or custard, with the addition of shaved chocolate, whipped cream, or dried fruit.

Gelato (Italian ice cream) is usually eaten as a between-meal snack, although, at least in the case of Meredith's children, it can also be an enjoyable and placating meal replacement. A true feast for the eyes, the local gelateria sells the rich, creamy, frozen confection in nearly every color and flavor (risotto gelato, anyone?).

When we're teaching Italian cooking, our students love the fact that we present the food in courses, much as it would be served in Italy. The combinations of colors and flavors are compelling, and the students enjoy savoring every bite. But more than the food itself, it's important that our students know they can go home and create a wonderful Italian meal from start to finish.

Here is one of our favorite Italian menus to get you started in your own kitchen:

FOOD *for* THOUGHT

- Pizzerias represent seventeen percent of all restaurants in the United States.

- Americans eat approximately 100 acres of pizza each day, or about 350 slices per second.

- Each man, woman, and child in America eats and average of 46 slices (23 pounds) of pizza per year.

- In eighteenth-century England, the word "macaroni" was a synonym for perfection and excellence. The feather in Yankee Doodle's cap was called "macaroni;" it must've looked amazing! In Italian, the word "macaroni" actually means "dearest darlings."

- Among his many other culinary gifts to the United States, Thomas Jefferson is also credited with introducing us to macaroni. He fell in love with it in Italy while serving as the American Ambassador to France. In fact, he ordered crates of "macaroni," along with a pasta-making machine, sent back to the States.

Basic Egg Pasta

Start to finish: 1 hour 20 minutes • Hands-on time: 40 minutes

We have been teaching students how to make pasta for years, but it's still a thrill to see the looks on their faces when they taste handmade pasta for the first time. This is something we love to do in classes because it's an easy sell. Once the students try it, they want to make it again and again. The silky, tender strands of pasta have a completely different texture than the rubbery, plastic-wrapped fresh pasta from a store. The delicacy of homemade pasta is especially delicious in sophisticated cream sauces, because its surface holds the sauce beautifully.

Using the proper equipment makes it so much easier to make pasta. You can roll pasta out by hand with a rolling pin, but having a pasta-rolling machine cuts the time and the sweat equity down to a minimum. We love pasta rollers with an attached motor or ones that attach to a stand mixer because you don't have to use one hand to crank the roller. It's fast and it's easy enough to make pasta alone, even on a Tuesday night.

YIELD: ABOUT 1¼ POUNDS, FOR 4 TO 6 SERVINGS

2¾ cups unbleached all-purpose flour, plus more if necessary

1 teaspoon plus 2 tablespoons salt

4 large eggs

Combine the flour, 1 teaspoon of salt, and the eggs in the bowl of a food processor and pulse several times until clumps of moist dough form.

Turn the dough out onto a lightly floured work surface, gather it into ball, and knead until smooth, about 3 minutes, sprinkling lightly with flour if the dough sticks. Wrap the dough in plastic and let it rest at room temperature for at least 20 minutes. (If you are making the Cannelloni on page 198 or the lasagnas on pages 199 to 201, stop here and continue with the directions in those recipes.)

Cut the dough into 4 equal pieces and cover each piece with plastic wrap to prevent it from drying. Set the pasta machine to its widest setting. Working with one piece at a time, flatten the dough into a rectangle and run it through the machine. Fold the dough in thirds, as if you are folding a letter. Dust the outside lightly with flour and, putting the shorter end through first, run it through the roller again. Repeat this process until the dough is smooth and elastic. It may take 3 or 4 times. (This is a continuation of the kneading process. It gives the dough a chance to absorb more flour if it is too sticky.)

Pass the dough through the machine, without folding it, using the narrower settings, one time through each setting. Dust lightly with flour as needed to prevent sticking, until the pasta sheet is the desired thickness.

Place the sheet on a lightly floured work surface. Repeat with the remaining dough. If the dough tears at any time during the rolling process, just fold it in half, dust both sides with flour, and run it through the setting you were just on one more time. (If you are making the Ravioli on page 196, stop here and continue with the directions in that recipe.)

Let the pasta sheets rest until they become slightly dry but are still pliable, about 20 minutes. Cut the sheets to the desired length. Fit the machine with the desired cutter and run the sheets through.

Using floured hands, toss the strands to separate.

Cook the pasta in a 6-quart pot of boiling water with the 2 tablespoons of salt, stirring occasionally, for 3 to 5 minutes, or until just tender and no longer rubbery. Drain and serve with desired sauce.

VARIATION: Spinach Pasta: Increase the flour amount to 3 cups. After adding the eggs, add ⅓ cup cooked, chopped spinach that has been thoroughly squeezed dry. Continue with recipe. Spinach pasta can be a little trickier to roll into sheets because the excess moisture in the spinach may be squeezed out during the process, making the dough sticky and hard to handle. This is particularly true the first few times you run the dough through the widest setting, so you may have to run it through the widest setting several times to get a nice, smooth, and elastic sheet of pasta. Just make sure you dust the dough with flour each time. If it tears while rolling, just fold it in half, dust thoroughly with flour and roll it through again.

TIP: Whenever possible, once you've pulled your cooked pasta from the pasta water, add it to the pan with your sauce and let it cook for another minute. This allows the pasta and the sauce to "marry"—in other words, it gives the flavors of the sauce a chance to seep into the pasta and makes for a much better finished dish.

Polenta

Start to finish: 50 minutes • Hands-on time: 15 minutes

Polenta is a variation on cornmeal mush that is easy to make and easy to dress up. One of our favorite meals is a big bowl of creamy polenta that has sidecar bowls of bolognese and pesto sauces, crumbled gorgonzola cheese, chopped toasted walnuts, dollops of mascarpone, and mountains of grated Parmigiano-Reggiano cheese. It's fun to let family and friends make a project out of dinner by adorning their own polenta.

YIELD: 6 TO 8 SERVINGS

2 teaspoons salt

1¾ cups polenta, or coarse- or
    medium-grained cornmeal

4 tablespoons unsalted butter

½ cup grated Parmigiano-
    Reggiano cheese

In a large saucepan, 7 cups of water to a boil over medium heat. Add the salt and gradually add the cornmeal, whisking constantly to prevent lumps. Lower the heat to a simmer, cover, and cook for 45 minutes, stirring occasionally to keep the polenta from sticking to the bottom of the pan. If the polenta becomes too firm, add some warm water to adjust the consistency. It should be thick, but not dry.

Add the butter and cheese, and stir to combine. Serve hot.

NOTE: The best Parmesan cheese you can buy is Parmigiano-Reggiano. This cheese comes from the city of Parma in the Emilia Romagna region of Italy and is aged for more than a year. You can tell it's the real deal by the dot-matrix pattern that spells its name on the rind. For best results in recipes it's important to find the real thing, and that most certainly does not come from a green cardboard cylinder.

TIP: Regular, everyday cornmeal will produce a decent polenta, but we like to mix it half and half with coarse ground cornmeal in order to give it an earthier taste and texture.

MAKE AHEAD: To make firm polenta that will be cut for baking, sautéing, or grilling, pour the cooked polenta into an oiled loaf pan and let cool. It can then be refrigerated for 2 days. When you're ready to serve, cut the polenta into slices, brush them with olive oil and sauté, grill, or bake as desired.

Bruschetta with Tomatoes and Basil

Start to finish: 1 hour 5 minutes • Hands-on time: 35 minutes

Bruschetta with tomatoes and basil is one of the most simple appetizers to make, and one of the best. But like most Italian dishes, the ingredients are so few that they must be of the highest quality for this dish to stand out. Don't even try to make this in winter when tomatoes are grainy and flavorless. Wait until late summer, when tomatoes and basil are both at their peak and can give their all to this classic Italian dish.

YIELD: 36 PIECES, 6 TO 8 SERVINGS

1 (22-inch) baguette, ends
    trimmed, angle-cut into
    36 (½-inch) slices
½ cup olive oil
3 large ripe tomatoes (about
    1½ pounds), trimmed, seeded,
    and cut into ¼-inch dice
¼ cup chopped fresh basil
2 tablespoons extra-virgin olive oil
1 tablespoon balsamic vinegar
1 garlic clove, finely minced
¼ teaspoon salt
Freshly ground black pepper

Preheat a grill or broiler. Brush the bread slices lightly on both sides with the ½ cup olive oil. Grill the bread, or place it on a pan 6 inches under the broiler, until lightly browned, about 3 to 4 minutes, turning once. Remove from the heat and let cool.

Meanwhile, make the topping. In a medium bowl, combine the tomatoes, basil, 2 tablespoons of extra-virgin olive oil, balsamic vinegar, garlic, salt, and a generous grinding of pepper. Cover and let stand at room temperature for 30 minutes. Taste and adjust the seasoning, if necessary.

To serve, spoon some of the topping onto the bread slices, or serve the topping in a bowl accompanied by the grilled bread slices.

> MAKE AHEAD: The bread can be toasted several hours in advance and kept in an airtight container at room temperature until ready to use. They should not be topped until just before serving.

Panzanella **BREAD AND TOMATO SALAD**

Start to finish: 1 hour • Hands-on time: 30 minutes

We love bread salads. What could be better than eating bread and getting credit for eating your vegetables? We use a rustic, chewy Italian loaf as the basis for this summertime salad. The cubes of bread are toasted, so they soak up all the delicious juices from the tomatoes and the vinaigrette. They're then tossed with fistfuls of fresh basil and colorful red onions.

YIELD: 6 SERVINGS

1 small loaf rustic Italian bread, cut into 1-inch cubes (about 6 cups)

3 tablespoons plus ½ cup extra-virgin olive oil

1½ teaspoons salt, plus more as needed

½ teaspoon freshly ground black pepper, plus more as needed

½ teaspoon Dijon mustard

3 tablespoons red wine vinegar

2 large, ripe tomatoes, cut into 1-inch cubes

1 English cucumber, unpeeled, seeded, and sliced ½ inch thick

½ red onion, cut in half and thinly sliced

20 large basil leaves, coarsely chopped

Preheat the oven to 375°F.

On a large baking sheet, toss the bread with the 3 tablespoons of oil, 1 teaspoon of the salt, and ¼ teaspoon of the pepper. Bake, stirring once or twice, until the croutons are crisp and lightly colored on the outside, but still soft within, about 8 or 9 minutes. Set aside to cool.

Meanwhile, make the vinaigrette. In a medium bowl, whisk together the mustard, vinegar, and remaining salt and pepper. Slowly drizzle in the remaining ½ cup of oil while whisking.

In a large bowl, mix the tomatoes, cucumber, onion, and basil. Add the breadcubes and the vinaigrette, and toss to coat. Taste and season with salt and pepper, if necessary. Allow the salad to sit for about 30 minutes at room temperature for the flavors to blend.

Fried Calamari

Start to finish: 35 minutes • Hands-on time: 20 minutes

When it comes to cooking squid, the saying goes, "Cook it for 1 minute or 1 hour, anything in between is too much or not enough." That's because squid, called calimari in Italian, is best cooked quickly or braised for a long time so that it's tender. We lightly coat our calamari in a cornmeal crust and fry it briefly to make it crispy on the outside but still delicate on the inside. We like it unadorned, with just a squeeze of fresh lemon, but if you prefer, you can certainly serve it with a side of Marinara Sauce (page 193).

YIELD: 4 TO 6 SERVINGS

1 pound whole small squid, bodies cleaned and cut into ¼-inch-wide rings, tentacles reserved

1 cup milk

1 large egg

1½ to 2 cups vegetable oil, for frying

1 cup unbleached all-purpose flour

1 cup cornmeal

1 teaspoon salt, plus more as needed

¼ teaspoon freshly ground black pepper

1 tablespoon chopped flat-leaf parsley

Lemon wedges, for serving

Rinse the squid under cool water and pat it dry with paper towels.

Combine the milk and egg in a bowl, mixing with a fork until lightly beaten. Add the squid and chill for about 15 minutes.

Pour 2 inches of oil into a large, heavy saucepan and heat to 360°F.

Mix the flour, cornmeal, salt, and pepper in a large, shallow bowl. Working in small batches, toss the squid in the flour mixture to coat. Carefully drop the squid into the oil and fry for 1 to 3 minutes, or until golden brown. Using a slotted spoon, transfer the fried squid to paper towels to drain. Season with salt to taste.

Place the squid onto serving plates or a platter, sprinkle with parsley, and serve immediately with lemon wedges.

Minestrone

Start to finish: 3 hours 30 minutes (plus 1 hour or 24 hours depending on the bean soaking method you choose) • Hands-on time: 50 minutes

Minestrone is the epitome of an "everything but the kitchen sink" soup. Even though we're giving you this great recipe, remember that at its essence, minestrone is a vegetable soup that needs to take advantage of what is in season to be great. If zucchini isn't in season, use yellow squash. If green beans aren't available, leave them out. The bones of this soup are quality tomatoes, olive oil, and Parmigiano-Reggiano cheese—the rest is up to you.

YIELD: 8 TO 10 SERVINGS

½ pound dried white beans

1 teaspoon salt

¼ pound pancetta or bacon, chopped

2 tablespoons olive oil

1 small onion chopped

2 carrots, diced

1 stalk celery, diced

2 garlic cloves, minced

2 cups boiling potatoes, peeled and diced

½ a head of green cabbage (preferably Savoy), shredded

1 (28-ounce) can whole tomatoes, chopped coarse, with juices

6½ cups chicken stock

2 cups zucchini, diced

1 cup green beans, trimmed and cut into ½-inch pieces

Freshly ground black pepper

Parmigiano-Reggiano cheese, freshly grated, for serving

Extra-virgin olive oil, for drizzling

In a large bowl, soak the beans overnight in enough water to cover by 2 inches, or quick-soak them (see tip below).

Drain the beans and place them in a saucepan. Add water to cover by 2 inches. Simmer, uncovered, for 45 minutes to 1 hour, or until the beans are tender. Add more water if necessary to keep them barely covered. Add the salt and simmer for 5 minutes. Remove from the heat and set aside, uncovered.

In a heavy soup pot over moderate heat, heat the oil and cook the pancetta, stirring, until it is crisp and pale golden. Add the onion and cook, stirring, until it softens, about 6 minutes. Add the carrots, celery, and garlic and cook, stirring, for 4 minutes. Add the potatoes and cabbage and cook, stirring, until the cabbage is wilted, about 5 minutes. Add the tomatoes and the stock and let the soup simmer, covered, for 30 minutes.

Add the beans, zucchini, and green beans and cook for 10 minutes. Season with salt and pepper to taste.

To serve, garnish with the cheese and drizzle with extra-virgin olive oil.

TIP: To quick-soak dried beans: Rinse the beans in a colander under cold water and discard any discolored ones. In a soup pot, combine the beans with enough cold water to cover them by 2 inches. Bring the water to a boil, and boil for 2 minutes. Remove from the heat and let the beans soak, covered, for 1 hour.

MAKE AHEAD: The soup may be made 3 days in advance and kept covered and chilled. Reheat the soup, thinning it with water as needed.

Wedding Soup MINESTRA MARITATI

Start to finish: 50 minutes • Hands-on time: 40 minutes

It turns out that wedding soup doesn't have anything to do with marriage. To say that things go well together in Italian is maritati, *or "married." In Italian, this soup is called* minestra maritati, *or "well-married soup" because of the happy marriage of the greens, stock, and meatballs. Whatever you want to call it, this dish is too good to save for special occasions.*

YIELD: 10 TO 12 SERVINGS

2 slices white bread,
   crusts removed, crumbled

¼ cup milk

1 large egg, beaten

½ pound ground beef

½ pound ground pork or veal

½ cup grated Parmigiano-
   Reggiano cheese, plus more
   for garnish

1 ounce prosciutto, minced

1 small onion, minced

2 garlic cloves, minced

1 teaspoon salt, plus more as
   necessary

Freshly ground black pepper

Pinch of nutmeg

¼ cup minced flat-leaf parsley

3 quarts chicken stock

1 head escarole, thinly sliced

1 cup acini de pepe pasta

In a large bowl, combine the bread and milk and set aside for 2 minutes. Add the egg, beef, pork, cheese, prosciutto, onion, garlic, salt, pepper, nutmeg, and parsley and mix with your hands until combined. Roll the mixture into small balls about 1 inch in diameter, and lay them out on a parchment-lined sheet pan.

In a large pot, bring the stock to a simmer and add the meatballs carefully. Try to keep the liquid at a simmer so that the meatballs are moving and don't stick together. Add the escarole and simmer for 10 minutes, or until the meatballs are done and the escarole is tender. Add the pasta and cook for 4 minutes, or until the pasta is tender. Season with salt and pepper to taste.

To serve, ladle the soup into bowls and top with Parmigiano-Reggiano cheese.

> MAKE AHEAD: The meatballs can be made a day ahead and kept covered and refrigerated, or they can be frozen on the sheet pan, transferred to a zip top bag, and kept frozen for up to 4 weeks. You can add them frozen to the simmering stock, just simmer a few minutes longer than directed in the recipe.

Risotto

Start to finish: 30 minutes • Hands-on time: 30 minutes

Risotto, should be rich, creamy, slightly al dente, and not at all gluey or watery—which is, unfortunately, what you get some-times in restaurants that aren't giving it the attention it deserves. This recipe will show you how easy it is to make the per-fect risotto. All you need is the right rice, a good stock, and a wooden spoon, because stirring is critical to a creamy risotto.

What you serve with risotto depends largely on the type of risotto you're making. The complex dish osso buco is tradition-ally served with saffron-scented risotto Milanese, which is a simple variation. More involved risotto additions, like wild mushrooms, sausage, or prosciutto and peas pair better with simple roasted or grilled meats. Of course, our idea of a lovely meal could very well consist of just risotto. But don't forget that good bread and a nice glass of wine make everything better.

YIELD: 6 TO 8 SERVINGS

5 cups chicken stock

4 tablespoons unsalted butter

2 tablespoons extra-virgin olive oil

1 medium onion, finely diced

½ teaspoon salt

Freshly ground black pepper

2 cups arborio rice

½ cup white wine

½ cup freshly grated Parmigiano-
  Reggiano, plus more for
  sprinkling

Heat the stock in a medium saucepan set over medium heat. Lower the heat and keep the stock hot while you are making the risotto.

In a large, heavy saucepan, heat 2 tablespoons of the butter and the olive oil over medium heat. Add the onion and cook until it is soft and translu-cent, about 6 minutes. Add the salt, pepper to taste, and the rice and stir to coat with the butter and oil. Cook, stirring, until opaque, about 3 to 4 minutes.

Add the wine and cook, stirring, until it has all been absorbed. Using a 4- to 6-ounce ladle, add one ladleful of the hot stock and cook, stirring, until it is mostly absorbed. Continue adding the stock one ladleful at a time, stirring constantly until the liquid is absorbed before adding more. Con-tinue to add stock, stirring as you go, until the rice is tender and creamy, yet still a little al dente, about 15 minutes.

Stir in the remaining 2 tablespoons butter and the cheese until well mixed. Taste and reseason with salt and pepper if necessary. Serve imme-diately with more cheese on the side.

VARIATIONS: There are a million different variations to risotto. It can be made with red wine or white. It can be made with vegetable stock for a vegetarian version. The sky's the limit. Really, what's important is for you to understand the process and then use your imagination. When adding vegetables to risotto, deciding when to add them depends on the vegetable itself. Risotto takes about 15 minutes to cook once you start adding the liquids. Vegetables like carrots or mushrooms that can withstand 15 minutes of cooking without getting mushy can be added at the beginning of the process. Asparagus or zucchini will be overcooked and it's best to sauté them separately and add at the end of the cooking process. How much to add depends on you, but we find about 2 cups of chopped or sliced vegetables for this amount of pasta suits our taste. If you like more, add more.

> MAKE AHEAD: Finished risotto waits for no one. If held too long, it will continue to absorb the liquid and become dry and mushy. You can, however, cook the risotto about three-quarters of the way done, then spread it out in a thin layer on a large cookie sheet and pop it into the refrigerator to chill down quickly. This will prevent the condensed heat from continuing to cook the rice. When it's cool, you can transfer it to a bowl and keep it covered for a day in the refrigerator. When ready to serve, heat the risotto in a saucepan and continue on with the end of the recipe, adding warm stock until the rice is al dente, then adding in the cheese and butter.

Here are a few variation ideas:

Risotto with Porcini: Soak ½ ounce of dried porcini mushrooms in 1 cup of warm water for 20 minutes, or until softened. Carefully lift them out of the water, leaving the grit at the bottom. Chop the mushrooms. Strain the water through cheesecloth. Use the strained water in place of some of the stock. Add the chopped mushrooms to the rice after it is sautéed and before you add the wine.

Risotto with Prosciutto and Peas: Add 1 cup frozen baby peas, thawed, and 2 ounces thinly sliced prosciutto, cut into ¼-inch-wide strips, to the risotto at the end when adding the cheese.

Risotto Milanese (Saffron Risotto): An Italian classic, traditionally served with osso buco. Add ½ teaspoon of saffron threads to the warm stock. Proceed with the recipe.

TIP: Stirring is what gives the risotto its creaminess. The starch that surrounds the outside of the rice is knocked off in the process of stirring and mixes with the stock to create a creamy and delicious "sauce." This is only true, though, if you use the right kind of rice. You need short-grain rice like Arborio or Carnaroli. Long-grain rice will not do. If you are using a canned stock, make sure it is the low-sodium variety.

Alfredo Sauce

Start to finish: 15 minutes • Hands-on time: 15 minutes

If you think you only have it in you to make handmade pasta one time, we beg you to serve it with this sauce. It's an experience you won't soon forget. Butter, cream, and cheese are cooked together with a dash of lemon juice and freshly ground nutmeg to make this perhaps the most incredibly luxurious sauce ever.

YIELD: ABOUT 2¾ CUPS

¼ pound (1 stick) unsalted butter

2 cups heavy cream

2 tablespoons fresh lemon juice

⅛ teaspoon ground nutmeg

½ teaspoon salt

¼ teaspoon freshly ground
   black pepper

1 cup finely grated Parmigiano-
   Reggiano cheese

Flat-leaf parsley, for garnish

Melt the butter in a large skillet over medium heat. Add the cream and bring to a boil. Cook until the sauce has reduced slightly, about 3 minutes. Remove from the heat. Stir in the lemon juice, nutmeg, salt, and pepper.

To serve with pasta: Add to the skillet the cooked pasta, half the cheese, and toss to combine. Adjust the seasonings if necessary. Sprinkle with the remaining cheese and garnish with parsley. Serve immediately.

FOOD *for* THOUGHT

PASTA EXISTED LONG BEFORE anyone in Europe had even seen a tomato, much less thought to make a sauce out of it. The Spanish explorer Hernan Cortez brought tomatoes back to Europe from Mexico in 1519. Even then, almost two hundred years passed before spaghetti with tomato sauce made its way into Italian kitchens.

Marinara Sauce

Start to finish: 40 minutes • Hands-on time: 20 minutes

What would Italian cooking be without a great tomato sauce? It just wouldn't be Italian. Feel free to double this recipe so you can freeze the extra and have it on hand whenever you need a quick pasta sauce, a braising sauce for almost any kind of meat, or even sauce for homemade pizza.

YIELD: ABOUT 3 CUPS

2 tablespoons extra-virgin olive oil

3 garlic cloves, minced

½ small onion, finely chopped

1 carrot, peeled and finely chopped

1 stalk celery, finely chopped

½ teaspoon dried oregano

½ teaspoon dried thyme

2 tablespoons tomato paste

1 (28-ounce) can crushed tomatoes

Salt and pepper

Heat the oil in a medium skillet over medium-low heat. Add the garlic, onions, carrots, and celery and cook about 5 minutes. Add the oregano, thyme, and tomato paste and cook, stirring frequently, for another 5 minutes or until the paste turns a brownish color. Add the tomatoes and cook over medium heat for about 20 minutes, or until the sauce thickens slightly and the flavors develop. Season with salt and pepper to taste.

VARIATIONS:

Marinara Basil Sauce: Add 3 tablespoons fresh basil, torn into bite-size pieces, to the sauce at the end of cooking.

Marinara Cream Sauce: Add ½ cup heavy cream to sauce, reheat over medium heat, and reduce down to sauce consistency.

Marinara Sauce with Wine: Before adding the tomatoes, add ½ cup white or red wine. Continue cooking until the wine has almost evaporated, and then proceed with recipe.

> MAKE AHEAD: This sauce can be made 3 days ahead and kept covered in the refrigerator. You can also freeze it for up to two months.

Pesto Sauce

Start to finish: 10 minutes • Hands-on time: 10 minutes

When summer is here and basil is abundant in our gardens and grocery stores, family and friends can count on pesto finding its way to the table in all sorts of forms. Of course, it's wonderful tossed with hot pasta, but we also love to mix it with Greek yogurt to serve on grilled salmon, or toss a tablespoon or two into vinaigrette and drizzle it over sliced tomatoes and fresh mozzarella. Its uses are endless.

YIELD: ABOUT 1 CUP

2 cups fresh basil leaves

½ cup extra-virgin olive oil

2 garlic cloves, chopped

1 teaspoon salt

2 tablespoons pine nuts

⅓ cup grated Parmigiano-
   Reggiano cheese

2 tablespoons grated Pecorino
   Romano cheese

Put the basil, olive oil, garlic, and salt in the bowl of a food processor and pulse until finely chopped. Add the pine nuts and cheeses and pulse again until finely chopped but not completely puréed. Stop from time to time and scrape down the bowl if necessary.

MAKE AHEAD: If you won't be using this sauce immediately, store it in an airtight container, drizzled over with a thin coating of olive oil to keep the sauce from turning dark. Pesto will keep well in the refrigerator for up to a week. Pesto also freezes well. We like to freeze it in ice cube trays for convenient use.

Bolognese Sauce

Start to finish: 3 hours 30 minutes • Hands-on time: 1 hour

We make this slow-cooked, meaty, and deliciously satisfying sauce in large quantities so we can save some in our freezer for cold winter nights when it will come in handy for easy pasta dinners. Made with a combination of meats, vegetables, and a little milk, every Italian household has its own version of this classic ragù.

YIELD: ABOUT 10 CUPS

2 tablespoons extra-virgin olive oil

2 tablespoons unsalted butter

2 medium onions, finely chopped

2 stalks celery, finely chopped

2 carrots, peeled and finely chopped

5 garlic cloves, chopped

1 pound ground veal

1 pound ground pork

½ pound ground beef

¼ pound diced pancetta

1 cup milk

2 (28-ounce) cans whole peeled tomatoes, crushed by hand, with the juices

1 cup dry white wine

1 quart chicken stock

Salt and freshly ground black pepper

In a 6- to 8-quart, heavy-bottomed saucepan, heat the olive oil and butter over medium heat. Add the onion, celery, carrot, and garlic and sweat over medium heat until the vegetables are translucent, about 10 minutes.

Add the veal, pork, beef, and pancetta to the vegetables and brown over high heat for about 15 to 20 minutes, stirring and breaking up the meat with the back of a wooden spoon.

Add the milk and simmer until the mixture is almost dry, about 10 minutes.

Add the tomatoes and their juices and simmer for 15 minutes. Add the wine and stock, bring to a boil, lower the heat, and simmer, skimming off excess fat as it accumulates, for 2 to 2½ hours, until the sauce has thickened. Season with salt and pepper to taste.

TIP: If you have an old-fashioned potato masher, use it to break up the meat as you're browning it. It will also crush your tomatoes in the pan if you don't want to get your hands messy.

> MAKE AHEAD: This sauce can be prepared up to 3 days ahead. Just let it cool to room temperature, then cover and refrigerate. It can also be frozen for up to 3 months.

Ravioli

Start to finish: 2 hours (includes time to make the pasta) • Hands-on time: 2 hours

Making these delightful, tender little pasta pockets isn't nearly as difficult as most people imagine it to be. However, it is a job best done with at least one friend and at least one bottle of wine. This recipe makes a lot, but it might as well—if the flour is going to fly in your kitchen, you should have more than one meal to show for it.

YIELD: 6 SERVINGS

Pasta sauce of your choice
   (pages 192-195)

CHEESE FILLING

1 large egg

2 cups ricotta cheese, drained

1 cup shredded mozzarella cheese

½ cup minced flat-leaf parsley

½ teaspoon salt

Freshly ground black pepper

Plain breadcrumbs, as needed

MEAT FILLING

1 tablespoon olive oil

½ pound ground veal

½ pound ground pork

1 cup dry white wine

Salt and freshly ground
   black pepper

2 garlic cloves, minced

1 ounce prosciutto or ham, minced

½ cup minced flat-leaf parsley

½ cup grated Parmigiano-
   Reggiano cheese

½ cup ricotta cheese

Prepare the sauce as directed in the recipe.

Prepare your choice of fillings.

To make the cheese filling: Combine the egg, ricotta, mozzarella, parsley, salt, and pepper to taste in a large bowl. If the mixture appears too loose to work with, add breadcrumbs, 1 tablespoon at a time, allowing the mixture to sit for a few minutes after each addition to absorb the moisture.

To make the meat filling: Heat the oil in a large, deep skillet. Add the veal and pork and cook for about 5 minutes, or until the meat loses its color, breaking up any clumps as it cooks.

Add the wine and salt and pepper, then turn the heat to low. Cook, stirring occasionally, until the meat is tender, about 45 minutes.

Add the garlic and prosciutto and cook for another 5 minutes. Remove from the heat and cool slightly, then add the parsley, Parmigiano-Reggiano, ricotta, and egg. If mixture is too loose and there is too much liquid, add the breadcrumbs, about a tablespoon at a time.

If you like a finer texture to your filling, pulse it several times in a food processor until it is the desired texture.

To assemble the ravioli: Prepare the dough as directed in the recipe, rolling it out to about ⅛-inch thickness.

Have a small bowl with water and a pastry brush handy. Dust your work surface lightly with flour and lay out a long sheet of pasta. Fold it in half and use your fingernail or a toothpick to mark the dough at the halfway point. Open the strip of dough out again and brush the top surface very lightly with water. Drop small spoonfuls of the filling about 1½ inches apart on one half of the pasta sheet, leaving at least a ½-inch border around the edges. Fold the other half of the sheet over the filling, making sure all the filling is covered.

1 large egg

Plain breadcrumbs, as needed

RAVIOLI ASSEMBLY

1¼ pounds Basic Egg or Spinach
   Pasta dough (pages 182-183)

Cornmeal, for dusting

2 tablespoons salt

> MAKE AHEAD: Ravioli can be made one day ahead and kept loosely covered on a cornmeal-dusted baking sheet in the refrigerator. It can also be frozen on a baking sheet in a single layer in the refrigerator. They can also be frozen in a single layer, then transferred to a zip top freezer bag and kept in the freezer for up to 2 weeks.

Using your index finger, gently press out air pockets around each mound of filling. Use a sharp knife, pizza cutter, or ravioli cutter to cut in between the pockets of filling, forming squares, where the dough has been pressed down to create a seal. Press down on the edges with your finger to make a tight seal.

Dust a sheet pan with cornmeal to prevent the ravioli from sticking and lay them out on the sheet, making sure not to let them touch. Repeat with the remaining dough and filling.

To cook the pasta, bring 6 quarts of water to a gentle boil. Add the salt and drop the ravioli into the water in batches (about 16 ravioli to a batch), being careful not to allow the water to come to a violent boil. Cook the ravioli until just tender, 4 to 6 minutes. Remove the cooked ravioli with a slotted spoon and continue with the remaining ravioli. Drain well. Serve with pasta sauce.

TIP: It's distressing to work so hard making ravioli and end up with them all coming apart in the water. Here are a few reasons why ravioli may come apart, and how to avoid the consequences:

• The seal on your ravioli may not be adequate. If they are coming apart, wet your finger with a little water, run it along the edge of the ravioli, and reseal.

• There are air pockets in the ravioli. Air expands when it's hot and if it is trapped in your ravioli, it will explode in boiling water. Make sure you carefully work your finger tightly around each mound of filling to push the air from the inside out to the edge of the pasta.

• Your water is boiling too violently and the force of the boil is bursting your ravioli open. Make sure the water is at a gentle boil.

Baked Cannelloni

Start to finish: 2 hours 20 minutes (includes the time to make the pasta and sauce) • Hands-on time: 1 hour 15 minutes

Cannelloni is an elegant baked pasta dish that will make everyone at your table feel special. Tender rolls of pasta are filled with a flavorful ground meat and cheese filling, sauced with a rich combination of tomato and béchamel, and baked until bubbly and golden. Like its kissing cousin lasagne al forno, it's an impressive dish for company that can be made ahead and popped into the oven as your guests are walking in the door.

YIELD: 6 SERVINGS

FILLING

1 ¼ pounds Basic Egg Pasta
    dough, (page 182)

1 ½ cups Marinara Sauce,
    (page 193)

1 cup Béchamel Sauce,
    (pages 140-141)

2 tablespoons unsalted butter

½ pound ground pork

½ pound ground beef

2 ounces prosciutto, finely chopped

1 garlic clove, minced

1 cup grated Parmigiano-
    Reggiano cheese

1 tablespoon unbleached
    all-purpose flour

1 cup whole milk

½ teaspoon plus 1 tablespoon
    salt

¼ teaspoon freshly ground
    black pepper

Pinch of nutmeg

1 egg, beaten

Prepare the pasta dough and sauces as directed in the recipes.

In a large skillet set over high heat, heat the butter until it foams and subsides. Add the pork and beef and cook for about 5 minutes, or until it begins to brown. Drain the excess fat and add the prosciutto, garlic, ½ cup of the cheese, the flour, and milk. Reduce the heat to a simmer and cook for 10 minutes, stirring regularly. Remove from the heat and allow to cool.

Season the meat mixture with ½ teaspoon of the salt, the pepper, and nutmeg. Stir in the egg. Set aside.

Preheat the oven to 350°F. Bring a large pot with 4 quarts of water to a boil.

Using a pasta rolling machine, roll the pasta dough out to the thickness of a dime (setting #5 on most pasta rollers) and cut it into 12 (4 x 6-inch) rectangles. Save any leftover pasta for another use.

Add 1 tablespoon of salt to the boiling water, and drop the pasta rectangles, 2 or 3 at a time, into the boiling water. Blanch the pasta for 1½ minutes, or until just tender. Remove them with a slotted spoon and immediately drop them into an ice water bath to stop the cooking. When the cooked pasta cools, place it on a clean dish towel (not one made of terry cloth, to avoid sticking) to soak up any excess liquid.

Divide the filling among the pasta, placing it in the middle of the rectangles, lengthwise. Roll the pasta around the filling, jelly-roll style.

Spread ½ cup of the marinara sauce evenly across the bottom of a 13 x 9-inch pan. Carefully lay each cannelloni in the pan so they are in a single layer. Top with the remaining cup of marinara sauce, then the béchamel sauce, and lastly with the remaining ½ cup cheese.

Bake for 20 to 25 minutes, or until the sauces and cheese are bubbling and the edges of the pasta are browned. Let sit for 10 minutes before serving.

Ricotta and Sausage Lasagna

Start to finish: 3 hours (includes the time to make the sauce) • Hands-on time: 50 minutes

This lasagna is really a big cheese pie, flavored with four kinds of cheese and lots of wine-infused, tomato-based meat sauce. For many years, Carla has made this recipe to feed her extended family on Christmas Eve. Because it can be made the day ahead, popped into the oven before the family goes to church, and brought out piping hot to serve as soon as the hungry hordes return, lasagna hits the spot for cook and guests alike. As far as we're concerned, nothing says lovin' like lasagna from the oven.

YIELD: 10 SEVINGS

6 cups Marinara Sauce with
    wine (page 193)

3 pounds ricotta cheese

3 large eggs, beaten

4 green onions, white and
    green parts thinly sliced

1½ teaspoons salt

Freshly ground black pepper
    to taste

Pinch of freshly ground nutmeg

⅓ cup flat leaf parsley,
    finely chopped

2 pounds Italian sausage, crumbled

2 cups grated mozzarella cheese

1 cup grated Asiago cheese

1 cup grated Parmigiano-
    Reggiano cheese

1 tablespoon salt

1 pound lasagna noodles

Prepare the Marinara Sauce with Wine variation as directed in the recipe (you will need to double the recipe).

In a large bowl, combine the ricotta, eggs, green onions, salt, pepper, nutmeg, and parsley; set aside.

Bring 4 quarts of water to a boil over medium-high heat.

Preheat the oven to 350°F.

In a large skillet over medium-high heat, cook the sausage for about 5 minutes, or until no longer pink.

Warm the marinara sauce in a large pot over medium heat. When the sausage is ready, add it to the sauce and heat until the sauce comes to a simmer. Turn the heat to low let the sauce simmer while you continue with the recipe.

In a large bowl, combine the mozzarella, Asiago, and Parmigiano-Reggiano cheeses and set aside.

Add the salt to the boiling water along with the lasagna noodles. Cook the noodles until they are almost cooked, about 10 minutes. Remove a noodle from the water and tear it open. You should see a fine line of white, un-cooked pasta in the center. (The pasta will continue to cook as the lasagna bakes.) Drain the pasta and rinse it under cold water to stop the cooking.

To assemble the lasagna, spread 1 cup of sauce evenly over the bottom of a lasagna pan or a 13 x 9-inch pan. Lay 3 noodles on top of the sauce to cover the bottom of the pan. Spread one-third of the ricotta mixture over the noodles and 1 cup of sauce, and sprinkle with 1 cup of the mixed cheese. Add another layer of noodles, half the ricotta, 2 cups of the sauce,

(continued on next page)

and 1 cup mixed cheese. For the third layer, add another layer of noodles, the remaining ricotta, and 1 cup of mixed cheese, then top with noodles. Spread 2 cups sauce on top of the lasagna and top with the remaining mixed cheese.

Butter a sheet of aluminum foil and lay it, buttered-side-down, on top of the lasagna. Seal the edges.

Bake the lasagna for 1 hour, or until it is hot in the center. Carefully remove the foil top so as not to disturb the cheese and return to the oven for another 15 to 20 minutes, or until the top has browned slightly.

Remove the lasagna from the oven and let it sit for 10 minutes. Serve directly from the pan.

Lasagna with Spinach Pasta   LASAGNE VERDI AL FORNO

Start to finish: 5 hours 15 minutes (includes the time to make the sauces and pasta) • Hands-on time: 2 hours 30 minutes

A classic dish from Bologna, this lighter, subtly flavored baked pasta dish is the more sophisticated version of the robust lasagna we're so often served in restaurants specializing in Southern Italian cooking. This lasagna is made up of verdant spinach noodles layered with a rich Bolognese and creamy béchamel. The whole dish is held together by a liberal dose of one our favorite cheeses: Parmigiano-Reggiano. This dish is so good that we often make two at a time and keep one in the freezer for future stress-free entertaining.

YIELD: 6 SERVINGS

1¼ pounds Spinach Pasta dough
   (pages 182-183)
5 cups Bolognese Sauce
   (page 195)
3 cups Béchamel Sauce
   (pages 140-141)
2 tablespoons salt
1 cup freshly grated Parmigiano-
   Reggiano cheese

Prepare the pasta dough and sauces as directed in the recipes.

Preheat the oven to 425°F. Set an oven rack in the middle of your oven.

Divide the pasta dough into 4 pieces and roll out to the thickness of a dime (this is setting #5 for most machines). Cut the pasta sheets into 6-inch-long pieces.

Bring 6 quarts of water to boil in a stockpot and add the salt. Allow the pasta to dry just long enough for the water to boil.

Lay out several clean, dry dish towels (not terry cloth, to avoid sticking) flat on your work surface. Set out a large bowl of ice water.

Cook each piece of pasta separately for 10 seconds after the water returns to a boil. Quickly remove the noodles and slip them into the cold

MAKE AHEAD: All the components of this dish may be made
one day ahead and kept,
unassembled and covered, in
the refrigerator. The dish can be
assembled and kept at room
temperature up to 1 hour before
baking, or up to 24 hours, covered, in the refrigerator. It can
be assembled and frozen for up
to 1 month. Thaw overnight in
the refrigerator before baking
and add 10 minutes to the
baking time.

water to stop the cooking. When the noodles are cool, remove them from the water, gently pat off the excess water, and lay flat on the towels, making sure they don't touch. Continue until all the noodles have been cooked.

To assemble: skim a ladleful from the top of the Bolognese Sauce (where the fat is), and smear it along the bottom of a 13 x 9-inch baking pan or lasagna pan. Line the pan with a layer of the noodles. (You may have leftover noodles at the end of the layering process.) Piece the noodle layers together if necessary. Spread with 1 cup of the Bolognese Sauce and ¾ cup of the Béchamel Sauce, and finish with a dusting of the cheese. Repeat the process about three more times (more or less, depending on the generosity of your previous layering efforts). End with a coating of Béchamel and a sprinkling of cheese.

Bake for 20 to 30 minutes, or until a golden, crusty layer forms on the top. Let the lasagna rest for 8 to 10 minutes before serving.

TIP: We always think it's important to buy quality products, but never more so than in the case of Parmesan cheese, and never more so than for a dish that so heavily relies on its intensely nutty flavor. See our note on page 184 for more on Parmigiano-Reggiano.

Potato Gnocchi

Start to finish: 1 hour 40 minutes • Hands-on time: 1 hour

Gnocchi are Italian dumplings that, at their best, are tender and light. Sadly, you might have only known them to be doughy little lumps of lead. This recipe will change your mind. Like dumplings all over the world, gnocchi are a comfort food. They can be simply tossed with brown butter (see note) and toasted breadcrumbs, or baked au gratin with tomato sauce and topped with mozzarella cheese, or bathed in Bolognese sauce and dusted with Parmigiano-Reggiano.

YIELD: 4 TO 6 SERVINGS

Pasta sauce of your choice
(pages 192–195)

2 pounds (about 4) baking
potatoes, preferably russets

1½ cups unbleached all-purpose
flour, plus more for dusting

1 large egg

1 teaspoon plus 1 tablespoon salt

Prepare the sauce as directed in the recipe.

Place the potatoes in a large pot and cover with cold water. Bring to a boil, then reduce the heat and simmer, uncovered, until the potatoes are tender, about 30 minutes. Drain the potatoes and, while they are still warm, peel them and pass them through a vegetable mill or potato ricer onto a clean work surface.

Gently gather the potatoes into a loose mound and make a well in the center. Sprinkle with the flour. Place the egg and 1 teaspoon of the salt in the center of the well and use a fork to stir them into the flour and potatoes (this process is similar to making pasta dough by hand). Bring the dough together, kneading gently until a ball is formed. Continue to knead for another 2 to 3 minutes, working in a little more flour if the dough is sticky, until the ball is smooth and no longer sticks to your hand.

Divide the dough into 4 pieces; wrap 3 pieces in plastic wrap. Working with one piece at a time, roll it into a rope about the thickness of your index finger. Cut the rope into 1-inch pieces. Gently roll each piece down the back of a floured fork with your thumb, so that the dough wraps around the tip of your thumb, creating a dimple on one side of the gnocchi and ridges from the tines of the fork on the other side. The gnocchi should be slightly curved and marked with ridges. Place the shaped gnocchi on a lightly floured baking sheet.

Bring 4 quarts of water plus the remaining tablespoon of salt to a boil. Cook the gnocchi in three batches. The gnocchi are done about 1 minute after they float to the surface. Remove them with a slotted spoon, and serve with your favorite sauce.

NOTE: Brown butter is butter that has been cooked over low heat until the milk solids brown, resulting in a light hazelnut color and a distinctively nutty flavor.

TIP: The kneading process is critical in making good gnocchi. This is where you determine how much flour should be worked into your dough. Too much flour, and the gnocchi will be leaden and tough. Too little flour, and the gnocchi can be mushy and possibly even disintegrate in the cooking water. You need (and knead) just enough to make the dough smooth and no longer tacky. It should still be soft and moist, just not sticky.

Basic Pizza Crust

Start to finish: 1 hour 25 minutes • Hands-on time: 15 minutes

All right, we confess, homemade pizza tastes nothing like the pizza in the cardboard box your deliveryman brings you. Our homemade pizza has a crisp bottom, hot, gooey cheese, and the best-quality toppings, is made specifically to suit your tastes, and will probably be ready in less time than it takes the delivery guy to ring your doorbell. It's so easy to make, you won't need the number for Dom . . . uh . . . your local pizza parlor anymore.

YIELD: 2 PIZZA CRUSTS

3⅓ cups unbleached
  all-purpose flour
1 tablespoon salt
1 tablespoon sugar
1 (2¼ teaspoon) package active
  dried yeast
1⅓ cups warm water (110°F.)
1 tablespoon extra-virgin olive
  oil, plus more as needed
Cornmeal for dusting

Place a pizza stone or unglazed tiles on the bottom rack of your oven. Preheat the oven to 450°F.

Combine the flour and salt in the bowl of a food processor and pulse a few times to blend.

In a small bowl, combine the sugar, yeast, and warm water and stir. Allow to sit for about 3 or 4 minutes. When it is foamy on top, add the olive oil and stir.

Turn on the food processor and quickly pour the yeast mixture through the feed tube. Process until the dough forms a ball. Remove the dough from the processor and bring together into the shape of a ball. Place in a large bowl that has been brushed with olive oil. Roll the ball around in the bowl to coat it with oil. Cover the dough with plastic wrap or a clean dish towel and let it rest for 45 minutes or until it doubles in size.

Punch the dough down and cut it into two pieces.

(continued on next page)

With a rolling pin, roll one half of the dough out on a floured surface to your desired shape and thickness.

Sprinkle the cornmeal over the surface of a rimless baking sheet or a pizza peel. Place the rolled-out dough on top of the cornmeal. (If you are making the Pizza Margherita on the next page, stop here and continue with the directions in that recipe.)

Top with your desired sauce and toppings. Brush the rim of the dough with olive oil. Place the pizza in the hot oven, sliding the dough off the baking sheet or pizza peel and onto the hot stone or tiles.

Repeat the process with the second piece of dough, or save it for later use.

Bake the pizza for about 10 to 12 minutes, or until the sauce is bubbly and the crust is golden brown. Take the pizza out of the oven and let it rest for about 3 minutes before slicing.

NOTE: Baking pizza on a hot pizza stone or tiles provides the best result, and if you plan on making pizza every now and then, the pizza stone and peel are well worth the investment. If you don't own either of those tools, though, you can still make a good pizza. Prepare the pizza directly on top of a baking sheet, place it in the oven, and cook for 5 minutes, or until the pizza dough has stiffened a bit. Then slide the whole thing off the baking sheet and directly onto the oven rack and continue cooking until the bottom is crisp and the top is golden and bubbly.

TIP: You can use the Marinara Sauce recipe on page 193 for your pizza sauce, but we also like to use Pesto (page 194). If you are adding fresh tomatoes, make sure they are sliced thinly so they cook properly. Topping possibilities are endless. You can top pizza with almost anything, but we like to use a combination of grated mozzarella, fontina, and Parmigiano-Reggiano cheeses.

Pizza Margherita

Start to finish: 1 hour 25 minutes (includes the time to make the sauce and dough) • Hands-on time: 15 minutes

This popular version of pizza, created in 1890 on honor of Italy's Queen Margherita, is a basic, but lovely pizza. Any dish that relies so heavily on just a few ingredients needs those ingredients to be great, so now is not the time to skimp!

YIELD: 2 (12-INCH) PIZZAS

Basic Pizza Crust (page 203)

1 cup Marinara Sauce (page 193)

12 ounces fresh mozzarella, cut into 16 slices

12 fresh basil leaves

Extra-virgin olive oil

Prepare the pizza crust and marinara sauce as directed in the recipes.

Place a pizza stone or unglazed tiles on the bottom rack of your oven. Preheat the oven to 450°F.

Spread ½ cup of sauce onto the dough, leaving a ½-inch border around the surface. Top with 8 slices of mozzarella. Tear 6 of the basil leaves into small pieces and sprinkle over the pizza.

Brush the edges of the pizza with olive oil.

Bake for about 10 to 12 minutes, or until the sauce is bubbly and the crust is golden brown. Take the pizza out of the oven and let it rest for about 3 minutes before slicing.

Repeat with second piece of dough and remaining sauce, cheese, and basil.

Eggplant Parmesan

Start to finish: 2 hours (including time to make sauce) • Hands-on time: 55 minutes

Eggplant parmesan is so good, we could eat it every day. Crisp, light breading surrounding hot, almost creamy eggplant is what makes homemade eggplant parmesan so worth making. A far cry from the rubbery, greasy version sometimes seen in restaurants, this dish will reacquaint you with eggplant parmesan as it was meant to be.

YIELD: 4 TO 6 SERVINGS

2 cups Marinara Sauce
   (page 193)
2 medium-sized eggplants (about
   2 pounds), trimmed and cut
   crosswise into ½-inch rounds
1½ teaspoons salt, plus more
   as needed
1½ cups unbleached
   all-purpose flour
½ teaspoon freshly ground black
   pepper
3 cups fine fresh breadcrumbs,
   lightly toasted
1¼ cups finely grated
   Parmigiano-Reggiano cheese
4 large eggs, lightly beaten
Vegetable or canola oil
2 cups shredded
   mozzarella cheese

Prepare the Marinara Sauce as directed in the recipe.

Preheat the oven to 350°F.

Toss the eggplant with 1 teaspoon of the salt in a colander set over a bowl, then let it stand 30 minutes to drain. Remove the eggplant from the colander, rinse it, and pat it dry with a paper towel. Set aside.

Combine the remaining ½ teaspoon salt, the flour, and pepper in a shallow bowl. Combine the breadcrumbs and ¾ cup of the Parmigiano-Reggiano cheese in another shallow bowl. Create an assembly line: starting with eggplant slices, then flour, eggs, breadcrumbs, and waxed paper. Dredge the eggplant slices in the flour, shake off the excess, then dip them in the eggs, letting the excess drip off, then dredge them in the breadcrumbs until they are evenly coated. Lay them side-by-side on the waxed paper.

In a large sauté pan, heat ½ inch of oil over medium-high heat until it shimmers. Carefully add 4 or 5 eggplant slices (don't overcrowd) and cook until they are light golden brown on both sides, about 2 minutes per side. Remove from the oil, drain on paper towels, and reseason with salt. Repeat with remaining eggplant.

On a baking sheet, lay out the 8 largest slices of eggplant. Smear a heaping tablespoon of the Marinara Sauce over each slice and sprinkle a heaping tablespoon of mozzarella on top, then a little Parmigiano-Reggiano cheese. Repeat the layering process, finishing with the Parmigiano-Reggiano cheese, until all of the ingredients have been used.

Bake for about 15 minutes, or until the top of each little stack is golden brown and bubbly.

Serve hot with a side of Marinara Sauce and spaghetti.

Chicken Parmesan

Start to finish: 2 hours (including time to make sauce) • Hands-on time: 55 minutes

Not many dishes can boast being crispy, juicy, and gooey all at the same time, but somehow chicken parmesan pulls it off. With a golden, crusty exterior and a moist, perfectly cooked interior, all slathered in delicious sauce and bubbly cheese, it's no wonder this dish is a restaurant favorite. Although we love it served with a side of pasta, it's also great in sandwiches wedged inside a warm, crusty Italian roll.

YIELD: 4 TO 6 SERVINGS

2 cups Marinara Sauce
   (page 193)
6 boneless chicken breast halves
Salt and freshly ground
   black pepper
1½ cups unbleached
   all-purpose flour
3 cups fine fresh breadcrumbs,
   lightly toasted
1¼ cups finely grated
   Parmigiano-Reggiano cheese
4 large eggs, lightly beaten
Vegetable or canola oil
2 cups shredded
   mozzarella cheese

Prepare the Marinara Sauce as directed in the recipe.

Preheat the oven to 350°F.

Using a flat meat pounder or a rolling pin, gently pound the chicken breasts between 2 sheets of plastic wrap to ½-inch thickness. Season each side with salt and pepper.

Place the flour and eggs in two shallow bowls.

In another shallow bowl, combine the breadcrumbs and ¾ cup of the Parmigiano-Reggiano cheese.

Create an assembly line: starting with chicken, then flour, eggs, breadcrumbs, and waxed paper. Dredge the chicken fillets in the flour, shake off the excess, then dip them in the eggs, letting the excess drip off, then dredge them in the breadcrumbs until they are evenly coated. Lay them side-by-side on the waxed paper.

In a large sauté pan, heat ½ inch of oil over medium-high heat until it shimmers. Carefully add the chicken, 3 pieces at a time, and cook, turning over once, until it is golden brown and just cooked through, about 6 minutes per batch. Remove from the oil and drain on paper towels.

Transfer the chicken to a baking sheet. Ladle some of the tomato sauce on top of each chicken piece, and sprinkle with the mozzarella and Parmigiano-Reggiano.

Bake for 15 minutes or until the top of each is golden brown and bubbly and the chicken is cooked through. Serve hot with a side of Marinara Sauce and spaghetti.

Veal Saltimbocca

SAUTÉED VEAL WITH PROSCIUTTO AND SAGE IN A WHITE WINE SAUCE

Start to finish: 25 minutes • Hands-on time: 25 minutes

While Americans often name dishes based on what's inside them or how they're made, the Italians take a different view, often naming them for how they make you feel. For instance, saltimbocca *literally means "jump in the mouth," which is a perfect name for this dish, because the combination of salty prosciutto, earthy sage, and rich, but slightly acidic wine sauce make you want to put one bite after another in your mouth without hesitation. That's* amore!

YIELD: 4 SERVINGS

8 (2-ounce) veal cutlets,
   thinly sliced
Salt and freshly ground
   black pepper
8 thin slices prosciutto
8 fresh sage leaves,
   plus more for garnish
1 cup unbleached
   all-purpose flour
2 tablespoons extra-virgin
   olive oil
2 tablespoons unsalted butter
½ cup dry white wine
Lemon wedges, for serving

> **VARIATION:** If veal is not available, or just not your favorite, feel free to substitute chicken or turkey cutlets.

Using a flat meat pounder or a rolling pin, gently pound the cutlets between two sheets of plastic wrap until they are ¼-inch thick. Remove the plastic wrap and season each cutlet with salt and pepper. Lay a slice of prosciutto on top of each cutlet, then place a sage leaf in the center of the prosciutto. Insert a toothpick in each cutlet to secure the prosciutto and sage.

Put the flour in a large, shallow platter. Dredge the veal in the flour, shaking off the excess.

Heat the oil and 1 tablespoon of the butter in a large skillet over medium heat. Cook the veal in batches, prosciutto side down first. Cook for 3 minutes, until golden, then turn the veal over and cook for 2 minutes. Transfer to a serving platter, remove the toothpicks, and keep warm.

Pour the wine into the pan and deglaze over high heat, scraping up any brown bits stuck to the bottom. Boil until the pan juices reduce and are thickened, about 2 minutes. Remove the pan from the heat and swirl in the remaining tablespoon of butter. Pour the sauce over the veal and garnish with sage leaves and lemon wedges. Serve immediately.

TIP: In this dish, the prosciutto is cooked and combined with other strong flavors, so spending money on the wonderful, but very expensive prosciutto de Parma is not worth it. Save that for when prosciutto is the lone star of the dish and use a domestic variety for this dish.

Osso Buco

Start to finish: 3 hours • Hands-on time: 1 hour

If you want to impress friends and family, these veal shanks, braised in a flavorful tomato stock, packed with vegetables, and spiked with orange zest, are the dish to serve. Great for entertaining, osso buco is best when made the day before and reheated just before serving. Gremolata, a powerhouse mixture of finely chopped garlic, parsley, and lemon zest, is generously sprinkled on top. Served along the traditional accompaniment of Risotto Milanese (pages 190-191) this sophisticated braise is fit for a king. This version was inspired by a recipe from one our favorite cooks, Anne Willan.

YIELD: 4 TO 6 SERVINGS

2 tablespoons olive oil

2 tablespoons unsalted butter

4 veal shanks, cut 3 inches thick

Salt and pepper

½ cup unbleached all-purpose flour

1 medium onion, finely chopped

2 carrots, finely chopped

2 stalks celery, finely chopped

1½ cups dry white wine

1 (14.5-ounce) can whole tomatoes, chopped, their juices reserved

2 garlic cloves, chopped

2 cups chicken stock, plus more if needed

Grated zest of 1 orange

GREMOLATA

3 garlic cloves

⅓ cup chopped flat-leaf parsley

Grated zest of 2 lemons

Preheat the oven to 350°F.

Heat the oil and butter over medium-high heat in an ovenproof, heavy-bottomed sauté or frying pan large enough to fit all the veal in a single layer.

Season the veal with salt and pepper to taste. Place the flour on a plate and dredge the veal shanks in the flour, patting to remove the excess. Add half the veal to the pan and brown, for 2 to 3 minutes per side. Remove to a platter and brown the remaining veal.

Lower the heat to medium and add the onion, carrots, and celery. Sauté until golden, 5 to 7 minutes. Add the wine and cook until reduced by half, about 3 to 5 minutes. Stir in the tomatoes and their juices, and add the garlic and stock. Season with salt and pepper.

Return the veal to the pan. The liquid should come at least halfway up the sides, so add more stock if necessary. Cover the pan and bring it to a boil.

Transfer the pan to the oven and cook for 1½ to 2 hours, or until the meat is nearly falling from the bone. Remove from the oven, add the orange zest, and taste the sauce to see if more seasoning is necessary.

To prepare the gremolata: Place the garlic, parsley, and lemon zest in a pile on a cutting board. Chop them together until they are finely chopped. The gremolata can be served separately from the osso buco, for guests to help themselves, or sprinkled on the dish just before it goes to the table.

> MAKE AHEAD: The osso buco can be cooked, cooled, and kept covered in the refrigerator for up to 3 days. Reheat on top of the stove.

Shrimp Scampi

Start to finish: 20 minutes • Hands-on time: 20 minutes

Carla has fond childhood memories of vacations to Florida where her family often dined at an Italian restaurant on the Intracoastal Waterway. One step into the restaurant, and they would be accosted by the scent of garlic, butter, and briny shrimp, in that order. Someone in the family would always order shrimp scampi, only to spend the entire meal defending their plate from the marauding forks of the rest of the family. Your family is sure to encounter the same phenomenon with this recipe.

YIELD: 4 SERVINGS

3 tablespoons unsalted butter

2 tablespoons extra-virgin
   olive oil

6 garlic cloves, minced
   (2 tablespoons)

1½ pounds large shrimp (about
   24), peeled and deveined

¾ teaspoon salt

¼ teaspoon freshly ground
   black pepper

½ cup chopped flat-leaf
   parsley leaves

Grated zest of 1 lemon
   (1½ teaspoons)

1½ tablespoons fresh lemon juice

¼ teaspoon red pepper flakes

In a large skillet set over medium-low heat, warm the butter and olive oil. When the butter is melted, add the garlic and sauté for 1 minute, making sure it does not brown. Add the shrimp, salt, and pepper, and sauté until the shrimp have just turned pink, about 3 minutes, stirring often. Remove from the heat; add the parsley, lemon zest, lemon juice, and red pepper flakes. Toss to combine, and serve.

VARIATION: Scampi with Linguini: When the shrimp are just done, remove them from the pan with a slotted spoon. Add one pound of cooked linguini to the pan and toss to coat with the sauce. Continue to cook with the sauce for 1 minute. If the sauce is too dry, add a ladleful of hot pasta water to thin it out. Transfer the pasta to a platter and spoon the shrimp and any accumulated juices onto the linguini.

Tiramisu

Start to finish: 4 hours 30 minutes • Hands-on time: 30 minutes

Italian for "pick me up," tiramisu has become one of the most popular desserts not just in Italy, but all over the world. Its beauty lies in its simplicity and its contrasting flavors. The cool, rich custard layered with espresso-soaked ladyfingers is a marriage made in heaven. Although there are a million different versions of this recipe, all include mascarpone, a rich, sexy Italian cousin to American cream cheese. In our recipe, we fold the cheese into light zabaglione custard, which is made by whisking egg yolks, sugar, and sweet Marsala wine over simmering water to make a flavorful and light foam. This is combined with whipped cream and spread over layers of the soaked ladyfingers. Despite the rich ingredients, this dish is surprisingly light and makes an elegant, stress-free dessert that can be made well ahead of serving time.

YIELD: 6 TO 8 SERVINGS

6 egg yolks

½ cup sugar

⅓ cup sweet Marsala wine

½ pound mascarpone cheese,
    at room temperature

1 cup heavy cream

2¼ cups brewed espresso

⅓ cup brandy

1 teaspoon vanilla extract

48 Savoiardi (crisp Italian
    ladyfingers)

2 ounces dark chocolate,
    grated (¾ cup)

To make the zabaglione: Combine the eggs, sugar, and wine in a large, heat-proof bowl. Set the bowl over a pot of simmering water, making sure that the bottom of the bowl does not touch the water (otherwise, you run the risk of scrambling the eggs). Whisk constantly until the mixture has thickened and doubled in volume, about 6 minutes. Remove from the heat, and with a mixer set on medium-high speed, continue to whip the zabaglione until it cools to room temperature.

In a small bowl, stir the mascarpone with a spoon until it is soft and smooth. Whisk a quarter of the zabaglione into the mascarpone to lighten it. Gently fold the mascarpone into the remaining zabaglione.

In another bowl, using a mixer, whip the cream to soft peaks. Fold the whipped cream into the mascarpone mixture.

In a shallow bowl, combine the espresso, brandy, and vanilla. Using a quick 1, 2 count, dip each ladyfinger in the espresso mixture, turning to coat it entirely, and arrange in a single layer in a 13 x 9-inch glass baking dish. (Do not soak the cookies, or they will become too moist and fall apart.)

Spread half the mascarpone cream evenly over the dipped ladyfingers. Sprinkle with half the chocolate. Repeat with a second layer of dipped ladyfingers and the remaining mascarpone cream. Sprinkle with the remaining chocolate.

Cover and refrigerate for at least 4 hours before serving.

(continued on next page)

VARIATION: This dish is best when made with the hard Savoiardi cookies, usually found in the cookie section of quality grocery stores. The French version of ladyfingers, which are soft and cakelike, are often found in the bakery section of the grocery store. They soak up more liquid and don't make for as nice a texture in the finished dish. That said, you can certainly make a worthwhile tiramisu with the soft ladyfingers, or even with slices of sponge or pound cake. Just make sure to dab them with a pastry brush rather than dipping them in the espresso mixture.

MAKE AHEAD: Tiramisu can be assembled completely and kept covered in the refrigerator up to 1 day ahead.

Gelato

Start to finish: 24 hours • Hands-on time: 30 minutes

We pity the poor souls who have never eaten gelato while strolling the streets of Siena under starry Tuscan skies. Even if you've never had the chance to eat gelato in any Italian city, this recipe will take you there in spirit if not in body. Gelato contains less fat than most ice creams, and much more flavor. Try to use the best ingredients and you will be rewarded with a texture and flavor straight from heaven.

YIELD: 1 QUART

2 cups whole milk

1 vanilla bean, split lengthwise

Pinch of salt

2 cups half-and-half

1 cup sugar

8 large egg yolks

Combine the milk, vanilla bean, and salt in a large, heavy-bottomed saucepan and cook over medium heat until the milk steams. Remove the bean from the milk and scrape down the length of it with the back of a knife to remove the vanilla seeds. Add the beans and pod back to the milk, cover, and let the milk steep for 15 minutes. Remove the pod from the milk. Add the half-and-half and stir to combine.

In a large bowl, combine the sugar and egg yolks. Whisk until the yolks are light and lemon-colored. Slowly whisk the milk mixture into the yolks. Return the custard mixture to the pan and cook over medium heat, stirring constantly, until the custard thickens and coats the back of a spoon, about 3 minutes. Don't let it boil or the eggs will curdle.

Pour the custard into a bowl and set it in a larger bowl filled with ice water. Stir until the custard cools. Remove the bowl from the ice bath, cover, and refrigerate overnight.

Process in an ice cream freezer according to the manufacturer's directions. Transfer to a container and freeze for 2 hours before serving.

The gelato will be best if served a few hours after churning. After freezing overnight, it will become hard to scoop.

VARIATIONS

Chocolate Gelato (gelato al cioccolato): Increase the sugar to 1½ cups and add ½ cup cocoa powder to the eggs and sugar. After cooking the custard, remove from heat and immediately stir in 3 ounces chopped bittersweet chocolate. Continue with the main recipe.

Pistachio Gelato (gelato al pistacchio): Coarsely grind 2 cups natural (green) pistachios in a food processor. Remove ½ cup and finely grind the remaining nuts. Heat the milk, half-and-half, and vanilla together with the finely ground nuts over medium heat until the milk steams. Remove the pan from the heat and cover. Let the milk steep for 30 minutes. Strain the milk and continue with the recipe. Add the chopped pistachios to the gelato right before it finishes churning. Freeze as directed in the recipe.

Hazelnut Gelato (gelato alla nocciola): Finely grind 2 cups skinned hazelnuts in a food processor. Heat the milk, half-and-half, and vanilla together with the ground nuts over medium heat until the milk steams. Remove the pan from the heat and cover. Let the milk steep for 30 minutes. Strain the milk and continue with the recipe.

Lemon Gelato (gelato al limone): Heat the milk, half-and-half, and vanilla along with the grated zest of 2 lemons until the milk steams. Remove the pan from the heat and cover. Let the milk steep for 30 minutes. Strain the milk and continue with the recipe.

Cannoli

Start to finish: 2 hours • Hands-on time: 1 hour

Who can forget the famous scene in The Godfather when, right after killing a man in the front seat of a car, one man turns to the other and says, "Leave the gun . . . take the cannoli"? Although we don't advocate killing for cannoli, if it were these cannoli and someone tried to take them . . . we might have grounds for murder. Often store-bought cannoli have a hard, tough shell and a too-sweet, bland filling. This shell is light and delicate, but not hard to work with, and the filling is rich and creamy with hints of orange and chocolate. These must be filled just before serving or the shells will become soggy.

SHELLS

1½ cups unbleached
    all-purpose flour

¼ teaspoon cinnamon

2 teaspoons sugar

½ teaspoon salt

1 teaspoon unsweetened
    cocoa powder

2 tablespoons unsalted butter

⅓ cup sweet Marsala wine

FILLING

1 pound firm whole milk ricotta
    cheese, drained 1 hour in a
    cheesecloth-lined sieve

¾ cup confectioners' sugar, plus
    more for dusting

2 teaspoons vanilla

4 tablespoons chopped candied
    orange peel, purchased or
    homemade (recipe follows)

¼ cup mini chocolate chips

ASSEMBLY

3 to 4 cups vegetable oil, for frying

1 egg white, lightly beaten

To make the shells: Combine the flour, cinnamon, sugar, salt, and cocoa powder in the bowl of a food processor. Pulse once to combine. Add the butter and pulse 3 or 4 times, until the mixture resembles coarse crumbs. Add the wine and pulse just to combine.

Remove the dough from the bowl and shape it into a ball. (The dough will be very firm.) Wrap the dough in plastic and let it rest at room temperature for 1 hour.

To make the filling: Combine all the filling ingredients in a large mixing bowl. Spoon into a pastry bag with an open tip and refrigerate.

Heat 3 inches of oil to 350°F. in a large, heavy pot.

To assemble: Divide the dough into 4 pieces. Working with one piece at a time and keeping the others covered with plastic wrap, roll the dough with a rolling pin to the thickness of a dime. Using a cookie cutter, cut 4-inch circles from the dough (see tip). Roll the rolling pin over each dough circle, once in one direction and once in the opposite direction to create a slightly oval shape.

Lay a metal cannoli mold (see note) on the dough lengthwise and brush one edge of the dough lightly with egg white. Wrap the dough around the mold by pulling the sides up and around so they touch in the middle. The egg white should work as glue to keep the edges together. (Don't get any egg white on the metal form itself, as this will make it more difficult to remove the shell from the mold when it is cooked.)

Gently drop 3 or 4 of the cannoli shells, still wrapped around the molds, into the hot oil and fry until dark golden brown, about 2 to 3 minutes. Transfer to paper towels with a slotted spoon. Repeat with the remaining shells.

When the cannoli are cool enough to touch, carefully twist the molds away from the shells. They will be hot, so be careful. The shells should come loose easily.

Just before serving, pipe the filling into the cannoli shells and dust with confectioners' sugar.

NOTE: Cannoli molds are metal tubes, about 5 or 6 inches in length. They are essential for making cannoli shells and can be purchased at most specialty kitchen shops.

TIP: Cannoli dough needs to be rolled quite thin. You can use a rolling pin to do this, but the job is made easier if you use a pasta rolling machine. Pat the dough into a rectangle and run it through the roller, starting at the widest setting and continuing to run it through each setting until it is thin enough (on our machine that is setting 6). The width should be 4 to 5 inches.

If you don't have the time to make the shells yourself, you can buy premade shells at the grocery store. They are not nearly as light and delicate as those you make yourself, but they still taste great.

CANDIED ORANGE PEEL

Start to finish: 1 hour

Hands-on time: 40 minutes

YIELD: 24 (2 X 3-INCH) PIECES

6 thick-skinned organic Valencia
    or navel oranges

3 cups sugar

1 cup light corn syrup

Cut the tops and bottoms off the oranges and score them into quarters, cutting only into the peel and not into the fruit. Pull the skin off the oranges in four segments. Put the orange peel in a large saucepan with cold water to cover, and bring to a boil over high heat. Pour off the water, cover with cold water, and boil again. Repeat this process 4 more times. Remove the orange peel from the pan.

Combine 2 cups of the sugar, the corn syrup, and ½ cup water in a large, heavy-bottomed pan and bring to a boil over medium-high heat. Add the orange peels and simmer over low heat for 20 minutes. Remove the peel from the syrup and lay out on a rack to dry. When cool enough to handle, roll the peels in the remaining 1 cup sugar. Store in an airtight container with the extra sugar.

❧JAPANESE❧

JAPANESE FOOD MAY NOT BE AS FAMILIAR to most Americans as, say, Italian, but sushi has certainly made its mark on our palates and taught us how the clean, fresh flavors of Japan's cuisine can provide a tasty and healthy backdrop to our everyday diets. Freshness of ingredients is key and the Asian discipline and attention to detail are evident in every recipe. Say sayonara to high-fat and over-processed fast food, we want a bento box for lunch!

About thirty years ago, sushi bars started popping up in the big cities and people loved them. The idea of sitting at a bar and watching a man with a very long, very sharp knife slice and dice your meal with the beauty and artistry of a painter with a brush captured the American public's imagination. This was not just a meal, it was a show, and it taught us to appreciate how a few incredibly fresh, high-quality ingredients could be satisfying on their own, unadorned with complicated sauces or other high-fat preparations.

This love affair with sushi sparked an interest in Japanese cuisine in general, and we as a country became familiar with terms like tempura and edamame. We learned to eat with chopsticks (you know, those things we played with at Chinese restaurants as children, until the waitperson brought us our forks) and drink sake (we were especially fast learners as we recall).

The beauty of Japanese cuisine is that all these things were taught to us in the most gracious way possible, which is the Japanese way. When we dropped our *gyoza* into a bowl of dipping sauce, splattering the brown liquid across the table, a gentle, quiet waitress would appear out of nowhere with a cloth to quickly clean up the mess. When we lost our piece of sushi under the table (it happens), an observant sushi chef discreetly turned his back to chuckle. Okay, so we've had a few "oops" moments at Japanese restaurants. We're much more adept now. A wise man once said that learning is not possible without a little spilt soy sauce. Well, maybe we said that, but you get the point.

Menu planning is fairly simple in Japan. As is true in many Asian countries, the center of a Japanese meal is white rice. Nothing else served during a meal is considered a main dish. Fish, meat, vegetables, and pickles are all seen as side dishes, meant to compliment one another. Soup, often miso soup, is also nearly always served. The simplest Japanese meal, for example, consists of soup, rice, and one accompanying side dish, and perhaps a pickled vegetable.

The most common meal, however, consists of soup, rice, and three side dishes, each of varying tastes and textures. The three side dishes are usually raw fish (sashimi), a grilled dish, and a simmered, steamed, or deep-fried dish. The meal often finishes with fresh fruit and green tea.

A Japanese meal begins and ends with sentiments of respect and gratitude. At the beginning, one would say, *Itadakimasu*, which is a polite word meaning, "I humbly receive this food." This expresses thanks to the person who prepared the food. At the end of the meal, the Japanese say, *Gochiso-sama*, which means, "I have feasted," an expression meant to give thanks for the delicious meal. We are always thankful when we are eating wonderfully fresh ingredients prepared with beauty and grace, as is the Japanese custom.

Here is a menu to get you started with Japanese cuisine in your own kitchen.

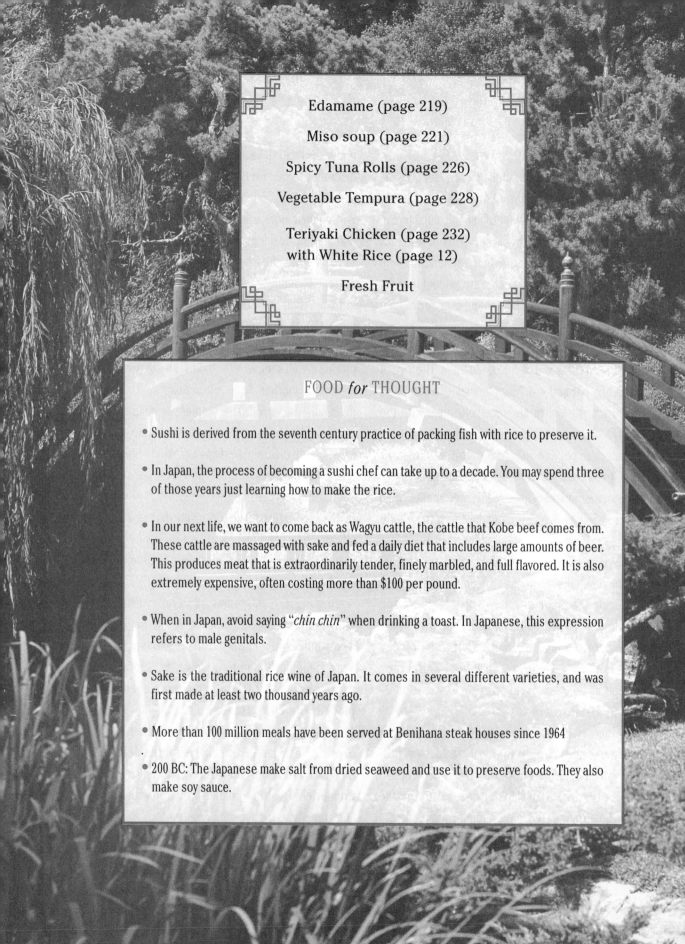

Edamame (page 219)

Miso soup (page 221)

Spicy Tuna Rolls (page 226)

Vegetable Tempura (page 228)

Teriyaki Chicken (page 232)
with White Rice (page 12)

Fresh Fruit

FOOD *for* THOUGHT

- Sushi is derived from the seventh century practice of packing fish with rice to preserve it.

- In Japan, the process of becoming a sushi chef can take up to a decade. You may spend three of those years just learning how to make the rice.

- In our next life, we want to come back as Wagyu cattle, the cattle that Kobe beef comes from. These cattle are massaged with sake and fed a daily diet that includes large amounts of beer. This produces meat that is extraordinarily tender, finely marbled, and full flavored. It is also extremely expensive, often costing more than $100 per pound.

- When in Japan, avoid saying "*chin chin*" when drinking a toast. In Japanese, this expression refers to male genitals.

- Sake is the traditional rice wine of Japan. It comes in several different varieties, and was first made at least two thousand years ago.

- More than 100 million meals have been served at Benihana steak houses since 1964
.

- 200 BC: The Japanese make salt from dried seaweed and use it to preserve foods. They also make soy sauce.

Edamame BOILED AND SALTED SOY BEANS

Start to finish: 15 minutes • Hands-on time: 5 minutes

Sit down at an American bar and you'll find a bowl of peanuts. Sidle up to a bar in Japan and you'll find edamame. The two things have a lot in common: both are thought to be good for you, in moderation, and both are addictive. Try to eat just one. Oh yes, and one more thing . . . they're both salty, which makes you thirsty, which adds up to higher bar bills.

YIELD: 6 SERVINGS

1 tablespoon salt

1 (1-pound) bag frozen edamame

Kosher salt

Bring a large pot of water to boil and stir in the 1 tablespoon salt. Have a bowl of ice and cold water ready.

Cook the frozen edamame in boiling water until bright green, 2 to 3 minutes. Immediately drain and place the edamame in the ice water. Drain the edamame well.

Just before serving, toss the edamame with kosher salt to taste.

> MAKE AHEAD: Edamame may be prepared 4 hours ahead and kept in a bowl, covered with a damp paper towel and plastic wrap, at cool room temperature.

Gyoza PORK AND CABBAGE DUMPLINGS

Start to finish: 2 hours • Hands-on time: 2 hours

A cousin to the Chinese pot sticker, gyoza are Japanese dumplings that have a slightly thicker wrapper, which can be found at most Asian markets. Much like pot stickers, these pork-and-cabbage-filled gyoza are typically pan-fried for crispy bottoms, then steamed right in the same pan until tender, and served with a sesame-soy dipping sauce.

YIELD: 60 DUMPLINGS

DUMPLINGS

1 pound ground pork

1 cup finely chopped cabbage

1 garlic clove, minced

½ cup finely chopped green onion

2 teaspoons toasted Asian
    sesame oil

1 tablespoon dry sherry

2 tablespoons soy sauce

3 garlic cloves, minced
    (1 tablespoon)

60 gyoza wrappers

2 tablespoons vegetable oil,
    for frying

DIPPING SAUCE

¼ cup seasoned rice vinegar

⅓ cup soy sauce

1 garlic clove, minced

1 (1-inch knob) fresh ginger,
    grated (2 teaspoons)

2 teaspoons toasted Asian
    sesame oil

To make the dumplings: Combine the pork, cabbage, garlic, green onion, sesame oil, sherry, soy sauce, and ginger in a bowl. Using your hands, mix the ingredients well.

Open the gyoza wrappers and keep them covered with a damp towel. Place one wrapper on a work surface. With a finger dipped in water, dampen the edges of the wrapper with water to help it adhere. Place about 1 heaping teaspoon of the filling into the center of each wrapper and fold it into a half-moon-shaped pouch. Make 3 or 4 pleats at each edge to gather the dough around the filling, then pinch around the top of the dumpling to seal it tightly. Arrange the dumplings on a parchment-lined sheet pan. Continue with the remaining filling and wrappers.

To make the sauce: Combine the vinegar, soy sauce, garlic, ginger, and sesame oil in a small bowl.

In a large sauté pan with a lid, heat 1 tablespoon of vegetable oil over medium-high heat. Place the dumplings in the pan so they aren't touching and cook until they are nicely browned on the bottoms about 3 to 5 minutes. Add ½ cup of water to the pan, cover, and steam the dumplings for about 3 minutes, or until firm and the pork is cooked through. Repeat with the remaining dumplings.

MAKE AHEAD: The filling can be made 8 hours ahead and kept in the refrigerator. The dumplings can be made up to one month ahead. Freeze them, uncooked, in a single layer on a baking sheet, then transfer them to a freezer bag. Cook them directly from the freezer, adding on another 2 to 3 minutes to the cooking time. The sauce can be made up to 5 days ahead and kept covered in the refrigerator.

Miso Soup

Start to finish: 20 minutes • Hands-on time: 20 minutes

If you eat at a Japanese restaurant, you will probably be served miso soup to start your meal. At its base is dashi, a simple soup stock flavored with kelp and dried bonito flakes (a type of tuna). Ichiban dashi is fundamental to Japanese cooking. Ichiban means "first" in Japanese and Ichiban dashi is the stock that results from the first brewing of the ingredients. It's used in clear soups. The first dashi can then be used again, adding more kelp for a second brewed stock that is considered a less refined version of Ichiban dashi. Miso, a salty, fermented paste made of soybeans, is also added. Of the few different varieties of miso available, we've chosen sweet white miso for this recipe. It is less salty than other types.

YIELD: 4 TO 6 SERVINGS,
6 CUPS DASHI

ICHIBAN DASHI

4 (6-inch) squares of *kombu*
   (dried kelp)

1 cup dried *katsuobushi*
   (bonito fish flakes)

MISO SOUP

2 tablespoons instant *wakame*
   (sea vegetable)

5 tablespoons sweet white
   miso paste

½ pound firm tofu,
   cut into ¾-inch cubes

¼ cup chopped green onion

To make the dashi: Line a strainer with cheesecloth and set it over a saucepan.

Wipe the surface of the kombu with a slightly damp kitchen towel, removing dirt and sand. Combine the kombu and 6 cups of water in a pot over medium-low heat and bring to a simmer. (Do not boil, as the kombu can become slimy and unpleasant.)

Remove the kombu once it has risen to the surface. Immediately add the katsuobushi. After 10 seconds, remove the pot from the heat and skim off any foam. When the katsuobushi sinks to the bottom of the pot, pour the mixture through the cheesecloth into the saucepan.

To make the miso soup: Soak the wakame in cold water for 5 minutes, then drain and set aside.

Bring 4 cups of the dashi to a boil over medium-high heat. Reserve the rest of the dashi for later use. Lower the heat, add the miso paste, and stir to dissolve. Add the tofu and bring to a simmer. Remove from the heat and add the green onion and wakame. Serve hot.

> MAKE AHEAD: Dashi can be made up to 4 days ahead and kept covered in the refrigerator. It can also be frozen for up to 1 month.

Sushi and Sashimi

Good sushi is a thing of beauty. Its simple, clean flavors are equaled only by its elegant appearance. No other food is as much a feast for the eyes, making sushi chefs, in our eyes at least, as much artists as chefs. Anyone who has spent time sitting at a sushi bar is aware that being a sushi chef is serious business. Knowing everything there is to know about fish and wielding a knife with the accuracy of a brain surgeon, all while listening to your sushi bar patrons' orders as they finish one bite and look for the next, are not skills that can be attained overnight. That said, there is no way for us to make you a sushi chef in a few short paragraphs, but we can teach you enough of the basics to get you started on the road to making good homemade sushi.

The best advice we can give you is to spend some time at a sushi bar. Eating sushi out will familiarize you with what it looks and tastes like. This will help you feel more comfortable when you go to make it. Once you become comfortable with the idea of sushi, you move on to the next and perhaps most important step in making sushi: buying the fish.

There are a number of things you need to know to buy the best fish for sushi, but the first of these is you must know your fish purveyor. Because sushi is often made up of raw fish, the potential for food-borne illness is great. Buying fish—whether it's for sushi or not—from someone who knows what they are selling is the best way to ensure that you buy high-quality fish that is as fresh as possible. If you are accustomed to buying fish at a large grocery store where it's all sold in plastic-covered Styrofoam trays, you may have a problem. There should be a fish counter and you should be able to find out from the person behind the fish counter what type of fish it is, where the fish is from, when it came in, and if it was frozen previously (it happens), when it was thawed. If you're lucky, he or she will also be able to tell you the best way to cook your fish.

It's also critical to know what you're looking for when you buy fish for sushi. Tell your fishmonger that it must be sushi-grade, which, in the United States, typically means the fish was flash frozen almost immediately after being caught. Often it will be sold still frozen in ½-pound blocks. Thaw the fish in the refrigerator, never at room temperature. Keep the fish cold at all times. Cold or even partially frozen fish is also easier to slice thinly. The fish should never have a fishy smell. Good, fresh seafood doesn't really have an odor.

Now, let's explore the different types of sushi.

SASHIMI

Sashimi consists of fresh raw seafood, thinly sliced into pieces about 1 inch wide by 1½ inches long and ¼ inch thick. It is served with soy sauce, wasabi paste, and pickled ginger.

NIGIRI SUSHI (FINGER SUSHI)

Nigiri sushi is simply made of sushi rice pressed into the shape of a finger and topped, most often, with a bit of wasabi paste and a thin slice of fresh raw fish or cooked shrimp.

To make your own *nigiri* sushi, slice the sushi-grade fish of your choice (tuna, yellowtail, and salmon are popular) into thin slices, about 2 inches long. Put a little wasabi paste on one side of the fish. Moisten your hands with water and place a small ball of sushi rice (recipe follows) in your palm, about 2 tablespoons. Form a slender oval with the rice. Press just firmly enough to get the rice to stick together. If the rice is too tight, it will be dense and unpleasant to eat. Press the fish, wasabi-side-down, onto the rice.

TIP: Cooked, butterflied shrimp are also a nice choice for a nigiri topping. When dipping your nigiri sushi in soy sauce, dip the fish first. The rice tends to fall apart in the soy sauce, making it hard to hold onto with your chopsticks.

MAKI SUSHI (SUSHI ROLLS)

Anyone who has ever eaten a California roll has eaten *maki* sushi. They are the type of sushi that has rice and fillings on the inside and nori, a seaweed wrapper, on the outside. There are inside-out rolls and hand rolls, but for the purposes of this discussion, we are focusing on the basic sushi roll.

To make your own maki sushi, lay a bamboo mat (used for rolling sushi) on a work surface so that the slats run horizontally. Put a piece of nori (dried seaweed) shiny side down on the mat, with a long side facing you. With dampened hands, spread ¾ cup sushi rice (recipe follows) onto the nori, leaving a 1½-inch border along the top edge.

Filling choices are largely up to you (a few specific recipes follow), but typically they include thin strips of sushi-grade raw fish, cucumber, avocado, crab, asparagus, cooked shrimp, or any combination of the above. Once you've chosen your filling or fillings and have lined them horizontally across the width of the rice, grasp the nori at the edge closest to you. (Don't overfill your sushi. Look at the following recipes below for an idea of quantities.) Lift the nori and the mat slightly, and roll evenly and tightly away from you, pressing down slightly with each quarter turn. Seal the roll with a drop of water on the far edge of the nori, press the seam closed, and transfer the roll to a cutting board. Using a wet, sharp knife, slice the roll in half, then into 6 equal pieces.

Sushi Rice

Start to finish: 1 hour 15 minutes •Hands-on time: 20 minutes

Sushi rice is a short-grain, polished white rice that has been steamed and tossed with a sweet-salty vinegar mixture. In the process of tossing the rice, you also need to fan it with a piece of cardboard, a magazine, or anything else lying around the house that will work as a large fan. This cools the rice quickly but avoids overcooking. Enlist the help of a friend; it makes it a lot easier.

YIELD: ABOUT 8 CUPS

⅓ cup rice wine vinegar

3 tablespoons sugar

1½ teaspoons salt

3 cups short-grain white rice
   or sushi rice

Combine the vinegar, sugar, and salt in a small saucepan set over low heat. Stir gently and cook to dissolve the salt and sugar. Cool to room temperature.

Place the rice in a large pot, or the inner pot of a rice cooker, and rinse with cold water as follows: Cover with water, let the rice settle, and carefully pour the cloudy water off. Repeat this process 3 or 4 times, or until the water runs clear. After you've drained the water from the final rinse, add 3 cups water and allow the rice to soak for 30 minutes.

Cook the rice, in the 3 cups water, on the stovetop or in an electric rice cooker according to package directions.

While the rice is still warm, transfer it to a large nonreactive (glass or stainless steel) bowl. Drizzle the vinegar mixture over the rice and gently fold it in, fanning as you fold. Make sure you don't crush the rice during this process. Continue folding and fanning until the rice cools to room temperature. Using a rice paddle or wooden spoon, gently break up and spread out the rice. Keep the rice covered with a damp cloth at room temperature until you are ready to make sushi. Do not refrigerate.

MAKE AHEAD: Rice can be made up to 4 hours ahead of time and left covered with a damp towel at room temperature.

California Rolls

Start to finish: 1 hour 30 minutes (includes time to make the rice) • Hands-on time: 35 minutes

One of the most popular choices among the "Eeew, icky raw fish!" crowd, this crab, avocado, and cucumber roll, created in the seventies in Los Angeles, is credited for easing Americans into the idea of sushi by giving them a slightly less "exotic" option.

YIELD: 36 PIECES, FOR 6 TO 8 SERVINGS

4½ cups Sushi Rice (opposite)

1 avocado, halved lengthwise, pitted, peeled, and cut lengthwise into ⅛-inch slices

1 tablespoon fresh lemon juice

6 (8 x 7-inch) sheets nori (roasted dried seaweed)

2 tablespoons wasabi paste, plus more for serving

2 frozen Alaskan king crab legs, thawed, shelled, and thick sections halved lengthwise; or ¾ pound frozen Alaskan king crabmeat, thawed and drained

½ cucumber, peeled and cut into matchsticks

Soy sauce, for serving

Pickled ginger, for serving

Prepare the sushi rice as directed in the recipe.

In a small bowl, combine the avocado with the lemon juice.

Lay a bamboo mat (used for rolling sushi and other foods) on a work surface so that the slats run horizontally. Put a piece of the nori shiny side down on the mat with a long side facing you. With dampened hands, spread ¾ cup sushi rice onto it, leaving a 1½-inch border along the top edge. Spread 1 teaspoon of wasabi paste horizontally across the center of the rice.

Arrange 3 avocado slices in a horizontal line over the wasabi paste, overlapping slightly, and top them with one-sixth of the crabmeat and one-sixth of the cucumber.

Grasp the nori at the edge closest to you. Lift the nori and the mat slightly, and roll the nori evenly and tightly away from you, pressing down on the mat slightly with each quarter turn. Seal the roll with a drop of water on the far edge of the nori, press the seam closed, and transfer the roll to a cutting board. Repeat with remaining ingredients to make 6 rolls.

Using a wet, sharp knife, slice each roll in half, then into 3 equal pieces.

Arrange the rolls decoratively on a platte, cut side up and serve with the soy sauce, wasabi paste, and pickled ginger on the side.

VARIATION: Philadelphia Roll: To make this restaurant favorite, substitute cream cheese and smoked salmon for the avocado, wasabi paste, and crab.

Spicy Tuna Rolls

Start to finish: 1 hour 30 minutes (includes time to make the rice) • Hands-on time: 35 minutes

Sorry, Charlie . . . but if there's one thing better than tuna in your sushi, it's spicy tuna.

YIELD: 24 PIECES, FOR 4 TO 6
SERVINGS

3 cups Sushi Rice (page 224)

3 tablespoons mayonnaise

1½ tablespoons Asian hot
    chili paste

½ teaspoon Asian hot chili oil

½ teaspoon toasted Asian
    sesame oil

½ pound sushi-grade fresh
    tuna, diced

2 tablespoons finely sliced
    green onions

4 sheets nori

Wasabi paste, for serving

Soy sauce, for serving

Pickled ginger, for serving

Prepare the sushi rice as directed in the recipe, cutting the recipe in half.

In a small bowl, combine the mayonnaise, chili paste, chili oil, and sesame oil. Add the tuna and green onions and carefully toss to coat.

Lay a bamboo mat (used for rolling sushi and other foods) on a work surface so that the slats run horizontally. Put a piece of the nori shiny side down on the mat with a long side facing you. With dampened hands, spread ¾ cup sushi rice onto it, leaving a 1½-inch border along the top edge. Lay one-quarter of the spicy tuna mixture in a horizontal line across the center of the rice.

Grasp the nori at the edge closest to you. Lift the nori and the mat slightly, and roll the nori evenly and tightly away from you, pressing down on the mat slightly with each quarter turn. Seal the roll with a drop of water on the far edge of the nori, press the seam closed, and transfer the roll to a cutting board. Repeat with remaining ingredients to make 4 rolls.

Using a wet, sharp knife, slice each roll in half, then into 3 equal pieces.

Arrange the rolls decoratively on a platter, cut side up and serve with the soy sauce, wasabi paste, and pickled ginger on the side.

Japanese Ginger Salad Dressing

Start to finish: 20 minutes • Hands-on time: 20 minutes

We are not usually big fans of iceberg lettuce, but when it's draped in this pink ginger-soy-sesame dressing, as you'll often find it in Japanese restaurants, we can't help but love it. Serve this over iceberg lettuce, tomatoes, cucumber, and grated carrot, and you're in heaven.

YIELD: ABOUT 1½ CUPS

¼ cup rice wine vinegar
   or white vinegar

2 tablespoons tomato paste

1 tablespoon soy sauce

½ teaspoon salt

1 (1-inch knob) fresh ginger,
   grated (2 teaspoons)

1 teaspoon sugar

1 teaspoon toasted Asian
   sesame oil

⅓ cup chopped celery

¼ cup chopped sweet onion

½ cup canola oil

Combine the vinegar, tomato paste, soy sauce, salt, ginger, sugar, sesame oil, celery, and onion in a blender. Pulse several times, until the celery and onion are finely chopped. With the blender running, slowly drizzle in the canola oil.

FOOD *for* THOUGHT

CHOPSTICK MANNERS: No sucking, waving, or poking with chopsticks.

Tempura with Dipping Sauce

Start to finish: 1 hour • Hands-on time: 1 hour

Tempura, the classic Japanese dish of lightly battered and fried vegetables and seafood, reflects all the essential qualities of Japanese cooking: using the freshest ingredients and paying close attention to the details and techniques employed. The best tempura is light, crispy, and not greasy. Making it is really not that complicated and is best done as a group activity, so rally the troops. Round up a few hands to cut vegetables while you dip and fry. You'll be an expert at making tempura in no time.

YIELD: 6 SERVINGS AS AN APPETIZER

2 to 3 cups vegetable or peanut
   oil, for frying

DIPPING SAUCE

1 tablespoon Ichiban Dashi
   (page 221)

2 tablespoons mirin or
   1 tablespoon sugar

3 tablespoons sake or dry
   white wine

¼ cup soy sauce

1 (1-inch knob) fresh ginger,
   peeled and grated (1 teaspoon)

BATTER

1 large egg

½ teaspoon salt, plus more
   as needed

1 cup club soda, chilled

¾ cup unbleached
   all-purpose flour

¼ cup cornstarch

To make the dipping sauce: Bring 1 cup of water to a boil and add the dashi. Boil for 3 minutes. Remove from the heat and add the remaining ingredients. Let cool and serve at room temperature.

In a 2-to 3-quart pot set over medium-high heat, heat 2 inches of oil to 360°F.

To make the batter: Combine the egg and salt in a medium bowl and beat with a fork until mixed. Add the club soda and stir gently to mix. Sift the flour and cornstarch into the egg mixture and, using chopsticks or the handle of a wooden spoon, stir briefly to mix. Do not overmix. There will be lumps. It should be the consistency of heavy cream.

To fry the tempura: Working with one type of food at a time, dip the vegetables, shrimp, or scallops in the batter one at a time, letting the excess batter fall back into the bowl. Carefully slide them into the hot oil. Work fast and fry no more than 6 or 7 pieces at a time to prevent the oil from plunging in temperature.

Turn the pieces when they are lightly golden on the bottom, about 1 minute. Fry on the second side for about 30 seconds to 1 minute and carefully remove with a spider (an Asian-style slotted spoon) or slotted spoon and drain on paper towels.

Here are some approximate frying times:

zucchini = 1½ minutes

yellow squash = 1½ minutes

sweet potato = 2 minutes

broccoli florets = 1½ minutes

small red onion = 1½ minutes

TEMPURA OPTIONS

1 zucchini, cut on the diagonal into 12 slices, no more than ¼ inch thick

1 yellow squash, cut on the diagonal into 12 slices, no more than ¼ inch thick

1 sweet potato, peeled and cut on the diagonal into 12 slices, no more than ¼ inch thick

1 head broccoli, separated into medium-sized (two-bite) florets

½ small red onion, peeled, cut in half, then sliced into ¼ inch slices

12 small mushrooms, wiped clean with a damp cloth and cut in half if large

12 medium shrimp, shelled, deveined, and butterflied

6 scallops, cut in half horizontally

Lemon wedges, for serving

Grated daikon radish, for serving

small mushrooms = 1½ minutes

shrimp = 1½ to 2 minutes

scallops = 1½ to 2 minutes

Return the oil to 360°F. and carefully add another 6 or 7 pieces of tempura. Fry the remaining ingredients in the same manner.

Serve the tempura hot with the dipping sauce, or with salt and freshly squeezed lemon. Grated daikon should be served alongside the fried vegetables. It can be added to the dipping sauce or on top of the vegetables.

VARIATION: Other vegetables to try are carrots, asparagus, and green beans. Cook them first in boiling water for about 1 minute, then put them in an ice bath to stop the cooking. Line up 4 or 5 carrots, asparagus, or green beans, side by side, and run a wooden skewer through them to connect. Dip them in the batter and fry them, then remove the skewer after frying. Other seafood possibilities include cod, crab, and squid.

MAKE AHEAD: The dipping sauce can be kept for up to 1 week in the refrigerator.

Tonkatsu FRIED PORK CUTLETS

Start to finish: 40 minutes • Hands-on time: 30 minutes

If you thought that Japanese cuisine didn't include comfort food, think again. This hugely popular dish, both here and in Japan, has a lot in common with our Southern chicken-fried steak. Pork cutlets are seasoned, breaded, and fried until golden brown, then served with a thick Worcestershire-based asian style barbecue sauce and shredded cabbage.

YIELD: 6 SERVINGS

TONKATSU SAUCE

⅓ cup ketchup

¼ cup soy sauce

¼ cup sugar

2 tablespoons mirin

⅓ cup Worcestershire sauce

¼ teaspoon allspice

1 teaspoon Dijon mustard

TONKATSU

6 (½-inch thick) pork loin cutlets
    or boneless pork chops

Salt and freshly ground
    black pepper

½ cup unbleached all-purpose flour

2 large eggs, beaten

1½ cups panko breadcrumbs

1 to 2 cups vegetable oil,
    for frying

Finely shredded cabbage,
    for serving

Lemon wedges, for serving

White Rice (page 12), for serving

To make the sauce: Whisk all the ingredients together in a bowl until the sugar is dissolved. Let stand for 30 minutes to allow the flavors to develop.

To make the tonkatsu: Heat ½ inch of oil in a large skillet to 360°F.

Pat the pork cutlets dry with paper towels, and make a few vertical slits on the outer rim of the cutlets to prevent them from curling when cooked. Season both sides of the pork with salt and pepper and dredge with flour, shaking off any excess.

Mix the eggs with 1 tablespoon water in a shallow bowl.

Dip the cutlets in the egg, then coat in panko breadcrumbs. Gently slide the cutlets into the oil and cook for 4 to 5 minutes per side until golden brown, or just cooked through. Drain on paper towels.

Cut each cutlet crosswise into 1-inch strips. Arrange on individual plates and garnish with cabbage and lemon wedges. Serve with a dish of tonkatsu sauce on the side for dipping. Accompany with rice.

Udon or Soba Noodles in Stock

Start to finish: 20 minutes • Hands-on time: 10 minutes

Noodles play a prominent roll in many Asian cuisines, and Japanese is no exception. There are many types of Japanese noodles, but the most common in the United States are udon and soba. Udon are thick wheat noodles, and soba are thin buckwheat noodles. Both are typically served in a mild stock seasoned with soy sauce, sake, and ginger.

Once you make your noodles in stock, topping them with more substantial ingredients makes for a heartier meal. Meredith's Japanese roommates in college topped them with slivered ham, slices of hard-boiled eggs, or leftover cooked vegetables. For something more elaborate, try sliced Tonkatsu (opposite) or Shrimp or Vegetable Tempura (page 228).

YIELD: 4 TO 6 SERVINGS

¾ pound dried udon or
    soba noodles

6 cups Ichiban Dashi (page 221)

¼ cup soy sauce

1½ tablespoons sugar

1 tablespoon of sake

6 quarter-sized slices fresh ginger

4 green onions, finely slivered

MAKE AHEAD: The noodles can be cooked, rinsed under cold water, and kept in a colander for up to 1 hour. The stock can be made 2 days ahead and kept covered in the refrigerator.

Cook the noodles according to the package directions, being careful not to overcook them (see tip). Drain, then rinse the noodles under cold water and transfer to serving bowls.

Heat the dashi, soy sauce, sugar, sake, and ginger in a small saucepan over medium-low heat. Pour the hot stock over the noodles and garnish with the green onions.

TIP: When cooking the noodles, test them for doneness a minute or so before the recommended cooking time is over. Do this by biting into a noodle and looking for a pin-sized vein of white uncooked noodle in the middle.

TIP: If you don't have any dashi on hand, try making these noodles with chicken stock instead.

Teriyaki Beef or Chicken

Start to finish: 2 hours 30 minutes • Hands-on time: 30 minutes

Take your kids to a Japanese restaurant and nine times out of ten they will order the teriyaki beef or chicken. We think the best part about teriyaki is the caramelized coating beef or chicken gets as it cooks with the sauce. Sometimes restaurants simply drizzle the meat with the sauce after it's cooked, which, in our minds, defeats the purpose.

YIELD: 4 SERVINGS

½ cup soy sauce

5 tablespoons mirin

3 tablespoons sake

3 tablespoons sugar

1½ teaspoons minced fresh ginger

1½ pounds sirloin beef, trimmed and cut into 1-inch cubes; or 1½ pounds boneless chicken thighs, whole

Combine the soy sauce, mirin, sake, sugar, and ginger in a large zip top bag. Add the beef or chicken and marinate for 2 hours in the refrigerator.

Remove the meat from the marinade, and pour the marinade into a medium-sized saucepan. Place over medium heat and reduce until slightly thickened, about 5 minutes. Reserve 2 tablespoons of reduced marinade and set aside.

Preheat the broiler.

For the beef teriyaki: Slide the beef onto wooden skewers that have been soaked in water for 1 hour and place on a broiler pan. Place the broiler pan on a rack 6 inches from the broiler and broil for 6 minutes. Turn the meat over, check for doneness, and baste with the reduced sauce. Continue cooking if necessary to desired doneness, checking every minute or two. Brush with the reserved sauce just before serving.

For the chicken teriyaki: Place the chicken on a broiler pan skin-side-down. Place the broiler pan on a rack 6 inches from the broiler and broil for 3 minutes. Turn the meat over and baste with the reduced sauce. Broil another 5 minutes. The skin should be dark brown in spots and the chicken should be cooked through. Brush with the reserved sauce just before serving.

TIP: Teriyaki is often cooked over a grill. For this technique, place the marinated meat directly on a barbeque grill rack situated 6 inches over hot coals. Turn and baste with sauce as instructed in the recipe.

* MEXICAN *

✳ MEXICAN ✳

IF YOUR ONLY EXPOSURE TO MEXICAN FOOD is "Combination Plate #5," this chapter is going to blow your mind. Mexican food is fresh, lively, and ready to salsa right into your kitchen.

For most of us, Mexican food is a welcome change of pace from our usual fare. We're excited not just by the heat, but also by the flavor of the chiles so often used in this food. No other cuisine highlights that combination more than the dishes of Mexico, where they not only use a lot of chiles, they use a lot of different kinds of chiles, each with its own unique flavor. Even if you're not a chile-head, you can't help but be charmed by the bold, comforting flavors and textures in this south-of-the-border cuisine.

Unless you live in a big city, it usually holds true that the farther you are from the Mexican border, the less likely you are to have access to good Mexican food. That's when it becomes important to take the bull by the horns (or the taco by the shell) and learn to make good Mexican food for yourself.

The best Mexican food, like every other cuisine, is largely dependent on the quality and freshness of the ingredients. But you don't need to go on a 5-day shopping safari to find what you'll need to make most of the dishes in this chapter. You will, however, need to familiarize yourself with a few key ingredients. Fresh chiles are key, so look for those

with smooth, shiny skins. Dried chiles should still be pliable. If they crumble in your hands, they've probably been sitting on the shelf too long. Fresh tortillas are important, so check the package to make sure they aren't as hard as rocks.

Although we hate to have to tell you this, a lot of the food you may think of as Mexican really isn't. Fajitas, burritos, and nachos? Decidedly not authentic Mexican. You may think they are because they share some of the same flavors and ingredients, but they are an American creation, born on this side of the border. That doesn't necessarily make them bad. In fact, they can taste great. That's why the food in this chapter is a combination of authentic Mexican cuisine, and a few Mexican-American dishes that most of us are used to seeing on the menu thrown in, too.

While many begin their Mexican culinary experience in a restaurant, filling up on chips and salsa before even thinking about ordering off the menu, when serving Mexican food at home, we think it's best to resist the urge to pile huge bowls with chips and set them on the table. Food is always better if you have an appetite for it.

So, turn up the mariachi music and pour the margaritas. Here's a menu to get you started in your own *cocina* (kitchen). Arriba!

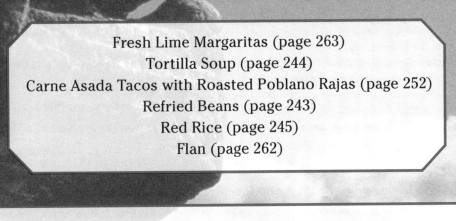

FOOD *for* THOUGHT

- The earliest evidence of chile peppers in our diet is from Mexico, where chile peppers were domesticated by at least 3300 BC.

- Columbus "discovered" chile peppers in the West Indies on his first voyage to the New World. By mistaking chiles for black pepper, he gave the chile the inaccurate name "pepper."

- In 2002, Americans consumed an average of 7.2 pounds of beans annually, according to the US Department of Agriculture. A package of Beano when you need it . . . priceless.

- Between 1864 and 1867, Mexico was ruled by the former Austrian archduke Ferdinand Maximilian, who was backed by the French. Though Maximilian's reign was brief, French cooking left its mark on Mexican dishes. Examples include stuffed chiles in a walnut sauce (*chiles en nogada*) and rabbit in mustard sauce (*conejo en mostaza*).

Corn Tortillas TORTILLAS DE MAIZ

Start to finish: 45 minutes • Hands-on time: 45 minutes

If you enjoy Mexican food and you've never tried homemade corn tortillas, you have to make them at least once, just so you know what you're missing. Homemade corn tortillas right off the griddle are things of beauty. Their warm, earthy aroma and chewy texture make them worth taking the time, even if it's just so you can slather them in butter and eat them while they're hot.

In a perfect world, we could all use fresh masa to make corn tortillas. Masa is corn dough that is made from dried field corn (corn that has not been hybridized to be made sweet) that has been boiled in calcium hydroxide (or lime). It's then rinsed and stone-ground into a paste, which is used to make flavorful and smooth tortillas. It's not an easy process to duplicate at home (although, with a great deal of work, it can be done). Fresh masa can be purchased from a local tortilla factory (or tortilleria*), but those can be difficult to find. If you can find fresh masa, it must be used the day you buy it because it sours quickly.*

Don't worry, though, if you can't find fresh masa. More often than not, we use masa harina, which is fresh masa that has been dried and ground into powder. It works very well and is fairly easy to find. In many parts of the country, you can find masa harina on the shelves of your local grocery store. Otherwise, look for it in specialty food shops or online. We like Maseca brand, but Quaker makes a good masa harina as well. You can then reconstitute it with warm water to make your tortillas. We add salt to our tortillas because we think it brings out the flavor of the corn, but it's not essential.

If you are really adept with your hands, you may find it possible to pat your tortillas manually. We must not be, though, because as many times as we've tried, we can't get our tortillas to come out as nicely and efficiently as they do with a tortilla press. Tortilla presses are usually made of metal, and are a fairly inexpensive tool to invest in. They're definitely worth it once you've tasted the end result. They can be purchased at specialty cookware stores, online, or in any Mexican market.

YIELD: ABOUT 1 DOZEN, VARIES
DEPENDING ON TORTILLA SIZE

1¾ cups masa harina, mixed with
   1 cup plus 2 tablespoons hot
   water, or 1 pound fresh masa
1 teaspoon salt

Mix the masa harina and the water together and knead to form your *masa* (dough). The dough should be slightly sticky and form a ball when pressed together. To test, flatten a small amount of dough between your palms. If the edges crack, add water to the dough, a teaspoon at a time, until your test piece does not crack. (Good masa dough has the consistency of homemade Play-Doh.) Keep the bowl of masa covered with a damp towel to prevent drying.

Preheat a cast-iron skillet (or griddle, not nonstick) over medium-low heat. Cut a large freezer bag down both sides so it is one long sheet of plastic. Please one half of the bag on the open tortilla press.

MAKE AHEAD: There is nothing like a tortilla right off the
griddle, but if you must, you can
make them several hours ahead
and keep them wrapped in
plastic wrap at room temperature. To reheat, remove the
plastic and wrap them in a
slightly damp paper towel, then
in foil. Heat in a 350°F. oven for
10 minutes, or until warm.

Pinch off a golf-ball-sized piece of masa and roll it into a ball. Set the masa ball on the plastic bag and cover it with the other half of the bag. Gently press the masa to flatten it into a disk (don't press too hard). Open the tortilla press and rotate the tortilla 180 degrees, plastic and all. Press down again. The tortilla should be about the thickness of a quarter.

Hold the pressed tortilla, with the plastic still on both sides, in one hand. Peel away the top plastic from the tortilla. (If it sticks to the plastic, your dough is too wet and needs more masa harina. If the tortilla seems crumbly and falls apart, add a little more water.) Flip the tortilla over onto your other hand, and peel away the other piece of plastic. Don't worry if your tortillas are not perfect circles. They'll look even more homemade!

Gently place the tortilla on the hot skillet or griddle. Cook for about 30 seconds on one side, or just until it moves easily on the skillet, then gently flip the tortilla and cook it for about 60 seconds. The tortilla should puff slightly after the second turn; if it doesn't, press down on the tortilla gently with a clean dish towel or spatula. This concentrates the heat and helps the tortilla to puff. (This technique is called "tickling the tortilla.") Flip the tortilla back to the first side and cook for another 30 seconds. Repeat with the remaining masa, using the same plastic bag.

As you remove the tortillas from the skillet, stack them together and keep them wrapped in a clean dish towel. The steam created in the towel will keep them soft and warm.

FOOD *for* THOUGHT

ACCORDING TO THE Tortilla Industry Association, "Tortillas are more popular today in the U.S. than all other ethnic breads, such as bagels, English muffins, and pita bread."

Flour Tortillas TORTILLAS DE HARINA

Start to finish: 1 hour 15 minutes • Hands-on time: 45 minutes

Homemade flour tortillas are easy to make and they are a world away from the tasteless flour tortillas we often find in the refrigerator case of the grocery store. Just getting the store-bought tortillas to separate can be a challenge. Make your own to experience how tender and flavorful they can be.

YIELD: 12 (8- TO 10-INCH) TORTILLAS

2¾ cups unbleached
    all-purpose flour
6 tablespoons vegetable
    shortening or lard (see tip)
1 teaspoon salt

MAKE AHEAD: Uncooked tortillas can be kept in the refrigerator, stacked between layers of wax paper and wrapped in plastic wrap, up to 1 day in advance. Although best eaten fresh, cooked tortillas can also be wrapped tightly in plastic wrap and frozen. To reheat, wrap in foil and heat for 10 minutes, or until warm in a 325°F. oven.

Combine the flour, shortening, and salt in a large bowl and mix with your hands until the mixture is crumbly. Gradually add 1 cup warm water and continue kneading, then turn the dough out onto a lightly floured surface and knead until the dough is smooth, about 3 minutes.

Divide the dough into 12 pieces, roll each piece into a ball, and place on a baking sheet or board. Cover with plastic wrap or a clean towel and let rest at room temperature for 30 minutes.

On a lightly floured work surface, roll each ball out into a circle about ⅟₁₆- to ⅛-inch thick.

Preheat a cast-iron skillet (or griddle, not nonstick) over medium-low heat.

Gently place a tortilla on the hot skillet and cook for about 30 seconds on one side, or just until it moves easily on the skillet. Gently flip the tortilla and cook it for about 30 seconds. The tortilla should puff slightly after the second turn; if it doesn't, press down on the tortilla gently with a clean dish towel or spatula. This concentrates the heat and helps the tortilla to puff. Flip the tortilla back to the first side and cook for another 30 seconds. Repeat with the remaining dough.

As you remove the tortillas from the skillet, stack them together and keep them wrapped in a clean dish towel. The steam created in the towel will keep them soft and warm.

NOTE: To use lard or not to use lard . . . that is the question. Lard is an animal fat produced from rendering the fat portions of the pig. While it doesn't sound good (or healthy), it can be good . . . *very* good. And it will make your tortillas amazing. The problem is that for most of us, it's gone entirely out of our culinary consideration. This may be because saturated fats are such a big dietary issue, but also because rendering down fat doesn't seem like a pleasant task and there's little reason to do it since vegetable shortening came on the scene. While we don't deny that lard can have great flavor, this is not true of the large sticks you find at the grocery store, which have been partially hydrogenated. If you're looking for the big advantages that come with using lard, buy pork fat from your butcher and render it yourself.

Pico de Gallo CHOPPED TOMATO SALSA

Start to finish: 50 minutes • Hands-on time: 20 minutes

Almost a salad, this colorful, uncooked salsa is often found as a side on almost any Mexican restaurant platter. For that reason, it's what most people think of when you say "salsa." It's fresh, attractive, and worthy of the attention.

YIELD: ABOUT 2 CUPS

1 pound ripe tomatoes, seeded and chopped

½ medium red or white onion, chopped (½ cup)

¼ cup chopped fresh cilantro

2 tablespoons fresh lime juice

1 garlic clove, minced

1 serrano chile, minced (1 tablespoon)

Salt

Combine all the ingredients in a medium bowl and toss to blend well. Season with salt to taste. Let stand at room temperature for at least 30 minutes to allow the flavors to develop.

TIP: This salsa is much better when all the ingredients are chopped with a knife as opposed to a food processor. The food processor turns everything into a uniform pink mass.

MAKE AHEAD: This salsa can be made up to 1 hour ahead.

Easy Tomato and Chipotle Salsa

Start to finish: 40 minutes • Hands-on time: 10 minutes

We find ourselves making this salsa more often than any other. Probably because it's so fast to put together, without the knife work or roasting that's necessary for other salsas, and the flavor doesn't suffer at all for the speed.

YIELD: ABOUT 2½ CUPS

1 (28-ounce) can whole tomatoes

1 tablespoon fresh lime juice,
 plus more if necessary

2 canned chipotle chiles
 in adobo

½ medium white onion, diced
 (½ cup)

½ cup chopped cilantro

Salt

In a blender, combine the tomatoes, lime juice, and chiles. Purée until smooth and pour into a bowl.

Rinse the onion under cold running water in a colander. Add the onion and cilantro to the salsa and season with salt to taste and more lime juice, if desired. If necessary, thin the salsa with a little water. Let the salsa sit for 30 minutes to allow the flavors to blend.

TIP: If you can find the fire-roasted type of canned tomatoes (Muir Glen brand), they work beautifully in this recipe.

MAKE AHEAD: The salsa can be made up to the point where the onion and cilantro are added 1 week ahead of time and kept covered in the refrigerator. Add the onions and cilantro just before serving.

David's Tomatillo Salsa

Start to finish: 40 minutes • Hands-on time: 30 minutes

Tomatillos—small, spherical, green fruits that are surrounded by paperlike husks—are the key to this spicy, sweet-tart salsa. This recipe is adapted from a recipe by Meredith's husband, David. It's a staple in the Deeds house and is requested often by family and friends.

YIELD: ABOUT 1½ CUPS

12 ounces tomatillos
    (6 to 10), husked and rinsed

2 serrano chiles

½ cup chopped cilantro

½ medium white onion, minced
    (½ cup)

4 garlic cloves, chopped

2 tablespoons fresh lime juice

2 tablespoons cider vinegar

¼ teaspoon salt, plus more
    if needed

1 teaspoon sugar

2 tablespoons vegetable oil

Preheat the broiler. Line a 13 x 9-inch pan with foil.

Place the tomatillos and chiles on the foil and broil for about 5 to 10 minutes, or until dark brown spots develop on the chiles and tomatillos. Cool, then transfer to a blender, including all the juices that have run out onto the baking sheet.

Add the cilantro, onion, garlic, lime juice, vinegar, salt, sugar, and ¼ cup water. Blend to a purée.

Heat the oil in a medium skillet set over medium heat. Add the tomatillo purée and bring to a boil. Continue to cook, stirring, until the salsa has thickened slightly, about 5 minutes. Remove from the heat and taste for seasoning; adjust if necessary. Transfer to a serving bowl and serve at room temperature or chilled.

> **MAKE AHEAD:** This salsa can be made ahead and kept covered in the refrigerator for up to a week, or frozen for up to 2 months.

Guacamole

Start to finish: 20 minutes • Hands-on time: 20 minutes

Think about how much guacamole you need, then double it, because this cool, creamy, mildly spicy dip is always the most popular thing on the table. We like to serve it with just chips, but we absolutely can't eat a taco or taquito without it.

YIELD: ABOUT 2½ CUPS

3 ripe California Hass avocados,
    quartered, pitted, and peeled
    (see tip)
½ cup chopped fresh cilantro
½ medium white onion, minced
    (½ cup)
1 fresh serrano chile, minced
1 tablespoon fresh lime juice,
    or to taste
1½ teaspoons salt, or to taste

Mash the avocados in a medium-sized bowl with a fork or potato masher until creamy, but with some lumps remaining. Add the cilantro, onion, chile, lime juice, and salt and stir to combine.

TIP: For the best guacamole, use the dark-skinned Hass avocados that give slightly when pressed. They are much creamier and more flavorful than the light, smooth-skinned variety.

MAKE AHEAD: Guacamole can be made 1 hour ahead and chilled, its surface covered with plastic wrap. Make sure to press the plastic directly onto the surface to avoid browning.

Refried Beans FRIJOLES REFRITOS

Start to finish: 2 hours 30 minutes (plus 1 hour or 24 hours depending on the bean soaking method you choose) • Hands-on time: 30 minutes

Refried beans are a matter of taste, and for those who grew up eating good Mexican food, they can also be a point of contention. Some think they should be spiced with cumin and chili powder, while others think the flavor of the bean should shine. Some think they should be mashed and refried to a thick, mortarlike paste, while others feel they should be kept loose, perhaps even adding extra water to thin them. We like ours simple, with just the flavor of caramelized onions in the background to give them depth.

YIELD: 6 SERVINGS

2 cups dried pinto beans
  or black beans
1 teaspoon salt
2 tablespoons vegetable oil
1 medium white onion,
  finely chopped
4 garlic cloves, finely chopped
Salt
½ cup crumbled Mexican *queso
  fresco, queso anejo*, dry feta,
  or Parmigiano-Reggiano
  cheese, for garnish

Let the beans soak overnight in a large bowl, in enough water to cover them by 2 inches or quick-soak them (see tip).

Drain the beans, pour them into a pan, and add enough water to cover them by 2 inches. Cook the beans over low heat, uncovered, for 30 to 45 minutes, or until almost cooked through. Add the salt and cook for 15 to 20 minutes, or until the beans are cooked and creamy inside. Add more hot water if necessary to keep the beans just covered.

Drain the beans and reserve the liquid. Put the beans back in the pot with about 1 cup of their cooking liquid. Mash them with a potato masher or the back of a wooden spoon until they are creamy. Add more liquid if necessary.

In a large nonstick skillet, heat the oil over medium heat. Add the onion and cook, stirring frequently, until deep golden, about 10 minutes. Add the garlic and cook for a minute or so, then add the mashed beans. Continue to cook, stirring about 10 minutes, or until the beans are the desired thickness. Add more bean liquid if you like your beans thinner. Taste and season with more salt if needed. Serve with the crumbled cheese.

TIP: To quick-soak dried beans: rinse the beans in a colander under cold water and discard any discolored ones. Combine the beans in a soup pot with enough cold water to cover them by 2 inches, bring the water to a boil, and let the beans boil for 2 minutes. Remove the pot from the heat and let the beans soak, covered, for 1 hour.

Tortilla Soup SOPA DE TORTILLA

Start to finish: 1 hour 35 minutes • Hands-on time: 45 minutes

So often in restaurants, tortilla soup is made with a starch or stabilizer that causes the soup to be goopy or gummy. It's much better without them. This simple chile and tomato soup is thickened with tortillas (hence the name!).

YIELD: 8 SERVINGS

- 4 dried ancho chiles
- 8 (6-inch) corn tortillas
- 2 tablespoons olive oil, plus more for brushing
- ½ large white onion, chopped
- 6 garlic cloves, chopped
- ½ teaspoon dried oregano, crumbled
- 1 teaspoon salt
- 1 (28-ounce) can whole plum tomatoes
- 8 cups low-sodium, fat-free chicken stock, plus more if necessary
- 2 tablespoons fresh lime juice
- 1 teaspoon chili powder
- 4 cups cooked and shredded chicken breast (about 3 breasts)
- 1 cup grated Monterey Jack cheese
- 1 ripe avocado, pitted, peeled, and cubed, for garnish
- ½ cup sour cream, for garnish
- ¼ cup chopped cilantro, for garnish

Remove the stems, seeds, and ribs from chiles.

Heat a griddle or heavy skillet over moderate heat until hot but not smoking. Place 1 or 2 chiles on the skillet and toast them, while pressing down on them with tongs or a spatula, for 20 to 30 seconds on each side, or until pliable. Repeat with the remaining chiles.

Chop the toasted chiles into small pieces and place them in a bowl. Pour enough hot water over the chiles to cover, and let them soak for about 20 minutes, or until they are soft.

Meanwhile, cut 4 of the tortillas into 1-inch squares.

Heat the oil in a heavy 5-quart pot over medium-high heat. Add the cut tortillas and sauté for 3 or 4 minutes, or until the tortillas turn golden brown. Add the onion, garlic, oregano, and ½ teaspoon of the salt and sauté for 3 minutes, or until the onions begin to brown. Remove from the heat.

Drain the chiles, discarding the liquid. Add the chiles, tomatoes, and stock to the pot and simmer uncovered for 30 minutes, stirring occasionally.

Remove the soup from the heat and purée it in batches in a blender. (Take care to fill the blender only halfway and cover the top with a towel in case soup leaks out while blending.) Return the puréed soup to the pot and keep it warm over low heat. Add the lime juice and taste for seasoning; adjust if necessary. Thin with additional stock if the soup looks too thick.

Preheat the oven to 400°F.

Brush both sides of the remaining 4 tortillas with olive oil. Cut the tortillas into matchstick-sized strips and arrange them on a baking sheet. Sprinkle with the chili powder and the remaining ½ teaspoon salt and toss so the strips are all seasoned. Bake the tortilla strips until they are crisp, about 15 minutes; set aside.

1 lime, cut into 8 wedges,
  for garnish

To serve, place ½ cup of shredded chicken and 2 tablespoons of cheese in each serving bowl. Ladle hot soup on top and garnish each serving with avocado, sour cream, cilantro, tortilla strips, and a wedge of lime. Serve hot.

> MAKE AHEAD: The soup base can be made up to 2 days ahead and kept covered in the refrigerator. Reheat over medium heat and proceed with the recipe.

Red Rice ARROZ ROJO

Start to finish: 1 hour 20 minutes • Hands-on time: 30 minutes

We bet the dishwashers in Mexican restaurants see a lot of rice go through their station. It must win the contest for the dish most frequently served, but least eaten. That's because it's usually mushy and flavorless, like it's just holding a spot on your plate where you can put the parsley garnish you're also not going to eat. Our version, with rice cooked to perfection in spiced tomato stock, is so good it could be the star of the plate. It also makes a great vegetarian addition to burritos.

YIELD: 8 TO 10 SERVINGS

3 tablespoons vegetable oil

1 medium onion, finely chopped

2 serrano chiles,
  stemmed and seeded

2 garlic cloves, chopped

3 cups long-grain rice, rinsed

1 (28-ounce) can whole tomatoes

1½ teaspoons salt

2 tablespoons fresh lime juice

Preheat the oven to 350°F.

Heat the oil in a large, heavy saucepan set over medium heat. Add the onion, chiles, and garlic and sauté until translucent, about 5 minutes, stirring constantly. Add the rice and cook until it begins to turn golden brown, about 5 more minutes.

Meanwhile, combine the tomatoes, salt, and lime juice in a blender and purée. Add the tomato purée and 1¼ cups water to the saucepan and stir to combine. Transfer the rice to a 4-quart baking dish or casserole, and cover with foil. Bake for 35 to 45 minutes, or until the liquid is absorbed and the rice is tender. Remove from the oven and let rest for 10 minutes. Fluff with a fork and serve hot.

NOTE: Leftover rice can be reheated in a microwave.

Tacos—Soft and Crispy Variations

Growing up in Southern California, Meredith and her family often enjoyed tacos filled with chili-spiced ground beef, and wrapped in warm, crispy, slightly chewy taco shells that were always homemade. For her and many others like her, that may be why it's such a disappointment to be served tacos in a restaurant that are wrapped in reheated, factory-made taco shells. The difference, in our minds, between homemade and store-bought taco shells is the difference between wanting to eat the taco and not. Of course, soft tacos are always a wonderful choice, and an easy way to make the dish more healthful. We give you both options here. While nothing is better for a soft taco than a homemade corn or flour tortilla, we use store-bought corn tortillas for our hard shells, because they are thinner and absorb less oil.

YIELD: 4 TO 6 SERVINGS

CRISPY TACO SHELLS

Start to finish: about 20 minutes

Hands-on time: 20 minutes

1 to 2 cups vegetable oil,
   for frying

12 (6-inch) corn tortillas

Salt to taste

To make crispy taco shells: In a heavy, medium-sized skillet over medium-high heat, heat about 1 inch of oil to 360°F.

Using tongs, place one tortilla into the oil. It should start to sizzle right away. Cook for about 15 to 30 seconds, then flip the tortilla over and fold the shell in half, using your tongs to hold the tortilla in a slightly open position (in order to form the familiar taco-shell shape). Cook one half until crispy, about 15 seconds. Now that your tortilla is in the shape of a taco, cook the other side of the tortilla (the side you were just holding) for 15 to 30 seconds, so both sides are crispy.

Remove the tortilla from the oil and place it on paper towels to drain. While the shell is still hot, sprinkle it with salt. Repeat with the remaining tortillas.

SOFT TACO SHELLS

Start to finish: 15 minutes

Hands-on time: 5 minutes

12 (6-inch) corn or flour tortillas

To make soft taco shells: Preheat the oven to 350°F.

Divide the tortillas into two stacks of 6, and wrap each stack in foil. Place the foil stacks on a baking sheet and heat in the oven for 5 to 10 minutes, or until heated through and pliable.

If the tortillas are dry, wrap them in a slightly damp paper towel before wrapping in foil.

TACO ASSEMBLY

3½ cups Chicken, Ground Beef,
    Shredded Beef, or Carnitas
    Filling (pages 250 to 251)
Shredded lettuce
Chopped tomatoes
Shredded cheddar,
    Monterey Jack, or crumbled
    queso fresco cheese
Guacamole (page 242)
Sour cream
Salsa (pages 239 to 241

To assemble the tacos: Place ¼ cup of filling in each taco shell. Top with desired amount of lettuce, tomato, and cheese. Garnish with guacamole, salsa, and sour cream and serve.

> MAKE AHEAD: Fried taco shells are best right after frying. If they get too cold, they have a tendency to get greasy and a little too chewy. If you need to make them ahead of time (2 hours at most), you can rewarm them in a 350°F. oven for 5 to 10 minutes. They will crisp up a bit.

FOOD *for* THOUGHT

WHAT CAUSES THE chile pepper to set our mouths, and sometimes eyes, noses, and fingers, on fire? Capsaicin is the culprit. It is found in the white "ribs," which hold the seeds on the inside of the pepper. Capsaicin tricks your brain into thinking you are in pain by stimulating the nerve endings in your mouth. The brain responds by releasing endorphins, which are similar in structure to morphine. That's why it hurts so good!

Taquitos and Flautas

Start to finish: 45 minutes (assuming the filling is made ahead) • Hands-on time: 45 minutes (assuming the filling is made ahead)

Taquitos and flautas are essentially the same thing. Flauta means "flute," and usually refers to a flour tortilla that has been rolled tightly around a filling and fried. The finished product closely resembles a flute. Taquitos, which means "little tacos," are made the same way, only with corn tortillas. On restaurant menus, the two terms are often interchangeable no matter what kind of tortillas are used. Whatever the name, these crispy rolls are a popular choice. Shredded beef and chicken are the two typical fillings, but carnitas and ground beef are a delicious choices as well.

YIELD: 4 TO 6 SERVINGS

TAQUITOS

1¾ cups Chicken, Ground Beef,
  Shredded Beef, or Carnitas
  Filling (pages 250 to 251)

1 to 2 cups vegetable oil,
  for frying

12 (6-inch) corn tortillas

Salt

Sour cream

Guacamole (page 242)

Salsa (pages 239 to 241)

Prepare the filling of your choice as directed in the recipe.

Heat 1 inch of oil in a medium-sized frying pan set over medium-high heat. Line a baking sheet with paper towels and set alongside your frying pan.

Use tongs to dip a tortilla in the hot oil for about 5 seconds to let it soften. Remove the tortilla from the oil and set it on paper towels to absorb any excess oil. Repeat with the remaining tortillas. Lower the heat while you assemble the taquitos.

Place a scant 2 tablespoons filling in the center of each tortilla. Roll the tortillas snugly around the filling and secure with toothpicks.

Increase the heat, and place 3 or 4 taquitos into the oil. Fry them, turning once, for about 2 to 3 minutes, or until the tortillas are slightly golden brown. Transfer the taquitos to the prepared baking sheet. Fry the remaining taquitos. Keep warm in a 180°F. oven for up to 30 minutes before serving.

To serve, remove the toothpicks and serve 2 to 3 taquitos on each plate, garnished with sour cream, guacamole, and salsa.

TIP: If you would like to avoid heating your tortillas in oil before frying them a second time, warm them in the oven as follows: Preheat the oven to 375°F. Lightly brush both sides of each tortilla with oil and place on a cookie sheet in stacks of two. Heat in the oven for about 3 minutes, until soft and pliable. Fill and fry as directed in the recipe.

FLAUTAS

1¾ cups Chicken, Ground Beef,
   Shredded Beef, or Carnitas
   Filling (pages 250 to 251)
1 to 2 cups vegetable oil,
   for frying
12 small (6-inch) flour tortillas
Salt to taste
Sour cream, for garnish
Guacamole (page 242)
Salsa (pages 239 to 241)

> **MAKE AHEAD:** Taquitos and flautas can be filled and rolled up to 8 hours ahead of time and kept covered in the refrigerator. For best results, fry just before serving. They can be fried up to half an hour ahead and kept on a baking sheet in a warm oven, but they will be chewier and less crispy.

Prepare the filling of your choice as directed in the recipe.

Heat 1 inch of oil in a medium-sized frying pan set over medium-high heat to 360°F. Heat an ungreased skillet over medium-high heat. Line a baking sheet with paper towels and set alongside your frying pan.

Warm both sides of the tortillas, on the skillet for 10 to 20 seconds to make them pliable. Place a scant 2 tablespoons filling into each tortilla. Roll the tortillas snugly around the filling and secure with toothpicks.

Place 3 or 4 flautas into the oil and fry them, turning once, for about 2 to 3 minutes, or until the tortillas are slightly golden brown. Transfer the flautas to the prepared baking sheet. Fry the remaining flautas. Keep warm in a 180°F. oven for up to 30 minutes before serving.

To serve, remove the toothpicks and serve 2 to 3 flautas on each plate, garnished with sour cream, guacamole, and salsa.

TIP: It's important for the oil to be hot enough when frying. Otherwise your taquito or flauta will absorb too much oil and be greasy and tough. To test the oil, we usually hold the end of a wooden spoon in the oil. If small bubbles appear around it, the oil should be hot enough.

Fillings for Tacos, Taquitos, and Flautas

YIELD: ABOUT 3½ CUPS
CHICKEN FILLING

Start to finish: 30 minutes

Hands-on time: 30 minutes

1 tablespoon vegetable oil

½ white onion, minced
   (½ cup)

2 garlic cloves, chopped

1 serrano chile, minced

½ cup prepared tomato sauce

1 teaspoon ground cumin

½ teaspoon salt

3½ cups shredded, cooked
   chicken (about 3 breasts)

GROUND BEEF FILLING

Start to finish: 35 minutes

Hands-on time: 35 minutes

1 tablespoon vegetable oil

¾ cup finely chopped onion

1 large garlic clove, minced

2 teaspoons ground cumin

2 teaspoons chili powder

1½ pounds lean ground beef

2 tablespoons tomato paste

½ teaspoon salt

Freshly ground black pepper

Heat the oil in a large skillet set over medium heat. Add the onion, garlic, and chile and sauté until the onions are translucent, about 6 minutes. Add the tomato sauce, cumin, and salt and continue to cook for one more minute. Add the chicken and cook just until heated through, about 2 minutes. Taste and adjust seasonings if necessary. Serve hot.

In an authentic Mexican restaurant, "American taco" usually refers to a crispy shell with ground beef filling, the filling with which most Americans are familiar. It's a great weeknight choice because it's quick to make. And if you're thinking, you can just buy an envelope of taco seasoning," remember they are loaded with sodium and still don't deliver the amount of flavor you will encounter in this recipe! So give it a try!

Heat the oil in a large skillet over medium-low heat. Add the onion and garlic and sauté until the onion has softened, about 6 minutes. Add the cumin and chili powder and cook, stirring, for another minute. Add the beef and cook, stirring and breaking up any lumps until the meat is no longer pink, about 5 minutes. Add the tomato paste, salt, and pepper to taste. Cook the mixture, stirring, until the meat is cooked through, about 5 minutes. Taste and reseason if necessary.

SHREDDED BEEF FILLING

Start to finish: 2 hours 40 minutes

Hands-on time: 40 minutes

2½ pounds boneless beef chuck, trimmed of excess fat and cut into 2-inch pieces

Salt and freshly ground black pepper

2 tablespoons vegetable oil

1 medium onion, finely chopped

3 garlic cloves, finely chopped

1 serrano chile, seeded and chopped

1½ teaspoons ground cumin

½ cup tomato sauce

CARNITAS FILLING

Start to finish: 2 hours 35 minutes

Hands-on time: 50 minutes

2½ pounds boneless pork butt, shoulder, or boneless country-style pork ribs

½ cup fresh orange juice

¼ cup milk

2 garlic cloves, chopped

1 teaspoon salt

¼ teaspoon freshly ground black pepper

Grated zest of 1 orange

MAKE AHEAD: These fillings can be made up to 1 day ahead and kept covered in the refrigerator, or frozen in a zip top bag for up to a month.

Season the beef with salt and pepper. Heat the oil in a large, heavy sauté pan over medium-high heat. Add the beef and cook, about 5 to 8 minutes, turning the meat so it browns on all sides. Do not crowd the beef in the pan or it will not brown properly. Work in two batches if necessary. Remove the beef from the pan. Add the onions, garlic, and chile to the pan. Cook until the onions are caramelized, about 10 minutes. Add the cumin and cook 1 minute. Return the beef to the pan and add the tomato sauce and 1 cup water. Bring to a boil, reduce the heat to low, and simmer partially covered, for 1½ to 2 hours, or until the beef is tender.

Let the beef cool in the liquid. Remove the beef from the pan and shred it using two forks. Return the beef to the pan and stir to combine. Taste and reseason if necessary. Serve hot

Meredith and her husband David have had a love affair with carnitas since they first began their own love affair over a plate at Old Town Mexican Café in San Diego. Carnitas is pork that has been slow-cooked with orange juice and garlic. It continues to cook in its own fat until it is crispy and browned. At Old Town Mexican Café (and at Meredith's house), it's served with white onion, avocado, cilantro, and lime. With a side of homemade tortillas and salsa, there is nothing better.

Cut the pork into large 4-inch pieces. Cut off any big chunks of fat and set them aside; leave small pieces of fat attached to the pork. Combine all of the ingredients, including the reserved fat, and 1 cup water, in a large, heavy saucepan or Dutch oven. Bring to a boil, then reduce the heat to low, cover, and simmer until the pork is tender, turning occasionally, about 1 hour 45 minutes.

Remove the meat from the liquid and turn the heat up to medium. Cook until the liquid is reduced by half, about 10 minutes. Return the meat to the pan (discarding the chunks of fat). Cook until the liquid evaporates and the meat browns and begins to crisp in the remaining fat, stirring often, about 15 minutes. Using a slotted spoon, transfer the meat to a platter. Using two forks, shred the meat (the meat will begin to shred while you're stirring in the pan). Season with more salt, if desired.

Carne Asada Tacos with Roasted Poblano Rajas

Start to finish: 5 hours • Hands-on time: 40 minutes

Similar to fajitas, these lime-and-beer-marinated steaks are cut into strips after they're grilled and served with rajas, which are sautéed roasted chiles, and onions for a memorable taco.

YIELD: 12 TACOS, 4 TO 6 SERVINGS

MARINADE

¼ cup fresh lime juice

3 garlic cloves, crushed

1 teaspoon salt

½ cup beer

1¼ pounds skirt steak
   or flank steak

RAJAS

5 to 6 poblano chile peppers

2 jalapeño chile peppers

1 white onion, sliced

2 tablespoons vegetable oil

1 tablespoon unsalted butter

1 garlic clove, crushed

COOKING AND ASSEMBLY

Vegetable oil

12 (6-inch) Corn or Flour Tortillas
   (pages 236 and 238)

Pico de Gallo (page 239)

Guacamole (page 242)

To make the marinade: Combine the lime juice, garlic, salt, beer, and meat in a large zip top bag. Close the bag and shake it to coat the meat. Marinate at least 4 hours or overnight.

To make the rajas: Char the chiles directly over a gas or electric burner, under a broiler, or on a very hot outdoor grill. Place in a plastic bag for 5 minutes. Gently remove the skins, seeds, and stems, and slice the chiles into ¼-inch strips.

In a medium sauté pan over medium-high heat, sauté the onion in the oil and butter until golden brown, about 5 minutes. Stir in the garlic and chile strips. Sauté for 5 minutes.

Remove the steak from the marinade, and dry with paper towels. Brush both sides of the steaks with the oil.

Preheat the oven to 350°F. Preheat a gas grill or an indoor grill to high.

Place the steaks on the hottest spot of the grill. Grill the steaks, turning once, for about 4 to 6 minutes per side for medium-rare steak, longer if desired. Let the steaks rest for 10 minutes, then cut into thin strips across the grain, then into 3- to 4-inch pieces.

Arrange the tortillas into two stacks of six. Wrap each stack in foil, and heat them in the oven for 5 to 10 minutes or until heated through and pliable. If the tortillas are dry, wrap them in a slightly damp paper towel before wrapping in foil.

To serve, place a few slices of meat into each warm tortilla, top with *rajas*, pico de gallo, and guacamole.

Fish Tacos TACOS DE PESCADO

Start to finish: 50 minutes • Hands-on time: 40 minutes

Although we've grilled fish many times for tacos with good success, there really is no fish taco like a fried fish taco. We can't explain how the better half of fish and chips landed in a taco, but we're glad it did. The light and crispy fish is settled into a warm, soft corn tortilla, covered in seasoned cabbage, and drizzled with a lime-spiked sour cream sauce. I think we'll pass on the malt vinegar and fries. Give us a fish taco any time.

YIELD: 12 TACOS, 4 TO 6 SERVINGS

SOUR CREAM SAUCE

1 cup sour cream

½ cup mayonnaise

3 tablespoons finely
  chopped cilantro

Zest of 1 lime

1 tablespoon fresh lime juice

2 tablespoons milk

TACOS

12 (6-inch) corn tortillas

2½ cups shredded green cabbage

2½ cups shredded red cabbage

1½ tablespoons fresh lime juice

2¼ teaspoons salt

2 to 3 cups vegetable oil, for frying

1 cup unbleached all-purpose flour

1 cup beer (not dark)

1 pound cod fillet (or other firm,
  white, flaky fish, such as had-
  dock, hake, or tilapia) cut into
  3 x 1-inch strips

Pico de Gallo (page 239)

4 limes, quartered

To make the sauce: Combine all of the ingredients in a bowl and whisk until smooth. Refrigerate until ready to use.

To prepare the tacos: Preheat the oven to 350°F.

Separate the tortillas into 2 stacks of 6. Wrap each stack in foil and heat in the oven for 10 minutes.

In a large bowl, combine the red and green cabbage. Toss with the lime juice and ¼ teaspoon of the salt. Set aside.

Heat 1 inch of oil to 360°F. in a large, heavy saucepan over medium heat.

In a large bowl, combine the flour and the remaining 2 teaspoons salt. Stir in the beer; the batter will be thick. Add the fish to the batter and toss gently to coat. Lift the fish out of batter, shaking off any excess. Carefully place it into the oil and fry in batches, turning once or twice, until golden, 3 to 4 minutes. Drain on paper towels.

To assemble: Place a piece of fish on each tortilla and top with sour cream sauce, pico de gallo, and cabbage. Squeeze lime over the filling, fold the tortillas, and enjoy.

Fajitas

Start to finish: 2 hours • Hands-on time: 1 hour

Fajitas are the perfect of example of the power of advertising. When you're sitting in a Mexican restaurant and a waitperson walks by with a sizzling skillet of fajitas, you have to have one, too. Who can blame you? The aroma of the garlic-and-lime-juice-marinated steak or chicken mingling with onions and peppers is irresistible.

YIELD: 6 SERVINGS

6 skinless boneless chicken
   breast halves, or 2 pounds
   skirt or flank steak

2 poblano chiles

1 large red bell pepper

1 large yellow bell pepper

1 large red onion

5 tablespoons vegetable oil

⅓ cup fresh lime juice

¼ cup chopped cilantro

3 garlic cloves, minced

1 canned chipotle chile, in adobo

1 teaspoon ground cumin

¾ teaspoon salt

¼ teaspoon freshly ground
   black pepper

12 (6-inch) Corn or Flour Tortillas,
   for serving (pages 236 and 238)

Salsa, for serving
   (pages 240 to 241)

Guacamole, for serving (page 242)

Sour cream, for serving

Flatten the chicken breast to ½-inch thickness or trim the steaks of fat and cut crosswise into 3 large pieces. Set aside.

Stem, seed, and cut the poblano chiles and bell peppers to ¼-inch-wide strips. Cut the onion into ¼-inch wedges. Set aside.

In a blender, combine 2 tablespoons of the oil, the lime juice, cilantro, garlic, chipotle chile, cumin, salt, and pepper to taste and blend until smooth. Pour into a large zip top bag, add the meat, and turn to coat. Refrigerate for at least 1 hour or overnight.

Heat 1 tablespoon of the oil in a heavy, large skillet over medium-high heat.

Add the meat to the skillet, making sure to not crowd the pan. You may have to cook it in 2 batches. Cook about 5 minutes per side for chicken (until cooked through) or 4 minutes per side for beef (or until desired doneness). Transfer the meat to a cutting board and let it rest while you continue with the peppers and onions.

Add the remaining 2 tablespoons oil to the skillet, and heat over medium-high heat. Add the onion and sauté for 3 minutes. Add the chiles and bell peppers and sauté until they are tender-crisp, about 4 minutes. Season with salt and pepper to taste. Transfer the vegetables to a large serving platter.

Cut the meat into ¼-inch-wide strips and combine with the vegetables on the serving platter. Serve with warm tortillas, salsa, guacamole, and sour cream.

Burritos and Chimichangas

Burritos are large flour tortillas that encase a multitude of fillings. In the United States they have become synonymous with Mexican food. Authentic Mexican burritos usually have only meat, but in America, we like to take everything we know about Mexican food and stuff it into a flour tortilla. We would chide this excessiveness ... but it kind of works. Because the sky's the limit when it comes to this topic, we won't give you a specific recipe, just the basics of how to put it together. A chimichanga is just like a burrito, only fried.

Large Flour Tortillas, homemade (page 238) or store-bought

FILLING IDEAS
Salsa (pages 239 to 241)
Sour Cream Sauce (page 253)
Fajitas (opposite)
Carne Asada (page 252)
Fish (page 253)
Guacamole (page 242)
Red Rice (page 245)
Refried Beans (page 243)
Shredded lettuce or cabbage
Chopped tomatoes
Chopped onions
Chopped cilantro
Cheese, such as shredded cheddar, Monterey Jack, or crumbled queso fresco
Sour cream

VARIATION: A wet burrito is covered with hot Red Chile Sauce or Green Tomatillo Sauce (page 257) and eat it with a fork and knife.

To make burritos: Heat a tortilla on a large skillet over low heat until warm and pliable. Add your choice of fillings down the center of the tortilla, leaving a margin around all sides of the filling. Be careful to not overfill the tortilla, or you won't be able to close (or fit your mouth around) your burrito.

Fold the bottom third of the tortilla over the filling, then fold in one side. Fold the top third of the tortilla down, then fold in the other side. This will leave you with one open end and one closed end. Begin eating your burrito at the open end to avoid your fillings and juice from falling out.

VARIATION: A wet burrito is covered with hot Red Chile Sauce or Green Tomatillo Sauce (page 256) and eaten with a fork and knife.

To make chimichangas: Do not put lettuce, sour cream, salsa, or guacamole inside a chimichanga. Stick with the basic meat, beans, rice, and cheese. Make sure your meat and /or beans are not cold when you fill the chimichanga. This will help ensure the fillings are hot after you fry it.

When you fold a chimichanga, enclose the whole thing so you can fry it without your filling leaking out. To do that, fold the bottom third of the tortilla over the filling, then fold in one side, the top third down, then the remaining side so that you have a completely closed packet. Secure your chimichanga with two toothpicks to make sure it stays closed during cooking.

Heat 1 inch of oil to 360°F. in a large sauté pan set over medium-high heat. Gently slide the chimichanga into the oil. Fry for about 2 minutes on each side, or until the chimichanga is golden brown. Drain on paper towels. Serve with salsa, sour cream, guacamole, and shredded lettuce.

Enchiladas

Enchilada translates to "seasoned with chiles" and this authentic dish lives up to its name. Traditionally, tortillas are fried, but we don't like the mess of dipping tortillas in hot oil, so we brush them with oil and bake them. We've given you recipes for green and red enchilada sauces as well as for chicken and cheese fillings. Mix and match them to suit your own taste.

GREEN TOMATILLO SAUCE

Start to finish: 45 minutes

Hands-on time: 35 minutes

YIELD: ABOUT 5 CUPS

2 pounds tomatillos

2 serrano chiles

1 tablespoon oil

1 medium onion, chopped

6 tablespoons chopped cilantro

1 teaspoon ground cumin

1 teaspoon sugar

½ teaspoon salt

1¼ cups chicken stock

½ cup heavy cream

Preheat the broiler. Remove the outer husks of the tomatillos. Rinse them under warm water to remove any stickiness or dirt. Place the tomatillos and chiles on a baking sheet lined with foil and broil 1 to 2 inches from the heat, turning once, until the tomatillos are softened and slightly charred, about 7 minutes.

Heat the oil in a large skillet over medium heat. Add the onion and sauté until golden brown, about 5 minutes.

Transfer the tomatillos and chiles to a blender along with the onions, cilantro, cumin, sugar, and salt and purée until smooth.

Return the tomatillo sauce to the skillet and cook over medium heat until thickened, about 5 minutes, stirring frequently to prevent sticking. Add the stock and cream and cook for 3 or 4 minutes, until slightly thickened. Taste, and add more salt if necessary.

RED CHILE SAUCE

Start to finish: 55 minutes

Hands-on time: 25 minutes

YIELD: ABOUT 3 CUPS

5 dried ancho chiles

3 dried guajillo chiles

2½ cups chicken stock

3 garlic cloves

1 teaspoon cumin

1 cup canned whole tomatoes

½ teaspoon salt

¼ teaspoon black pepper

1 teaspoon sugar

2 tablespoons vegetable oil

Stem and seed the chilies, make a slit down their sides, and open them so they are as flat as possible. Place them on a skillet over medium heat and press them flat for a few seconds with a metal spatula. Flip them and press down to toast the other side. Transfer to a bowl, cover with hot water, and set aside to rehydrate for 30 minutes.

Drain the chiles and discard the water.

Combine the chiles, stock, garlic, cumin, tomatoes, salt, pepper, and sugar in a blender and purée.

In a large skillet, heat the oil over medium heat. Add the purée and cook for 10 minutes, stirring to prevent sticking. Taste, and add more salt if necessary.

CHICKEN ENCHILADA FILLING

Start to finish: 15 minutes

Hands-on time: 15 minutes

YIELD: ABOUT 4 CUPS

2½ cups shredded cooked chicken

½ cup grated mild Cheddar cheese

½ cup grated Monterey Jack cheese

½ onion, minced (½ cup)

½ teaspoon salt

½ cup Green Tomatillo Sauce
   or Red Chile Sauce

Combine all the ingredients in a large bowl.

CHEESE ENCHILADA FILLING

Start to finish: 15 minutes

Hands-on time: 15 minutes

YIELD: ABOUT 3½ CUPS

1½ cups grated cheddar cheese

1½ cups grated Monterey Jack cheese

½ onion, minced (½ cup)

Combine all the ingredients in a large bowl.

ENCHILADA ASSEMBLY

Start to finish: 40 minutes

Hands-on time: 20 minutes

YIELD: 6 TO 8 SERVINGS

12 (6-inch) corn tortillas

2 tablespoons vegetable oil

½ cup grated Cheddar cheese

½ cup Monterey Jack cheese

White onions, for garnish

Chopped cilantro, for garnish

Prepare the sauce and filling of your choice.

Preheat the oven to 375°F.

Brush both sides of the tortillas lightly with oil and lay them on a baking sheet in stacks of two. Heat them in the oven just until soft and pliable, about 3 minutes.

Spread ½ cup sauce in the bottom of a 13 x 9-inch baking dish. Dip a corn tortilla into the remaining sauce.

Place ¼ cup of cheese filling or ⅓ cup of beef or chicken filling in the center of the tortilla. Roll the tortilla around the filling. Place seam side down in the baking dish. Repeat with the remaining tortillas and filling.

Pour the remaining sauce over the enchiladas and sprinkle them with the cheese.

Bake until the cheese melts and the enchiladas are heated through, about 15 to 20 minutes. To serve, sprinkle with onions and cilantro.

> **MAKE AHEAD:** Enchiladas can be assembled and kept covered in the refrigerator up to 1 day ahead. They will be more fragile and will not hold together as well, however.

Quesadillas

Start to finish: 5 minutes • Hands-on time: 5 minutes

Grilled cheese sandwiches in some form or another are popular all over the world. In Mexico they predictably like theirs with flour tortillas. Quesadillas are so simple, but easy to doll up. Like grilled cheese, quesadillas can come with a variety of fillings. We like ours with pico de gallo and guacamole.

YIELD: 4 SERVINGS

2 cups grated cheddar cheese

2 cups grated Monterey Jack
   cheese

8 (8-inch) flour tortillas

Olive oil

Pico de Gallo, for garnish
   (page 239)

Guacamole, for garnish
   (page 242)

Heat a large nonstick skillet over medium heat.

In a medium bowl, combine the cheeses.

Brush the tortillas lightly on one side with oil. Place 1 tortilla on the skillet, oiled side down. Top with ¼ cup of each cheese and another tortilla, oiled side up. Cook about 3 minutes per side, until the tortillas are browned and the cheese begins to melt. Serve hot, garnished with Pico de Gallo and Guacamole.

Chiles Rellenos STUFFED PEPPERS

Start to finish: 40 minutes • Hands-on time: 40 minutes

Sometimes bad things happen to good dishes. Chiles rellenos are a case in point. When a canned green chile is stuffed with a slice of American cheese, dipped in a heavy batter, fried, and then drenched in a strangely translucent, flavorless sauce . . . that's bad. And unfortunately, that's the impression most Americans have of chiles rellenos. They couldn't be more wrong. A good chile relleno starts with a fresh chile that is roasted, peeled, and stuffed with real cheese. It's then dipped in a soufflé-like batter and fried until light and crispy. Instead of covering up this little beauty with a gloppy sauce, we like to set it on top of homemade salsa. Now that's doing the dish justice.

YIELD: 6 SERVINGS

6 poblano chiles or New Mexico
   chiles (Hatch, preferably),
   roasted and peeled
2 to 3 cups shredded
   Monterey Jack cheese
1 to 2 cups vegetable oil
½ cup plus 1 tablespoon
   unbleached all-purpose flour
3 large eggs, separated,
   at room temperature
¼ teaspoon salt
2 cups Salsa (pages 239 to 241)

Make a T-shaped slit on the side of each chile. Carefully remove the seeds and set the chiles aside.

Take a handful of cheese and press it together so it fits into the chile; stuff the chile with the cheese.

Preheat the oven to 180°F.

In a heavy and deep large skillet, heat 1 inch of oil to 360°F.

Spread the ½ cup flour on a plate.

Add the salt to the egg whites and beat them on high speed with a mixer until they hold stiff peaks. With the mixer still going, add the remaining 1 tablespoon flour, then add the egg yolks, one at a time.

Working quickly, dredge the chiles in the flour, shake off any excess, then dip them into the batter to coat and lay them in the hot oil. After about 2 minutes, use a spoon to gently bathe the tops of the chiles with hot oil. Turn the chiles over and fry the other side until golden brown, about 2 minutes.

Transfer the fried chiles to a foil-lined baking sheet and keep them warm in the oven until all are done and ready to serve.

To serve, spoon salsa onto individual plates, set a warm chile on top, and serve.

Tamales

Start to finish: 2 hours 40 minutes • Hands-on time: 1 hours 10 minutes

When you eat a tamal (which is the singular form of tamales), there's something so basic about the dish, it makes you feel as though you're sharing an experience with Mayan ancestors (even if your ancestors aren't Mayan). Perhaps it has something to do with the process of unwrapping the corn husk the tamal is cooked in, or maybe it's the rustic masa-based dough that encase the flavorful fillings. Whatever the case, tamales are an ancient dish that many still love today.

YIELD: ABOUT 30 TAMALES

Carnitas, Shredded Beef, or
    Chicken Filling (pages 250
    to 251), or Refried Beans
    (page 243)

1⅓ cups lard or solid vegetable
    shortening (see note on page
    238)

1½ teaspoons salt

1½ teaspoons baking powder

4 cups freshly ground masa
    dough, or 3½ cups masa
    harina mixed with 2½ cups
    warm water

1¼ to 2 cups low-sodium
    chicken stock

1 (8-ounce) package dried
    corn husks (see note)

NOTE: Often, many of the corn husks in the package are torn or too small to fill, so be sure to buy enough, just in case.

Prepare the filling of your choice as directed in the recipe.

To make the dough: Combine the lard, salt, and baking powder in a large bowl and beat with an electric mixer set on medium speed until fluffy, about 3 minutes.

Beat in the masa a handful at a time. Gradually beat in ½ cup of the stock. Continue to beat in enough stock until the dough resembles a thick (not runny) cake batter. Test by dropping a small spoonful in a cup of cold water. The dough should float to the surface. If it sinks, continue beating for a minute and retest.

To assemble the tamales: Place the corn husks in a large pot or bowl and add enough hot water to cover. Place a heavy plate on the husks to keep them submerged. Let stand until the husks soften, turning occasionally, about 20 minutes.

Fit a large stockpot with a vegetable steamer insert and fill it with enough water so it reaches the bottom of the insert (about 2 inches). Line the bottom of the insert with a few softened corn husks.

Tear 4 or 5 large husks into ¼-inch-wide strips to use as ties and set aside.

Open 2 large husks on a work surface. Spread ¼ cup of the dough in a 4-inch square in the center of each husk, leaving a 2-inch border at the husk's pointed end.

Spoon 2 tablespoons of the filling down the center of each dough square. Fold the long sides of the husk and dough over the filling, bringing the sides together in the middle so that the dough completely encompasses the filling. Then fold both ends over in the same direction. Tie each tamal with a strip of husk to secure, leaving the wide end of the tamale open.

Place the tamal in the steamer basket standing open end up. Repeat with the remaining husks, dough, and filling until all of the filling has been used. If necessary, to keep tamales upright in steamer, insert pieces of crumpled foil between them.

Bring the water in the pot to a boil. Cover the pot and steam the tamales, adding more water as necessary, until the dough is firm to touch and separates easily from the husk, about 1 hour. Let stand in the pot for 10 minutes.

Sopaipillas

Start to finish: 40 minutes • Hands-on time: 20 minutes

These puffy pillows of fried dough dusted with cinnamon sugar and drizzled with honey are always popular with kids, but we've seen just as many adults come out of Mexican restaurants with cinnamon sugar on the tips of their noses and the corners of their mouths.

YIELD: 6 SERVINGS

2 cups unbleached all-purpose flour

1 teaspoon baking powder

1 teaspoon salt

1 tablespoon plus 1 to 2 cups vegetable oil

¼ cup warm milk

½ cup warm water

Confectioners' sugar, for dusting

Ground cinnamon, for dusting

Honey, for serving

Combine the flour, baking powder, and salt in a large bowl. Add the 1 tablespoon oil, the milk, and water and stir until a dough forms. Turn the dough out onto a lightly floured work surface and knead until soft but no longer sticky. Divide the dough into two balls, cover with plastic wrap, and let rest for 20 minutes.

Pour about 1½ inches of oil into a medium pot and heat to 360°F.

Working with one ball of dough at a time and keeping the other one covered, roll out the dough on a lightly floured surface to about ⅛-inch thickness. With a sharp knife or pizza cutter, cut the dough into 2½- to 3-inch squares.

Working in batches, carefully slide 3 or 4 squares of dough into the hot oil, being careful not to overcrowd the sopaipillas. Cook, turning once, until golden brown on both sides, about 1 minute per side. Transfer the sopaipillas to paper towels using a slotted spoon.

Dust with confectioners' sugar and cinnamon and serve with honey for drizzling.

Flan

Start to finish: 4 hours 15 minutes • Hands-on time: 30 minutes

The French dessert, crème caramel, would definitely recognize this dish as family. What might set the Mexican version apart is the intense richness of the custard. Made with an unlikely pairing of sweetened condensed and evaporated milk, flan is gloriously dense and silky. A whole vanilla bean thoroughly infuses this custard and sets it apart from those made with extract.

YIELD: 8 SERVINGS

CARAMEL

1 cup sugar

2 tablespoons light corn syrup

CUSTARD

1 (14-ounce) can sweetened
  condensed milk

1 (12-ounce) can evaporated milk

¾ cup whole milk

½ cup sugar

1 vanilla bean, split lengthwise

3 large egg yolks

4 large eggs

⅛ teaspoon salt

Boiling water

MAKE AHEAD: The custards can be cooked 1 day ahead and kept covered in the custard cups in the refrigerator.

Preheat the oven to 325°F. Set aside 8 (6-ounce) custard cups.

To make the caramel: Combine the sugar, corn syrup, and ⅓ cup water in a medium, heavy-bottomed saucepan over medium-high heat. Stir just to combine. Cook until the mixture becomes light brown, about 4 minutes. Immediately pour the caramel into the custard cups, tilting and rotating the cups to coat the bottoms. Reheat the caramel over medium heat if it gets too thick. Set the custard cups aside.

To make the custard: In a medium saucepan, combine the milks. Add the sugar and scrape in the seeds from the vanilla bean, then add the bean. Bring to simmer, then remove from the heat and steep for 10 minutes.

Meanwhile, in a large bowl, whisk the egg yolks and whole eggs together. Slowly whisk in the warm milk mixture. Strain the resulting custard through a fine mesh strainer into another bowl. Ladle the custard into the prepared custard cups.

Set the custard cups into 2 baking pans lined with kitchen towels (they should fit into one 13 x 9-inch pan, plus one 9 x 9-inch pan). Place the pans in the middle of the oven. Pour enough boiling water into the pans to come halfway up the sides of the custard cups.

Bake for 35 to 45 minutes, or until the sides are set and the custard looks slightly jiggly in the middle. Remove the custards from the water bath and let cool completely on a wire rack. Cover and chill for at least 3 hours.

To serve, run a thin knife around the edge of each flan to loosen, then invert them onto individual serving plates.

Fresh Lime Margaritas

Start to finish: 20 minutes • Hands-on time: 20 minutes

Most restaurant margaritas are made with a mix that is overly sweet and toxically sour. But this margarita is the real deal. With fresh lime and premium tequila, these margaritas are smooth and zippy. Many margarita recipes include Triple Sec, but we've replaced that with the much more flavorful and smooth orange-infused Cointreau or Grand Marnier.

YIELD: 6

3 limes, quartered lengthwise
    and sliced
¼ cup kosher or coarse salt
2 cups premium tequila,
    such as 1800 Silver
⅔ cup Cointreau or
    Grand Marnier liqueur
½ cup plus 2 tablespoons
    lime juice
Crushed ice

Lay 8 lime slices on a plate that matches the circumference of the glasses in which you will serve the drinks. Pour the salt onto another plate.

Gently press the rims of the glasses down onto the limes, twisting to make the rims juicy. Lightly dip the wet rims into the salt to coat. Place the glasses in the freezer for at least 15 minutes.

Combine the tequila, liqueur, and lime juice in a pitcher. Pour 4 ounces of this tequila mixture into a shaker with about ½ cup crushed ice and shake until the shaker is frosty and cold.

Pour the mixture into one of the prepared glasses and repeat with the remaining ice and tequila mixture.

Garnish with lime slices and serve immediately.

MIDDLE EASTERN
& MOROCCAN

WHEN WE THINK OF THE MIDDLE EAST, visions of prayer rugs, colorful courtyards, and camels mingle with the scents of spices, mint, and roasted lamb. Although the origins of much of this cuisine began with Bedouin "tent cooking," that doesn't mean the food is any less sophisticated than other cuisines. In fact, we feel the combination of spices and herbs is intricate and intriguing enough to peak any cook's interest. So we encourage you to enjoy the fragrant flavors of this beautiful region.

What we love the most about Middle Eastern and Moroccan food is how the romance of the region extends into the cuisine. Middle Eastern cooking seems clean and savory all at once. The meats are often grilled and eaten with vegetables, pita bread, and a tahini sauce made of sesame seed paste. Once you've tasted these simple elements together, you can't wait to have them again. The beauty is the simplicity with which you can bring them into your own kitchen, since Middle Eastern and Moroccan cuisines include many spices and other ingredients you may already have in your pantry.

Moroccan food is the jewel of North African cuisine. Not only does the food stand out, but the way it is served is equally fascinating. In fact, Moroccan meals have probably accounted for some of the most memorable dinner parties we have ever

hosted. What could be more fun than setting up a plywood table on cinder blocks, dressing it with a beautiful tablecloth, and tossing pillows around it for your friends to sit on?

If you choose to do this, here's our suggestion for the evening's feast: because most Moroccan food is eaten with the fingers, start the meal by presenting your guests with an urn of warm, rose-scented water so that diners may wash their hands. Then, we believe that no Moroccan meal should start without *b'steeya*, which is perhaps the star of all Moroccan cooking. It's a phyllo pastry layered with spiced shredded chicken and cinnamon-scented ground almonds. Follow that with skewers of beef or lamb kebabs, or bowls of soup, then bread and salad. Then serve couscous, the granular form of semolina, with a spiced vegetable stew. Both the couscous and stew may be eaten with large spoons. Then, just when you thought you couldn't eat one more bite, a chicken tagine, or stew with preserved lemons and olives appears. Finally, you and your guests can lean back on your pillows and enjoy dates and fresh fruit for dessert and perhaps a cup of mint tea. Life doesn't get much better than this.

We've already given you an idea for a Moroccan meal, so here's a Middle Eastern meal to get you started in your own kitchen.

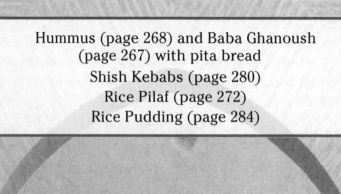

Hummus (page 268) and Baba Ghanoush (page 267) with pita bread
Shish Kebabs (page 280)
Rice Pilaf (page 272)
Rice Pudding (page 284)

FOOD *for* THOUGHT

• Lentils have been found in Egyptian tombs that date from 2400 BC. They may have been used as an aphrodisiac. Egyptians also believed that eating lentils enlightened the minds of children, making them more cheerful and studious. What's for dinner tonight? Lentils!

• Chickpeas made their first appearance in the Middle Eastern diet in 5500 BC.

• There are ninety-one shawarma restaurants in Ottawa, Canada.

• The most popular side dish for falafel in the Middle East is French fries.

Baba Ghanoush EGGPLANT DIP

Start to finish: 1 hour • Hands-on time: 30 minutes

Most often served as a dip, this smoky Egyptian eggplant dish is as fun to eat as it is to say. It's served in much the same way as you would present hummus. In fact, you'll often find it on a platter alongside hummus in Middle Eastern restaurants, with a pile of fresh pita wedges on the side for dipping.

YIELD: 2 CUPS

2 medium eggplants,
    about 1 pound total
3 garlic cloves, coarsely chopped
¼ cup tahini
3 tablespoons fresh lemon juice
⅓ cup chopped flat-leaf parsley
½ teaspoon ground cumin
1 teaspoon salt
¼ teaspoon freshly ground
    black pepper
½ cup extra-virgin olive oil,
    plus more for drizzling
Pita bread, cut into wedges

MAKE AHEAD: The baba ghanoush can be made 1 day ahead and kept covered in the refrigerator.

Prepare a medium-hot fire in a grill and preheat the oven to 375°F.

Prick the eggplants with a fork in several places and place on the grill rack 4 to 5 inches from the fire. Grill the eggplant, turning frequently, until the skin blackens and blisters, and the flesh just begins to feel soft, about 10 to 15 minutes.

Transfer the eggplant to a baking sheet and bake until very soft, 15 to 20 minutes. Remove from the oven, let cool slightly, and peel off and discard the skin. Place the eggplant flesh in a colander to drain for 15 minutes.

In a food processor, combine the garlic, tahini, lemon juice, parsley, cumin, salt, and pepper. Pulse until smooth. Add the eggplant; pulse 4 times to combine. Pour in the oil and pulse again to incorporate. Do not overprocess. The mixture should still be a bit chunky. Taste and adjust the seasoning, as needed.

To serve, pour the baba ghanoush into a serving bowl, drizzle with a little extra-virgin olive oil, and serve with pita wedges for dipping.

TIP: If the weather is hot and you don't want to turn on your oven, you can leave the eggplant on the grill an additional 15 minutes to complete its cooking. We like to use the oven because we find it cooks the eggplant evenly, giving it a more consistent texture.

Hummus CHICKPEA DIP

Start to finish: 15 minutes • Hands-on time: 15 minutes

Hummus is the perfect party food. This garlicky chickpea spread is delicious, inexpensive, easy to make, and loved by everyone. Make a more upscale hummus by sprinkling toasted pine nuts and chopped parsley on top.

YIELD: 2 CUPS

2 (16-ounce) cans garbanzo
    beans, drained

1 garlic clove, chopped

¼ teaspoon salt

2¼ tablespoons fresh lemon juice,
    plus more if necessary

2 tablespoons tahini

¼ cup extra-virgin olive oil,
    plus more for garnish

In a food processor, combine the garbanzo beans with the garlic, salt, lemon juice, tahini, olive oil, and ⅓ cup water. Process to a smooth purée. Taste for seasoning and add more salt or lemon juice if necessary. If the hummus is too thick, add water, one tablespoon at a time, until it is the desired consistency.

To serve, transfer the hummus to a serving bowl and drizzle with additional olive oil. Serve with pita toasts or crudités.

MAKE AHEAD: Hummus can be made up to 2 days ahead and kept covered in the refrigerator.

Harissa

Start to finish: 10 minutes • Hands-on time: 10 minutes

Harissa, a fragrant, devilishly hot sauce is the condiment of choice in Meredith's house. It's typically served with stews and couscous, but we love it on eggs, in soups, and spread on pita sandwiches filled with Falafel or Kefta Kebabs (pages 276 and 277). It's only good for about 1 week in the refrigerator, but because we make it in small batches, it's always gone before the week is up.

YIELD: ½ CUP

2 tablespoons red pepper flakes

1 garlic clove, crushed

½ teaspoon ground coriander

½ teaspoon ground caraway
    seed

¼ teaspoon ground cumin

1 roasted red bell pepper
    from a jar, drained

1 teaspoon salt

Olive oil

Place the red pepper flakes, garlic, coriander, caraway seed, cumin, bell pepper, and salt in the bowl of a blender or mini food processor and process until you have a thick paste. Pack the mixture in a small dry jar. Cover the harissa with a thin layer of oil, close the lid, and keep refrigerated.

> MAKE AHEAD: Harissa can be made and kept in the refrigerator for up to 1 week.

Tahini Sauce

Start to finish: 5 minutes • Hands-on time: 5 minutes

Like ketchup in the United States, tahini sauce is the preferred condiment for most Middle Eastern sandwiches. Sesame paste is its base, lending it a warm, nutty flavor. The lemon juice cuts through the richness and gives it a tang.

YIELD: ABOUT 1 CUP

½ cup tahini

½ cup water

2 tablespoons fresh lemon juice

1 garlic clove, minced

Pinch of salt

Combine all the ingredients in the work bowl of a food processor. Pulse until smooth and creamy. Adjust seasoning to taste.

MAKE AHEAD: Tahini sauce can be made 3 days ahead and kept covered in the refrigerator.

Yogurt Sauce

Start to finish: 10 minutes • Hands-on time: 10 minutes

Although this yogurt sauce is traditionally served over vegetables or stews, we also enjoy it on pitas filled with Kefta Kebabs (page 277).

YIELD: ABOUT 1 CUP

1 cup plain yogurt, strained
   (see directions on page 155)

1 garlic clove, crushed

1 tablespoon olive oil

1 tablespoon chopped cilantro

1 tablespoon chopped fresh mint

Salt and freshly ground
   black pepper

Combine the yogurt, garlic, olive oil, cilantro, and mint in a bowl. Season with salt and pepper, cover, and chill until needed.

MAKE AHEAD: This sauce can be made 1 day ahead and kept covered in the refrigerator.

Tabbouleh HERB AND BULGUR SALAD

Start to finish: 20 minutes • Hands-on time: 15 minutes

Loads of fresh herbs and wholesome grains are what make this light and easy salad so appealing. If you're not familiar with bulgur, it's a whole grain that plumps up in warm water in a matter of minutes, which makes this salad perfect for a last-minute dinner. Try eating this as they do in Lebanon, by scooping it up with crisp leaves of romaine lettuce.

YIELD: 6 SERVINGS

2 cups bulgur (cracked wheat)

½ cup finely chopped
   flat-leaf parsley

½ cup finely chopped
   fresh mint leaves

4 green onions, green part
   only, finely chopped

2 cups cherry tomatoes,
   cut in half

¼ cup fresh lemon juice

¼ cup extra-virgin olive oil

¾ teaspoon ground cumin

½ teaspoon salt

Freshly ground black pepper

Place the bulgur in a large bowl and pour enough warm water over to cover generously. Let it stand until the bulgur softens, about 15 minutes. Drain well, pressing down gently to extrude any excess liquid.

In a large bowl, combine the parsley, mint, green onions, tomatoes, lemon juice, olive oil, cumin, salt, and pepper. Add the bulgur and toss. Taste and reseason with salt and pepper if necessary.

> **MAKE AHEAD:** Tabbouleh can be made up to 3 hours ahead and kept at room temperature.

FOOD *for* THOUGHT

THE LARGEST RECORDED bowl of tabbouleh was made on June 9, 2006, in Ramallah, West Bank, Israel. The previous record was set on February 24, 2001, in Qurnet Shahwan, Lebanon. It weighed 1,514 kilograms and earned a Guinness World Record.

Rice Pilaf

Start to finish: 35 minutes • Hands-on time: 15 minutes

Rice pilaf is the go-to dish for most Middle Eastern meals. It goes so much better with the spices and flavors of the cuisine than plain rice.

YIELD: 4 SERVINGS

3 tablespoons unsalted butter

½ onion, minced (½ cup)

¼ teaspoon ground cardamom

1 cup long-grain rice

2 cups chicken stock

½ teaspoon salt

½ cup golden raisins

¼ cup slivered almonds, toasted

2 green onions, white and
   green parts, thinly sliced

Freshly ground black pepper
   to taste

In a small, heavy saucepan over medium low heat, melt the butter, then add the onion and the cardamom and cook, stirring, until the onion is softened, about 6 minutes. Add the rice and stir until the rice is coated with the butter and the grains look opaque. Add the stock and salt, and bring to a simmer. Cover and cook for 17 minutes, or until the liquid is absorbed and the rice is tender.

Soak the raisins in boiling water to cover for 1 minute. Discard the water and add the raisins, almonds, green onions, and salt and pepper to the rice. Stir to combine and serve warm.

Fattoush BREAD SALAD

Start to finish: 45 minutes • Hands-on time: 30 minutes

In an effort to be frugal and never waste a crumb of food, peasants around the world have created ingenious dishes that utilize day-old bread. Hence the birth of bread pudding, bread soup, and even bread salads. Fattoush is a perfect example of the latter. Its name means "moistened bread," and it is made of pita that is crisped in the oven and tossed with tomatoes, cucumbers, and an invigorating vinaigrette made of olive oil, lemon juice, and mint.

YIELD: 6 SERVINGS

2 garlic cloves, crushed

½ cup olive oil

3 tablespoons fresh lemon juice

¼ cup chopped fresh mint

Salt and freshly ground pepper

3 (6-inch) pitas, torn into
    1-inch pieces

2 tomatoes, cut into ½-inch dice

1 cucumber, peeled and cut into
    ½-inch dice

¼ cup chopped flat-leaf parsley

¼ cup chopped green onions

Preheat the oven to 400°F.

In a small bowl, combine the garlic, olive oil, lemon juice, and mint. Season with salt and pepper to taste and set aside.

Place the pita pieces on a baking sheet and bake for 5 to 10 minutes, or until the pita is slightly browned.

In a large bowl, combine the pita, tomatoes, cucumber, parsley, and green onions. Add the dressing and gently toss to coat. Allow the salad to sit for 15 minutes so the pita can absorb the flavors of the vegetables and vinaigrette.

> MAKE AHEAD: Fattoush can be made up to 30 minutes ahead of time.

Harira Soup LENTIL AND CHICKPEA SOUP

Start to finish: 1 hour • Hands-on time: 25 minutes

In the United States, you'll often find harira, *a traditional Moroccan soup, as the opener to a Moroccan meal. In Morocco,* harira *is typically served during the holy month of Ramadan to break the day of fasting. If we were fasting, this soul-satisfying lentil and chickpea soup would be just what we would want. Its earthy flavor comes from the exotic mix of spices.*

YIELD: 8 SERVINGS

2 tablespoons unsalted butter

1 tablespoon olive oil

2 onions, sliced

1 (28-ounce) can whole tomatoes

3 tablespoons chopped fresh
   cilantro

1 teaspoon salt

¼ teaspoon freshly ground
   black pepper

¼ teaspoon ground ginger

½ teaspoon ground cinnamon

½ teaspoon ground turmeric

½ teaspoon ground cumin

1 cup lentils,
   rinsed and picked over

1 (14-ounce) can chickpeas,
   drained

½ cup angel hair pasta,
   broken into 1-inch pieces

Lemon wedges, for serving

Heat the butter and oil in a large stockpot set over medium-high heat. Add the onions and cook, stirring occasionally, until they soften, about 6 minutes.

Meanwhile, in a blender or food processor, combine the tomatoes, cilantro, salt, and pepper. Process until smooth.

Add the ginger, cinnamon, turmeric, and cumin to the onions and cook for 1 minute, stirring. Add the tomato mixture to the onions and bring to a boil. Add the lentils and 8 cups water. Cover and reduce the heat to low. Simmer until the lentils are tender, about 30 to 35 minutes.

Add the chickpeas and raise the heat, bringing the soup to a low boil.

Add the pasta and cook until tender, 6 to 8 minutes.

Ladle the soup into bowls and serve with lemon wedges.

> **MAKE AHEAD:** *Harira* soup can be made up to 2 days ahead and kept covered in the refrigerator. For best results, hold off on adding the pasta until just before serving. Bring the soup back to a simmer over medium heat, add the pasta, and cook as directed.

Lentil Soup with Garlic and Cumin

Start to finish: 50 minutes • Hands-on time: 20 minutes

Cuisines all over the world have some version of this warming, garlicky soup. It's the scent of cumin that makes this one Middle Eastern at the heart. The soup is so fast and easy to make, and the ingredients are ones you are likely to already have in your pantry, so you'll find it the perfect solution to the eternal question: "What's for dinner?"

YIELD: 6 SERVINGS

2 tablespoons olive oil

1 large onion, finely chopped

2 garlic cloves, finely chopped

1 teaspoon cumin

1¾ cups dried lentils

8 cups chicken stock

1 teaspoon salt

Freshly ground black pepper

2 tablespoons fresh lemon juice

Extra-virgin olive oil, for drizzling

Heat the olive oil in a large pot set over medium heat. Add the onion and garlic and cook for 6 minutes, until the onions become translucent. Add the cumin and continue to cook for another minute. Add the lentils, stock, salt, and pepper, and simmer for 30 minutes, or until the lentils have broken down. Add water if the soup needs thinning.

Stir in the lemon juice, taste, and reseason if necessary.

Ladle into soup bowls and drizzle with olive oil to serve.

TIP: There are many varieties of lentils: red, green, yellow, and black. Although green is the easiest to find, any variety will work well in this soup.

MAKE AHEAD: This soup can be made up to 2 days ahead and kept covered in the refrigerator.

Falafel

Start to finish: 24 hours 40 minutes • Hands-on time: 40 minutes

Years ago, when Meredith lived in Seattle, Pikes Place Market, the wonderful downtown farmers' market, became her second home. Tucked away in one of the recesses of the market is a tiny restaurant that specializes in falafel sandwiches. Although the seats are few and the lines are often long, these crisp little golden orbs made of ground, spiced chickpeas, stuffed into fresh pita bread and drizzled with tahini sauce made this restaurant a required stop nearly every time she passed by. Having left Seattle years ago, she learned the hard way that it's not easy to find good falafel, so she learned how to make them herself in order to satisfy the craving. These falafel are light, crisp, and full of happy Seattle memories.

YIELD: 8 SERVINGS

2 cups dried chickpeas

½ onion, chopped (½ cup)

6 garlic cloves, minced

¼ cup coarsely chopped
   flat-leaf parsley

¼ cup coarsely chopped cilantro

1 teaspoon baking powder

2 teaspoons ground cumin

2 teaspoons ground
   coriander seeds

¼ teaspoon cayenne pepper

1½ teaspoons salt

¼ teaspoon freshly ground black
   pepper

3 to 4 cups vegetable oil,
   for frying

8 warm pita breads

Tahini Sauce (page 270),
   for serving

Shredded lettuce, for serving

Chopped tomatoes, for serving

Chopped cucumbers, for serving

Put the chickpeas in a large bowl and add cool water to cover by 2 inches. Soak in the refrigerator for at least 18 hours or up to 24; they will swell to triple their original size. Drain and rinse.

Combine the chickpeas with the onion, garlic, parsley, cilantro, baking powder, cumin, coriander, cayenne pepper, salt, and pepper in the bowl of a food processor. Process to a smooth paste, scraping the sides down if necessary. Refrigerate for 15 minutes.

Pour 3 inches of oil in a deep fryer or deep, heavy pot and heat to 375°F.

Roll the falafel mixture into balls, just smaller than a ping-pong ball. Carefully slip 4 or 5 at a time into the hot oil, making sure they don't stick to the bottom. Fry until they are crusty brown on all sides, turning as needed, about 3 to 5 minutes. Transfer the falafel to a platter lined with paper towels using a slotted spoon.

Open the pita bread to make pockets (don't split all the way) and put 2 or 3 fried falafel into each. Drizzle with tahini sauce and layer with lettuce, tomatoes, and cucumbers. Serve immediately.

Kefta Kebabs

Start to finish: 35 minutes • Hands-on time: 35 minutes

Ground meat mixed with herbs and spices, formed onto skewers, grilled, and stuffed into a pita makes for a wonderfully juicy Middle Eastern version of a hamburger. We like to serve warm kefta kebabs with a salad, Tahini or Yogurt Sauce (page 270), and warm pita bread.

YIELD: 4 TO 6 SERVINGS

1½ pounds ground lean beef
   or lamb
½ cup finely chopped fresh
   flat-leaf parsley
¼ cup finely chopped cilantro
1 onion, minced
1 teaspoon ground cumin
1 teaspoon paprika
½ teaspoon freshly ground
   black pepper
1 teaspoon salt

Preheat the broiler, or prepare the grill.

Combine the ingredients in a large bowl and mix well. Moisten your hands and mold about ¼ cup of the meat mixture into a sausage shape around a flat metal skewer. Repeat with the remaining meat mixture.

Place the skewers on the broiler rack about 4 inches from the heat source on a grill or over hot grill. Cook, turning once, until the meat is cooked through, about 4 to 6 minutes on each side.

TIP: If you don't have flat metal skewers, simply shape the meat into oval patties and proceed with the recipe.

MAKE AHEAD: The recipe can be assembled up to 1 day ahead and kept covered in the refrigerator. Let sit at room temperature for 30 minutes before cooking.

B'steeya (or Bisteeya)

Start to finish: 3 hours 15 minutes • Hands-on time: 1 hour 25 minutes

Reading the description of this dish on a Moroccan menu could give a diner pause. Although "chicken pie with eggs, almonds, and a coating of confectioners' sugar and cinnamon" may sound like an unusual pairing of tastes, once you've tried this dish, you will find yourself waking up in the middle of the night with an insatiable urge to eat it again. Traditionally, b'steeya *is served as a first course and placed in the center of the table, where everyone digs in with their fingers. Of course, you can eat it with a fork as well, but we think something is lost in the translation. This recipe is an adaptation of one we have made many times from Paula Wolfert's wonderful book,* Couscous and Other Good Food from Morocco.

YIELD: 10 TO 12 AS AN APPETIZER

5 pounds chicken legs and thighs

5 garlic cloves, peeled

2 tablespoons plus ½ teaspoon salt

¾ cup chopped flat-leaf parsley

¼ cup chopped cilantro

1 medium onion, finely chopped

Pinch of saffron threads

¼ teaspoon turmeric

1 teaspoon freshly ground
    black pepper

1 teaspoon ground ginger

3 cinnamon sticks

½ pound (2 sticks) butter

1 pound whole blanched
    almonds, toasted

½ cup confectioners' sugar,
    plus more for dusting

2 teaspoons ground cinnamon,
    plus more for dusting

Trim as much excess fat from the poultry as possible. Combine the garlic and 2 tablespoons of salt and smash together with a fork or mortar and pestle to make a paste. Rub the chicken with the paste and let sit for 30 minutes. Rinse the chicken well and drain.

In a large, heavy pot set over high heat, combine the chicken, parsley, cilantro, onion, saffron, turmeric, pepper, ginger, cinnamon sticks, ¼ pound of butter, the remaining ½ teaspoon salt, and 3 cups water. Bring to a boil, then reduce the heat to low, cover and simmer for 1 hour.

Meanwhile, place the almonds in the bowl of a food processor and pulse until finely ground. Do not overprocess or you will make a paste. In a small bowl, combine the almonds with the confectioners' sugar and ground cinnamon and set aside.

Remove the chicken, cinnamon sticks, and any loose bones from the pot. Discard the cinnamon sticks and bones and set the chicken aside to cool. Raise the heat to medium-high and reduce the sauce to approximately 1¼ cups. Add the lemon juice.

In a separate bowl, beat the eggs until frothy, then pour them into the simmering sauce and stir continuously until the eggs cook and curdle. (They should become curdy, stiff, and dry.) Drain the eggs, taste for salt, and set aside.

Remove the chicken from the bones and discard the skin and bones. Shred the meat into bite-size pieces.

¼ cup fresh lemon juice

10 large eggs

½ pound phyllo pastry sheets

MAKE AHEAD: The individual components of the dish (except the phyllo) can all be made the day before. The meat and the eggs should be kept covered in the refrigerator. The almonds can be kept at room temperature. Assemble and bake the dish as directed in recipe.

Melt the remaining ¼ pound of butter.

Preheat the oven to 425°F.

Unroll the phyllo pastry, cover it with a large sheet of plastic and then put a damp towel on top to prevent the pastry sheets from drying out. Fold 4 phyllo pastry sheets in half. Brush each lightly with the melted butter, place on a large baking sheet and bake for 1 or 2 minutes, or until crisp but not too browned. Set aside.

Brush melted butter over the bottom and sides of a 12-inch ovenproof skillet. Cover the bottom of the pan with one sheet of uncooked phyllo pastry, then brush lightly with the butter. Arrange 6 more phyllo sheets (each brushed with the butter) offset around the skillet, so that half of the sheet covers the bottom of the skillet and half extends over the side. (The entire bottom of the skillet should be covered, as this will end up being the top of the *b'steeya*.)

Spread the shredded chicken over the phyllo on the bottom of the skillet, then add the well-drained egg mixture, and cover with the 4 baked phyllo sheets. Sprinkle the almond-sugar mixture over baked leaves, then fold the overlapping leaves in over the top to cover the pie. Brush the top lightly with butter.

Bake for 20 minutes, or until the pastry is golden brown. Set aside to cool for 10 minutes.

Place a large plate on top of the skillet and carefully invert the skillet to remove the *b'steeya*. Sift a heavy layer of confectioners' sugar over the *b'steeya*, then draw a crisscross pattern of ground cinnamon over the confectioners' sugar. Wipe excess sugar from the edges of the plate and serve immediately.

Shish Kebabs

Start to finish: 4 hours 10 minutes (or longer depending on marinating time) • Hands-on time: 30 minutes

A literal translation of the Turkish words shish kebab is "roasted meat on a skewer," which is a pretty apt description of this dish. These Middle Eastern skewers of flavorfully marinated meat are so popular in the United States that there are restaurants dedicated solely to serving them. We love to serve them alongside Rice Pilaf (page 272) with Yogurt Sauce (page 270) on the side for dipping.

YIELD: 4 TO 6 SERVINGS

4 tablespoons olive oil

1 tablespoon fresh lemon juice

1 teaspoon cumin

1 teaspoon coriander

¼ teaspoon turmeric

½ teaspoon red pepper flakes

1½ teaspoons salt

1 garlic clove, minced

2 pounds beef sirloin or tenderloin, cut into 1-inch cubes

2 medium red onions,
cut into quarters

1 pint cherry tomatoes

In a large bowl, combine the olive oil, lemon juice, cumin, coriander, turmeric, red pepper flakes, salt, and garlic. Add the beef and toss to coat. Cover and chill for at least 4 hours, or up to 24 hours.

Soak wooden skewers in water for 1 hour.

Prepare a grill.

Skewer the meat, onions, and tomatoes, alternating each, onto the skewers. Place the kebabs onto an oiled grill about 6 inches from the coals and cook for 8 minutes, turning every 2 minutes.

VARIATION: The beauty of shish kebabs is that the recipe is so clean and basic you can feel free to substitute almost any other kind of meat or seafood for the beef. Try lamb, chicken, or even shrimp. If you use seafood, shorten the marinade time to 30 minutes. Almost any vegetable will work too. Mushrooms, chunks of zucchini, red peppers, or eggplant are wonderful alternatives or additions.

TIP: Baby new potatoes, carrots, and many other types of dense vegetables need to be boiled for 2 to 3 minutes before skewering so that they are fully cooked when you pull the kebabs from the grill. If you like your beef rare, you might consider skewering your vegetables separately from your meat so you can cook them at different times.

Chicken with Preserved Lemons and Green Olives

Start to finish: 1 hour 15 minutes (not including time to make the lemons) • Hands-on time: 30 minutes

Lemons preserved in salt and lemon juice are a common ingredient in many classic Moroccan dishes. Preserving them in this fashion captures their essence and enlivens this intricately spiced chicken braise. Green olives add further color and interest to a dish that would make a wonderful centerpiece to any Moroccan meal. The warm hues and complex flavors make this standout dish perfect for any occasion. Note that the preserved lemons need to be made a week in advance.

YIELD: 4 TO 6 SERVINGS

8 pieces Preserved Lemons
   (page 283)
1 whole chicken, quartered
Salt and freshly ground
   black pepper
2 tablespoons olive oil
1 large onion, finely chopped
4 garlic cloves, finely chopped
1 teaspoon ground ginger
½ teaspoon Hungarian
   sweet paprika
¼ teaspoon turmeric
Pinch of saffron
¼ teaspoon freshly ground
   black pepper
1 cup chicken stock
16 green olives, pitted
   and halved
2 tablespoons fresh lemon juice
2 tablespoons finely chopped
   flat-leaf parsley
2 tablespoons finely chopped
   fresh cilantro

Prepare the preserved lemons as directed in the recipe.

Pat the chicken dry, then season with salt and pepper. Heat 1 tablespoon of the oil in a 12-inch sauté pan set over moderately high heat. Sauté the chicken until golden brown, about 3 minutes on each side. Transfer the chicken to a plate and keep warm, covered.

Add the remaining tablespoon of oil to the pan and reduce the heat to medium. Add the onion and garlic and cook for 3 to 4 minutes. Add the ginger, paprika, turmeric, saffron, and ¼ teaspoon pepper and cook for 1 minute, stirring. Add the chicken and stock to the pan, reduce the heat to low and simmer for about 40 minutes, or until the chicken is tender.

Scrape the pulp from the preserved lemons, and discard or reserve for another use. Cut the lemon rind into slivers and add to the chicken, along with the olives. Cook for 5 minutes, uncovered.

Transfer the chicken to a serving dish and spoon the olives and lemons around them. Add the lemon juice, taste for seasoning, and add more salt if necessary.

Pour the sauce over the chicken. Sprinkle with the parsley and cilantro and serve.

> **MAKE AHEAD:** This dish can be made up to 2 days ahead and kept covered in the refrigerator. Reheat on the stove over low heat until warmed through.

Seven-Vegetable Couscous

Start to finish: 55 minutes • Hands-on time: 25 minutes

Seven is a lucky number, and when you eat this fragrant stew, you'll feel lucky, too. At home it's not hard to cook these vegetables to perfection.

YIELD: 4 TO 6 SERVINGS

STEW

3 garlic cloves

1 medium yellow onion

3 small turnips

2 large carrots

1 pound butternut squash

1 small zucchini

½ fennel bulb, root end intact

1 (15½-ounce) can chickpeas

1 cup canned whole tomatoes

2 tablespoons butter

1 tablespoon peeled, chopped
   fresh ginger

1 teaspoon salt

1 teaspoon ground cumin

2 teaspoons paprika

½ teaspoon ground turmeric

¼ teaspoon cayenne pepper

2 small cinnamon sticks

⅛ teaspoon ground cloves

COUSCOUS

1½ cups instant couscous

1 tablespoon unsalted butter

1 teaspoon salt

2 cups boiling water

Harissa (page 269), for serving

To make the stew: Mince the garlic and onion. Peel the turnips, carrots, and butternut squash and cut them into 2-inch chunks. Cut the zucchini into 2-inch rounds. Cut the fennel lengthwise into thick slices. Rinse and drain the chickpeas and chop the canned tomatoes. Set all aside.

Heat the butter in a large soup pot over medium heat. Add the onion and garlic and cook until the onion is softened, about 6 minutes. Add the ginger, salt, cumin, paprika, turmeric, cayenne pepper, cinnamon sticks, and cloves, and continue to cook for another minute. Add the turnips, carrots, fennel, raisins, and 2 cups water and bring to a boil over high heat. Reduce the heat and simmer until the vegetables are just beginning to soften, about 10 minutes.

Add the butternut squash and cook for 5 minutes, then add the zucchini, chickpeas, and tomatoes. Simmer the stew, covered, until it has thickened slightly and the vegetables are fork tender but not mushy, about 15 minutes. Remove the cinnamon sticks.

To prepare the couscous: Combine the couscous, butter, and salt in a medium bowl; pour the hot water over it and stir to combine. Cover and let sit for 5 to 10 minutes. Uncover and fluff with a fork.

To serve, place the couscous on a platter, forming a well in the middle. Spoon the vegetables into the well. Pour some stock over the vegetables. Serve with harissa and pass the remaining stock at the table.

Quick and Easy Preserved Lemons

Start to finish: 7 days • Hands-on time: 20 minutes

This fast and easy technique, inspired by Paula Wolfert, allows you to make preserved lemons in much less time then many traditional techniques.

6 small lemons (preferably
thin-skinned), scrubbed
⅔ cup kosher salt
1 cup fresh lemon juice (from
about 5 large lemons)

Wash the lemons, place them in a saucepan. and cover with cold water. Bring to a boil and cook for 5 minutes, or until the rinds have begun to soften.

Drain and dry the lemons well and cut each into 8 wedges. In a bowl, toss the wedges with the salt and transfer to a large glass jar. Add the lemon juice and cover the jar with a tight-fitting glass lid or plastic-coated lid. Let the lemons stand at room temperature 5 days, shaking jar each day to redistribute the salt and juice. Store the lemons, covered, in the refrigerator.

> MAKE AHEAD: Preserved lemons will keep covered and chilled for up to 6 months.

Rice Pudding ROZ BI LABAN

Start to finish: 2 hours 20 minutes • Hands-on time: 20 minutes

A different take on the traditional rice pudding, roz bi laban *is made with rice flour, which gives it a silky texture. Rose water is added, as well as saffron, turning a dish that could otherwise fall into the comfort food category into something quite exotic.*

YIELD: 8 SERVINGS

¾ cup rice flour

¾ cup sugar

¼ teaspoon salt

6 cups milk

⅛ teaspoon ground cardamom

Pinch of saffron threads

2 tablespoons rose water

1 tablespoon fresh lemon juice

2 tablespoons honey, plus more
    for drizzling

Finely chopped pistachios,
    to garnish

In a heavy, medium-sized saucepan, whisk together the rice flour, sugar, and salt. While continuing to whisk, gradually add in the milk, cardamom, and saffron. Slowly bring to a boil and cook, whisking vigorously, for 3 minutes. Be careful not to burn the bottom. Remove from the heat and add the rose water, lemon juice, and honey.

Pour the pudding into 8 individual serving glasses and let cool. Cover and refrigerate for about 2 hours.

Right before serving, sprinkle the top with the chopped pistachios and drizzle with a little honey.

MAKE AHEAD: The pudding can be made up to 1 day ahead and kept covered in the refrigerator.

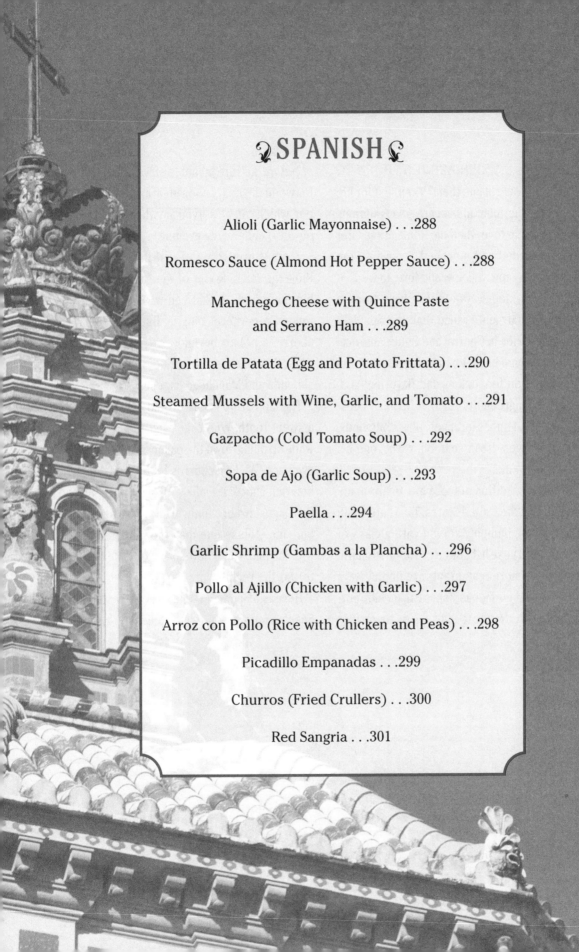

SPANISH

℘ SPANISH ℘

IT SEEMS THE SPANISH ARE JUST BORN TO party, and who could blame them? Their lust for life is inspired by the food, music, art, and traditions that go back to the time when the Romans and later the Moors invaded and morphed Spain into the tapas-rich landscape we know and love so well.

That's why the foodways of Spain have more in common with Italy and France than the Spanish-speaking countries in Central and South America. The unifying theme between these regions is a reliance on olive oil for cooking and flavoring food. The essential ingredients for real Spanish cooking are olive oil, lemons, oranges, olives, almonds, pork and sausages, fresh seafood, garlic, onions, tomatoes, and wine.

The Spanish tradition of tapas has finally made its mark here in the United States. Tapas are small plates of food commonly served with a glass of wine or sherry. These light bites continue to charm us as more and more restaurants are finding ways to fit them into their menus. Tapas can include anything from pickled squid to light salads to *tortillas*

de patata, and are meant to stave off hunger pangs between the heavy noon meal and the lighter supper, which can be served anywhere from seven to eleven o'clock in the evening.

Spain is primarily a wine-drinking country, with Rioja the reigning king of wine and an indispensable ingredient in that red-wine-and-fruit punch found everywhere, sangria. But the popularity of sherry is not to be underestimated, especially when this ambrosial fortified wine is paired with almonds and Manchego cheese.

The land of Don Quixote and bullfights also has a sweet tooth. Who can resist the churro stands while strolling down the paseo on a balmy summer evening? (We love churros for breakfast dipped in hot, rich chocolate milk.) Also not to be missed is flan, a custard brimming with vanilla and caramel, but since this is one dish they share in common with Mexico, you'll have to visit the Mexican chapter for the recipe!

Here is a Spanish menu to get you started with Spanish food in your own kitchen.

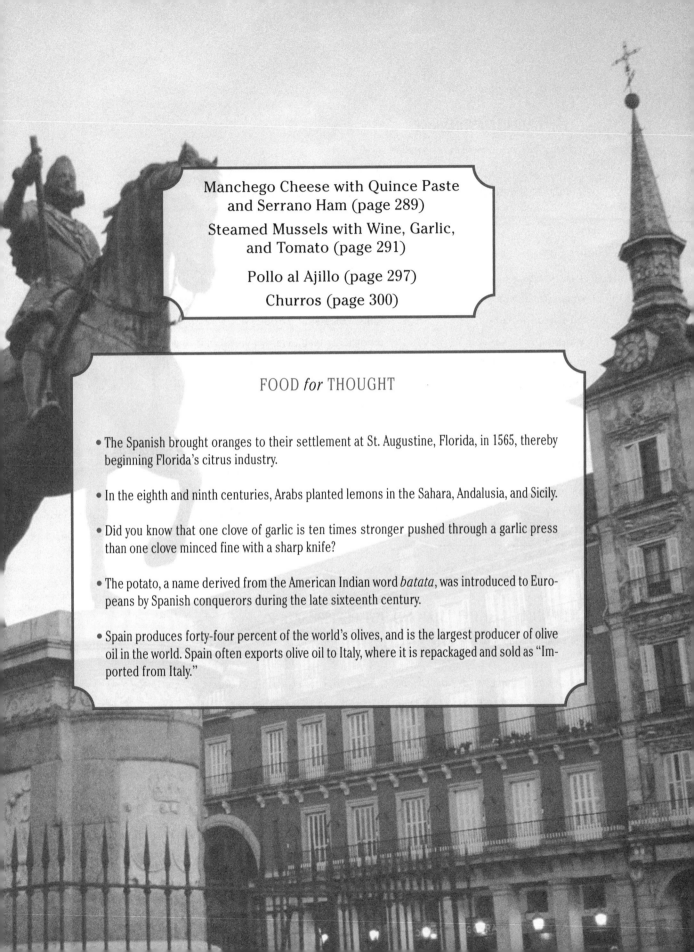

FOOD *for* THOUGHT

- The Spanish brought oranges to their settlement at St. Augustine, Florida, in 1565, thereby beginning Florida's citrus industry.

- In the eighth and ninth centuries, Arabs planted lemons in the Sahara, Andalusia, and Sicily.

- Did you know that one clove of garlic is ten times stronger pushed through a garlic press than one clove minced fine with a sharp knife?

- The potato, a name derived from the American Indian word *batata*, was introduced to Europeans by Spanish conquerors during the late sixteenth century.

- Spain produces forty-four percent of the world's olives, and is the largest producer of olive oil in the world. Spain often exports olive oil to Italy, where it is repackaged and sold as "Imported from Italy."

Alioli GARLIC MAYONNAISE

Start to finish: 10 minutes • Hands-on time: 10 minutes

Spaniards like to serve alioli, a garlic mayonnaise, with grilled meats and seafood.

YIELD: ABOUT 1 CUP

5 garlic cloves, peeled

1 tablespoon lemon juice

1 tablespoon water

¼ teaspoon salt,
   plus more as needed

2 pasteurized egg yolks

1 cup olive oil

Freshly ground black pepper

> MAKE AHEAD: Romesco sauce can be made up to 3 days in advance, kept covered, and refrigerated.

Run an empty food processor, then add the garlic cloves through the feed tube and process until finely minced, about 15 seconds. Turn the machine off, scrape down the sides, and add the lemon juice, water, salt, and egg yolks. Process the mixture and, with the motor on, add half of the oil through the feed tube very slowly in a steady stream. The mayonnaise should begin to emulsify and make a slapping sound as it processes. Continue to slowly add the remaining oil until the sauce is thick. Taste for seasoning and adjust with salt and pepper.

TIP: If you add your oil too quickly to the egg and garlic mixture, it may not emulsify and become thick and smooth. To remedy the situation, scrape the sauce from the bowl of the food processor and transfer it to a measuring cup. Add another yolk to the bowl of the food processor and reintroduce the sauce slowly through the feed tube.

Romesco Sauce ALMOND HOT PEPPER SAUCE

Start to finish: 10 minutes • Hands-on time: 10 minutes

Romesco is a spicy sauce made from almonds, hot peppers, vinegar, and oil. Sometimes we like to add a tablespoon or so of romesco to alioli for a little hit of heat. It tastes great with grilled shrimp or chorizo.

YIELD: ABOUT 1 CUP

2 tablespoons plus ¾ cup olive oil

1 small onion, minced (¼ cup)

1 red bell pepper, minced (¼ cup)

In a skillet set over medium heat, heat 2 tablespoons of olive oil. Add the onion, bell pepper, tomato, and garlic, and cook, stirring, until the vegetables have softened, about 3 minutes. Add the cayenne pepper, salt, and pepper to taste and continue to cook until the mixture has dried a bit,

1 tomato, seeded and diced

2 garlic cloves, peeled

¾ teaspoon cayenne pepper

¼ teaspoon salt

Freshly ground black pepper

¼ cup blanched almonds

2 tablespoons red wine vinegar

about 2 more minutes. Remove from the heat.

Add the almonds to the bowl of a food processor and process until they are finely ground. Add the vegetables to the bowl and process.

In a separate bowl, combine the remaining ¾ cup olive oil with the vinegar. With the food processor motor running, add the oil and vinegar in a steady, thin stream. The mixture should thicken and emulsify to form a rust-colored, thick sauce. Taste for seasoning and adjust with salt and pepper.

> **MAKE AHEAD:** Romesco sauce can be made up to 3 days in advance, kept covered, and refrigerated.

Manchego Cheese with Quince Paste and Serrano Ham

Start to finish: 5 minutes • Hands-on time: 5 minutes

Manchego is a sheep's milk cheese that's been aged for 3 or more months. It's a semi-hard cheese that's perfect for nibbling. Serrano ham is Spain's answer to prosciutto, and like prosciutto, should be sliced so thin that you could read a newspaper through it (well, not really, but you get the idea). Quince paste, membrillo, *is sweet and tart and makes the perfect accompaniment to the smooth, nutty cheese. Each of these three ingredients is wonderful on its own, but they're even better combined.*

YIELD: 4 TO 6 SERVINGS

¾ pound Manchego cheese

1 (14.1-ounce) package quince paste (*membrillo*)

¼ pound serrano ham

Cut the cheese into ¼-inch-thick wedges, discarding the rind, and cut the quince paste into ⅛-inch-thick rectangles. Roll the ham into cigar shapes.

To serve, top the cheese wedges with quince paste and arrange on a platter alongside the rolled ham. Serve at room temperature.

> **MAKE AHEAD:** The cheese, quince, and ham can be assembled up to 8 hours ahead, covered in plastic wrap, and kept in the refrigerator. Allow 30 minutes for the cheese to come to room temperature before serving.

Tortilla de Patata EGG AND POTATO FRITTATA

Start to finish: 45 minutes • Hands-on time: 25 minutes

A traditional tapas favorite, this egg and potato dish can be found in almost every tapas bar in Spain. Although called a tortilla, it doesn't resemble in the least what most Americans refer to as a tortilla. This dish more closely resembles a frittata, and is so sturdy that it is often eaten out of hand.

YIELD: 6 SERVINGS

1 large russet potato, peeled and
   diced (1½ cups)

¼ cup plus 3 tablespoons olive oil

2 onions, chopped

1 red bell pepper, chopped

3 garlic cloves, minced

2 tomatoes, seeded and diced

1½ teaspoons salt

½ teaspoon freshly ground
   black pepper

7 large eggs

2 tablespoons chopped chives

¼ cup chopped flat-leaf parsley

MAKE AHEAD: The tortilla will keep for 1 day, covered and refrigerated. Let it come to room temperature before serving, or reheat it wrapped in foil in a 350°F. oven for about 10 minutes.

Steam the potatoes over simmering water for 20 minutes, or until they are tender and easily pierced with a fork. Transfer them to a large bowl to let them cool slightly.

Meanwhile, heat ¼ cup of olive oil in a 10-inch nonstick skillet set over medium-high heat. Add the onion and bell pepper and sauté for 3 minutes. Lower the heat to medium, add the garlic, and sauté for another 2 minutes. Add the tomatoes, 1 teaspoon of the salt, and ¼ teaspoon of the pepper. The mixture will be wet from the tomatoes. Turn the heat down if it cooks too fast and starts to spatter. Simmer for about 10 minutes, or until the tomato juices have reduced and the vegetables are tender. Transfer to the bowl containing the potatoes and mix well. Wipe the skillet with a paper towel.

In a large bowl, beat the eggs with the remaining salt and pepper, and the chives.

Preheat the broiler with a set on the second-highest rung of the oven.

Heat the skillet over medium heat, then add the remaining 3 tablespoons olive oil and tilt the pan to coat the bottom with oil. Add the potato-onion mixture and spread evenly in the pan. Quickly pour in the eggs, cover, and cook over low heat for 10 minutes. Turn off the heat, uncover the skillet, and transfer it to the oven.

Broil for 3 minutes, or until the tortilla is set. Let stand, covered, for 15 minutes. Slide the tortilla onto a serving plate, garnish with the parsley, and cut into wedges. Serve warm or at room temperature.

Steamed Mussels with Wine, Garlic, and Tomato

Start to finish: 30 minutes • Hands-on time: 30 minutes

The first time Carla had this dish, she was traveling through Spain as a twenty year old. An old fisherman she befriended invited her and a traveling companion to his home, where the mussels that he'd caught that morning glistened in a bucket of shallow water. Miguel cooked them simply in a little garlic, onion, and wine over a little one burner stove in the middle of the one-room house. It was a memorably divine meal of fresh food, simply prepared in a rustic atmosphere. This recipe evokes the same. Make sure you serve this dish with lots of crusty bread for dipping into the juice at the bottom of the plate.

YIELD: 4 TO 6 SERVINGS

3 pounds fresh mussels, scrubbed and debearded (see note)

1 cup dry white wine

¼ cup olive oil

⅓ cup finely chopped shallots

3 plum tomatoes, seeded and diced

6 large garlic cloves, minced

Pinch of salt and freshly ground black pepper

4 tablespoons chopped flat-leaf parsley

1 teaspoon grated lemon zest

2 tablespoons fresh lemon juice

Crusty bread, for serving

Combine the mussels and the wine in a large, heavy Dutch oven set over high heat. Cover and cook, shaking the pan occasionally, until the mussels open, about 5 minutes. Drain the mussels, reserving the liquid. Transfer the mussels to a large serving bowl and discard any that are not open. Tent the bowl with foil to keep warm.

Heat the oil in the same Dutch oven over medium-high heat. Add the shallots, tomatoes, garlic, and salt and pepper and sauté until tender, about 3 minutes. Add 3 tablespoons of the parsley, the lemon zest, lemon juice, and the reserved liquid from the mussels and bring to a boil. Taste for seasoning and adjust if necessary.

Drizzle the sauce over the mussels and sprinkle with the remaining tablespoon parsley. Serve immediately with crusty bread.

NOTE: Live mussels should be tightly closed. If any of the mussels are open and won't close when tapped, they are dead and should be discarded before cooking. If the mussels do not open after cooking, they should also be discarded.

Gazpacho COLD TOMATO SOUP

Start to finish: 2 hours 30 minutes • Hands-on time: 30 minutes

Sometimes called a "liquid salad," gazpacho hails from sunny Andalusía, where the long, hot summers make even the hardiest of souls search for cooling, wet refreshment. This healthy concoction descended from the Romans, who built roads and aqueducts across southern Spain in the second century BC. As slaves labored for the good of the Roman Empire, they were given a form of gazpacho to replenish the necessary salt and vitamins lost through their exertion (making this soup an ancient rendition of Gatorade, perhaps).

There are many versions of gazpacho. Some are left hearty and chunky with vegetables, others are strained and smooth, but all styles converge on this point: gazpacho is tart and tangy, cold and refreshing. Because tomato is the main ingredient, it is best made when tomatoes are plentiful and in season. Fortunately, you no longer have to work like a Roman slave to enjoy a bowl of this refreshing, colorful soup.

YIELD: 6 TO 8 SERVINGS

2 pounds (about 7) medium tomatoes

1 large baguette or country-style bread, crusts removed and cut into cubes (3 cups)

1 cucumber, peeled, seeded, and chopped (1 cup)

1 small green bell pepper, seeded and diced (¾ cup)

1 small red onion, chopped (¾ cup)

1 garlic clove, minced

3 tablespoons sherry vinegar

2 teaspoons salt

¼ teaspoon freshly ground black pepper

¼ cup extra-virgin olive oil

Bring a medium pot of water to a simmer over medium-high heat. Cut an X into the bottom of each tomato and drop them 3 at a time into the simmering water. Cook the tomatoes for 1 minute, remove them with a slotted spoon, and transfer them to a bowl of cold water to stop the cooking. Repeat with the remaining tomatoes. Peel the skin from the tomatoes, discard the skin, and cut each tomato in half through its center.

Set up a bowl with a strainer over it and squeeze the tomatoes so that the seeds and juices run into the strainer. Discard the seeds and drop the tomato halves into the bowl with the juice. Add 1 cup of the bread cubes to the bowl, along with the cucumber, bell pepper, onion, garlic, sherry vinegar, salt, pepper, and 1 cup water.

Transfer the mixture to a food processor or blender and purée, in batches if necessary, until smooth. Pour the soup into a large bowl and whisk in the olive oil. Taste the gazpacho and adjust the seasoning with salt, pepper, and more vinegar if necessary. Cover and refrigerate for at least 2 hours.

Just before serving, toast the remaining 2 cups bread cubes. Ladle the chilled soup into bowls and garnish with the toasted bread cubes.

> MAKE AHEAD: The soup can be made and kept for 2 days, covered and refrigerated.

Sopa de Ajo GARLIC SOUP

Start to finish: 45 minutes • Hands-on time: 15 minutes

A simple soup of garlic, thickened with bread and enriched with eggs, sopa de ajo *is peasant food at its best. Here, we make it more flavorful with chicken stock, but in Spain (or Italy or Greece) many cooks would use water as the main ingredient. Soups in this genre generally come about as a way of using leftover or day-old bread. Remember, waste not, want not is a rule strictly adhered to in most parts of the world, where filling the stomach is one of the day's many hurdles.*

YIELD: 6 SERVINGS

⅓ cup olive oil

9 garlic cloves, finely chopped
(to yield 3 tablespoons)

1 large French or Italian bread,
crusts removed and cut into
cubes (3 cups)

1 teaspoon paprika

6 cups chicken or vegetable stock

3 large eggs, lightly beaten

½ teaspoon salt

¼ teaspoon freshly ground
black pepper

2 tablespoons minced
flat-leaf parsley

Heat the olive oil, in a large, heavy-bottomed stockpot set over medium heat. Add the garlic and bread and cook, stirring, for about 2 minutes, or until the garlic is soft but not brown and the bread has begun to color and crisp.

Add the paprika and stock and continue to cook until the mixture comes to a boil. Turn the heat to low and let the soup simmer for 20 minutes. Remove the soup from the heat and allow it to sit for 10 minutes.

Whisk the soup to break up the bread, then slowly add 2 cups of the hot soup to the beaten eggs. Slowly add the egg mixture to the soup. Taste for seasoning and add the salt and pepper. Garnish with the parsley and serve hot.

NOTE: Simple soups enriched with bread can sometimes have a slippery feel in your mouth. If you find this unpleasant, process the soup in a food processor or blender to make it smooth and silky. Also, the eggs may curdle if the soup is too hot. It doesn't affect the taste of the soup, but may be alarming visually. A whir in the blender can also fix this.

Paella

Start to finish: 1 hour • Hands-on time: 30 minutes

Paella is a terrific dish to serve when having people over because there are so many elements to it: chicken, shrimp, mussels, and chorizo sausage are all mixed up with peppers, onions, and peas in a saffron-scented rice. It's a festival of flavors, and contains so many ingredients that there is literally something for everyone. In Spain, paella can be simple or elaborate, so feel free to substitute or use additional seafood such as lobster, clams, or squid. We like to serve paella at the table directly from the pan in which it cooked. That way your guests can serve themselves, picking the parts of the dish that most appeal to them.

YIELD: 6 TO 8 SERVINGS

2 tablespoons olive oil

Salt and freshly ground
   black pepper

1 chicken fryer, cut into
   8 pieces (breasts cut in half)

¾ pound chorizo
   sausage inks (see note)

1 onion, chopped

1 red bell pepper, cut into
   thin strips

1 green bell pepper,
   cut into thin strips

3 garlic cloves, minced

1 (14.5-ounce) can diced
   tomatoes, with juice

2 cups chicken stock

2 cups long-grain rice

1 teaspoon salt

¼ teaspoon saffron threads,
   crumbled

1 pound raw shrimp, shelled

Preheat the oven to 400°F.

Heat the olive oil in a large, heavy skillet or paella pan over medium-high heat (see tip). Season both sides of the chicken with salt and pepper. Add the chicken to the pan, skin side down, and cook until the skin has crusted over and is nicely browned, about 10 minutes. If the pan begins to turn black, lower the heat to medium. Turn the chicken and cook the second side for another 7 minutes. Transfer the chicken to a plate.

Meanwhile, combine 2 cups water and the chorizo in a medium saucepan. Bring to a simmer and cook for 5 minutes. Remove from the heat and cut the sausage into bite-sized pieces.

Add the onion, bell peppers, and garlic to the hot fat in the paella pan, and sauté for about 5 minutes, or until they begin to soften. Add the tomatoes with juice and the stock and stir to mix.

Place the rice in a colander and rinse under cold running water until the water runs clear. (This step removes some of the starch from the rice.) Add the rice, salt, pepper, and saffron to the paella pan and bring the mixture to a simmer. Return the chicken and sausage to the pan, cover the pan, and place it in the oven for 15 minutes.

Add the shrimp and mussels to the pan and bake for another 10 minutes.

Sprinkle the peas over the paella and cover the dish. Let the paella sit for about 5 minutes for the peas to heat through. Serve the paella at the table, directly from the pan.

12 mussels, shells scrubbed
and debearded (see note
on page 291)

1 cup frozen peas

TIP: Paella is traditionally made in a large, shallow pan that looks something like a big skillet without the long handle. We use a 6-quart sauté pan, which works well. If you don't have a large skillet or sauté pan, you may need to divide the recipe between two smaller skillets.

NOTE: In the United States, chorizo typically comes in two varieties. One is a precooked spicy sausage, which is often used in Spanish recipes and the other is a fresh sausage, more often called for in Mexican dishes. For this recipe we are calling for the precooked chorizo, but you can use fresh if that's all you can find.

FOOD *for* THOUGHT

THE MOST EXPENSIVE widely used spice is saffron, which is made from the dried stigmas of the crocus sativus flower. One ounce of saffron includes the stigmas from approximately 5,000 crocuses, and it takes an acre of flowers to produce a pound. Although it's usually purchased in very small quantities of fractions of an ounce, you can stock up for $500 a pound.

Garlic Shrimp GAMBAS A LA PLANCHA

Start to finish: 30 minutes • Hands-on time: 15 minutes

Gambas a la plancha can be found in most Spanish bars serving tapas. These shrimp are usually served with their shells on, but we prefer our shrimp peeled and ready to go. This classic is so easy and so good that you will say, Adios! to boiled shrimp with cocktail sauce forever.

YIELD: 6 TO 8 SERVINGS
AS AN APPETIZER

1 pound uncooked large shrimp (about 28 to 30), peeled and deveined

1 teaspoon kosher salt

⅓ cup olive oil

6 garlic cloves, chopped (2 tablespoons)

1 small bay leaf

1 (2-inch) piece of dried red chile pepper, seeded

2 tablespoons minced flat-leaf parsley

Place the shrimp in a bowl and sprinkle with the salt. Toss and let stand for 15 minutes.

Heat the oil in a medium skillet over high heat. Add the garlic, bay leaf, and chile pepper and stir for 1 minute. Add the shrimp and stir until just cooked through, about 3 minutes.

Transfer to a serving dish. Sprinkle with parsley and serve immediately.

Pollo al Ajillo CHICKEN WITH GARLIC

Start to finish: 45 minutes • Hands-on time: 15 minutes

Chicken with garlic is the kind of dish the Spanish share together on Sunday afternoons . . . traditionally, the big dinner-with-the-family day. They would also include the chicken backs and necks, picking all the tasty meat from the bones. We know this seems like a lot of garlic, and it is, but most of the garlic is left whole so it becomes sweet and aromatic, not strong and sharp. We serve this dish with some rice, a side dish of our favorite vegetable, and a nice salad of oranges, olives, and bitter greens.

YIELD: 4 SERVINGS

¼ cup olive oil

Salt and freshly ground
   black pepper

1 chicken, cut into 8 pieces
   (breasts cut in half)

1 head garlic, separated into
   cloves, skinned

3 bay leaves

2 tablespoons sherry vinegar

1½ cups dry white wine

2 garlic cloves, minced

2 tablespoons minced flat-leaf
   parsley

Heat a large skillet with a lid or a Dutch oven over medium heat and add the olive oil. Season both sides of the chicken with salt and pepper.

When the oil smokes, add the garlic cloves to the pan along with the chicken, skin side down. Tuck the bay leaves in between the chicken and cook for about 10 minutes, or until the chicken is browned on one side. Watch that the garlic and chicken don't burn, and turn the heat down accordingly. Turn the chicken and garlic to color them evenly and cook for another 7 minutes.

Transfer the chicken and garlic to a plate, discard the bay leaves, and drain the excess fat from the pan. Return the pan to the heat and add the sherry vinegar, letting it deglaze the browned bits in the bottom of the pan. Add the wine and minced garlic, and return the chicken and garlic cloves to the pan. Cover and simmer over low heat for about 15 minutes, or until the chicken is cooked through.

Arrange the chicken on a platter garnished with the browned garlic, the parsley, and wine sauce. Serve immediately.

> MAKE AHEAD: The chicken can made ahead and kept warm in a 200°F. oven for 30 minutes.

Arroz con Pollo RICE WITH CHICKEN AND PEAS

Start to finish: 1 hour • Hands-on time: 30 minutes

Arroz con pollo is one of those easy, one-dish meals that busy cooks love. We remember making a version of this dish over and over again back in the seventies. It is a simpler version of paella, minus the seafood and sausage, but its stick-to-your-ribs character also makes it a weeknight favorite. This recipe has definitely made the short list for easy weeknight dinners, but good enough for company.

YIELD: 4 SERVINGS

1 chicken fryer, cut into 8 pieces
   (breasts cut in half)
Salt and freshly ground
   black pepper
2 tablespoons olive oil
6 slices bacon, chopped
1 onion, diced (1 cup)
3 garlic cloves, minced
½ cup white wine
2 teaspoons paprika
1 (14.5-ounce) can diced
   tomatoes with juice
2 cups chicken stock
¼ teaspoon saffron threads
¼ cup green olives, chopped
1 cup long-grain rice
1 cup frozen peas, thawed
2 tablespoons chopped
   flat-leaf parsley

Pat the chicken pieces dry and season them with salt and pepper.

In a large skillet set over medium-high heat, heat the olive oil, then add the bacon and fry it until the bacon has rendered its fat and is crispy. Transfer the bacon with a slotted spoon to a plate covered with paper towels.

Add the chicken to the pan, skin side down, and cook until the chicken browns, about 10 minutes. Don't let the pan get too hot, or it will blacken. Adjust the heat as necessary. Turn the chicken and cook for another 7 minutes. Transfer the chicken to the plate with the bacon. Drain all but 2 tablespoons of fat from the pan and discard it.

Add the onion and garlic to the hot pan and cook for 3 minutes, or until it has softened. Add the wine and cook until it has reduced by half, about 2 minutes. Add the paprika, tomatoes, stock, saffron, and olives and bring to a simmer.

Place the rice in a colander and rinse under cold running water until the water runs clear. (This step removes some of the starch from the rice.) Add the rice to the tomato mixture and stir just until combined.

Top the rice with the chicken and bacon. Cover, reduce the heat to medium-low or low, and simmer for 20 minutes, or until the chicken is tender and the rice has absorbed most of the liquid in the pan.

Sprinkle the peas over the top, re-cover, and let sit undisturbed for 3 minutes. Garnish with parsley and serve directly from the pan at the table.

Picadillo Empanadas

Start to finish: 2 hours 30 minutes (including the time to make the pastry) • Hands-on time: 1 hour 30 minutes

Empanadas are hefty pies that can be filled with almost anything. We use ground pork seasoned with a mix of spices, raisins, and olives, giving the filling a subtly sweet and salty flavor.

YIELD: 6 TO 8 SERVINGS

2 batches Flaky Pastry (page 65)

2 tablespoons vegetable oil

1 small onion, finely chopped

3 garlic cloves, minced

2 teaspoons ground cumin

1 tablespoon paprika

1 teaspoon crumbled dried
   oregano

¾ teaspoon cinnamon

¼ teaspoon allspice

¼ teaspoon red pepper flakes

½ teaspoon salt, plus more to taste

¼ teaspoon freshly ground black
   pepper, plus more to taste

1 pound ground pork

1 (6-ounce) can tomato paste

1 (28-ounce) can plum tomatoes
   including the juice, chopped

½ cup raisins

½ cup finely chopped pimiento-
   stuffed green olives

1 egg

3 large eggs, hard-boiled and cut
   into ¼-inch slices

Prepare the pastry as directed in the recipe. Heat the oil in a large skillet over medium heat. Add the onion and cook until softened, about 3 minutes. Add the garlic, cumin, paprika, oregano, cinnamon, allspice, red pepper flakes, salt, and pepper and cook, stirring, for 1 minute. Add the pork and cook, stirring and breaking up any lumps, until the meat is no longer pink, about 3 minutes. Add the tomato paste, tomatoes, raisins, and olives, and simmer, stirring occasionally, for 20 to 25 minutes, or until the mixture is thickened and most of the liquid is evaporated. Let the mixture (called a *picadillo*) cool. Season with salt and pepper to taste.

In a small bowl, combine the raw egg and 2 tablespoons water, and set aside. Preheat the oven to 425°F.

Working with half of the dough at a time, roll out the dough to a 12 x 8-inch rectangle on a lightly floured surface. Cut into 4 (6 x 4-inch) rectangles. Lightly brush the egg wash around the edges of each rectangle. Put 3 table-spoons of the *picadillo* onto the short half of each rectangle and top with a slice of hard-boiled egg. Fold the top half over, enclosing the filling, and crimp the edges with a fork to seal. Repeat with the remaining pastry and filling. For the flakiest pastry, refrigerate the empanadas as they are assembled.

Transfer the empanadas to a parchment-lined baking sheet. Cut a small slit on the top of each one and brush lightly with egg wash. Bake in the middle of the oven for 20 to 25 minutes, or until they are golden. Transfer to a rack and let them cool. Serve warm or at room temperature.

> **MAKE AHEAD:** Picadillo may be made 1 day in advance and kept covered and refrigerated. Return it to room temperature before using. Empanadas can be assembled and frozen for 1 month.

Churros FRIED CRULLERS

Start to finish: 1 hour • Hands-on time: 30 minutes

It seems that in Madrid, churros are sold on every street corner. They taunt you with their crispy, sugary goodness . . . a Spanish version of a doughnut. If only they weren't so yummy dipped into rich, hot chocolate milk. This is a battle you definitely want to lose.

Churros have crept into Mexican cuisine by way of the Spanish conquistadors. In Mexico and parts of the American Southwest, the addition of cinnamon to the sugar coating is a welcome spice from south of the border. We like them with the cinnamon, but either way, they are a treat.

YIELD: 4 TO 6 SERVINGS

6 tablespoons unsalted butter

¾ cup unbleached all-purpose flour

¼ teaspoon salt

⅛ teaspoon grated nutmeg

3 large eggs

1 large egg yolk

Vegetable oil, for frying

1 cup granulated sugar

1 teaspoon ground cinnamon

Hot chocolate, for serving

In a large saucepan set over medium-high heat, bring 1 cup water and the butter to a boil. Reduce the heat to medium and add the flour, salt, and nutmeg. Beat vigorously with a wooden spoon until the paste comes together and forms a ball. Cook the dough, stirring, until a film forms on the bottom of the pan, about 2 minutes. Remove the pan from the heat and continue to stir vigorously for another 2 minutes to cool the dough before adding the eggs.

Add the eggs and the egg yolk one at a time, beating with the wooden spoon until each egg is incorporated. The batter should be stiff enough to hold a soft peak. Transfer the mixture to a pastry bag with a star tip.

In a large, heavy-bottomed pot, heat the oil to 360°F.

Mix the sugar and cinnamon together on a large plate.

Squeeze 5 inches of dough into the hot oil, cutting it from the end of the tip with a knife. Squeeze 3 more 5-inch dough pieces and fry them, turning occasionally, for 3 minutes, or until they are golden brown. Remove them from the oil with a slotted spoon or kitchen tongs, and immediately dredge the churros in the sugar mixture. Continue with the remaining dough.

Serve the churros warm with hot chocolate.

Red Sangria

Start to finish: 1 hour 40 minutes • Hands-on time: 10 minutes

Sangria is a wine punch containing sliced fruit, sugar, and some form of liqueur. If you're having a big party in the summer, this refreshing drink is sure to be a crowd-pleaser.

YIELD: 8 SERVINGS

2 bottles chilled dry red wine,
   such as merlot
1 cup brandy
½ cup orange liqueur
½ cup orange juice
2 tablespoons honey
2 oranges, cut into thin rounds
1 lemon, cut into thin rounds
1 lime, cut into thin rounds
2 cups club soda, chilled

In a large pot or bowl, combine the wine, brandy, orange liqueur, orange juice, and honey and stir. Add the orange, lemon, and lime slices, and refrigerate until well chilled, about 1 hour 30 minutes.

To serve, add the club soda, and pour over ice.

❧THAI❧

EATING THAI FOOD IS LIKE HAVING AN orchestra play in your mouth. The flavors are so vibrant; they come alive with each bite in a series of bright notes, each one clear on its own, but in perfect harmony together. Perhaps that's why so many people love Thai food. Why is it then, that often the most devoted fans of this cuisine will not cook it at home? In this chapter, we will take the mystery out of this food and bring its tastes and smells into your own kitchen.

When we are creating a menu for a Thai dinner, we think about it in much the same manner as we think about an individual dish. It must have balance. With that in mind, we want to incorporate a hot dish, a cool or cold dish, maybe something crunchy or fried, and perhaps something steamed. Although in western countries, Thai food may be served in traditional courses, as we do in the United States, it is not so in Thailand. All the courses, even soups and salads, are served and meant to be consumed together, of course with a large bowl of jasmine rice. Jasmine rice is literally and figuratively the center of the Thai table. It is served in large amounts, with the more boldly flavored dishes served in smaller amounts. Even soups are often spooned over rice.

Thais don't eat with chopsticks. So if you don't know how to maneuver those little wooden dowels, you won't need to know here. Thai food is eaten with a fork and big soup-sized spoon. The food is never served in large chunks because there are no knives at the table. Everything is served in easy-to-eat, bite-sized pieces. Whew, the pressure's off!

Teaching the cooking of Thailand has been one of our greatest joys for years. It allows us to illustrate how flavors work together in the most elemental way. The Thais play the balance of sweet, sour, salty, and spicy in every dish like a musical instrument. And you can, too. Once you know what note each ingredient brings to the dish, you can adjust it to suit your own tastes. If you like things a bit sweeter, add more brown sugar, a bit hotter, bring on the chiles. A little more salt, you say? A few dashes of fish sauce should do the trick. How about more acid? Lime juice or tamarind will pucker you up. With any of these recipes, when you get to the end of the cooking and give it that final taste, we encourage you to take the reins into your own hands and make the dish yours.

Here is one of our favorite Thai meals to get you started in your own kitchen.

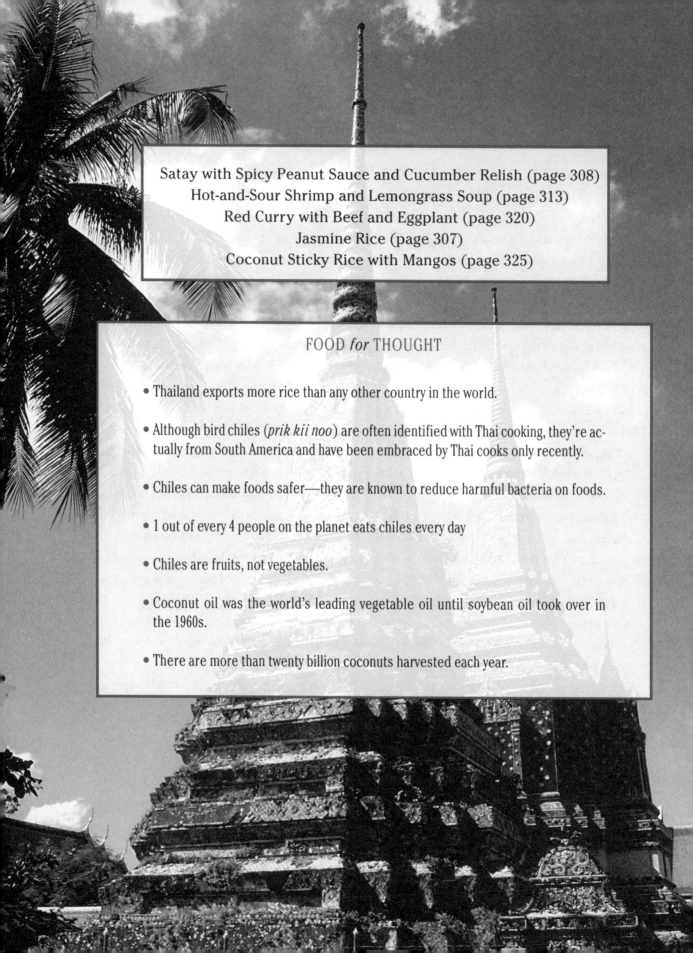

FOOD *for* THOUGHT

- Thailand exports more rice than any other country in the world.

- Although bird chiles (*prik kii noo*) are often identified with Thai cooking, they're actually from South America and have been embraced by Thai cooks only recently.

- Chiles can make foods safer—they are known to reduce harmful bacteria on foods.

- 1 out of every 4 people on the planet eats chiles every day

- Chiles are fruits, not vegetables.

- Coconut oil was the world's leading vegetable oil until soybean oil took over in the 1960s.

- There are more than twenty billion coconuts harvested each year.

Spicy Peanut Sauce

Start to finish: 10 minutes • Hands-on time: 10 minutes

Prepare yourself for something decadent. This spicy peanut sauce, made with coconut milk and red curry paste, is so good you'll want to slather it on anything that doesn't move.

YIELD: ABOUT 2¼ CUPS

1 (14-ounce) can unsweetened coconut milk

1 tablespoon light brown sugar

1 tablespoon Thai red curry paste

1 tablespoon fish sauce

1 teaspoon grated fresh ginger

1 garlic clove, minced

½ cup crunchy peanut butter

In a small saucepan set over medium heat, combine the milk, brown sugar, curry paste, fish sauce, ginger, and garlic. Bring to a simmer and cook for 2 minutes. Reduce the heat to low and stir in the peanut butter. Continue to cook for 3 more minutes, or until the peanut butter is well blended. Serve warm.

TIP: This sauce is great on hot or cold cooked spaghetti noodles. We also like to toss in a handful of fresh cilantro.

> MAKE AHEAD: This sauce can be made 1 day ahead and kept covered in the refrigerator. Reheat over medium-low heat until warm.

Cucumber Relish

Start to finish: 1 hour • Hands-on time: 15 minutes

Chopped peanuts and cilantro are scattered generously on top of this spicy, sweet, salty relish. We always serve this with satay, but it also goes especially well with fried foods like Shrimp Spring Rolls (page 309).

YIELD: ABOUT 4 SERVINGS

½ cup white vinegar

½ cup sugar

1 teaspoon salt

1 pound English cucumbers,
   peeled and thinly sliced

2 small Thai bird chiles or
   1 serrano chile, finely chopped

2 tablespoons finely chopped
   roasted unsalted peanuts

2 tablespoons chopped cilantro

In a small saucepan, bring the vinegar, sugar, and salt to a boil. Reduce the heat to low and continue to cook, stirring to dissolve the sugar and salt, for 2 minutes. Remove from the heat and let cool to room temperature.

Place the cucumbers and chiles in a bowl and mix with the dressing. Sprinkle with the peanuts and cilantro and serve.

> **MAKE AHEAD:** This relish can be made up to 2 hours ahead and kept covered in the refrigerator. Sprinkle with peanuts and cilantro at the last minute to keep them fresh and crunchy.

Jasmine Rice

Start to finish: 25 minutes • Hands-on time: 10 minutes

You absolutely cannot eat Thai food without a big bowl of jasmine rice. It's the staple of the Thai diet and almost every dish is meant to be served with it. Different than typical white rice, jasmine rice has a flowery perfume and nutty flavor.

YIELD: 6 TO 8 SERVINGS

2½ cups (1 pound) jasmine rice

Wash the rice in several changes of water, swirling it around with your fingers until the water runs almost clear. Drain.

Put the rice and 3½ cups water into a heavy-bottomed saucepan and bring to a boil. Cover tightly and reduce the heat to low. Simmer for 18 minutes.

Lift the lid to check for doneness; continue to cook for another minute or two if necessary.

Coconut Rice

Start to finish: 45 minutes • Hands-on time: 15 minutes

Although not a traditional Thai accompaniment, we like to serve Nancie McDermott's deliciously rich coconut rice alongside the Green Papaya Salad with Chiles and Limes (page 314). The creamy, mild flavor of the rice makes a nice foil to the spicy, citrusy salad.

YIELD: 6 TO 8 SERVINGS

1 (14-ounce) can unsweetened
   coconut milk

6 quarter-sized slices fresh ginger

1 teaspoon salt

2 cups jasmine rice, or basmati
   or another long-grain rice

½ cup coarsely chopped
   fresh cilantro

In a saucepan with a tight-fitting lid, combine the coconut milk, ginger, salt, and 1¾ cups water, and bring to a rolling boil over medium heat. Add the rice and stir well.

When the liquid boils again, cover, reduce the heat to low, and cook for 25 minutes, or until the rice is tender and the liquid has been absorbed.

Remove the saucepan from the heat and let stand, covered, for 10 minutes. Uncover, and remove and discard the ginger. Add the cilantro and toss the rice gently with a fork to distribute the cilantro. Serve hot or warm.

Satay with Spicy Peanut Sauce and Cucumber Relish

Start to finish: 50 minutes • Hands-on time: 25 minutes

Even though the origins of satay may not lie in Thailand (it is probably from Indonesia), satay skewers are still a very popular Thai street food and are certainly on the menu in Thai restaurants in America. The appeal is easy to understand: tender, grilled meat dunked in the most delicious peanut sauce and served with a sweet, salty cucumber relish. What's not to love? Sometimes satay is served with white toast points. That may seem strange at first, but when you taste the peanut sauce, you begin to understand that they are just vehicles meant to get more of the sauce into your mouth.

YIELD: 6 TO 8 SERVINGS

Spicy Peanut Sauce (page 305)

Cucumber Relish (page 306)

1 pound boneless chicken breast, beef sirloin, or lean pork

1 cup unsweetened coconut milk

2 tablespoons light brown sugar

2 tablespoons fish sauce

1 tablespoon ground coriander seed

1 teaspoon ground cumin

½ teaspoon turmeric

Wooden skewers, soaked in water for 1 hour

Prepare the Peanut Sauce and Cucumber Relish as directed in the recipes. Place the meat in the freezer for 20 minutes.

Combine the coconut milk, brown sugar, fish sauce, coriander, cumin, and turmeric in a bowl and mix well to dissolve the sugar. Set aside.

Slice the meat into thin strips about 3 inches long. Add the meat to the coconut milk marinade and refrigerate for at least 2 hours.

Preheat the broiler or a grill. Thread 1 or two pieces of meat like a ribbon onto the skewers. Grill or broil them for about 3 to 5 minutes, turning once, until the chicken or pork is cooked through or, if using beef, until it is medium-rare.

Transfer the skewers to a large platter and serve with Spicy Peanut Sauce and Cucumber Relish.

TIP: Meat is much easier to slice thinly if you partially freeze it for a short amount of time.

MAKE AHEAD: The meat can be marinated, threaded onto skewers, and kept covered in the refrigerator for up to 8 hours.

Shrimp Spring Rolls with Chile Sauce

Start to finish: 1 hour 15 minutes • Hands-on time: 1 hour 15 minutes

What makes these rolls different from Chinese egg rolls are their little, finger-sized shape, and the simple filling of shrimp, cilantro, and bean sprouts. Making these little gems is a great activity for family and friends to get in on, too.

YIELD: 60 MINI ROLLS

CHILE SAUCE

1 cup sweet chile sauce

1 tablespoon fish sauce

1 tablespoon lime juice

1 tablespoon chopped cilantro

1 serrano chile, seeded and
   minced (1 teaspoon)

SPRING ROLLS

1¼ pounds medium shrimp,
   peeled and deveined

½ cup chopped cilantro

½ teaspoon salt

1 cup bean sprouts

15 (10-inch) egg roll wrappers,
   each cut into 4 even squares

1 to 2 cups vegetable oil,
   for frying

To make the chile sauce: Combine the chile sauce, fish sauce, lime juice, cilantro, and serrano chile in a bowl and stir to combine. Cover and refrigerate until needed.

To make the spring rolls: Combine the shrimp, cilantro, and salt in the bowl of a food processor. Pulse until the mixture is chopped to ½-inch pieces, about 8 pulses. Pour the shrimp mixture into a large bowl and stir in the bean sprouts.

Lay an egg roll wrapper square on a work surface with a point facing you. Keep the remaining wrappers covered with plastic wrap while you are working to keep them from drying out. Arrange a rounded teaspoon of the shrimp filling across the center of the wrapper, fold up the point end to cover the filling, and fold in the pointed sides to enclose the filling. Roll the wrapper around the filling as tightly as possible. Dip a finger into some water and run it along the open pointed end of the wrapper. Continue to roll tightly and seal the egg roll. Transfer the roll seam side down to a parchment-lined baking sheet. Continue with the remaining filling and wrappers.

Heat 2 inches of oil in a heavy saucepan set over medium-high heat until it is hot, but not smoking. Fry 4 or 5 spring rolls until golden, about 1 minute, and turn to fry the other side, about 1 minute. Transfer the egg rolls to paper towels to drain. Fry the remaining egg rolls in the same manner.

Serve hot with chile sauce.

MAKE AHEAD: The rolls can be assembled and kept in a single layer on a baking sheet, covered, and refrigerated for up to 8 hours. The cooked rolls may be kept hot in a 200°F. oven for up to 1 hour.

Mango Summer Rolls

Start to finish: 1 hour • Hands-on time: 45 minutes

Soft and sumptuous, summer rolls are just the thing when it's hot outside and you're making dinner inside. No need to turn on the stove, you just need hot tap water to soften the wrappers and the noodles for the filling and you're ready to go. Mango, cucumber, cilantro, and mint give this vegetarian version of traditional spring rolls a refreshing, light taste. You can add cold cooked shrimp if you want to make it more of a meal.

YIELD: 10 ROLLS

Spicy Thai Dipping Sauce
    (opposite)
3 ounces vermicelli rice
    stick noodles
2 tablespoons fresh lime juice
1 tablespoon fish sauce
1 tablespoon sugar
10 (8-inch) rice-paper rounds
2 mangos, peeled, seeded,
    and cut into matchsticks
Large bunch fresh cilantro leaves
Large bunch fresh mint leaves
1 medium seedless cucumber,
    peeled, cored, and cut into
    matchsticks
4 green onions, thinly sliced
    on the diagonal
2 carrots, peeled and coarsely
    grated (1 cup)

Prepare the dipping sauce as directed in the recipe.

In a large bowl, soak the noodles in enough hot water to cover for 15 minutes, or until softened and pliable. Drain in a colander, then rinse under cold running water and drain again.

In a large bowl, combine the lime juice, fish sauce, and sugar. Add the noodles and toss to coat.

Put a double thickness of paper towels on a work surface and fill a shallow baking pan with warm water. Soak 1 rice paper round in water until pliable, 30 seconds to 1 minute. Carefully transfer to paper towels.

Arrange 6 mango sticks, 3 cilantro leaves, 3 mint leaves, and 6 cucumber sticks across the bottom third of the soaked rice paper (the part nearest you). Spread ¼ cup of noodles on top and sprinkle some green onion and carrot on top of the noodles. Fold the bottom of the rice paper over the filling and begin rolling up tightly, stopping at the halfway point. Arrange 3 more mint leaves and 3 more cilantro leaves along the crease, then fold in the ends and continue rolling. Transfer the roll, seam side down, to a plate and cover with dampened paper towels. Make 9 more rolls in the same way.

Serve the rolls whole or halved diagonally, with dipping sauce.

> MAKE AHEAD: Summer rolls can be made 4 hours ahead and chilled, covered with lightly dampened paper towels and then with plastic wrap. Let sit at room temperature for 30 minutes before serving.

Spicy Thai Dipping Sauce

Start to finish: 40 minutes • Hands-on time: 10 minutes

This hot sauce is easy to make and nice to have in the refrigerator to add zing to anything from white rice to grilled fish.

YIELD: ABOUT ⅔ CUP

4 serrano chiles (about
    2 inches long), finely chopped

1 tablespoon chopped
    green onion

1 garlic clove, finely minced

3 tablespoons sugar

2 tablespoons fish sauce

⅓ cup fresh lime juice

In a small bowl, whisk together all the ingredients until the sugar has dissolved. Let the sauce sit for 30 minutes before serving to allow the flavors to blend.

> MAKE AHEAD: This sauce can be made 1 week ahead and kept covered in the refrigerator.

FOOD *for* THOUGHT

TOO MUCH HEAT? Don't drink water—capsaicin, which is the oil from which chiles get their heat, will not mix with water, but will instead distribute to more parts of the mouth. Try drinking milk instead. The protein in dairy products, casein, is thought to break the bond the chile oil has on your palate.

Chicken, Coconut, and Lemongrass Soup TOM KHA KAI

Start to finish: 30 minutes • Hands-on time: 20 minutes

Rich and spicy . . . we like our soup like we like our men! Although a long way from the traditional restorative chicken noodle soup, we guarantee this creamy coconut-milk–based soup, studded with lemongrass, lime leaves, and chile peppers, will cure anything that ails you.

YIELD: 4 TO 6 SERVINGS

3 cups chicken stock

8 slices galangal (see note)

1 large stalk lemongrass, trimmed
   to 12 inches and angle-cut into
   2-inch pieces

12 kaffir lime leaves

2 (14-ounce) cans unsweetened
   coconut milk

1½ tablespoons roasted
   chile paste

⅓ cup fresh lime juice

1½ tablespoons light brown sugar

2½ tablespoons fish sauce

1 pound boneless, skinless
   chicken breast, cut into
   bite-sized pieces

½ pound button mushrooms,
   sliced

5 small Thai bird chiles
   or serrano chile, stemmed

Combine the stock, galangal, lemongrass, and lime leaves in a soup pot set over medium heat. Bring to a simmer and cook for 1 minute. Add the coconut milk and return to a simmer, then add the chile paste, lime juice, brown sugar, and fish sauce. Stir to dissolve the chile paste and sugar. Add the chicken and mushrooms and simmer about 3 minutes, or just until the chicken is cooked through.

Remove from the heat and top with the chiles.

NOTE: Galangal is a flavorful root, used often in Thai cooking. Although it looks like ginger, its flavor is distinctly different with a much more pungent, hot peppery flavor. It can be purchased fresh in Asian markets and many specialty food stores. It can also be purchased dried, in slices. We like to use the fresh galangal whenever possible, but use dried if that's what is available.

TIP: If you have a novice Thai eater at the dinner table, it may be a good idea to mention that the lemongrass, galangal, and lime leaves should not be eaten. Chile eating is encouraged only for the brave of heart.

Hot-and-Sour Shrimp and Lemongrass Soup TOM YUM GUNG

Start to finish: 40 minutes • Hands-on time: 25 minutes

We always serve this soup when we are having a Thai dinner party. It's light, and whets everyone's appetite, but the best part is that it's so easy to make.

YIELD: 6 TO 8 SERVINGS

8 cups chicken stock

6 thin slices fresh galangal

2 stalks lemongrass cut into
  2-inch sections

8 kaffir lime leaves

4 small serrano chile peppers,
  cut into quarters lengthwise

2 tablespoons fish sauce

1½ tablespoons light brown sugar

1 pound medium shrimp, peeled
  and deveined

½ pound button mushrooms,
  thinly sliced

⅓ cup freshly squeezed lime juice

In a large pot set over medium heat, combine the stock, galangal, lemongrass, lime leaves, and chiles and bring to a gentle boil. Reduce the heat to low and simmer for 10 minutes.

Add the fish sauce and brown sugar. Simmer for 5 minutes. Toss in the shrimp and mushrooms and cook for about 3 minutes, or until the shrimp turn pink. Remove from the heat and add the lime juice. Taste and season with salt if necessary.

TIP: Thai food is all about the balance of flavor. If the soup tastes too acidic for you, add a little sugar and maybe a touch more fish sauce. If it's too sweet, add a little more lime juice. Work with the flavors so the end result suits your tastes.

Green Papaya Salad with Chiles and Lime SOM TUM

Start to finish: 35 minutes • Hands-on time: 35 minutes

When Meredith first started cooking Thai food, one of the first books she bought was Nancie McDermott's essential cookbook Real Thai: The Best of Thailand's Regional Cooking. *Years later, Meredith interviewed Nancie for a piece in* Chile Pepper *magazine that included this refreshing, but definitely hot, green papaya salad. Since then, it has been one of Meredith's favorites. Its flavor and intriguing, but accessible, ingredients make it a welcome addition to any Thai meal. Nancie uses the traditional mortar and pestle method in the recipe, but she has been kind enough to offer another method for those of us who don't have a large mortar and pestle (see tip).*

YIELD: 4 TO 6 SERVINGS

6 fresh whole Thai bird chiles, or

2 fresh serrano chiles, thinly
    sliced

2 garlic cloves, coarsely chopped

1 teaspoon coarsely chopped
    shallot

1 small, hard, green, unripe
    papaya, peeled and finely
    shredded (about 2 cups), or
    1 cup each finely shredded
    cabbage and carrot

9 green beans, trimmed and cut
    into 2-inch lengths

1 teaspoon light brown sugar

¼ teaspoon salt

2 tablespoons fish sauce

½ lime, quartered lengthwise

7 cherry tomatoes, quartered
    lengthwise

In the bowl of a large, heavy mortar, combine the chiles, garlic, and shallot. Grind and pound with a pestle until they are broken down, but not completely mushy. Use a spoon to scrape the sides now and then and mix everything in well.

Add the papaya and pound until the stiff shreds become limp and soft, about 3 minutes. Use the spoon to scrape and turn the mixture over as you work.

Add the green beans and pound to bruise them. One at a time, add the brown sugar, salt, and fish sauce, pounding and scooping a little after each addition. Squeeze in the juice from each piece of lime, then add the lime pieces to the mortar as well.

Add the tomatoes and pound another minute, turning the mixture as before. Pound more gently so the liquid from the tomatoes doesn't splash.

Taste the sauce from the bottom of the mortar and adjust the seasonings, which should be an interesting balance of sour, hot, salty, and sweet. Using a slotted spoon, transfer the salad to a small serving platter. Drizzle on some of the sauce remaining in the mortar and serve.

ALTERNATE METHOD: If you do not have a large mortar and pestle, here are instructions on how to complete the recipe using a rolling pin:

Mince the chiles, garlic, and shallots and place them in a medium bowl.

Spread the shredded green papaya out on a cutting board, and pound it gently with a rolling pin for a minute or two. Press down hard, moving back and forth, to bruise and wilt the papaya shreds so that they will absorb the seasonings well. Stop to gather up the shreds, squeeze them hard, and then spread them out again for another pass or two. When the shreds are wilted, transfer them to the bowl along with the garlic, chiles, and shallots.

Repeat with the green beans, pressing down just enough to split them open and wilt them a bit, and then add them to the bowl as well. Add the fish sauce, juice from the half lime, and sugar and use your hands to squeeze the mixture a few times and work in the seasonings. Add the cherry tomatoes and toss well.

Mound the salad on a small serving platter, juices and all. Serve at room temperature.

Curries

We can't remember ever going to a Thai restaurant without ordering at least one curry dish. The aromatic blend of fresh and dried herbs, chiles, and spices intermingled with the richness of coconut milk make a compelling centerpiece to any meal. A fresh curry paste, usually cooked in coconut milk, is what gives Thai curry its bold flavor. There are many types of curry pastes, each with its own unique character, and they are often named for their colors. The most popular curries in American restaurants are a stoplight selection of red, green, and yellow curries to accompany beef, poultry, shrimp, or tofu.

When making Thai curry dishes at home, you have to decide whether to make your curry paste by hand, or buy a premade curry paste. Homemade curry pastes are more delicate and nuanced than store-bought pastes, and are worth making, especially as you delve deeper into the cuisine. Premade curry pastes are a good option, though, and one we've used ourselves when time is a factor. Although homemade curry pastes are quite hot, we've noticed that packaged pastes can be a good bit hotter, tablespoon for tablespoon. That said, every brand on the store shelf is different and you have to expiriment with each one in order to know exactly how much to add to your curry dish.

In this section, we've tried to give you the same options you would see on a Thai menu. Similarly, when making a curry, you must decide which curry paste to use and what you want to have as a protein and vegetable.

Red and Green Curry Pastes

Start to finish: 30 minutes • Hands-on time: 25 minutes

The difference between the red and green curry is subtle: red curry is made with dried red chiles, while green is made with fresh Thai bird chiles (or serranos). Although the taste difference is hard to detect, the heat in either one is not—they can both be incendiary. That said, the amount of curry paste you add may be the difference between some of your guests being able to eat the dish or not. Unless you know that your guests are hotheads, it may be wise to start with a smaller amount of curry paste, maybe 2 or 3 tablespoons if using homemade, 1 tablespoon for most store-bought brands. If you add 4 tablespoons of a hot store-bought curry paste, all bets are off.

YIELD: ABOUT 1 CUP

RED CURRY PASTE

⅓ cup small dried red chiles

1 teaspoon whole black
  peppercorns

Soak the chiles in hot water until softened, about 20 minutes. Drain well and discard the water.

In a small, heavy skillet set over medium heat, toast the peppercorns, cumin seeds and coriander seeds until fragrant, 3 to 4 minutes, shaking the skillet often. Remove the spices to a small bowl to cool.

1 teaspoon cumin seeds

1 tablespoon coriander seeds

3 stalks lemongrass

1 thumb-sized piece of galangal
   or fresh ginger, peeled and
   sliced

1 tablespoon chopped cilantro

2 tablespoons chopped shallots

6 garlic cloves, chopped

2 teaspoons shrimp paste

2 teaspoons fish sauce

GREEN CURRY PASTE

2 tablespoons coriander seeds

1 teaspoon cumin seeds

1 stalk lemongrass,
   root end cut off

8 Thai bird chiles or serrano
   chiles

2 garlic cloves

1 thumb-sized piece of galangal or
   fresh ginger, peeled and sliced

2 teaspoons grated lime zest

½ cup loosely packed fresh
   cilantro, including the stems

1 teaspoon shrimp paste

1 tablespoon fish sauce

Cut the root end off the lemongrass, thinly slice the lower 6 inches of the stalks, and finely chop them.

Using a mortar and pestle or a spice mill, finely grind the toasted peppercorns, cumin seeds, and coriander seeds (see note on page 000). Place the ground spices into the bowl of a food processor along with the lemongrass, galangal, cilantro, shallots, garlic, soaked dried chiles, and ¼ cup water. Process until smooth, adding more water a tablespoon at a time if the mixture is too thick to process into a paste. Add the shrimp paste and fish sauce and pulse until combined well.

In a small, heavy skillet set over medium heat, toast the coriander and cumin seeds, until fragrant, 3 to 4 minutes, shaking the skillet often. Transfer the spices to a small bowl to cool.

Thinly slice the lower 6 inches of the lemongrass stalks and finely chop them.

Using a mortar and pestle or a spice mill, finely grind the cumin and coriander (see note on page 154). Place the ground spices in the bowl of a food processor with the lemongrass, chiles, garlic, galangal, lime peel, cilantro, and ¼ cup water and process until smooth, adding more water a tablespoon at a time if the mixture is too thick to process into a paste. Add the shrimp paste and fish sauce and pulse until combined well.

> MAKE AHEAD: These curry pastes can be made up to 1 week ahead and kept covered in the refrigerator.

Yellow Curry Paste

Start to finish: 25 minutes • Hands-on time: 25 minutes

Yellow curry is typically the mildest of all the curries, although it can still be hot. It is the most reminiscent of an Indian curry, as it employs many of the same spices, like turmeric (which gives the yellow color), cinnamon, cumin, and black mustard. It's always served with potatoes and onions, and its mellow nature is best suited to chicken or shrimp. Although not exactly the same, this curry is similar to massaman curry, another mild curry, influenced by Indian curries, that also includes sweet spices like cinnamon.

YIELD: ABOUT 1 CUP

1 tablespoon coriander seeds

2 teaspoons cumin seeds

3 whole cloves

¼ teaspoon ground cinnamon

1 teaspoon turmeric

½ teaspoon black mustard seed

1½ teaspoons salt

1 stalk lemongrass, root end cut off

2 tablespoons dried
small red chiles

¼ cup chopped shallots

1 thumb-sized piece galangal or
fresh ginger, peeled and sliced

3 garlic cloves

1 teaspoon shrimp paste

In a small, heavy skillet set over medium heat, toast the coriander and cumin seeds until fragrant, 3 to 4 minutes, shaking the skillet often. Transfer the spices to a small bowl to cool.

Using a mortar and pestle or a spice mill, finely grind the cumin and coriander (see note on page 154). Place the ground spices in the bowl of a food processor with the remaining ingredients and ¼ cup water. Process until smooth, adding more water a tablespoon at a time if the mixture is too thick to process into a paste.

MAKE AHEAD: Can be made up to 1 week ahead and kept covered in the refrigerator.

Red or Green Curry with Beef, Chicken, Shrimp, or Tofu

Start to finish: 1 hour 10 minutes (including time to make the curry paste) • Start to finish: 45 minutes (using premade curry paste)

Hands-on time: 45 minutes (including time to make the curry paste) • Hands-on time: 25 minutes (using premade curry paste)

YIELD: 4 SERVINGS

1 to 4 tablespoons Red or Green Curry Paste (pages 316-317)

2 (14-ounce) cans unsweetened coconut milk (see tip)

3 tablespoons fish sauce

2 tablespoons light brown sugar

Possible vegetable additions to equal ½ to ¾ pould total: bamboo shoot slices; Japanese or Thai eggplant, cut into 1 inch pieces; zucchini, cut into ½ inch rounds; red bell pepper, julienned; or tomatoes, seeded and cut into large bite-size pieces

1 pound lean beef, thinly sliced and cut into 2-inch pieces; or 1 pound boneless, skinless chicken breast, thinly sliced and cut into 2-inch pieces; or 1 pound medium shrimp, peeled and deveined; or 1 pound extra-firm tofu, cut into 1-inch cubes

4 Thai bird chiles or serrano chiles, stemmed and sliced in half lengthwise

¾ cup loosely packed Thai, purple, or Italian basil

Jasmine Rice (page 307), for serving

If you are making homemade curry paste, prepare it as directed in the recipe.

Skim the "thick" coconut milk (or coconut cream) off the top of the cans and put it in a wok or a large sauté pan over medium-high heat. Set aside the remaining "thin" coconut milk. Add the curry paste, fish sauce, and brown sugar to the wok and bring to a boil. Let the mixture cook and reduce for about 10 to 15 minutes, or until tiny pockets of oil appear on the surface. Stir to prevent burning.

Add the desired vegetables and cook for 2 minutes.

Add the beef, chicken, shrimp, or tofu and cook, stirring often, for 2 minutes, or until just cooked through. Add the remaining coconut milk and return to a boil. Remove from the heat and add the chiles and basil. Taste and adjust the seasonings if necessary, adding more fish sauce to make it saltier, or sugar if you like it a bit sweeter.

Transfer the curry to a serving bowl and serve with plenty of steamed jasmine rice.

TIP: Canned coconut milk usually separates in the can into thick and thin milk, much the same way as the cream rises to the surface of milk. Some brands use stabilizers to prevent this separation, but we prefer those that don't. If you open a can and it isn't separated, you can still use it in this recipe, just use half of the can to cook the curry paste and add the other half as directed in the recipe.

Yellow Curry with Chicken, Shrimp, or Tofu

Start to finish: 1 hour 10 minutes (including the time to make curry paste) • Start to finish: 45 minutes (using premade curry paste)

Hands-on time: 45 minutes (including the time to make curry paste) • Hands-on time: 25 minutes (using premade curry paste)

YIELD: 4 SERVINGS

2 to 4 tablespoons Yellow Curry
  Paste (page 318)

2 (14-ounce) cans unsweetened
  coconut milk

2 tablespoons fish sauce

2 tablespoons light brown sugar

Optional additions: carrots, peeled
  and sliced into ¼-inch rounds;
  red bell peppers, julienned; or
  fresh pineapple chunks, especially if using shrimp

12 ounces Yukon Gold
  potatoes, peeled and
  cut into ¼-inch slices

1 large onion,
  cut into ¼-inch slices

1 pound boneless, skinless chicken
  breast, sliced thinly and cut into
  2-inch pieces; or 1 pound
  medium shrimp, peeled and deveined; or 1 pound extra-firm
  tofu, cut into 1-inch cubes

Jasmine Rice (page 307),
  for serving

If you are making homemade curry paste, prepare it as directed in the recipe.

Skim the "thick" coconut milk (or coconut cream) off the top of the cans and add it to a wok or a large sauté pan set over medium-high heat. Set aside the remaining "thin" coconut milk. Add the curry paste, fish sauce, and brown sugar to the wok and bring to a boil. Let the mixture cook and reduce for about 10 to 15 minutes, or until tiny pockets of oil appear on the surface. Stir to prevent burning.

Add the remaining coconut milk, the potatoes, onion, and any optional additions (except for the pineapple, which should be added at the end and just warmed through) and bring to a gentle boil. Cook for 6 to 8 minutes, or until the potatoes are just tender.

Add the chicken, shrimp, or tofu and cook, stirring often, for 2 minutes, or until just cooked through. Taste and adjust the seasonings if necessary, adding more fish sauce to make it saltier, or sugar if you like it a bit sweeter.

Transfer the curry to a serving bowl and serve with plenty of steamed jasmine rice.

VARIATION: Sometimes fresh pineapple chunks are added to shrimp curries.

Pad Thai STIR FRIED RICE NOODLES

Start to finish: 55 minutes • Hands-on time: 45 minutes

Pad thai is a stir-fried noodle dish that has caught on like wildfire in the United States. It's got to be one of the most ordered dishes in any Thai restaurant, and it usually doesn't disappoint. Its appeal lies in the sweet-sour sauce, roasted peanuts, and large amount of other goodies like fried tofu and shrimp you find as you dig through the deliciously silky rice noodles.

YIELD: 6 SERVINGS

½ pound dried rice stick noodles, ¼-inch wide

1 to 2 cups plus 4 tablespoons vegetable oil

4 ounces extra firm tofu, sliced crosswise into ¼-inch slices

3 tablespoons tamarind paste

¾ cup boiling water

¼ cup fish sauce

2 tablespoons fresh lime juice

3 tablespoons sugar

¾ teaspoon cayenne pepper

1 pound medium shrimp, peeled and deveined

Salt

6 garlic cloves, peeled and minced

2 shallots, minced

2 large eggs, beaten

½ cup peanuts, preferably un-salted and roasted, chopped

5 green onions, green part only, thinly sliced on the diagonal

3 cups bean sprouts

Lime wedges, for garnish

Place the noodles in a large bowl and cover with hot water. Soak for 30 minutes, or until they soften. Drain the noodles and set them aside.

Heat ½ inch of oil in a heavy saucepan set over medium-high heat.

Dry the tofu with paper towels. When the oil is hot, fry the tofu on both sides until golden brown, about 3 or 4 minutes total. Drain the fried tofu on paper towels, then cut each slice crosswise into ½-inch strips and set aside.

Soak the tamarind paste in the boiling water for 10 minutes. Work the paste with a fork so the pulp dissolves. Drain through a sieve into a small bowl. Add the fish sauce, lime juice, sugar, cayenne pepper, and 2 tablespoons of oil to the tamarind liquid and set aside.

Heat 1 tablespoon of the oil in a 12-inch nonstick skillet set over high heat. Add the shrimp and sprinkle with salt. Sauté the shrimp until they are opaque, about 2 minutes. Remove from the skillet and set aside.

In the same nonstick skillet, set over medium heat, add the remaining tablespoon of oil. Toss in the garlic and shallots and cook until they are golden brown, about 30 seconds. Add the eggs and stir constantly until they are scrambled. Add the noodles and toss to combine, about 1 minute. Pour the fish sauce mixture over the noodles, raise the heat to high, and cook, tossing constantly until the noodles are coated. Toss in the tofu, ¼ cup of the peanuts, all but ¼ cup of the green onions, half the bean sprouts, and the shrimp and continue to cook for 2 minutes, tossing constantly. Check if the noodles are tender. If they aren't, add 2 tablespoons water to the skillet and cook until tender.

Transfer the noodles to a warm serving platter and sprinkle with the remaining peanuts, green onions, and bean sprouts. Garnish with lime wedges and serve immediately.

Fiery Thai Beef Salad

Start to finish: 35 minutes • Hands-on time: 25 minutes

They say that the heat from chiles (from the capsaicin*), prompts the release of endorphins, those "feel-good" chemicals naturally released by the body. If that's true, then my, oh my, does this salad feel good! To make this light and refreshing salad, we combine cooked flank steak with lemongrass and mint on a bed of romaine and drizzle with a chile-lime vinaigrette. Add as many chiles as you dare. This is the perfect dish for those trying to cut back on fat, because the steak is lean and the dressing is fat free.*

YIELD: 4 TO 6 SERVINGS

1 pound lean flank steak

¼ teaspoon salt

⅛ teaspoon freshly ground pepper

¼ cup cilantro, plus additional
   for garnish

2 to 4 Thai bird chiles or
   serrano chiles

5 garlic cloves

1 tablespoon fish sauce

1½ tablespoons light brown sugar

⅓ cup fresh lime juice

6 cups romaine lettuce, torn into
   bite-sized pieces

16 cherry tomatoes, quartered

½ medium red onion, thinly sliced

1 stalk lemongrass, tough outer
   leaves removed, finely chopped
   (see tip)

¼ cup chopped fresh mint

Preheat a grill or broiler and season the steak with salt and pepper.

Place the steak on a grill rack or broiler pan and cook for 5 minutes on each side, or until the meat is medium-rare. Transfer to a cutting board and let rest for 15 minutes.

Meanwhile, combine the cilantro, chiles, garlic, fish sauce, brown sugar, and lime juice in a blender and blend until smooth. Set aside.

Cut the steak thinly across the grain.

Mound the lettuce in the middle of a serving tray. Drape the beef slices on top of the lettuce and surround with the tomatoes, onion, lemongrass, and mint. Drizzle with the dressing and garnish with additional cilantro leaves. Serve immediately.

TIP: When working with fresh lemongrass, it's important to use the tender part of the inner stalk. When you trim the root end, you should be able to see rings. If you still see a woody center, you're not far enough up the stalk. Once you trim the root end, you should have about 4 inches of tender stalk before you get to the tough section toward the end.

MAKE AHEAD: The steak can be cooked up to 1 day ahead and kept in the refrigerator. Slice just before serving.

Ground Meat Salad with Toasted Rice Powder LARB

Start to finish: 30 minutes • Hands-on time: 30 minutes

More of a Thai "taco" than what we think of as a salad, larb's spicy, lime-infused meat filling, wrapped in a tender let-tuce leaf, makes this a dish we could eat every day. We try to resist the urge to sprinkle chopped peanuts on all of our Thai dishes, so we haven't included them in this recipe. But we have to admit, if you like peanuts as much as we do, they make a nice addition. Toasted rice powder is easy to make and, along with soaking up the lively dressing in this ground meat salad, it also lends a unique texture.

YIELD: 4 SERVINGS

3 tablespoons uncooked
   jasmine rice

⅓ cup fresh lime juice

3 tablespoons fish sauce

1 tablespoon light brown sugar

¾ teaspoon cayenne pepper

1 pound ground chicken or pork

½ onion, thinly sliced
   (⅓ cup)

¼ cup very thinly sliced tender
   inner stalk of fresh lemongrass

¼ cup chopped fresh mint

¼ cup chopped cilantro

12 Boston lettuce leaves, washed

To prepare toasted rice powder, heat the rice for 3 minutes in a small skil-let over medium-high heat, shaking the pan so the rice colors evenly to a toasty light brown. Let the rice cool, then grind it to a sandy powder in a spice grinder.

In a bowl, combine the lime juice, fish sauce, brown sugar, and cayenne pepper, stirring until the sugar is dissolved. Set aside.

In a saucepan set over medium heat, cover the chicken or pork with water and simmer for about 7 minutes, or until all the pink is gone from the meat, stirring to break up lumps. Remove from the heat and drain.

In a large bowl, combine the cooked meat with the dressing. Add the toasted rice powder, green onions, lemongrass, mint, and cilantro.

To serve, spoon the meat mixture into the lettuce leaves and serve.

Coconut Sticky Rice with Mangoes

Start to finish: 5 hours • Hands-on time: 20 minutes

Although many more sweets exist in Thai cuisine, for many in the United States, this warm sticky rice mixed with a sweet, slightly salty coconut sauce and served with cool, fresh mango slices is the only Thai dessert we know and love. This recipe is adapted from Kasma Loha-Unchit's beautiful book It Rains Fishes: Legends, Traditions and the Joys of Thai Cooking.

YIELD: 6 SERVINGS

2 cups white sticky rice (see tip)

1 (14-ounce) can unsweetened coconut milk

½ cup sugar

1 teaspoon salt

2 to 3 ripe mangos, peeled and sliced

Rinse the rice a couple of times, then cover with 2 to 3 inches of water. Let the rice soak for at least 4 hours. It will absorb much of the water.

Drain the rice and place in a shallow, heatproof dish. Place the dish on a steamer rack in a large pot with 2 inches of water on the bottom. Cover and steam the rice for about 30 minutes over medium heat, or until the rice is translucent and soft, but chewy.

About 10 minutes before the rice is done, prepare the coconut sauce by heating the coconut milk, sugar, and salt together in a saucepan, while stirring until it is well blended and smooth. Keep the sauce warm.

When the rice is done and while it's still hot, pour half the sauce over the rice. Stir until the rice is well coated. Let stand for 15 to 20 minutes to allow the grains to absorb the flavoring.

To serve, dish the rice into bowls, spoon some of the remaining sauce over each portion, and garnish with slices of mango. Serve warm or at room temperature.

TIP: You cannot use regular long-grain white rice in place of the sticky rice; it just won't work. You have to get the Thai rice, sometimes sold as sweet or glutinous rice.

Thai Iced Tea or Coffee

Start to finish: 20 minutes • Hands-on time: 10 minutes

More often than not, Thai tea or coffee is made by steeping the tea leaves or coffee powder in hot water and then pouring it into a glass of ice with sweetened condensed milk. Although it is good made that way, we like our version, made with a sugar syrup and half-and-half, even better.

YIELD: 4 TO 6 SERVINGS

¾ cup sugar

¼ cup Thai coffee powder or
   Thai spiced tea (see tip)

Ice

1 to 1½ cup half-and-half

MAKE AHEAD: The coffee or tea can be brewed, strained, and combined with the sugar syrup up to 1 day ahead and kept covered in the refrigerator.

Bring the sugar and ¾ cup water to a simmer in a small saucepan, stirring until the sugar is dissolved, about 5 minutes. Remove from the heat and let the syrup cool completely.

In a large saucepan, bring 4 cups water to a boil over medium heat. Stir in the coffee powder or tea and return to a boil. Immediately remove the pan from the heat and set it aside to cool. When it reaches room temperature, strain through a fine mesh strainer. Add the sugar syrup and stir. Cover and chill until ready to serve.

To serve, fill 4 to 6 glasses with ice. Add about ¾ cup of the chilled, sweetened coffee or tea to each glass. Top off each glass with 3 to 4 tablespoons of half-and-half. Serve as the half-and-half swirls down into the coffee or tea.

TIP: Although you can use strongly brewed regular coffee or black tea in this recipe, they will not have the same flavor as their Thai counterparts. Thai coffee has chicory and, sometimes, toasted sesame seeds incorporated. Thai tea is black tea mixed with spices such as star anise and cardamom. They can both be purchased in Asian or specialty grocery stores.

GLOSSARY

Ancho chile: A dried poblano chile with a deep reddish-brown color. Ranges in heat from mild to medium.

Andouille: A spiced, heavily smoked pork sausage popularized in the United States from its use in Cajun cuisine.

Anthotiros: A dry Greek cheese; it is used grated, much like Parmigiano-Reggiano.

Arborio rice: A short-grained rice most often used in risotto dishes.

Basmati rice: An aromatic long-grained rice often used Indian cuisine. Its name means "queen of fragrance" in Hindi.

Black mustard seed: Of all the mustard plant seed varieties, black seeds have the strongest flavor. Often used in creating Indian spice mixes, such as curry powder.

Black vinegar: A dark, mild, slightly sweet vinegar used in Chinese cuisine.

Bok choy: A member of the cabbage family, bok choy has long, wide, white and dark green leaves.

Brown bean sauce: A salty brown sauce made from soybeans.

Cardamom: A light green pod containing small black seeds. Sold as a whole pod, seeds, or a ground spice. Used frequently in Indian and Middle Eastern cooking.

Chili garlic sauce: A very spicy red chile sauce flavored with garlic. *Sambal oelek* and *Sriracha* sauce are good substitutes.

Chili oil: A chile-flavored oil used in Asian cuisine.

Chinese mustard: An extremely hot, smooth mustard typically served with egg rolls.

Chinese or napa cabbage: An elongated and tightly packed cabbage with pale green leaves.

Chinese wheat noodles: Often used in Northern Chinese cuisine, wheat noodles can be white or yellow, thin as spaghetti or thick as fettuccine.

Chipotle chile: A dried, smoked jalapeño pepper. It is sold both dried, and canned in adobo sauce (a tomato, vinegar sauce). It is a hot chile.

Chorizo: A popular, spicy pork sausage flavored with garlic and chili powder. Spanish dishes calling for chorizo typically call for the cooked variety using smoked pork. Mexican dishes more often rely on the fresh, uncooked variety.

Coconut milk: Although it can be made at home, canned, unsweetened coconut milk is a worthwhile product that is often the basis for Thai curries and other dishes. Do not confuse it with the sweetened coconut milk used to make piña coladas.

Corn husk, dried: The outer covering of corn, dried and used as a wrapper for tamales.

Cornichon: French for "gherkin," these tiny, tart pickles are often an accompaniment to pâte.

Couscous: This tiny granular pasta is often mistaken for a grain. It features prominently in Middle Eastern cuisine.

Daikon radish: A large, white Asian radish often used raw in salads and accompaniments.

Demerara sugar: A coarse, textured raw sugar from the Demerara region of Guyana.

Edamame: The Japanese word for fresh soybeans, these are often served in the pod as a snack or out of the pod as part of a stir-fry or salad.

Egg roll wrapper: A thin sheet of dough, either square or round, used to wrap fillings.

Farmer cheese: A soft-textured cottage-cheese-style cheese made from cow's milk.

Fenugreek: A spice native to the Mediterranean region often used in Indian cuisine.

Fish sauce: Made from anchovy extract, fish sauce is very salty and is often added to Southeast Asian dishes as a flavor boost. Even though it smells fishy, it doesn't taste that way in the dish.

Galangal: A root native to Southeast Asia, galangal has a peppery, almost medicinal flavor. Fresh ginger can be used as a substitute.

Ghee: Butter that has the water and milk solids removed so that it can be heated to a higher heat without burning. Clarified butter with a nutty flavor.

Grape leaves: Grape leaves that have been blanched and brined to use as a wrap for fillings.

Greek yogurt: Made either with whole milk or low-fat milk, Greek yogurt is strained to make it thicker and richer than most American brands.

Gruyère: A cow's milk cheese made in the Swiss style, Gruyère has a nutty, sweet flavor.

Guajillo chile: A tough, thick-skinned dried chile that must be soaked longer than most dried chiles to be usable. Its heat ranges from mild to medium.

Gyoza wrapper: Thicker than a wonton skin and round in shape, gyoza wrappers are used to make the popular Japanese dumpling, or pot sticker.

Hoisin: The Chinese version of barbeque sauce, made with soybeans, garlic, chiles, and other spices. It often is used as a condiment for Peking duck and mu shu pork, or as an ingredient in other dishes.

Hungarian paprika: A blend of ground dried red chiles, often from Hungary. Their flavor can be anywhere from mild to hot, and color from light to deep red. Quality paprika will be labeled Hungarian Paprika and will come in either the sweet or hot variety.

Jalapeño chile: A medium-sized, green, smooth-skinned chile. Its heat can range from very mild to extremely hot.

Its unpredictability causes the authors to avoid using them.

Jasmine rice: Tender long-grained rice with a flowery fragrance and nutty flavor often used in Thai and Vietnamese cuisines.

Kaffir or wild lime leaves: The leaf of the Kaffir lime looks like two leaves joined together, base to tip, and has a citrus aroma. It is used as a flavoring in Southeast Asian cuisine.

Katsuobushi or bonito fish flakes: Tiny flakes of boiled, smoked, and then sun-dried tuna often used to flavor *dashi*, the basis for many Japanese soups and sauces.

Kefalotyri: A hard Greek cheese similar to Parmigiano-Reggiano.

Kirshwasser: A clear cherry brandy used to flavor Black Forest cake.

Konbu: Dried seaweed used to flavor stocks and other dishes in Japanese cuisine.

Lemongrass: Long green-colored stalks with a lighter-colored root-end flavored of lemon, fresh lemongrass is used in Southeast Asian cuisines.

Manchego cheese: A semi-hard, mild sheep's milk cheese.

Marsala wine: A fortified Italian wine ranging in flavor from sweet to dry. The sweet version is often used in desserts and the dry version enjoyed as an aperitif.

Marscarpone: Italy's richer, more decadent answer to cream cheese.

Masa and masa harina: Masa is the traditional dough used to make tortillas and tamales. It is made from corn kernels soaked in lime-water and ground to a thick paste. Masa harina is masa that has been dried and ground into a powder.

Matzo meal: Ground matzo, which is a thin, unleavened bread often eaten during Passover. Matzo meal is the basis for matzo balls.

Mirin: A Japanese sweet rice wine used in a variety of dishes. Sometimes it can be found in the wine section of the grocery store and sometimes in the Asian section.

Miso paste: A fermented soybean paste with the consistency of peanut butter. It ranges in color from white to dark brown. The lighter the color, the sweeter the flavor.

New Mexico or Hatch chile: A long, green chile with moderate heat.

Nori: Paper-thin sheets of dried seaweed used as a wrapper for sushi.

Ouzo: A strong Greek liqueur with anise flavor.

Oyster sauce: A thick brown sauce made from oysters, brine, and soy, used to flavor Chinese dishes.

Pancetta: The Italian version of bacon, it's pork belly cured in salt, but not smoked.

Panko: Crispy, large-flaked, dried, unseasoned Japanese breadcrumbs.

Parmigiano-Reggiano cheese: A hard cow's milk cheese with rich, nutty flavor, Parmigiano-Reggiano is aged for 2 to 3 years. When a recipe calls for Parmesan, this is the best cheese to use.

Phyllo or filo pastry: Paper-thin layers of pastry brushed with butter and often used in Greek and Middle Eastern pastries.

Pickled ginger: Thin, pink slivers of ginger that has been pickled in a rice vinegar brine. Almost always served as an accompaniment to sushi.

Plum sauce: Often referred to as duck sauce, this sweet, tart sauce is made from plums, chiles, vinegar, and sugar and is often used as a dip.

Poblano chile: A large, dark, mild, heart-shaped chile often used in Mexican cuisine. Substitute New Mexico or Anaheim chiles if necessary.

Polenta: Italian for cornmeal, it can be purchased finely ground to coarsely ground.

Prosciutto: Salt-cured and air-dried ham from the Parma region of Italy.

Queso anejo: An aged white Mexican cheese with a crumbly texture and salty flavor.

Queso fresco: A soft, mild, crumbly cheese from Mexico.

Quince paste or *membrillo*: A firm preserve made from quince, which has a pear-apple-like flavor, often served with cheese as part of a tapas menu.

Rice flour: Finely ground white or brown rice used for baking, or as a thickener for sauces or desserts.

Rice noodles: Thin noodles made from finely ground rice and water. They can be fried or soaked, and are used in a variety of Asian dishes.

Rice paper: A thin, translucent, plastic-like sheet that is soaked in water until soft and used as a wrapper for Thai and Vietnamese summer or spring rolls.

Rice vinegar: Vinegar made from rice wine.

Roasted chili paste: A very spicy chili paste made from dried roasted chiles and sometimes tamarind, used in a variety of Asian dishes.

Rose water: A strongly perfumed flavoring made from distilled rose petals. Rose water is used in Asian and Middle Eastern dishes.

Saffron: A yellow-orange spice derived from the stigma of the crocus, saffron has a strong aroma and flavor. It is used in Spanish and Middle Eastern cuisines.

Sake: A Japanese wine made from fermented rice. Sake can be served hot or cold.

Salt: Kosher salt has a larger flake and milder taste than sea salt, which is granular with a strong, clean salty taste.

Serrano chile: A small, green, smooth-skinned chile that can be very hot. They are typically easy to find in grocery stores.

Serrano ham: Spain's answer to prosciutto, serrano ham is salt-cured and air-dried ham.

Shrimp paste: A paste made from fermented, sun-dried shrimp that is often used in Thai curries. It can be found in Asian grocery stores.

Soba noodles: Thin, flat Japanese noodles made from buckwheat flour.

Soy sauce: A dark, salty sauce made from fermented soybeans, roasted wheat, or barley.

Sweet chili sauce: A sweet, thick sauce made from chiles and often served as a dipping sauce with Southeast Asian dishes.

Szechuan peppercorns: The dried berry and husk from a type of ash tree, these hot and spicy peppercorns are one of the ingredients in five-spice-powder.

Tahini: A paste made of ground sesame seeds. Used in Middle Eastern and Greek cuisine.

Tamarind: The secret ingredient of Worcestershire sauce, tamarind paste is extracted from the long pods of a tree native to Asia. Its flavor often lends a sour element to Indian, Asian, and Southeast Asian dishes.

Thai basil: A variety of basil with purple-colored leaves and a licorice flavor. Regular or purple basil can be substituted.

Thai bird chile: An extremely hot chile used in Thai cooking. Substitute serrano chiles if necessary.

Thai coffee: Strongly brewed coffee served over ice with sweetened condensed milk.

Thai curry paste: An aromatic herb and chili paste typically used to flavor Thai coconut-based curries. The paste can be homemade or purchased. The store-bought varieties tend to contain more heat than the homemade varieties. There are many versions, but the most popular are the red, a hot curry with dried red chiles as the base, the green , possibly the hottest curry with fresh green chiles as the base, and yellow curry, which is the mildest and most familiar of Indian curries.

Thai tea: Strongly brewed black tea served over ice with sweetened condensed milk.

Toasted Asian sesame oil: Made from toasted sesame seeds, this oil has a light brown color and a warm, nutty flavor.

Tofu: A custard like product made from soybean curd. It's texture can range from silky and soft to dense and firm.

Tomatillo: A small, green, tomato-like fruit encased in a papery husk, this tart member of the nightshade family is a favorite in Mexican salsas.

Turbinado sugar: A raw, coarse, light-brown sugar.

Udon noodles: A wide, flat, Japanese wheat-flour noodle most often served with stock.

Wakame: Dried or salted kelp used in many Japanese dishes, most notably miso soup.

Wasabi paste or powder: Derived from the root of an Asian plant similar to horseradish, when ground and mixed with water, wasabi is served as a condiment to sushi and other Japanese dishes.

White sticky rice: Also known as glutinous or sweet rice, this type is used in Southeast Asia in savory and sweet dishes.

Wonton skin: A thin square of dough used to wrap a variety of fillings. Wonton skins are most often found in the refrigerator case near the produce section of your grocery store.

PHOTOGRAPHY CREDITS

INDEX